T0215836

Business Process Management

Mathias Weske

Business Process Management

Concepts, Languages, Architectures

Third Edition

 Springer

Mathias Weske
Hasso Plattner Institut (HPI)
Universität Potsdam
Potsdam, Germany

ISBN 978-3-662-59434-6   ISBN 978-3-662-59432-2   (eBook)
https://doi.org/10.1007/978-3-662-59432-2

This Springer imprint is published by the registered company Springer-Verlag GmbH, DE part of Springer
Nature.
The registered company address is: Heidelberger Platz 3, 14197 Berlin, Germany

For DJET

Foreword

Business Process Management (BPM) is a "hot topic" because it is highly relevant from a practical point of view while at the same it offers many challenges for software developers and scientists. Traditionally information systems used information modeling as a starting point, i.e., data-driven approaches have dominated the information systems landscape. However, over the last decade it has become clear that processes are equally important and need to be supported in a systematic manner. This resulted in a "wave" of workflow management systems in the mid-nineties. These systems aimed at the automation of structured processes. Therefore, their application was restricted to only a few application domains. However, the basic workflow concepts have been adopted by different types of "process-aware" information systems. BPM addresses the topic of process support in a broader perspective by incorporating different types of analysis (e.g., simulation, verification, and process mining) and linking processes to business and social aspects. Moreover, the current interest in BPM is fueled by technological developments (service oriented architectures) triggering standardization efforts (cf. languages such as BPMN and BPEL).

Given the huge interest in BPM it is good that Mathias Weske took on the challenge to write a comprehensive book on BPM. The textbook covers the broad space of BPM in-depth. Most books on BPM are rather superficial or closely linked to a particular technology. In this book the topic is viewed from different angles without becoming superficial. Therefore, it is a valuable contribution to BPM literature.

The book "Business Process Management: Concepts, Languages, and Architectures" is motivated by practical challenges and is grounded in both computer science and business administration. The subtitle of the book adequately describes its scope. Unlike many other books in this space the focus is not on a particular notation or XML syntax. Instead the book focuses on the essential concepts. Different process languages are described (Petri nets, EPCs, Workflow nets, YAWL, BPMN, etc.) on the basis of these concepts. Moreover, the different languages are characterized and related using meta models. This is very important because it provides a view on the essence of business process models and prepares the reader for new languages and standards that will emerge in the future. Interestingly, the book also contains a chapter on process analysis. Here different soundness notions relevant for process verification are described and related. The last part of the book is related to architectures and methodologies. Two critical topics are discussed in detail: flexibility and service composition. Process flexibility is very important for the application of BPM in less structured domains. Through service composition a bridge is established between the service-oriented architecture and workflow technology.

The book provides an excellent introduction into BPM. On the one hand, the book covers many topics and links concepts to concrete technologies. On the other hand, the book provides formal definitions and relates things through meta modeling. This makes it a superb textbook for students in both computer science and business administration. Moreover, it is also a very useful book for practitioners since it provides a comprehensive coverage of BPM independently of industry hypes around workflow management, business process management, and service-oriented architectures. Therefore, I expect that this book will help organizations in addressing the BPM topic in a more mature way.

Prof. dr.ir. Wil van der Aalst
Eindhoven University of Technology, July 15th, 2007

Preface to Third Edition

Since the second edition of this book was published in 2012, business process management has enjoyed widespread adoption across many industries and markets. Today, process models are an essential instrument to understand, evaluate, improve, and automate business processes. They also play an important role in process improvement, where process analytics techniques allow us to compare the actual process behaviour with process models. The increasing uptake of business process management concepts and techniques has also been fueled by the digital transformation that continues to impact many aspects of how businesses are run today.

At the same time, industry faces increasing reporting requirements, mainly related to auditing and compliance. Companies have to report in a comprehensible and convincing way to third parties, like auditors, how they run their businesses. Process models have traditionally played a key role in auditing scenarios, because they represent how work is organized, including activities conducted, responsibilities assigned, and data processed. While process models cover many aspects of work in organizations, one of the most essential aspects is not covered by process models: decisions.

To close this gap, business decision management emerged recently to help companies not only fulfill their auditing requirements but also ease process automation. To reflect these developments, this book contains a new chapter on business decision modeling. The Decision Model and Notation (DMN) standard is covered that allows us to define the structure of decisions and concrete decision logic. Both levels of abstraction are useful to communicate decisions but also to implement them. We will discuss how business decision models are tied to process models. Based on a behavioural description of business processes with decisions, decision soundness is introduced as a novel correctness criterion.

In addition to these major enhancements of the book, there are numerous clarifications and corrections. The chapter on process choreographies is streamlined and improved, in particular related to sub-choreographies. Since conversation diagrams do not contribute significantly to the understanding of interacting processes, the respective section has been dropped. The definition of relaxed soundness is now much more concise and, I think, also much more elegant than it was in the previous edition of this book.

To conclude, I am happy to acknowledge the support of our students and members of the Business Process Technology research group. HPI student Leon Bein not only spotted a subtle error in the mapping of an EPC to a Petri net in the relaxed soundness section, but he also helped drafting figures in the business decision modeling chapter. Thanks to Adriatik Nikaj and Jan Ladleif for their feedback on the updated and improved choreography chapter. The comments by Kimon Batoulis and Luise Pufahl on business decision modeling and decision soundness helped improving the readability and consistency of these additions to the BPM book.

Potsdam, March 2019 *M. W.*

Preface to Second Edition

Since the first edition of this book was published in late 2007, the business process management area has enjoyed an amazing development, both in industry and academia. To organize change and to achieve higher degrees of automation, more and more companies and public administrations put processes in the centre of their attention.

While changing business requirements, paired with cost and time pressure are the driving forces of this development, important factors are dependable standards, sophisticated tools, and well educated people. Many young professionals graduating in computer science, business engineering, or related fields have enjoyed an education in business process management, focusing on complementary topics that range from technical aspects to business aspects.

The business process management area is also fueled by the BPM Academic Initiative, which provides a professional process modeling and analysis tool free of charge for users in teaching and academic research. Today more than ten thousand students, lecturers, and researchers use this platform. I thank my colleagues in the core team for their involvement, namely Wil van der Aalst, Frank Leymann, Jan Mendling, Michael zur Mühlen, Jan Recker, Michael Rosemann, and Gero Decker. Also in the name of the platform users, a special thanks to the Signavio team for providing this service to the BPM community.

Just like the first edition, this book does not contain any teaching exercises. However, students and lecturers working with this book can register at the BPM Academic Initiative at academic.signavio.com to access a comprehensive set of teaching material related to this book, and beyond. The material is published under a Creative Commons license, allowing lecturers to use and adapt the exercises according to their syllabi. All figures of this book can be downloaded from bpm-book.com.

It is interesting to see that the increasing adoption of business process technology poses interesting challenges to the research community. One of these challenges is to closer relate process models with the actual execution of the business processes. Since about a decade, an impressive body of work was done in process mining and business process intelligence. There are further topics that have emerged as challenges in real-world settings, such as compliance checking of process models, process model abstraction, and the management of process repositories, where issues like behavioural similarity and indexing of process models are investigated. Unfortunately, a text book on business process management cannot cover all these topics.

Still, this second edition contains a number of enhancements and modifications. The increasing importance of the BPMN in Version 2 is matched by extending significantly the respective section in the process orchestrations chapter. I also added a section on BPMN in the process choreographies chapter to discuss the language constructs for expressing process interactions, conversations, and choreographies. A concrete consistency criterion for process orchestrations implementing behavioural interfaces is introduced, which makes the discussion of the consistency property more tangible. In the process properties chapter, I extended the section on data in processes, which now also covers properties of a business process with respect to the data objects it works on. To improve the integration of the business process management methodology with the concepts introduced in the first part of the book, I rewrote the methodology chapter. It now discusses the relationships between business processes in much more detail and it also introduces performance indicators for business processes and concepts on how to measure them.

In addition to these extensions of the book, there are many minor changes, which, I hope, will increase its readability and soundness. Quite a number of them were triggered by readers, whose feedback I am happy to acknowledge. Thanks to all members of my research group at HPI; your comments and remarks on earlier versions of this manuscript have helped improving the book. Special thanks to Matthias Kunze and Alexander Lübbe for their feedback, mainly on the BPMN sections. I would also like to thank the Berliner BPM Offensive for providing me with the stencil set of the BPMN shapes. The shapes are much nicer than I could ever do them, they helped a lot!

Potsdam, March 2012   *M.W.*

Preface

The extensive ground covered by business process management is divided between representatives from two communities: business administration and computer science. Due to the increasingly important role of information systems in the realization of business processes, a common understanding of and productive interaction between these communities are essential.

Due to different viewpoints, however, the interaction between these communities is seldom seamless. Business administration professionals tend to consider information technology as a subordinate aspect in business process management that experts will take care of. On the other hand, computer science professionals often consider business goals and organizational regulations as terms that do not deserve much thought, but require the appropriate level of abstraction.

This book argues that we need to have a common understanding of the different aspects of business process management addressed by all communities involved. Robust and correct realization of business processes in software that increases customer satisfaction and ultimately contributes to the competitive advantage of an enterprise can only be achieved through productive communication between these communities.

By structuring business process management, this book aims at providing a step towards a better understanding of the concepts involved in business process management—from the perspective of a computer scientist.

If business persons find the book too technical, software people find it too non-technical, and formal persons find it too imprecise, but all of them have a better understanding of the ground covered by our discipline, this book has achieved its goal.

The Web site bpm-book.com contains additional information related to this book, such as links to references that are available online and exercises that facilitate the reader's getting into deeper contact with the topics addressed. Teaching material is also available at that Web site.

This book is based on material used in the business process management lectures that the author has conducted in the Master's and Bachelor's program in IT Systems Engineering at the Hasso Plattner Institute for IT Systems Engineering at the University of Potsdam. I am thankful for the critical remarks by my students, who encouraged me to shape the content of my lectures, which ultimately led to this book.

Many people contributed to this book. First of all, I like to thank my colleague researchers in business process management for developing this area in recent years, most prominently Wil van der Aalst, Alistair Barros, Marlon Dumas, Arthur ter Hofstede, Axel Martens, and Manfred Reichert. The chapter on case handling is based on joint work with Wil van der Aalst and Dolf Grünbauer. I am grateful to Barbara Weber for her detailled comments on the manuscript that have led to improvements, mainly in the chapter on process orchestrations.

I acknowledge the support of the members of my research group at Hasso Plattner Institute. Gero Decker, Frank Puhlmann, and Hilmar Schuschel were involved in the preparation of the assignments of the business process management lectures. Together with Dominik Kuropka and Harald Meyer, they provided valuable comments on earlier versions of the manuscript. Special thanks to Gero Decker for contributing the first version of the process choreographies chapter.

The lion's share of my acknowledgements goes to my family, and foremost to Daniela.

Potsdam, July 2007   *M.W.*

Contents

Part I

Foundation

1

Introduction

Business process management has received considerable attention recently by both business administration and computer science communities.

Members of these communities are typically characterized by different educational backgrounds and interests. People in business administration are interested in improving the operations of companies. Increasing customer satisfaction, reducing cost of doing business, and establishing new products and services at low cost are important aspects of business process management from a business administration point of view.

Two communities in computer science are interested in business processes. Researchers with a background in formal methods investigate structural properties of processes. Since these properties can only be shown using abstractions of real-world business processes, process activities are typically reduced to letters. Using this abstraction, interesting observations on structural properties of business processes can be made, which are very useful for detecting structural deficiencies in real-world business processes.

The software community is interested in providing robust and scalable software systems. Since business processes are realized in complex information technology landscapes, the integration of existing information systems is an important basis for the technical realization of business processes.

The goal of this book is to narrow the gap between these different points of view and to provide a step towards a common understanding of the concepts and technologies in business process management.

The introductory chapter looks at the motivation for business process management from a high-level point of view. The background of business process management is explained, and major concepts and terms are introduced. An example featuring an ordering process is used to illustrate these concepts. The phases in setting up and maintaining business process management applications are discussed. A classification of business processes and an overview of the structure of this book complete this chapter.

© Springer-Verlag GmbH Germany, part of Springer Nature 2019
M. Weske, *Business Process Management*,
https://doi.org/10.1007/978-3-662-59432-2_1

1.1 Motivation and Definitions

Business process management is based on the observation that each product that a company provides to the market is the outcome of a number of activities performed. Business processes are the key instrument to organizing these activities and to improving the understanding of their interrelationships.

Information technology in general and information systems in particular deserve an important role in business process management, because more and more activities that a company performs are supported by information systems. Business process activities can be performed by the company's employees manually or by the help of information systems. There are also business process activities that can be enacted automatically by information systems, without any human involvement.

A company can reach its business goals in an efficient and effective manner only if people and other enterprise resources, such as information systems, play together well. Business processes are an important concept to facilitating this effective collaboration.

In many companies there is a gap between organizational business aspects and the information technology that is in place. Narrowing this gap between organization and technology is important, because in today's dynamic markets, companies are constantly forced to provide better and more specific products to their customers. Products that are successful today might not be successful tomorrow. If a competitor provides a cheaper, better designed, or more conveniently usable product, the market share of the first product will most likely diminish.

Internet-based communication facilities spread news of new products at lightning speed, so traditional product cycles are not suitable for coping with today's dynamic markets. The abilities to create a new product and to bring it to the market rapidly, and to adapt an existing product at low cost have become competitive advantages of successful companies.

While at an organizational level, business processes are essential to understanding how companies operate, business processes also play an important role in the design and realization of flexible information systems. These information systems provide the technical basis for the rapid creation of new functionality that realizes new products and for adapting existing functionality to cater to new market requirements.

Business process management is influenced by concepts and technologies from different areas of business administration and computer science. Based on early work in organization and management, business process management has its roots in the process orientation trend of the 1990s, where a new way of organizing companies on the basis of business processes was proposed.

In their seminal book *Reengineering the Corporation*, Michael Hammer and James Champy advocate the radical redesign of the business processes of a company. They define a business process as a collection of activities that take one or more kinds of input and create an output that is of value to the customer.

While it has been argued that a radical redesign of business processes is, in many cases, not the best choice and that evolutionary improvements are more promising, the business process definition by Hammer and Champy is a good starting point for our investigations.

This definition puts emphasis on the input/output behaviour of a business process by stating its precondition (inputs) and its postcondition (output). The process itself is described in an abstract way by a collection of activities. Assuming that the term "collection" neither implies an ordering of the activities nor any other execution constraints, the definition by Hammer and Champy is quite liberal with regard to the process aspect.

Execution constraints between activities are identified by Davenport, who defines a business process as "a set of logically related tasks performed to achieve a defined business outcome for a particular customer or market."

The term "logically related" puts emphasis on the process activities, while associating the outcome of a business process with a requestor of a product, that is, a customer. Davenport also considers the relationship of process activities, including their execution ordering, by defining a business process as "a specific ordering of work activities across time and place, with a beginning, an end, and clearly identified inputs and outputs." He continues, "business processes have customers (internal or external) and they cross organizational boundaries, that is, they occur across or between organizational subunits."

Based on these characterizations of business processes, we adopt the following definition.

Definition 1.1 A *business process* consists of a set of activities that are performed in coordination in an organizational and technical environment. These activities jointly realize a business goal. Each business process is enacted by a single organization, but it may interact with business processes performed by other organizations.   ◇

After a first consideration of business processes, their constituents, and their interactions, the view is broadened. Business process management not only covers the representation of business processes, but also additional activities.

Definition 1.2 *Business process management* includes concepts, methods, and techniques to support the design, administration, configuration, enactment, and analysis of business processes.   ◇

The basis of business process management is the explicit representation of business processes with their activities and the execution constraints between them. Once business processes are defined, they can be subject to analysis, improvement, and enactment. These aspects of business process management will be introduced in Section 1.2.

Traditionally, business processes are enacted manually, guided by the knowledge of the company's personnel and assisted by the organizational regulations and procedures that are installed.

Enterprises can achieve additional benefits if they use software systems for coordinating the activities involved in business processes. These software systems are called business process management systems.

Definition 1.3 A *business process management system* is a generic software system that is driven by explicit process representations to coordinate the enactment of business processes.   ◇

The definitions introduced so far are illustrated by a sample business process. Because of its clarity and limited complexity, a simple ordering process is well suited. In the ordering process, an order is received, an invoice is sent, payment is received, and the ordered products are shipped.

This textual representation lists the activities of the business process, but it does not make explicit the ordering according to which these activities are performed. Graphical notations are well suited to expressing orderings between activities of a business process.

The ordering process of a reseller company is shown in Figure 1.1. The process consists of a set of activities performed in a coordinated manner. The coordination between the activities is achieved by an explicit process representation using execution constraints. The process starts with the company receiving and checking an order, followed by activities in concurrent branches. In one branch, the invoice is sent and the payment is received; in the other branch, the products are shipped. When both branches complete their activities, the order is archived, and the business process terminates. At this point in time, the reseller has processed an incoming order, including shipping the product and receiving the payment, which realizes a business goal of the reseller.

While there are several graphical notations for business process modelling, their essence is quite similar. This introductory chapter uses a simplified variant of the Business Process Model and Notation, BPMN. In this notation, activities are represented by rounded rectangles, marked with the name of the activity. Events can be used to mark the start and end of the process. Events are represented by circles. An event can be marked with a symbol indicating the type of the event. In the example, we use a start event with an envelope mark ("message start event" in BPMN) to represent that the process starts on receiving a message. Execution ordering of activities is expressed by directed arrows.

Branching and joining of nodes is represented by diamonds that can be marked with different symbols. In the sample process shown in Figure 1.1, a diamond with a plus sign, a single incoming arc, and multiple outgoing arcs represents a parallel split, which means that the follow-up activities can be executed concurrently. Concurrent activities can be executed in any order, and any overlap in the execution time of concurrent activities is allowed.

The same symbol with multiple incoming arcs and a single outgoing arc is the respective join node, merging the concurrent branches. In the example, this join node makes sure that the archiving of the order can only be started once both concurrent branches have completed. The Business Process Model and Notation will be discussed in detail in Chapter 4.

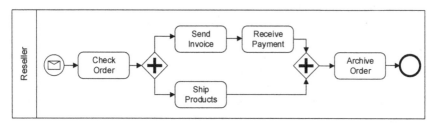

Fig. 1.1. Simple ordering process of reseller

The ordering process shown can be used as a blueprint that allows the reseller company to organize its work. The company will receive many orders, each of which can be processed as described in the blueprint. This observation gives rise to important concepts in business process management: business process models and business process instances.

The blueprint shown in Figure 1.1 is the business process model. Each order that is processed according to this model is a business process instance. Therefore, there is a one-to-many relationship between business process models and business process instances. Conceptual models of business process models and instances will be the subject of Chapter 3.

Definition 1.4 A *business process model* consists of a set of activity models and execution constraints between them. A *business process instance* represents a concrete case in the operational business of a company, consisting of activity instances. Each business process model acts as a blueprint for a set of business process instances, and each activity model acts as a blueprint for a set of activity instances.   ◇

If no confusion is possible, the term *business process* is used to refer to either business process models or business process instances. Analogously, *activity* is used to refer to either activity models or activity instances.

Business process models are the main artefacts for implementing business processes. This implementation can be done by organizational rules and policies, but it can also be done by a software system, using a business process management system. In this case, according to Definition 1.3, the software system is driven by explicit process representations.

The business process model shown in Figure 1.1 can be used to configure the process management system accordingly. The resulting system makes sure that all business process instances are executed as specified in the business process model and that, for instance, after receiving an order, the *Send Invoice* and the *Ship Products* activities are executed concurrently.

Since business processes are performed in a single organization by definition, the ordering of activities can be controlled by a business process management system as a centralized software component run by the reseller company. This centralized control is very similar to a conductor who centrally controls the musicians in an orchestra; therefore, business processes are also called *process orchestrations*. Chapter 4 will investigate languages to express process orchestrations.

The business process model shown in Figure 1.1 represents activities that a reseller performs to process an incoming order. This business process interacts with the business process of a corresponding buyer. The buyer sends an order, receives payment information, settles the invoice, and receives the ordered products.

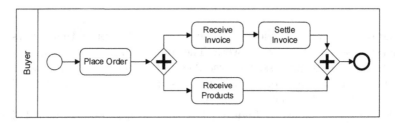

Fig. 1.2. Ordering process of a buyer

The business process of the buyer is shown in Figure 1.2. It starts with its placing an order, before two concurrent branches are opened. In one branch, the invoice is received and the invoice is settled. In the other branch, the product is received. When both branches complete, the business process of the buyer completes.

Definition 1.1 indicates that each business process is enacted by one organization, and that business processes can interact with each other. The business processes of the reseller and the buyer can, for instance, interact with each other in the following way.

1. The buyer sends an order message to the reseller.
2. The reseller receives that message in a start event. The order information is then extracted from the message, and order processing starts.
3. The reseller sends an invoice and ships the ordered products.
4. The buyer receives the invoice.
5. The buyer settles the invoice.
6. Finally, the buyer receives the ordered products.

The interacting business processes are shown in Figure 1.3. Interacting activities of the reseller business process and the buyer business process are related to each other by dotted arcs, representing the flow of messages. Message flow can represent electronic messages sent and received, but also the transport of physical objects, such as ordered products.

The interactions of a set of business processes are specified in a *process choreography*. The term choreography indicates the absence of a central agent that controls the activities in the business processes involved. The interaction is only achieved by sending and receiving messages. In order to realize correct interactions, the interacting business processes need to agree on a common choreography before they start interacting.

This situation is similar to dancers who need to agree on a common choreography before the show starts. During the performance, however, each dancer behaves autonomously but in line with his or her part in the choreography. Process choreographies will be discussed in detail in Chapter 6.

The representation of the business process choreography is shown in Figure 1.3; it also represents start events and end events of the interacting business processes, marked by circles.

This process choreography allows for multiple concrete implementations, in which the degree of software support can differ. Traditional ways of ordering goods that are not supported by information systems are well captured by this business process interaction. A buyer browses a paper catalogue of a reseller, selects a set of products, fills a postcard with ordering information, and sends the postcard to the reseller.

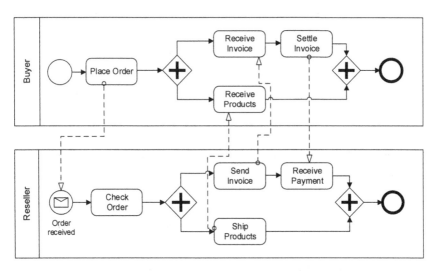

Fig. 1.3. Interacting business processes form process choreography

This postcard effectively implements the message flow from the buyer to the reseller. On receiving the postcard, the reseller sends the products and the invoice. The buyer receives the products and, assuming everything is fine, settles the received invoice, for instance, by money transfer. Once the money arrives at the reseller, the interacting business processes complete.

Large parts of the interacting business processes shown in Figure 1.3 can also be implemented by software systems. The buyer might use a Web browser to search the online catalogue of the reseller; she fills her shopping basket, provides address and billing information, and presses the submit button.

Pressing the submit button submits the order, that is, it realizes the message flow from the buyer to the reseller. The message flow from buyer to reseller is no longer implemented by surface mail, but by Internet protocols. The buyer's Web browser sends a message to the reseller's Web server, which calls a software module that places the order in the reseller's ordering system.

In case intangible goods have been ordered, such as music or software, sending the products can also be realized by software systems. The same applies for invoicing and billing, where online billing services can be integrated into the business process.

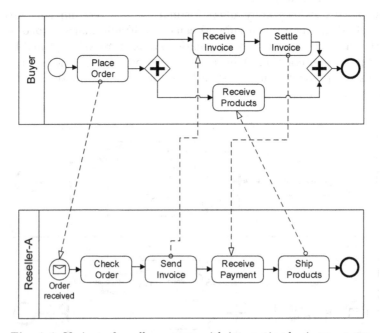

Fig. 1.4. Variant of reseller process with interacting business process

Graphical representations of business processes, as shown in the examples, focus on the process structure and the interactions of the participating parties rather than on technical aspects of their realization. This is an important aspect in business process modelling, since the definition of business processes and their interaction behaviour does not prescribe certain implementation strategies or platforms.

The realization of business processes by participants can change without affecting the externally visible behaviour of the process, that is, without affecting the business process interaction. To illustrate this property, the buyer interacts with a different reseller, called *Reseller-A* in Figure 1.4. The business process of this reseller performs the activities in a sequential order; there are no concurrent activities as in the business process of the original reseller.

Reseller-A realizes the following business rule: a product is sent only after the payment has been received. This is a sensible approach that protects the reseller from fraudulent buyers. The business process of *Reseller-A* also works well with the buyer process, since the concurrent branches allow the products to be received after the invoice is settled. However, overall execution might take longer than in the first case, since fewer activities can be performed concurrently.

The examples discussed so far have shown how to represent individual business processes that realize process orchestrations. We have also looked at interacting business processes that realize process choreographies. These examples focus on the activities of business processes and their relationships and on the business partners involved. The next section will consider the development of business processes and software platforms that realize them by introducing the business process lifecycle.

1.2 Business Process Lifecycle

The goal of this section is providing an overall understanding of the concepts and technologies that are relevant in business process management, using a business process lifecycle. This lifecycle is also useful for scoping the contents of this book.

The business process lifecycle is shown in Figure 1.5; it consists of phases that are related to each other. The phases are organized in a cyclical structure, showing their logical dependencies. These dependencies do not imply a strict temporal ordering in which the phases need to be executed. Many design and development activities are conducted during each of these phases, and incremental and evolutionary approaches involving concurrent activities in multiple phases are not uncommon.

Chapter 9 extends this lifecycle by proposing a methodology for the development of business process applications.

Design and Analysis

The business process lifecycle is entered in the *Design and Analysis* phase, in which surveys on the business processes and their organizational and technical environment are conducted. Based on these surveys, business processes are identified, reviewed, validated, and represented by business process models.

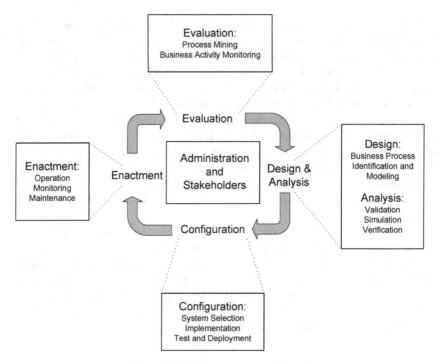

Fig. 1.5. Business process lifecycle

Explicit business process models expressed in a graphical notation facilitate communication about these processes, so that different stakeholders can communicate efficiently, and refine and improve them. Chapter 4 investigates languages to express business process models.

Business process modelling techniques as well as validation, simulation, and verification techniques are used during this phase. Business process modelling is the core technical subphase during process design. Based on the survey and the findings of the business process improvement activities, the informal business process description is formalized using a particular business process modelling notation.

Once an initial design of a business process is developed, it needs to be validated. A useful instrument to validate a business process is a workshop, during which the persons involved discuss the process. The participants of the workshop will check whether all valid business process instances are reflected by the business process model.

Simulation techniques can be used to support validation, because certain undesired execution sequences might be simulated that show deficits in the process model. Simulation of business processes also allows stakeholders to walk through the process in a step-by-step manner and to check whether the process actually exposes the desired behaviour. Most business process management systems provide a simulation environment that can be used in this phase.

Business processes involving multiple participants play an increasing role to foster the collaboration between enterprises. The design and analysis of interacting business processes is subject of Chapter 6.

Business process modelling has an evolutionary character in the sense that the process model is analyzed and improved so that it actually represents the desired business process and that it does not contain any undesired properties. Deadlock is such a property, in which all activities in a business process come to a halt. Chapter 7 investigates the verification of business process models with respect to correctness properties.

Configuration

Once the business process model is designed and verified, the business process needs to be implemented. There are different ways to do so. It can be implemented by a set of policies and procedures that the employees of the enterprise need to comply with. In this case, a business process can be realized without any support by a dedicated business process management system.

In case a dedicated software system is used to realize the business process, an implementation platform is chosen during the configuration phase. The business process model is enhanced with technical information that facilitates the enactment of the process by the business process management system.

The system needs to be configured according to the organizational environment of the enterprise and the business processes whose enactment it should control. This configuration includes the interactions of the employees with the system as well as the integration of the existing software systems with the business process management system.

The latter is important, since in today's business organizations, most business processes are supported by existing software systems. Depending on the information technology infrastructure, the process configuration phase might also include implementation work, for instance, attaching legacy software systems to the business process management system.

The configuration of a business process management system might also involve transactional aspects. Transactions are a well-known concept from database technology, where a transaction manager guarantees that application programs run as transactions and obey the ACID principle: atomicity, consistency, isolation, and durability. This means that transactions are executed in an atomic all-or-nothing fashion, they transfer a consistent database state into another consistent database state, they do not interfere with other transactions, and transaction results are durable and survive future system failures.

While in business process management database applications with transactional properties play an important role to realize process activities, transactional properties can also be defined at the business process level; a subset of the process activities form one business transaction, so that either all activities in this set are performed successfully or none is executed, realizing the atomicity property.

Unfortunately, the techniques that guarantee transactional behaviour in database systems cannot be used for business process transactions, since they are based on preventing access to data objects by locking, and locking data objects during process instances is no valid option. Business transactions are currently at the research stage; therefore, this book does not investigate them further.

Once the system is configured, the implementation of the business process needs to be tested. Traditional testing techniques from the software engineering area are used at the level of process activities to check, for instance, whether a software system exposes the expected behaviour.

At the process level, integration and performance tests are important for detecting potential run time problems during the configuration phase. Once the test subphase is complete, the system is deployed in its target environment. Depending on the particular setting, additional activities might be required, for instance, training of personnel and migration of application data to the new realization platform.

The configuration of business process management systems and the respective software architectures are investigated in Chapter 8.

Enactment

Once the system configuration phase is completed, business process instances can be enacted. The process enactment phase encompasses the actual run time of the business process. Business process instances are initiated to fulfill the business goals of a company. Initiation of a process instance typically follows a defined event, for instance, the receipt of an order sent by a customer.

The business process management system actively controls the execution of business process instances as defined in the business process model. Process enactment needs to cater to a correct process orchestration, guaranteeing that the process activities are performed according to the execution constraints specified in the process model.

A monitoring component of a business process management system visualizes the status of business process instances. Process monitoring is an important mechanism for providing accurate information on the status of business process instances. This information is valuable, for instance, to respond to a customer request that inquires about the current status of his case.

Detailed information on the current state of process instances are available in a business process management system. In Section 3.4, the states and state transitions of activity instances are investigated, while Section 3.5 covers process instances. State information can be used to visualize and monitor process instances. Visualization techniques can be based on colours, so that, for instance, an enabled activity is shown in green, a running instance is marked in blue, and a completed process instance is represented in grey. Most business process management systems provide monitoring information that is based on states of active business processes.

During business process enactment, valuable execution data is gathered, typically in some form of log file. These log files consist of ordered sets of log entries, indicating events that have occurred during business processes. Start of activity and end of activity is typical information stored in execution logs. Log information is the basis for evaluation of processes in the next phase of the business process lifecycle.

Evaluation

The evaluation phase uses information available to evaluate and improve business process models and their implementations. Execution logs are evaluated using business activity monitoring and process mining techniques. These techniques aim at identifying the quality of business process models and the adequacy of the execution environment.

For instance, business activity monitoring might identify that a certain activity takes too long due to shortage of resources required to conduct it. Since this information is useful also for business process simulation, these phases are strongly related.

Similar considerations apply to process mining, which has recently developed into an active field of research. There are different applications of process mining. If the execution logs are generated by traditional information systems, they collectively can be used as a starting point to develop business process models. The evaluation of existing business process models is another application area of process mining. The evaluation phase is not covered in detail in this book; for further information, the reader is referred to the bibliographical notes in the end of this part.

Administration and Stakeholders

There are numerous artefacts at different levels of abstraction in business process management scenarios that need to be organized and managed well. Structured storage and efficient retrieval of artefacts regarding business process models and information on business process instances as well as the organizational and technical execution environment need to be taken into account.

Especially in large organizations with hundreds or thousands of business process models, a well-structured repository with powerful query mechanisms is essential. In addition to business processes, knowledge workers with their organizational roles and skills, as well as the information technology landscape of the enterprise, need to be represented properly.

The business process domain is characterized by several types of stakeholders with different knowledge, expertise, and experience; these are classified into the following roles:

- *Chief Process Officer*: The chief process officer is responsible for standardizing and harmonizing business processes in the enterprise. In addition, he or she is responsible for the evolution of business processes in the presence of changing market requirements. Installing an explicit role of chief process officer acknowledges the importance of business process management at the top level management.

- *Business Engineer*: Business engineers are business domain experts responsible for defining strategic goals of the company and organizational business processes. Often, business engineers have a nontechnical educational background, so that convenient and simple-to-use process modelling notations are required to communicate about business processes with these stakeholders.

- *Process Designer*: Process designers are responsible for modelling business processes by communicating with business domain experts and other stakeholders. Very good analytical capabilities and excellent communication skills are important for a process designer.

- *Process Participant*: Process participants conduct the actual operational work during the enactment of business process instances. They also play an important role during business process modelling, because they are knowledgeable about the activities conducted and their interrelationships with activities conducted by other process participants. It is the task of the process designer to assemble from this information a consistent overall view and capture it as a business process model.

- *Knowledge Worker*: Knowledge workers are process participants who use software systems to perform activities in a business process. Knowledge workers are equipped with detailed knowledge of the application domain, and they can perform activities, or even parts of business processes, autonomously.

- *Process Owner*: Each business process model is assigned an individual who is responsible for the correct and efficient execution of the process. He or she is responsible for detecting inefficiencies in the process and for improving it, in close collaboration with the process participants and the process designers.

- *System Architect*: System architects are responsible for developing and configuring business process management systems so that the configured business process management system enacts the business processes in the context of the information systems infrastructure at hand.

- *Developers*: Developers are information technology professionals who create software artefacts required to implement business processes. The implementation of interfaces to existing software systems is an important area of work for developers.

These different types of stakeholders need to cooperate closely in designing business processes and in developing adequate solutions for enacting them. The business process lifecycle provides a rough organization of the work conducted and the concepts used in this endeavour. In Chapter 9 the specific properties of development methodologies for business process management applications are discussed in more detail.

1.3 Classification of Business Processes

In this section, the main dimensions along which business processes can be classified are investigated.

Organizational versus Operational

Different levels of abstraction can be identified in business process management, ranging from high-level business goals and business strategies to implemented business processes. These levels are depicted in Figure 1.6. At the highest level, business goals and strategies are specified. Business goals refer to the long-term objectives of the company, while business strategies refer to its plans for achieving these goals.

At the second level, organizational business processes can be found. *Organizational business processes* are high-level processes that are typically specified in textual form by their inputs, their outputs, their expected results, and their dependencies on other organizational business processes. These business processes act as supplier or consumer processes. An organizational business process to manage incoming raw materials provided by a set of suppliers is an example of an organizational business process.

Informal and semiformal techniques are used at these high levels. The strategy of a company, its goals, and its organizational business processes can be described in plain text, enriched with diagrams expressed in an adhoc or semiformal notation. A forms-based approach to express organizational business processes is discussed in the next chapter.

While organizational business processes characterize coarse-grained business functionality, typically there are multiple operational business processes required that contribute to one organizational business process. In *operational business processes*, the activities and their relationships are specified, but implementation aspects of the business process are disregarded. Operational business processes are specified by business process models.

Operational business processes are the basis for developing implemented business processes. *Implemented business processes* contain information on the execution of the process activities and the technical and organizational environment in which they will be executed.

As discussed earlier in this chapter, there are multiple ways to implement business processes, ranging from written procedures and policies of the organization to the use of process enactment platforms. In any case, implemented business process refers to a specification that allows the enactment of the process on a given platform, be it organizational or technical.

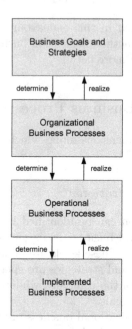

Fig. 1.6. Levels of business processes: from business goals and strategies to implemented business processes

Intraorganizational Processes versus Process Choreographies

As defined above, each business process is performed by a single organization. If there is no interaction with business processes performed by other parties, then the business process is called *intraorganizational*. Most business processes, however, interact with business processes in other organizations, forming process choreographies. The ordering process choreography discussed earlier in this chapter is an example of interacting business processes.

The primary focus of intraorganizational business processes is the streamlining of the internal processes by eliminating activities that do not provide value. The personnel of the enterprise is represented in organizational models used to allocate activities to persons who are skilled and competent to perform these activities. Traditional process management systems can be used to support intraorganizational business processes.

There are a number of issues to address when dealing with interacting business processes, including not only communication aspects related to the process structures, but also legal matters. Interactions between business processes need to be protected by legally binding contracts between the companies involved.

Also, the technical layer requires more thought, since multiple organizations have most likely a heterogeneous software infrastructure that hampers interoperability in the software layer. Process choreographies are discussed in detail in Chapter 6.

Degree of Automation

Business processes can diverge in the level of automation. There are business processes that are fully automated, meaning that no human is involved in the enactment of such a business process. An example is ordering an airline ticket using Web interfaces. While the process is fully automated on the side of the airline, the customer is involved with manual activities, such as providing address information via Web browser interfaces.

Enterprise application integration is another area where automated business processes can be found. The goal is to integrate the functionality provided by a heterogeneous software landscape. While there are different techniques to integrate enterprise applications, process technology is an important technology, especially since the emergence of service-oriented software architectures that allow composing services to processes.

Many business processes require manual activities; but they also include automated activities. Processing an insurance claim is an example of such a process. Manual activities enter the customer data and determine the settlement of the damage, while automated activities are used to store data on the damage in the software systems of the company.

The interaction with the human user is essential in these settings. Early approaches that prescribe to human users "what to do next" often failed. User interfaces that accept the knowledge worker as an important source to improve and control the process provide more user acceptance.

Degree of Repetition

Business processes can be classified according to their degree of repetition. Examples of highly repetitive business processes include business processes without human involvement, such as online airline ticketing. However, business processes in which humans are involved can occur frequently, for example, insurance claim processing. If the degree of repetition is high, then investments in modelling and supporting the automatic enactment of these processes pay off, because many process instances can benefit from these investments.

At the other end of the repetition continuum, there are business processes that occur a few times only. Examples include large engineering efforts, such as designing a vessel. For these processes it is questionable whether the effort introduced by process modelling does in fact pay off, because the cost of process modelling per process instance is very high.

Since improving the collaboration between the persons involved is at the centre of attention, these processes are called *collaborative business processes*.

In collaborative business processes, the goal of process modelling and enactment is not only efficiency, but also tracing exactly what has actually been done and which causal relationships between project tasks have occurred.

This aspect is also present in the management of scientific experiments, where data lineage is an important goal of process support. Since each experiment consists of a set of activities, an increasing fraction of the experimentation is performed by analyzing data using software systems. The data is transformed in a series of steps. Since experiments need to be repeatable, it is essential that the relationship of the data sets be documented properly.

Business processes with a low degree of repetition are often not fully automated and have a collaborative character, so that the effort in providing automated solutions is not required, which lowers the cost.

Degree of Structuring

If the business process model prescribes the activities and their execution constraints in a complete fashion, then the process is structured. The different options for decisions that will be made during the enactment of the process have been defined at design time. For instance, a credit request process might use a threshold amount to decide whether a simple or a complex credit check is required, for instance, 5000 Euros. Each process instance then uses the requested amount to decide on the branch to take.

Leymann and Roller have organized business processes according to dimensions structure and repetition. They coined the term *production workflow*. Production workflows are well structured and highly repetitive. Traditional process management system functionality is well suited to supporting production workflows.

If process participants who have the experience and competence to decide on their working procedures perform business process activities, structured processes are more of an obstacle than an asset. Skipping certain process activities the knowledge worker does not require or executing steps concurrently that are ordered sequentially in the process model is not possible in structured business processes.

To better support knowledge workers, business process models can define processes in a less rigid manner, so that activities can be executed in any order or even multiple times until the knowledge worker decides that the goals of these activities have been reached. So-called *adhoc activities* are an important concept for supporting unstructured parts of processes.

Case handling is an approach that supports knowledge workers performing business processes with a low level of structuring and, consequently, a high level of flexibility. Rather than prescribing control flow constraints between process activities, fine-grained data dependencies are used to control the enactment of the business process. These aspects will be discussed in more detail in Chapter 8.

1.4 Structure, and Organization

The book is organized into three parts, providing a foundation of business process management, looking at concepts and languages for business process modelling, and investigating architectures and methodologies.

Part I continues with Chapter 2, which looks at business process management from a software systems point of view by investigating the evolution of enterprise systems architectures. The role of business process management systems and the relationships to other types of information systems are highlighted.

Part II covers business process modelling. Chapter 3 presents the foundation of business process modelling by introducing abstraction concepts. It also introduces a way to describe process models and process instances based on fundamental concepts, such as events that occur during the execution of business process instances and their dependencies.

Chapter 4 looks at process orchestrations by first discussing control flow patterns. The meaning of these patterns is expressed by properties of process instances using these patterns. A metamodel is used to specify the semantics of control flow patterns. An important part of this book deals with process modelling techniques and notations. The most important ones are discussed in a concise manner, including Petri nets, event-driven process chains, workflow nets, YAWL, a graph-based workflow language, and the modelling elements of the Business Process Model and Notation (BPMN), which are related to process orchestrations.

Chapter 5 covers business decision modelling. After a motivating section, the Decision Model and Notation (DMN) is introduced, which allows us to represent business decisions on different levels of abstraction, focusing on the structure of decisions and on decision logic, respectively. Decision tables are investigated in detail, since these allow us to express decision logic in a formally precise, yet well understandable manner.

Process choreographies are covered in Chapter 6. Process choreographies describe the interaction of multiple business processes and, as such, are an important concept for supporting business-to-business collaboration. After introducing high-level choreographies that specify dependencies between interactions of choreographies, service interaction patterns are discussed. Interesting issues occur with regard to the correctness of combined execution when combining multiple business processes. These issues are addressed by discussing the notions of compatibility and consistency. The public-to-private approach is introduced, a concrete technique to develop process orchestrations that are consistent with their behavioural interfaces. This chapter is complemented by introducing language elements of the Business Process Model and Notation that are related to process choreographies.

Properties of business process models are investigated in Chapter 7. Correct data dependencies within a process are a simple type of correctness property of a business process. With object lifecycle conformance, a property of business processes with respect to the data objects they operate on, is introduced. Other correctness criteria have been proposed as different types of soundness criteria. If a business process is sound, then each process instance enjoys certain execution guarantees, for instance, freedom from deadlock. There are different types of soundness properties, each of which takes into account some specific aspect of the business process executed. With the development of business decision management, the traditional soundness criteria have to be extended to decision soundness, which is motivated, defined, and illustrated by examples.

Part III investigates architectures of business process management systems and methodologies to develop business process applications. Chapter 8 introduces traditional workflow management architectures. Based on a discussion of Web services as the current implementation of service-oriented architectures, Web services composition is discussed as the mechanism to realize business processes whose activities are implemented by Web services. To ease the composition of services, advanced service composition, which takes advantage of semantic annotations of services, is discussed. Chapter 8 completes by introducing data-driven process control and its realization in case handling systems.

Chapter 9 introduces a methodology for the development of business process applications involving human users. This methodology provides an understanding of the complexity and of the technical and organizational difficulties in the design and development of business process applications.

Evolution of Enterprise Systems Architectures

Process orientation in general and business process management in particular are parts of a larger development that has been affecting the design of information systems since its beginning: the evolution of enterprise systems architectures.

Enterprise systems architectures are mainly composed of information systems. These systems can be distinguished from software systems in the area of embedded computing that control physical devices such as mobile phones, cars, or airplanes. Business process management mainly deals with information systems in the context of enterprise systems architectures.

The guiding principle of this evolution is separation of concerns, a principle identified by Edsger Dijkstra and characterized by "focusing one's attention upon some aspect." It is one of the key principles in handling the complexity of computer systems.

While this principle has many applications in theoretical and applied computer science, in the context of software systems design—and therefore also in information systems design—it means identifying sets of related functionality and packaging them in a subsystem with clearly identified responsibilities and interfaces. Using this approach, complex and powerful software systems can be engineered. Separation of concerns also facilitates reuse at a level of coarse granularity, because well-specified functional units provided by subsystems can be used by different applications.

Separation of concerns also facilitates response to change and is therefore an important mechanism to support flexibility of software systems, because individual subsystems can be modified or even exchanged with another subsystem providing the same functionality without changing other parts of the system—provided the interfaces remain stable.

Since local changes do not affect the overall system, a second guiding principle of computer science is realized: information hiding, originally introduced by David Parnas. Reasons for changes can be manifold: new requirements in an ever-changing dynamic market environment, changes in technology, and changes in legal regulations that need to be reflected in software systems.

M. Weske, *Business Process Management*,
https://doi.org/10.1007/978-3-662-59432-2_2

While effective response to change is an important goal of any software system, it is of particular relevance to business process management systems, as will be detailed below.

Before addressing the evolution of enterprise systems architectures, the understanding of software architectures as used in this book is described. In general, software architectures play a central role in handling the complexity of software systems.

Definition 2.1 A *software architecture* defines a structure that organizes the software elements and the resources of a software system. Software elements and resources are represented by subsystems. In a given software architecture, these subsystems have specific responsibilities and relationships to other subsystems.   ◊

Software architectures do not detail the internal structure of a subsystem; but they detail their externally visible behaviour and, thus, their relationships to other subsystems of the architecture. Internal aspects of a subsystem can, however, be represented in the software architecture of the particular subsystem.

2.1 Traditional Application Development

The main goal of this section is to categorize business process management systems from a software systems point of view into major developments that information systems design underwent in the last decades. Figure 2.1 depicts the first stages in the evolution of information systems. The dates in that figure provide only rough estimates—the respective systems architectures were not uncommon at the dates given.

In the early days of computing, applications were developed from scratch, without taking advantage of prior achievements other than subroutines of fine granularity. Application programmers needed to code basic functionality such as, for instance, access to persistent storage and memory management. Basic functionality needed to be redeveloped in different applications, so that application programming was a costly and inefficient endeavour. As a result of the tight coupling of the programmed assembler code with the hardware, porting an application to a new computer system results in a more or less complete redevelopment.

Operating systems were developed as the first type of subsystem with dedicated responsibilities, realizing separation of operating systems concerns from the application. Operating systems provide programming interfaces to functionality provided by the computer hardware. Applications can implement functionality by using interfaces provided by the operating system, realizing increased efficiency in system development.

Specific properties of the computer hardware could be hidden from the application by the operating system, so that changes in the hardware could be reflected by a modified implementation of the operating system's interface, for instance, by developing a new driver for a new hardware device. An operating systems (OS) layer is depicted in Figure 2.1 as the lowest level subsystem.

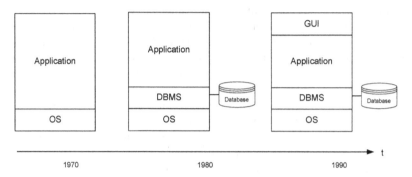

Fig. 2.1. Early systems architectures

The next step in the evolution of systems architectures considers the management of data. Before dedicated subsystems for handing data were developed, each application program was responsible for storing its data persistently and for retrieving it. Programming interfaces were used to store data. Since the structure of the stored data matches the data structure in the application program, each change in the data structures of the application results in a change of the data structures in persistent memory, and vice versa. Due to the strong link between the data structures in the application and the data structures in persistent memory, any modification requires implementation or reorganization effort.

Two additional problems are associated with this approach: the design and implementation of data management takes considerable implementation effort because dedicated storage and retrieval functionality need to be implemented in each application. In addition, data consistency issues arise if multiple applications store related data redundantly. In this case, the modification of a data item needs to be realized by a modification of each copy of the data item by different systems, introducing the potential for data inconsistency issues.

To provide a reusable set of functionality and to overcome the data inconsistency problem, database management systems were introduced. Following early data models, like the hierarchical data model and the network data model, relational databases were developed. Relational database systems allow modification of the structures of the physically stored data without affecting the application programs. This important property is known as physical data independence.

At the same time, logical data independence is covered, that is, the ability to change the logical organization of the data without the need to change applications. Efficient and convenient access to large amounts of data, declarative query languages, most prominently the Structured Query Language SQL, transaction processing capabilities to cater for concurrent access and recovery from failure situations, security aspects, and many more features are realized in today's database management systems. Today, relational database systems are an important backbone of modern information systems.

The layering of the subsystem—applications sit on top of database systems that sit on top of operating systems, as shown in Figure 2.1—is simplified. Applications do not only use the functionality provided by the database management system—as the layering might indicate. Applications also directly use functionality provided by the underlying operating system.

The next step in the evolution of information systems is dedicated to graphical user interfaces which were developed to ease human interaction with application systems. Before the advent of graphical user interfaces, users interacted with application programs on the basis of mostly textual interfaces that required extensive user training before work could be done efficiently.

Since until then applications covered a comparatively narrow ground and the users of these systems were highly specialized employees, textual or simple graphical interfaces were adequate for most applications. Due to increased functionality of applications and the associated broadening of the competence and skills of the personnel, more elaborate user interfaces were required.

The new role of the employees can be characterized as that of a knowledge worker. Knowledge workers have a large set of capabilities and skills at their disposal, from which they can choose the one that best suits the current task. In order to be effective, knowledge workers require advanced user interfaces to access the required functionality from powerful information systems.

The separation of the business logic covered in applications and the interaction between the system and the knowledge worker led to the development of graphical user interfaces, which also foster reuse of functionality at the user interface layer. Today, graphical user interfaces are developed using elaborate frameworks, increasing the efficiency of graphical user interface development.

2.2 Enterprise Applications and their Integration

Based on operating systems and communication systems as a basic abstraction layer, relational database management systems for storing and retrieving large amounts of data, and graphical user interface systems, more and more elaborate information systems could be engineered.

Most of these information systems host enterprise applications. These applications support enterprises in managing their core assets, including customers, personnel, products, and resources. Therefore, it is instructive to look in more detail at enterprise information systems, starting from individual enterprise applications and addressing the integration of multiple enterprise applications. The integration of multiple enterprise applications has spawned a new breed of middleware, enterprise application integration systems. Enterprise application integration proves to be an important application area of business process management.

These developments can be illustrated with an enterprise scenario. In the early stages of enterprise computing, mainframe solutions were developed that hosted monolithic applications, typically developed in assembler programming language. These monolithic applications managed all tasks with a single huge program, including the textual user interface, the application logic, and the data. Data was mostly stored in files, and the applications accessed data files through the operating system.

With the advent of database systems, an internal structuring of the system was achieved: data was managed by a database management system. However, the application code and the user interface code were not separated from each other. The user interface provides the desired functionality through textual, forms-based interfaces.

With lowering cost of computer hardware and growing requirements for application functionality, more application systems were developed. It was typical that an enterprise had one software system for human resources management, one for purchase order management and one for production planning. Each of these application systems hosted its local data, typically in a database system, but sometimes even on the file system. In large enterprises, in different departments, different application systems were sometimes used to cope with the same issue.

What made things complicated was the fact that these application systems hosted related data. This means that one logical data object, such as a customer address, was stored in different data stores managed by different application systems. Dependencies between data stored in multiple systems were also represented by dedicated links, for instance through a contract identifier or an employee identifier.

It is obvious that in these settings changes were hard to implement, because there are multiple data dependencies between these disparate systems, and changes in one system had to be mirrored by changes in other systems. Detecting the systems affected and the particular change required in these systems was complex and error-prone. As a result, any change of the data objects, for instance, of a customer address, needed to be reflected in multiple applications. This lack of integration led to inconsistent data and—in many cases—to dissatisfied customers. An application landscape showing these dependencies between multiple applications is shown in Figure 2.2.

2.2.1 Enterprise Resource Planning Systems

In this setting, Enterprise Resource Planning systems (ERP systems) were developed. The great achievement of enterprise resource planning systems is that they provide an integrated database that spans large parts of an organization. Enterprise resource planning systems basically reimplemented these

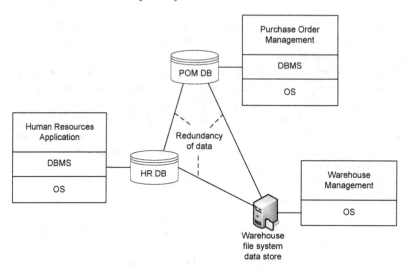

Fig. 2.2. Enterprise applications with redundant data and data dependencies

disparate enterprise application systems on the basis of an integrated and consistent database.

An enterprise resource planning system stores its data in one centralized database, and a set of application modules provides the desired functionality, including human resources, financials, and manufacturing. Enterprise resource planning systems have effectively replaced numerous heterogeneous enterprise applications, thereby solving the problem of integrating them.

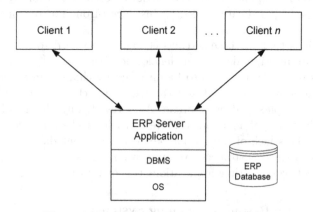

Fig. 2.3. Two-tier client-server architecture

Enterprise resource planning systems are accessed by client applications, as shown in Figure 2.3. These client applications access an application server that issues requests to a database server. We do not address the architectures of enterprise systems in detail but stress the integrated data storage and the remote access through client software.

With the growth of enterprises and new market requirements, driven by new customer needs around the year 2000, the demand for additional functionality arose, and new types of software systems entered the market. The most prominent types of software systems are supply chain management systems, or SCM systems, and customer relationship management systems, or CRM systems. While basic functionality regarding supply chain management has already been realized in enterprise resource planning systems, new challenges due to increased market dynamics have led to dedicated supply chain management systems. The main goal of these systems is to support the planning, operation, and control of supply chains, including inventory management, warehouse management, management of suppliers and distributors, and demand planning.

Regarding the evolution of enterprise systems architectures, the main point is that new types of information systems have entered the market, often developed by different vendors than that of the enterprise resource planning system many companies run. At the technical level, the supply chain management system hosts its own database, with data related to supply chains. Since large amounts of data are relevant for both enterprise resource planning and supply chain management, data is stored redundantly. As a result, system architects face the same problems as they did years ago with the heterogeneous enterprise applications.

As with the settings mentioned, in order to avoid data inconsistencies and, at the end of the day, dissatisfied customers, any modification of data needs to be transmitted to all systems that host redundant copies of the data. If, for example, information on a logistics partner changes that is relevant for both the enterprise resource planning system and the supply chain management system, then this change needs to be reflected in both systems. From a data integrity point of view, this change even needs to take place within a single distributed transaction, so that multiple concurrent changes do not interfere with each other.

The source of the problem is, again, redundant information spread across multiple application systems. Since this information is not integrated, the user of an enterprise resource planning system can access only the information stored in this system. However, the customer relationship management system also holds valuable data of this customer.

When the customer calls and the call centre personnel can only access the information stored in one system, and is therefore not aware of the complete status of the customer, the customer is likely to become upset; at least, he does not feel well served. The customer expects better service, where the personnel is aware of complete status and not just of partial status that happens to be stored in the software system that the call centre agent can access. In the scenario discussed, the call centre agent needs to know the complete status of the customer, no matter in which software system the information might be buried.

To characterize this unsatisfactory situation, the term *siloed applications* has been coined, meaning that data is stored redundantly in different systems, and these systems are not related at all. Figure 2.4 shows siloed enterprise applications customer relationship management, supply chain management, and enterprise resource planning systems. While these application systems can be physically connected by, for instance, a local network, they are not logically integrated.

As a result, the only way to integrate the information stored in these systems is through the user, who accesses the information in the various systems and does the integration manually. Obviously, this manual integration consumes considerable resources and is error-prone, so that other solutions are sought.

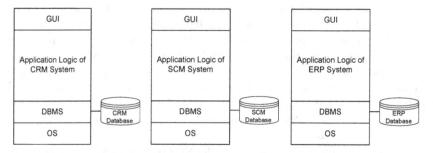

Fig. 2.4. Siloed enterprise applications

With enterprise resource planning systems, this problem had already been solved by redeveloping an integrated solution. Unfortunately, due to the large complexity of the systems at hand, the same approach to reimplementing systems functionality in an integrated way is not feasible in the new context. The only option is to integrate these systems, which leads to a new breed of middleware system, the enterprise application integration system.

2.2.2 Enterprise Application Integration

Enterprises are facing the challenge of integrating complex software systems in a heterogeneous information technology landscape that has grown in an evolutionary way for years, if not for decades. Most of the application systems have been developed independently of each other, and each application stores its data locally, either in a database system or some other data store, leading to siloed applications.

Data heterogeneity issues occur if a logical data item—for instance, a customer address—is stored multiple times in different siloed applications.

Assume that customer data is stored in an enterprise resource planning system and a customer relationship management system. Although both systems use a relational database as storage facility, the data structures will be different and not immediately comparable.

These differences involve both the types of particular data fields (strings of different length for attribute `CustomerName`), but also the names of the attributes. In the customer example, in one system the attribute `CAddr` will denote the address of the customer, while in the other system the attribute `StreetAdrC` denotes the address.

The next level of heterogeneity regards the semantics of the attributes. Assume there is an attribute `Price` in the product tables of two application systems. The naming of the attribute does not indicate whether the price includes or excludes value-added tax. These semantic differences need to be sorted out if the systems are integrated. Data integration technologies are used to cope with these syntactic and semantic difficulties.

Data integration is an important aspect in enterprise application integration. In this section, the traditional point-to-point enterprise application integration approach and an approach based on message brokers following the hub-and-spoke paradigm will be discussed.

Point-to-Point Integration

A typical enterprise scenario is represented in Figure 2.4, where siloed applications are shown; typically, many more application systems need to be integrated, often even several instances of a specific type of application system, such as enterprise resource planning systems, which in many cases run different versions of the software.

Enterprise application integration technology is based on middleware technology that has been around for years. The goal is to take advantage of these technologies so that data in heterogeneous information technology landscapes can be integrated properly. In addition to data integration, the processes that the application systems realize also need to be integrated. This means that one system performs certain steps and then transfers control to another system which takes the results and continues operation. In the context of this book, the process integration part of enterprise application integration is at the centre of attention.

Enterprise application integration faces the problem that each integration project requires design and implementation efforts that might be considerable. When directly linking each pair of applications, system integrators run into the $N \times N$ problem, meaning that the number of interfaces to develop rises to the square of the number N of applications to be integrated.

A sketch of this integration issue is represented in Figure 2.5, where $N = 6$ of siloed applications and their integration links are shown. Each link represents an interface that connects the application systems associated with it. Therefore, the number of interfaces between pairs of application systems to realize grows to the order of $N \times N$, incurring considerable overhead. If there were links between any pairs of application systems, then the number of interfaces to develop would be $5 + 4 + 3 + 2 + 1 = 15$. In the general case, the number of links between N application systems is

$$\sum_{i=1}^{N-1} i = \frac{1}{2}N(N-1)$$

and therefore rises to the square of the number of application systems. In the scenario shown, not all pairs of application systems are connected, but the problem of the large number of interfaces can nevertheless be seen.

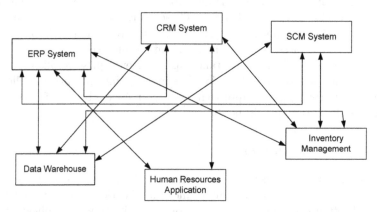

Fig. 2.5. Early enterprise application integration: hard-wiring of application systems results in $N \times N$ problem

In enterprise computing, changes are abundant, and a systems architecture should support changes in an efficient and effective manner. The enterprise application integration architecture resulting from point-to-point integration does not respond well to changes. The reason is due to the hard-wiring of the interfaces. Any change in the application landscape requires adaptation of the respective interfaces. This adaptation is typically realized by reprogramming interfaces, which requires considerable resources.

A specific realization platform of enterprise application integration is message-oriented middleware, where applications communicate by sending and receiving messages. While conceptually the middleware realizes a centralized component, the direct connection between the applications—and therefore the point-to-point integration—is still in place, because each sender needs to encode the receiver of a message.

The main aspect of message-oriented middleware is execution guarantees, such as guaranteed message delivery. However, the problem mentioned above is not solved, since any change in the application landscape needs to be implemented by changing the communication structure of applications.

A sample architecture of message-oriented middleware is shown in Figure 2.6. The sender of a message specifies the recipients of the message. As a result, the supply chain management system defines in its interface that a certain message needs to be received by a particular enterprise resource planning system and a particular customer relationship management system, hard-wiring these application systems via the implemented interfaces.

Message queues are used to store messages persistently and to realize guaranteed delivery. A client uses an application that integrates a number of application systems; this application is called *Integration Application* in Figure 2.6. In order to realize this integration, the integration application sends a message to another application system, for instance, to an enterprise resource planning system.

In order to do so, it inserts the message into the message queue of the enterprise resource planning system. The message is then relayed to the ERP system, which invokes the requested functionality and returns a result message to the integration application. This result message is inserted into the incoming message queue of the integration application. Receiving this message, the integration application prepares a message and sends it to the supply chain management system. Because each sender of a message needs to encode the receiver of the message, effectively a point-to-point connection between the applications is realized. Therefore, the problems of point-to-point connections in supporting change do not diminish in message-oriented middleware.

This example shows that the cooperation of the application systems is realized in the integration application. As in the early days of information systems evolution, the process that describes how this cooperation takes place is implemented by an application—in this case an integration application. As a result, the process is hardwired within an application, so that there is no explicit process model that can be easily communicated and changed, if required.

While message-oriented middleware provides important run time guarantees, response to change is not considerably improved. Still, any change in the application structure or in the process behaviour needs to be mirrored by a change in the communication structure, implemented for each application.

Hub-and-Spoke Integration

The *hub-and-spoke* paradigm is based on a centralized hub and a number of spokes that are directly attached to the hub; the spokes are not connected. The centralized enterprise application integration middleware represents the hub, and the applications to be integrated are reflected by the spokes. The applications interact with each other via the centralized enterprise application integration hub.

It is an important feature of hub-and-spoke architectures that the sender of a message need not encode the receiver of the message. Instead, each message is sent to the enterprise application integration hub. The hub is configured in

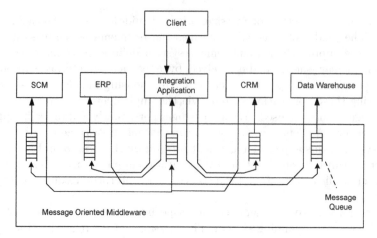

Fig. 2.6. Message-oriented middleware for reliable communication between applications. Senders of messages encode receivers, and process logic is encoded in applications

such a way that the message structure and content can be used to automatically detect the receiver or receivers of a message.

The advantage of these centralized middleware architectures is that the number of connections can be reduced. No longer are connections in the order of $N \times N$ required to connect N application systems. Since each application system is attached to the centralized hub, N interfaces will suffice. Using these interfaces, the specific relationships between the applications can be reflected in the configuration of the middleware.

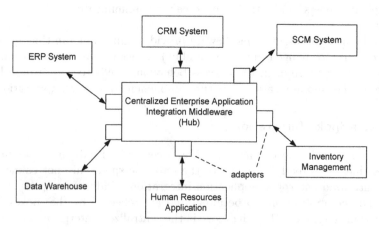

Fig. 2.7. Hub-and-spoke enterprise application integration architecture

A centralized enterprise application integration middleware following the hub-and-spoke paradigm is shown in Figure 2.7. The centralized hub provides adapters that hide the heterogeneity of the application systems from each other. Each application system requires the development of a dedicated adapter to attach to the hub.

Depending on the complexity of these systems—and the availability of generic adapters provided by the enterprise application integration vendor— the development of the adapter might consume considerable resources. When the adapters are in place and the hub is configured, the applications can interact with each other in an integrated manner.

On a technical level, message brokers can be used to realize a hub-and-spoke enterprise application integration system. Message brokers are software systems that allow a user to define rules for communication between applications. Therefore, the burden of implementing—and changing—communication structures is taken away from applications. By defining in a declarative way how communication between applications takes place, implementation is redeemed by declaration, that is, by the declaration of the communication structures. Response to change is improved, because the sender is not required to implement these changes locally. These changes can be specified in a declarative way in the central hub, rather than by coding in the applications.

The hub uses rules to manage the dependencies between the applications. Based on these rules, the hub can use information on the identity of the sender, the message type, and the message content to decide on which message queues to relay a message received. Besides relaying messages to recipients, message brokers also transform messages to realize data mapping between the applications, so that data heterogeneity issues can be handled appropriately. Adapters of application systems are used to perform these message transformations.

As shown in Figure 2.8, each application is linked to the message broker, reflected by the directed arcs from the applications to the message broker, in particular, to the rule evaluation component of the message broker. On receipt of a message, the message broker evaluates the rules and inserts the message into the queues of the recipients.

The queues are used for guaranteed delivery of messages. Note that any change in the communication is handled through the message broker: by establishing new rules or by adapting existing rules, these changes can be realized. There is no implementation effort required for realizing these changes; just a modification of the declarative rules.

Publish/subscribe is a mechanism to link applications to message brokers. The idea is that applications can subscribe to certain messages or types of messages. Applications can also publish messages. The information received by publish and subscribe are used by the enterprise application integration hub to realize the relaying of messages. Figure 2.8 also shows that at a technical level enterprise application integration with a message broker relies on

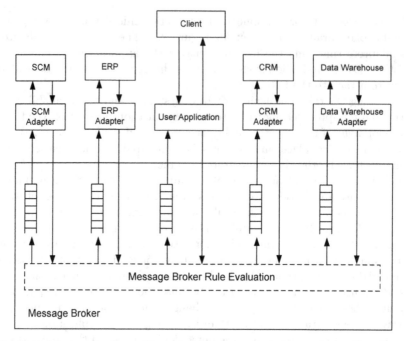

Fig. 2.8. Message broker with declarative rules that de-couples senders from receivers and eases response to change

adapters that are used for transforming data and protocols between senders and receivers.

Based on a message broker in which adapters for the applications to be integrated are in place, applications can be integrated by developing an integration application. This integration application communicates with the message broker and, via the message broker and the adapters of the respective systems, with the backend application systems.

Various types of interaction between the applications are possible, ranging from simple invocations to complex interactions between multiple applications. These complex interactions consist of a series of activities, each of which is represented by an invocation of an application system. These activities can be ordered, so that execution constraints are in place between the respective invocations. These execution constraints might be determined by data dependencies, so that a particular function of the enterprise resource planning system can only be started when particular customer information is extracted from the customer relationship management system.

While message brokers are a feasible solution to the enterprise application integration problem, there are also some drawbacks with them. First of all, the message broker contains considerable application logic. This application logic is hidden in the rules that the message broker uses to relay messages. The configuration and management of these rules becomes hard and cumbersome, since complex dependencies between rules can emerge, so that changing one rule might have undesired implications on the overall system behaviour.

The main reason for these issues is the missing conceptual underpinning of enterprise application integration. Despite rule mechanisms, enterprise application integration technologies to a large extent rely on programming and low-level configuration of adapters and message brokers. This applies to both data integration and process integration.

Data integration is typically performed using data mapping tools. These tools allow the mapping of data structures of the application to data structures of the message broker. Conceptually, this approach requires a data model hosted by the message broker that all applications have agreed upon, that is, a global data model. In many cases the global data model is not explicitly developed, but somehow hidden in the data mapping rules realized in the adapters.

In typical enterprise application integration scenarios, the functionality provided by the integrated applications is organized by a sequence or partial order of steps, realizing a process. This process consists of activities that are executed based on a set of execution constraints, and the execution of these activities achieves an overall business goal. While in traditional enterprise application integration scenarios, like the ones discussed so far, these process structures are buried in rules that the message broker hosts, an explicit representation of processes proves more appropriate.

As the next step in the evolution of information systems, workflow management, which identifies process specifications as first-class citizens that contribute to solving the process integration problem in enterprise application integration scenarios is addressed. However, before addressing workflow management, a second influencing factor for business process management is introduced that emerges from business administration rather than from software technology, that is, enterprise modelling and process orientation.

2.3 Enterprise Modelling and Process Orientation

In addition to developments in software architecture, business administration also contributed to the rise of business process management. There were two major factors that fuelled workflow management and business process management. Value chains as a means to functionally break down the activities a company performs and to analyze their contribution to the commercial success of the company, and process orientation as the way to organize the activities of enterprises.

2.3.1 Value Chains

Value chains are a well-known approach in business administration to organize the work that a company conducts to achieve its business goals. *Value chains* were developed by Michael Porter to organize high-level business functions and to relate them to each other, providing an understanding of how a company operates.

Porter states that "the configuration of each activity embodies the way that activity is performed, including the types of human and physical assets employed and the associated organizational arrangements" and he continues to look at the enterprise and its ecology by stating that "gaining and sustaining competitive advantage depends on understanding not only a firm's value chain but how the firm fits in the overall value system."

In order to fulfill their business goals, companies cooperate with each other, that is, the value chains of these companies are related to each other. The ecology of the value chains of cooperating enterprises is called *value system*. Each value system consists of a number of value chains, each of which is associated with one enterprise.

The value chain of a company has a rich internal structure, which is represented by a set of coarse-grained business functions. These high-level business functions, for instance, order management and human resources, can be broken down into smaller functional units, spanning a hierarchical structure of business functions of different granularity.

The process of breaking down a coarse-grained function into finer-grained functions is called functional decomposition. Functional decomposition is an important concept to capture and manage complexity. For instance, order management can be broken down into business functions to obtain and store an order and to check an order.

Figure 2.9 depicts a typical value system of an enterprise E, shown at the centre of the value system. This enterprise manufactures goods. In order to do so, it cooperates with suppliers $S1$ and $S2$ that provide raw material. To bring the products to its customers, enterprise E cooperates with transport and logistics companies that realize a channel from the manufacturer E to the buyers.

The graphical arrangements of value chains in the context of a value system are centred at the enterprise under consideration, enterprise E in the example. If channel enterprise $C1$ was addressed, then $C1$ would have been drawn in the centre, and it would have E among its incoming value chains and a set of buyers among its outgoing value chains. Value systems provide a very high-level characterization of the relationship of a particular enterprise to its business environment.

The arrangement of the value chains in a value system does not imply any particular ordering of the functions that the respective companies conduct. Therefore, value chains do not have a formal meaning as far as the ordering of the business functions is concerned. The arrangement of the value chains in Figure 2.9 is quite obvious in a manufacturing environment, where enterprise E receives raw material from its suppliers (incoming value chains) and delivers products via its channels to its buyers (outgoing value chains).

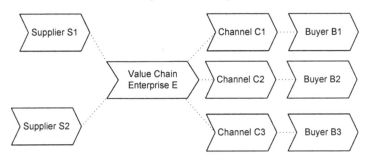

Fig. 2.9. Value system

In order to realize collaboration between suppliers, the manufacturer, channel companies, and buyers, many activities have to be performed in a coordinated fashion. The manufacturing enterprise E needs to negotiate a contract with each supplier, and the flow of incoming raw material must be planned and controlled properly. As a result, there are multiple interactions between the enterprise and its business partners.

Although the ordering of the value chains indicates that the flow of information and goods is from left to right, that is, from supplier to enterprise E, in this case the start of interaction is in the opposite direction, that is, from E to the supplier. The ordering of the value chains in a value system loosely follow the overall impression the modeller wants to communicate with the value system. The concrete interactions that realize the business collaboration are complex interactions.

In the sample value system shown, the overall flow of goods and information is from left to right. There are, however, also interactions in the opposite direction. For instance, the ordering of raw material by the enterprise E from Supplier 1 is realized by an interaction between these companies that originates from E. This interaction is performed if the need for raw material is determined.

This situation is depicted in Figure 2.10, in which the logical ordering of the value chains in a subset of the value system shown above in Figure 2.9 is enriched by arrows between the value chains, representing interactions between Enterprise E and Suppliers 1 and 2.

The value chain of a company subsumes all activities that the enterprise conducts to fulfill its business goals. The organization of the business functions within a value chain is shown in Figure 2.11. (Porter uses the term *activity* for these highest-level business functions. To provide a consistent terminology and to be in line with business process terminology, the term *business function* is used in this book.) The value chain is based on a functional organization of an enterprise, where the activities that are conducted are organized into business functions.

From a business administration point of view, the business functions that a company performs can be partitioned into primary functions and support

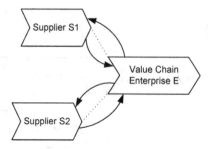

Fig. 2.10. Value system with interactions represented by arcs

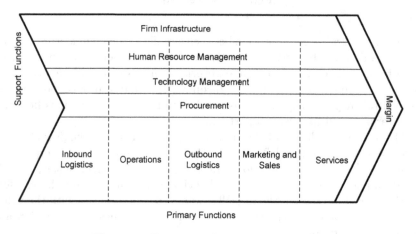

Fig. 2.11. Internal structure of value chain

functions. Primary functions contribute directly to the competitive advantage of the company, while secondary functions provide the environment in which the primary functions can be performed efficiently. The secondary business functions include human resources, technology development, procurement, and the infrastructure, all of which are required for supporting the primary business functions.

All functions that a company performs need to contribute to the success of the company, and the margin is the difference between the resources invested and the revenue generated by the company. The primary business functions of a value chain are as follows.

- *Inbound Logistics*: Business functions that collectively make sure the company receives raw material, goods and information, required for performing its business. For instance, in order to realize inbound logistics, a set of suppliers needs to be identified, contracts need to be negotiated, and operational procedures need to be in place. Inbound logistics interact significantly with business partners to request quotations, to collect and select offers, to negotiate contracts, to organize transportation, and to manage incoming goods and information.

- *Operations*: Operations aggregate business functions responsible for producing added-value products that contribute directly to the revenue of the company. In a manufacturing company, the products are produced by the operations business function.
- *Outbound Logistics*: Once products are manufactured, outbound logistics take care of distributing these products to warehouses or other distributing centres so that they can be distributed to the customers.
- *Marketing and Sales*: In marketing and sales, the business functions for marketing the company's products and for selling them in a competitive market are organized. The typical function in this primary business function is organizing and conducting a campaign to market a new product.
- *Services*: Once a product is sold, the company needs to keep in touch with buyers, both to cater to problems with the sold product and to provide valuable customer information for developing and marketing future products.

While Porter explains very well the functional decomposition of business functions, he does not identify the role of processes, although processes fit very well into the value chain approach. Below, the relationships of business functions that a firm performs in the context of a value system are identified and captured in business processes.

Due to the complexity inherent in large-scale organizations, the granularity of business processes needs to be in line with the particular goals associated with the business function that a particular business process supports. By doing so, a complete picture of the work conducted by a company and the processes that contribute to it can be developed.

While the approach by Porter is tailored towards traditional enterprises, for instance, manufacturing, there is a rich set of extensions of Porter's work. Due to the technical scope of this book, these extensions and the business implications of value chains and value systems are not discussed in detail. However, value systems provide an appropriate holistic setting for the business administration background of business process management.

2.3.2 Organizational Business Processes

The early 1990s saw process orientation as a strong development not only to capture the activities a company performs, but also to study and improve the relationships between these activities.

The book *Reengineering the Corporation*, which was briefly discussed in Section 1.1, proved instrumental in this development. The general approach of business process reengineering is a holistic view on an enterprise where business processes are the main instrument for organizing its operations. Business process reengineering is based on the understanding that the products and services a company offers to the market are provided through business processes, and a radical redesign of these processes is the road to success.

Process orientation is based on a critical analysis of Taylorism as a concept to organize work, originally introduced by Frederick Taylor to improve industrial efficiency. This approach uses functional breakdown of complex work to small granularities, so that a highly specialized work force can efficiently conduct these work units of small granularity. Taylorism has been very successful in manufacturing and has, as such, fuelled the industrial revolution in the late eighteenth and early nineteenth century considerably.

Small-grained activities conducted by highly specialized personnel require many hand-overs of work in order to process a given task. In early manufacturing in the late eighteenth and early nineteenth century the products were typically assembled in a few steps only, so that hand-overs of work did not introduce significant delays. In addition, the task were of a rather simple nature, so that no context information on previously conducted steps was required for a particular worker.

Using Taylorism to organize work in modern organizations proved inefficient, because the steps during a business process are often related to each other. Context information on the complete case is required during the process. The hand-overs of work cause a major problem, since each worker involved requires knowledge on the overall case. For this reason, the functional breakdown of work in fine-granular pieces that proved effective in early manufacturing proves inefficient in modern business organizations that mainly process information.

From a process perspective, it is instrumental to combining multiple units of work of small granularity into work units of larger granularity. Thereby, the hand-over of work can be reduced. But this approach requires workers to have broad skills and competencies, that is, it requires knowledge workers who have a broad understanding of the context and the ultimate goals of their work.

At an organizational level, process orientation has led to the characterization of the operations of an enterprise using business processes. While there are different approaches, they have in common the fact that the top-level business processes are expressed in an informal way, often even in plain English text. Also each enterprise should not have more than about a dozen organizational business processes. These processes are often described by the same symbols as those used for value systems, but the reader should be aware of the fact that different levels of abstraction are in place.

The structure of organization-level business process management is shown in Figure 2.12. The business process management space is influenced by the business strategy of the enterprise, that is, by the target markets, by business strategies opening new opportunities, and, in general, by the overall strategic goals of the enterprise.

Information systems, shown in the lower part of Figure 2.12, are valuable assets that knowledge workers can take advantage of. An important aspect of business process reengineering is combining small granular functions conducted by several persons into functional units of larger granularity, and supporting knowledge workers in performing these tasks with dedicated information systems.

Business process management is based on the resources of an enterprise, most prominently its knowledge workers and information systems. Information systems enable knowledge workers to perform business process activities in an effective manner. Information systems also have implications on business processes, since some business processes might not be possible without appropriate information system support.

Stakeholders are among the most important influential factors of business process management. The stakeholder box in the left hand side in Figure 2.12 represents the fact that stakeholders have implications on the organizational business processes. But business processes also have implications on the stakeholders, as shown in that figure, too. Stakeholders include external business partners, customers, and the personnel of the enterprise.

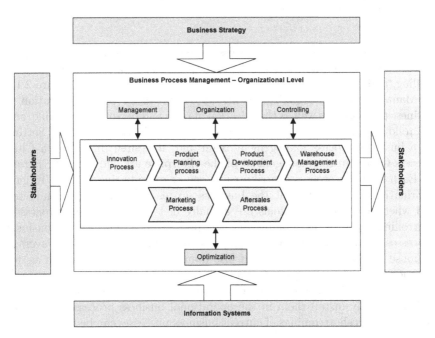

Fig. 2.12. Organization-level business process management, based on Schmelzer and Sesselmann (2010)

The internal structure of the business process management box in Figure 2.12 contains the organizational business processes of an enterprise. Sample organizational business processes for a manufacturing company are innovation process, product planning process, product development process and, purchase order process and service process.

Process Name: Product Development Process	**Responsible Process Manager:** Dr. Myers
From: Requirements **To:** Rollout	**Type:** Development Project
Process Inputs: Requirements Document, Product specification, Budget Plan, Prototypes	**Supplier Processes:** Product Planning Process, Innovation Process
Process Results: Integrated and completely tested innovative product with complete documentation	**Customer Processes:** Order Management Process, After-Sales Service Process

Fig. 2.13. Forms-based description of organizational business process, based on Schmelzer and Sesselmann (2010)

The organizational business processes are influenced by a number of activities that the company performs: the management, the organization, the controlling, and the optimization of business processes, as shown in Figure 2.12.

Management and organization include activities for the identification of business processes, as well as the selection of roles and persons responsible, and the rollout of the implemented business processes in the enterprise. Setting up a business process management team and, if desired, installing a Chief Process Officer in the management of the enterprise are additional activities.

Each business process contributes to one or more business goals. To gain information on how efficient the business processes are actually conducted and whether the business goals are actually met by the business processes, controlling activities are conducted. Key performance indicators of business processes are determined, for instance technical indicators, such as average response time and throughput, but also domain-specific aspects, such as, for instance, reduction of error rate, and cost savings.

Controlling also develops methods to measure key performance indicators and to actually install them in the operational business processes. Valuable information on shortcomings of current business processes can be found, which can be used to continuously improve and optimize them.

Organizational business processes have a large granularity, and they involve many persons and activities in a company. Therefore, they are typically described in a textual form, often using a forms-based approach. This means that individual process activities and their orderings are not addressed. The elements of these forms include the name of the business process, a person responsible for it, the objects addressed, the inputs and the results of the process, and the suppliers and customers of the process, both of which are organizational business processes.

A sample description of an organizational business process is shown in Figure 2.13, where a product development process is described. This process takes input and generates output that is of value to the enterprise. From this point of view, it is a valid characterization of a business process.

However, at this top level, the business process is treated as a black box, so that no details on the internal structure of the process are given. As a consequence, the property that a business process consists of activities with execution constraints does not immediately apply. This definition is appropriate at a lower level of abstraction where operational business processes are at the centre of attention.

To represent the relationships between the organizational business processes, their dependencies are depicted by a process landscape diagram. It contains each organizational business process as a block; dependencies are represented by arrows. There are different forms of dependencies, including information transfer and the transfer of physical goods.

The interfaces of the organizational business processes need to be designed carefully, since unclear interfaces are a source of inefficiency. These interfaces need to be broken down into interfaces of the operational business processes that actually realize the organizational business process. A process landscape

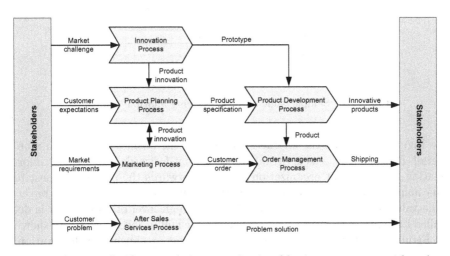

Fig. 2.14. Process landscape relating organizational business processes with stakeholders, based on Schmelzer and Sesselmann (2010)

is represented in Figure 2.14, showing the main business processes of a manufacturing company and their dependencies. Stakeholders such as customers are also depicted, as are interfaces, because the external behaviour of the company—which to a large extent is responsible for the commercial success of the company—is specified at exactly these interfaces.

2.3.3 Business-to-Business Processes

The business motivation behind interacting business processes stems from value systems, which represent collaborations between the value chains of multiple companies. These high-level collaborations are realized by interacting business processes, each of which is run by one company in a business to business process scenario. This section studies interactions between business processes performed by different companies.

For the sake of concreteness, this section uses an example from the area of order processing, described as follows. A buyer orders goods from a reseller, who acts as an intermediary. The reseller sends a respective product request to a manufacturer, who delivers to product to the buyer. In addition, the reseller asks a payment organization to take care of the billing. The value chain of this business scenario is shown in Figure 2.15. Notice that the arrangement of the value chains in this figure is somewhat arbitrary, because there are various interactions between the participating organizations.

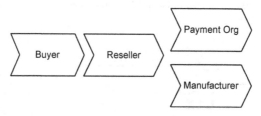

Fig. 2.15. Sample value system involving multiple companies

Figure 2.16 shows the interactions between the business partners in more detail. Reseller-B acts as a virtual company that forwards the payment information to a payment organization and that forwards the product request to the manufacturer. The manufacturer then ships the products to the buyer. The value system shown in Figure 2.15 on a high level of abstraction is detailed in Figure 2.16. Note that for each value chain in the value system shown in Figure 2.15 there is a participant in the business-to-business collaboration, detailing its internal structure and its contribution to the collaboration.

There are many interesting issues to study: how do we make sure that the business-to-business process created by putting together a set of existing business processes really fulfills its requirements? Structural criteria, for instance, absence from deadlock, need to be valid for these processes.

The problem is aggravated by the fact that internal business processes are an important asset of enterprises. Therefore, few enterprises like to expose their internal processes to the outside world. This means that the properties

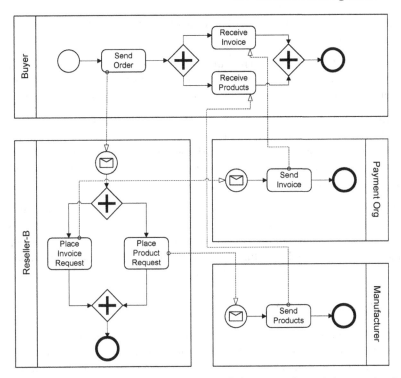

Fig. 2.16. Example of business-to-business collaboration through interacting business processes

of the overall business-to-business collaboration cannot be based on the actual detailed local processes run by the enterprises, but rather on the externally visible behaviour and the associated models to represent it. There are different approaches to tackle this problem, some of which are discussed in Chapter 6.

2.4 Workflow Management

The developments in enterprise software architectures and in organization-level business process management laid out in the previous sections led to workflow management. The important achievement of workflow management is the explicit representation of process structures in process models and the controlled enactment of business processes according to these models.

The model-driven approach facilitates a high degree of flexibility, because process models can be adapted to fulfill new requirements, and the modified process models can immediately be used to enact business processes.

In the 1990s, the Workflow Management Coalition (WfMC) was founded to bundle workflow related activities by vendors, users, and academia. The

Workflow Management Coalition defines workflows and workflow management systems as follows.

Definition 2.2 *Workflow* is the automation of a business process, in whole or in part, during which documents, information, or tasks are passed from one participant to another for action, according to a set of procedural rules.   ◇

Definition 2.3 A *workflow management system* is a software system that defines, creates, and manages the execution of workflows through the use of software, running on one or more workflow engines, which is able to interpret the process definition, interact with workflow participants, and, where required, invoke the use of IT tools and applications.   ◇

Workflow technology is capable of supporting business processes within a given application system or between a set of application systems, effectively integrating these systems. But workflow technology can also be used to enact business processes in which humans are actively involved, thus improving the collaboration between knowledge workers.

2.4.1 Workflows and Applications

Traditionally, application systems are designed and implemented not only by coding functions that the application carries out, but also by coding the ordering of these functions, that is, the process logic realized by the application.

With growing complexity of the application systems and increasing demand for adapting application systems to new requirements, the coding of process logic in applications has a severe drawback: any modification of the process realized by the application requires a modification of the programming code. The code not only needs to be modified, but also tested and maintained, so that each modification consumes considerable resources.

Workflow management technology can be used to ease the modification of the process logic realized by applications. The functions of an application system are the steps in the workflow, and a workflow component uses a workflow model to enact the functions. By modification of the process logic specified in workflow models, the behaviour of the application system can be modified without coding.

Today, most enterprise application systems, such as enterprise resource planning systems, host a workflow component that facilitates the flexible customization of business processes within these systems. Observe that instead of the term *workflow management system* the term *workflow component* is used, because a workflow component is not a stand-alone software system; rather, it is embedded in the application.

Definition 2.4 A *single-application workflow* consists of activities and their causal and temporal ordering that are realized by one common application system. *Multiple-application workflows* contain activities that are realized by multiple application systems, providing an integration of these systems.   ◇

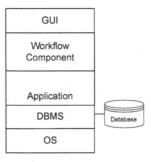

Fig. 2.17. Single-application workflow systems achitecture

The architecture of an single-application workflow system is shown in Figure 2.17. There is a dedicated workflow component that is fed with workflow models that capture the process logic as well as technical execution information. The workflow component uses functions realized by the application and provides processes to the higher level, the graphical user interface.

In the case of multiple-application workflows, a dedicated workflow management system makes sure that the application systems are invoked as specified in the process model. In addition, data transfer between application systems is also taken care of by the workflow management system.

The relationships of the subsystems involved in a workflow application are shown in Figure 2.18. The integration of the application systems is performed by the workflow management system, using adapters similar to those used in traditional enterprise application integration scenarios. The detailed architecture of workflow management systems will be discussed in Chapter 8.

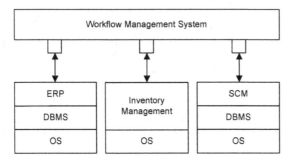

Fig. 2.18. Multiple-application workflow systems architecture

2.4.2 System Workflows

In system workflows, the workflow activities are performed automatically by software systems. Therefore, knowledge workers do not interact with the application, and graphical user interfaces in general and work item lists in particular are not required. The execution constraints are specified in a process model, and the workflow management system makes sure that the ordering of calls to the software systems is in line with the process model.

Figure 2.19 shows a scenario of a system workflow, with a dedicated workflow management system that invokes for each activity a defined application system. Each of these software systems provides an interface that the workflow management system can use, similar to the adapter in the enterprise application integration scenario sketched above. The workflow management system behaves like a centralized hub in an enterprise application integration scenario, but with explicit process representation and enactment control.

Definition 2.5 A *system workflow* consists of activities that are implemented by software systems without any user involvement.   ◇

Enterprise application integration scenarios are typical candidates for system workflows. The design and implementation of system workflows can be regarded as a type of high-level programming, where functionality provided by application systems characterize the building blocks that are organized within a system workflow.

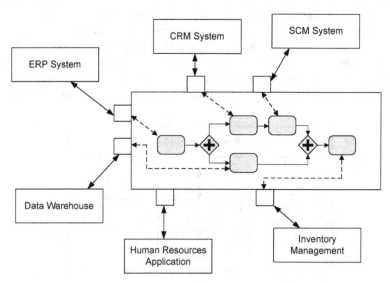

Fig. 2.19. System workflow integration scenario; a process model defines if and when enterprise applications are invoked

In enterprise application integration platforms without a dedicated process component, the interaction between the application systems is represented by rules, which are used to forward messages based on their type or content. From these rules, the overall process structure cannot be derived easily, and realizing change is cumbersome, because rules might trigger other rules, so that undesired side effects can occur.

Process modelling techniques can be used to provide an explicit representation of the relationships between enterprise applications. Process models provide the conceptual basis for defining when and under which conditions enterprise applications are actually invoked in the context of an integration scenario.

Therefore, a dedicated process component responsible for modelling and enacting processes in enterprise application integration scenarios is adequate. Workflow management systems are well equipped to act as this component. Today, most enterprise application integration middleware systems host a dedicated workflow component.

2.4.3 Human Interaction Workflows

In order to introduce human interaction workflows, it is useful to discuss its development. An early predecessor of human interaction workflow management systems is the office automation system, developed in the early 1980s. The goal of these systems was supporting the organization and the collaboration of work involving multiple persons. Until then, supporting office work of individuals was at the centre of attention. It turned out that it is not sufficient to equip workers with adequate software for their individual workplace, but also to consider the relationship of the work activities that are performed by different workers and provide support for their collaboration.

By shared, consolidated data repositories and by improving the hand-over of work between employees, a considerable speed-up in office procedures could be realized. However, the scope of office automation was still quite narrow: workers of a given organization process information objects, primarily using forms-based applications.

Today, human interaction workflows typically realize parts of a larger business process that has automated as well as nonautomated parts. The goal of human interaction workflows is to effectively support the automated parts of business processes by actively controlling the activities performed according to process models.

Definition 2.6 Workflows in which humans are actively involved and interact with information systems are called *human interaction workflows*.   ◇

Workflow management systems also take into account the organization in which the process runs. In particular, for each step in a workflow process, the role responsible for executing is defined. Roles are groups of employees that qualify for this responsibility.

The role concept introduces an additional type of flexibility, because at run time of the workflow, a person currently available can be offered to work on the respective activity, and one of the persons can select the activity to actually start working on it. Organizational aspects are discussed in more detail in Chapter 3.

Goals attributed to human interaction workflows are reduction of idle periods, avoiding redundant work such as the entering of data multiple times by different knowledge workers, and improved integration of human work with underlying information systems.

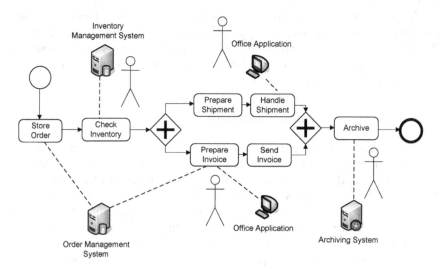

Fig. 2.20. Sample human interaction workflow

A sample human interaction workflow is shown in Figure 2.20. In addition to the activities and their logical ordering in a process model, the information system required to enact the workflow for each activity is represented. This information is required, since the workflow management system at run time will invoke these applications and will feed the required process data to these applications.

In the workflow at hand, first an order is stored in an order management system. Then the inventory is checked to find out whether the order can be fulfilled. To keep the process simple, the process design assumes that the order can be fulfilled, that is, there is no alternative modelled if this is not the case. Then, concurrently, the shipment is prepared, the parcel is handed to the shipper, and the invoice is prepared and sent. The fulfilled order is archived, completing the human interaction workflow.

Human interaction workflows require particular graphical user interface concepts. The main concept is the work item list. Knowledge workers interact with the system using work item lists, which are also called in-baskets. Whenever a knowledge worker can perform a process activity, he or she is informed by an item in his or her work item list. When the item is selected, the respective application is started, and the input data is provided. When the activity is completed, the knowledge worker informs the workflow application. The workflow management system then computes the current state and determines the activities next due.

2.4.4 Challenges for Workflow Management

As discussed in the previous sections, workflow management has considerable benefits due to explicit process representation and process enactment control. However, workflow management has also spawned criticism that has led to a broader perspective in business process modelling, organization, and control realized by business process management.

Lack of Adequate Support for Knowledge Workers

In contrast to many developments in software architecture and technology, workflow management systems have massive effects on the daily work for their users. The method of data storage and whether the program was developed with a procedural programming language or an object oriented programming language are relevant only for system designers and developers; these implementation aspects do not matter for the users of these systems. Therefore, special care has to be taken in the rollout of workflow applications; early participation of users in the design of these systems is important to avoid user acceptance issues.

Workflow management systems represent not only processes but also the organizational environment in which these processes are executed. This means that persons are represented by their skills, competences, and organizational positioning. This information is used to select persons to perform certain activities. The active selection of persons by the workflow management system has not been considered appropriate, since human workers felt that a machine burdened them with additional work. This feeling might also be due to crude interfaces of early workflow management systems.

The role of knowledge workers is another area where traditional workflow management systems scored low. Workflow models prescribe the process flow, and a workflow management system makes sure that the workflow is performed just as it is described. This also means that there is little room for creativity for the knowledge worker. Any process instance that has not been envisioned by the process designer cannot be realized. This might lead to situations where certain parts of the overall business process are not handled by the workflow management system. Sometimes, even paper-based solutions were used by the knowledge workers, leading to inconsistent states in the overall process.

These shortcomings of traditional workflow management systems have spawned a number of developments, some of which are reported in Chapter 8.

Technical Integration Challenges

While system workflows are well equipped to support the process aspect of enterprise application integration scenarios, the same technical integration problems need to be solved in system workflow projects as those in traditional enterprise application integration projects.

Application systems that need to be integrated are typically not equipped with well-documented interfaces that can be used to get hold of the required functionality. Functionality of application systems might also be implemented in the graphical user interfaces, so that low-level implementation work is required to access the application system functionality.

Another important source of trouble is relationships between different applications at the code level. Direct invocation between software systems is an example of these relationships, so that an invocation of an application system automatically spawns off an invocation of another application system. In these settings, the overall process flow is in part realized at the application code level, so that the workflow management system is capable of controlling only parts of the actual process flow, but not the complete process.

The granularity of the workflow activities and the granularity of the functionality provided by the underlying application systems might be different. Fine-granular business activities might have been designed in the process model that cannot be realized, because the underlying application system only provides coarse-grained functionality. In some cases, the interface to the application can be modified so that fine-grained functionality is available. This alternative is likely to incur considerable cost, or it might be impossible for some applications. Another alternative is changing the granularity of the business activities. In this case, certain properties of the process might not be realizable—for instance, the concurrent execution of two fine-granular activities. As a result, the run time of the workflow will not be optimal.

Service-oriented architectures and service-enabling of legacy applications are important concepts currently being investigated to address these technical problems.

Process Support Without Workflow Systems

Not all environments ask for a workflow management system. In cases where no changes to the process structure are envisioned, a coding of the process flow can be an attractive and adequate choice.

In database administration there are predefined procedures that are enacted following a process model. Similar developments can be found in publishing environments where print workflow is a common tool to describe and perform the steps that lead to publishable results. Most enterprise resource planning systems feature a dedicated workflow component that allows us to model new processes and enact them in the system environment. Due to their close link to particular applications, these systems are also called embedded workflow management systems.

Business processes are also realized in online shops, such as train reservation systems or electronic book stores, where steps of an interaction process are depicted in graphical form. This graphical representation guides the user in his interaction with the Web site. In a train reservation online shop, for instance, there are interaction steps for querying train connections, for getting detailed information on the connections, for selecting connections, for providing payment information, and for booking and printing the train ticket. Since this type of interaction process can easily be realized using traditional Web page design, workflow management systems are not required. However, these examples show that the business process paradigm is helpful also in application scenarios that do not require dedicated workflow support.

Enterprise application systems, such as enterprise resource planning systems, realize literally thousands of business processes. These processes can be customized to fit the particular needs of the company that runs the system. In most cases, the business processes are realized within the system, so no integration issues emerge. If the predefined business processes cannot be tailored in a way that fits the needs of the company, then integrated process modelling functionality can be used to model new processes.

2.5 Enterprise Services Computing

Service-oriented computing is one of the major trends both in business engineering and software technology. The main idea of service orientation is to capture business relevant functionality as a service and provide sufficiently detailed information so that customers can use it. This definition of service orientation goes well beyond services that are realized by software systems.

Consider a real-world service, for example, one to fix a car. The service the garage provides needs to be specified in a way that the customer can find and use. Once the car is fixed, the customer pays the bill and the service is completed. There are specific registries for finding real-world services, for instance, yellow page directories. This general idea of service orientation is applied to services provided by software systems. The requirements that apply to real-world services also need to be satisfied for services realized by software systems.

Service-oriented computing uses well-specified service interfaces that rely on common interface definition languages to combine several services to new service-oriented applications. If service-oriented computing is used in large-scale environments, an organizing principle is useful; this principle is introduced by service-oriented architectures, discussed next.

2.5.1 Service-Oriented Architectures

Steve Burbeck, one of the early advocates of service-oriented architectures, defines service-orientation as follows.

> *Services* are loosely-coupled computing tasks communicating over the internet that play a growing part in business-to-business interactions. [...] We reserve the term *service-oriented* for architectures that focus on how services are described and organized to support their dynamic, automated discovery and use. We do not address systems based on manually hardwired interactions, such as those used in EDI systems.

In this definition, services communicate over the Internet. This means that services are expected to be used in business-to-business scenarios, where the participants are connected by the Internet. Although not explicitly ruled out, services that are provided and used within a company do not fully qualify in Burbeck's definition.

The second interesting aspect of this definition is the high degree of flexibility provided by late, run time finding and binding of services. Matching a service request to a set of service specifications in a service registry is a complex task, especially if automated discovery and use are sought, as implied by the definition.

Burbeck's definition mirrors the long-term vision of service-oriented architectures. But this architectural style is not only useful in Internet settings, where the services are provided by different organizations in business-to-business scenarios, but also in intracompany settings. Therefore this book adopts the following definitions.

Definition 2.7 A *service* captures functionality with a business value that is ready to be used. Services are made available by service providers. A service requires a service description that can be accessed and understood by potential service requestors. *Software services* are services that are realized by software systems.

Service-oriented architectures are software architectures that provide an environment for describing and finding software services, and for binding to services. Descriptions of software services provide a level of detail that facilitates service requestors to bind to and invoke them.   ◇

Service-oriented architectures are especially important in environments where many services are available and where the set of available services changes over time. Burbeck investigates this aspect in more detail and states as follows.

> To work easily, flexibly, and well together, services must be based on shared organizing principles that constitute a service-oriented architecture.

In a service-oriented architecture, organizations may use services offered by other companies, and companies may provide services to a growing services market. The vision is for information systems to use business functionality of service providers, so that reuse of functionality is realized at a level of coarse granularity. New applications can be built with less effort and existing applications can be efficiently adapted to changing requirements, reducing maintenance and development cost.

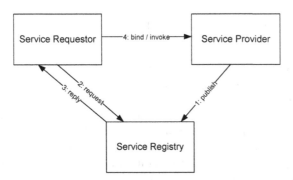

Fig. 2.21. Roles in service-oriented architectures

Figure 2.21 depicts the classical service-oriented architecture, as introduced by Burbeck. This architecture is based on roles that participating organizations can play. Service providers offer services. To enable service requestors to find and use them, they are specified, and their descriptions are stored in a service registry.

The interactions between the three primary roles in service-oriented architecture are publish, request/reply, and bind. The service provider publishes service specifications in a service registry, and the service requestor searches the service registry and finds suitable services. The service registry provides the service requestor with information that allows the service requestor to bind to the service and, eventually, invoke it.

In this section, service-oriented computing is characterized in an informal way. Web services as the current implementation of service-oriented architectures will be covered in Chapter 8.

2.5.2 Enterprise Services

In enterprise computing environments, the functionality of application systems can be described and provided by services. Figure 2.22 visualizes a service-enabled application system. The functionality of the application system is provided through services, depicted by semicircles on top of the application system. Services need to be specified in a way that the specification of services

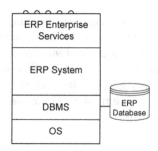

Fig. 2.22. Service-enabled application system

is decoupled from their implementation. Detailed specification of services facilitates the flexible configuration of services by composing services to achieve complex functionality.

In an existing application built with several services provided by different business partners, the partners can modify the realization of their services, as long as the service specification does not change. Based on the service specification, an improved service implementation can be integrated seamlessly in a service-based application. New potential business partners can use publicly available service specifications to offer their own implementations of the services. As a result, individual parts of a complex service-based application can be exchanged without redesigning the application.

Service orientation is also one of the main influencing factors for enterprise application integration. Enterprise services architecture characterizes the development of added-value applications that take advantage of existing functionality provided through standardized interfaces.

Enterprise services architecture is based on the understanding that complex applications will be increasingly built on top of existing functionality. This functionality is provided by legacy systems, which are an important asset of companies. Making this functionality reusable is a challenging task. The idea is to encapsulate the functionality of existing software systems in a service, realizing enterprise services. Enterprise services can be used to realize enterprise application integration scenarios.

As pointed out by Woods, there are a number of business drivers that foster the development of enterprise services. The main driver is change: the ability to change the enterprise application system infrastructure is a competitive advantage for an enterprise. There are a number of current trends that motivate the development of enterprise services:

- *Rise in the power of the customer*: Value-added services are essential, because customers can change suppliers easily, without much effort. Positive user experience is important, as the success of online auctioning sites and online shops with community building indicates.

- *Systems transparency*: The Internet has brought customers and suppliers inside a company's IT infrastructure. Weak or missing integration of enterprise application systems will be immediately exposed to the customer.
- *Rise in computer mediated interaction with customers and suppliers*: Companies differentiate themselves on their service to their customers. Dan Woods indicates that "Outsiders can now peer into the glass house of the data centre and see if it is a mess." An example of a messy situation is one where a customer cannot be serviced well, because the client interface provides information only about one aspect of the customer, and the other aspects are hidden in application systems that are not accessible. Due to lack of integration, this valuable information is not available, so the customer does not feel well cared for.
- *Products as services*: Corporations are increasingly perceived by the set of services they provide. These services exposed to the market can be realized by enterprise services, which provided by the back end application systems of the enterprise. But also services provided by third parties can be integrated, so that better applications and end user services can be provided to the customer.
- *Multi-tier applications*: There is also a trend towards multi-tier applications, where each tier is provided by a different enterprise. This means that the tier 1 company provides value-added services directly to a customer, using the tier 2 services from a set of business partner companies. These companies might use tier 3 services provided by other companies. By flexible integration based on the service paradigm, many new applications and services can be realized.

Composite Service-Based Applications

With this background in enterprise services architectures, an intra-company scenario is sketched, where new applications should be built on top of an existing customer relationship management system, a supply chain management system, and an enterprise resource planning system. These systems expose enterprise services via standardized interfaces. The applications built on top are known as composite applications, as shown in Figure 2.23. Composite applications invoke enterprise services that provide the functionality of the underlying back-end systems. User interaction is realized by dedicated graphical user interfaces that sit on top of composite applications.

Technological advance has paved the way for enterprise services. The main cornerstones of these developments are the full suites of enterprise applications that are available off-the-shelf today. There are rich middleware and enterprise application integration products that can be used for technical integration, most of which host a dedicated workflow component for process enactment. To integrate multiple application systems, data transformation is essential. With the advent of the extensible markup language (XML), there is an industry standard for data and message format specifications. While this

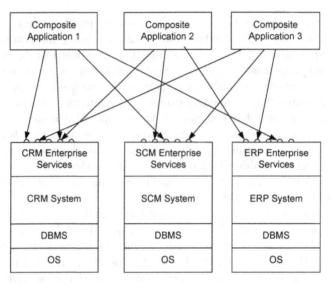

Fig. 2.23. Enterprise systems expose functionality through enterprise services

base technology is in place, the integration logic still needs to be defined and implemented in each integration project.

As shown in Figure 2.23, applications that use the functionality of existing application systems are called composite applications. Processes are a key factor in realizing composite applications, because they provide a link from high-level business processes to the information technology layer.

The structure of composite applications can in many cases be expressed as a business process. The activities of these processes are implemented by invoking enterprise services. Additional execution constraints like conditional execution can be represented by business process models; these can be realized by process orchestrations.

Enterprise services can also be used to realize business interactions of multiple enterprises. In multi-tier scenarios for realizing innovative applications, interactions between the software systems of the business partners involved are required. These interactions are governed by a process choreography. Process choreographies have been defined informally above; they are subject of further investigation in Chapter 6.

While the vision for enterprise services includes business-to-business processes, most enterprise services today are used in an intra-company setting, where the goal is to develop composite applications on top of well-specified business functionality represented by enterprise services.

Enterprise Services and Service-Oriented Architectures

The roles in service-oriented architectures as discussed above are not completely filled in typical enterprise scenarios. The specification of services is typically done by the provider of the service, that is, by the system architects responsible for service-enabling the particular application.

The service registry is installed locally, and its access by other companies is usually disallowed. The most striking difference to service-oriented architectures as defined by Burbeck is the absence of dynamic matchmaking. As enterprise services are developed, they are specified and registered in a local registry. When a new composite application is developed, the designers consult the registry to find suitable services that can be used to perform certain tasks in the composite application. This search is a manual process, which in some cases is assisted by a taxonomy and a textual description of the services.

There are a number of hard problems in this context that are unsolved today. One of the main problems regards the scoping of services: the functionality provided by one or more application systems that is suitable for an enterprise service. If the granularity is small, then the level of reuse is small too, because many enterprise services need to be composed to achieve the desired functionality.

If on the other hand the granularity is large, then there might be only few scenarios where the enterprise service fits well and where using it makes sense. Tailoring of services of large granularity is also not a valid option, since extensive tailoring hampers reuse. As in many related cases, there is no general answer to this question. The choice of a suitable service granularity depends on the particular usage scenario and on the properties of the application systems to integrate and the composite applications to develop.

In enterprise services architectures, each enterprise service is typically associated with exactly one application system. This is a limitation, since building an enterprise service on top of a number of related back-end application systems involves system integration, so that reuse is simplified.

To illustrate this concept, an example is introduced. Consider a purchase order enterprise service in which an incoming purchase order needs to be stored in multiple back-end application systems. In this case, the enterprise service can be used with ease, since it is invoked once by a composite application and it automatically provides the integration of the back-end system by storing the purchase order—with the relevant data mappings to cater to data type heterogeneity—in the respective back-end application systems.

An integration of legacy systems can be realized within an enterprise service. This allows using enterprise services at a higher level of granularity, so that integration work can actually be reused in multiple composite applications.

2.5.3 Enterprise Services Bus

In a recent development, enterprise application integration middleware provides standardized software interfaces to the enterprise applications that it integrates. As the term enterprise service bus indicates, each of these enterprise applications is then attached to this bus, which acts as a centralized component to integrate these applications, as shown in Figure 2.24.

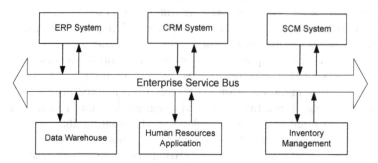

Fig. 2.24. Service!Enterprise service bus

An enterprise service bus hides the heterogeneity of the enterprise applications by introducing service interfaces. To realize these service interfaces, traditional enterprise application integration adapter technology is typically used that is also in place in traditional enterprise application integration middleware, as discussed in Section 2.2.2.

By introducing standardized interfaces to the outside world using services, however, an enterprise service bus goes one step beyond traditional enterprise application integration middleware. It must not be overlooked, however, that the term enterprise service bus is also used by software vendors to rebrand existing technologies for marketing reasons.

2.5.4 Service Composition

To realize composite applications in service-oriented enterprise computing environments, service composition techniques are appropriate. The general principle of service composition is depicted in Figure 2.25, where application systems in the lower part of the figure represent services that can be used to realize composite applications.

The composite application shown uses functionality provided by a CRM system, an SCM system, and an ERP system. The application logic realized in the composite application defines a process consisting of three activities. The ordering of these activities can be specified in a process model.

Since the business process is realized by a composition of services, processes of this kind are also called service compositions. The service composition shown in Figure 2.25 realizes a business process that can be embedded in a composite application, which adds a graphical user interface to the service layer.

Enterprise application integration middleware in general and enterprise service bus middleware in particular provide a good technical basis to realize

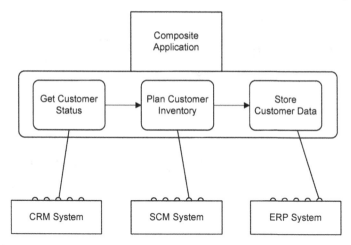

Fig. 2.25. Using service composition to realize composite applications

service compositions, because they provide standardized services interfaces that can be used in service compositions. Typical enterprise application integration middleware features a system workflow component that uses either a proprietary format for system workflows or, if it is based on services, the Business Process Execution Language for Web services, discussed in Chapter 8.

2.6 Summary

In this section, the technological subdomains of business process management introduced so far are summarized. These subdomains are also related to each other, resulting in an overall organization of business process management that serves as an environment for the detailed discussion of individual aspects of business process management in the remainder of this book.

The overall organization of business process management is shown in Figure 2.26. Since company strategies, business rules, and organizational business processes are not considered in detail in this book, these organizational levels are not represented.

At the lowest level of the business process management landscape, applications can be found. Typically, there are heterogeneous application landscapes that contain typical enterprise applications like enterprise resource planning systems and customer relationship management systems, but tailor-made applications to cover specific functionalities are not uncommon. The application subdomain was covered in Section 2.1. Because each of these applications potentially hosts its data in a dedicated database, data integration issues emerge.

Integration issues are covered at the enterprise application integration level, discussed in Section 2.2. Enterprise application integration middleware can be used to realize adapters for applications that hide their heterogeneity

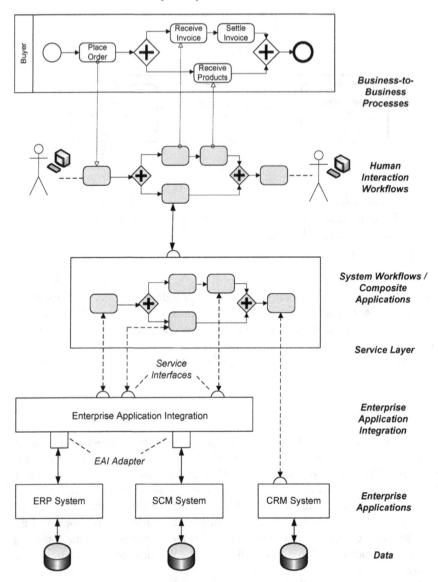

Fig. 2.26. Business process management landscape

from one another and, thus, solve the integration problem. Data mapping is an essential part of the realization of these adapters.

In modern enterprise application infrastructures based on the service-orientation paradigm, the functionality of enterprise applications is provided through services. Therefore the concepts introduced in Section 2.5 can be used in enterprise application integration. In Figure 2.26, it is assumed that the customer relationship management system provides a service interface, which can be used by the upper layers.

Composite applications use the functionality provided by multiple application systems. In order to do this, composite applications invoke enterprise applications, either by directly using standardized interfaces or via enterprise application integration middleware. The invocation behaviour of composite applications can be described as a system workflow. There are also traditional implementation strategies for composite applications, but flexible response to change and well-specified behaviour by explicit process models are important advantages of using system workflow technology. These aspects have been discussed in Section 2.4 in the context of system workflows and in Section 2.5 in the context of service-oriented computing.

Composite applications can have dedicated user interfaces, but they can also expose service interfaces to be used by higher levels. In Figure 2.26, a composite application realizes a value-added service described by a service interface that makes it usable to the higher levels.

The next level contains human interaction workflows. The activities of human interaction workflows can be associated with knowledge workers, but there can also be activities that are realized by application systems. The example shown in the figure realizes an activity by a composite application that realizes a system workflow.

Activities in human interaction workflows can also be part of a business-to-business process interaction. For instance, activities can send messages to or receive messages from business partners. The interaction behaviour of a set of business processes was discussed in Section 2.3; they will be further investigated in Chapter 6.

While the scenario sketched organizes the business process management area from a technical point of view, different variations are possible. For instance, system workflows can also interact with processes run by business partners, and not only with human interaction workflows.

This characterization of the technical aspects of business process management deliberately abstracts from business strategies, goals, and organizational business processes. However, business-to-business processes, human interaction workflows, and system workflows are associated with operational business processes. Therefore, they contribute to organizational business processes and, eventually, to the business goals and the realization of the business strategies.

Bibliographical Notes

Porter (1998) focused on the operation of enterprises and the interaction between business partners from a high-level perspective. To some extent, Porter, with his holistic view on the activities an enterprise performs, paved the way for process orientation. The high-level business functions of value chains are broken down to smaller-grained business functions, where the granularity is subject to design decision, indicated by the observation that "appropriate degree of disaggregation depends on the economics of the activities and the purposes for which the value chain is being analyzed."

Process orientation dates back to as early as 1932, when Fritz Nordsieck looked at the goal-oriented cooperation of workers in an organization; see Nordsieck (1932). Based on his work, Erich Kosiol developed organizational principles for corporations in Kosiol (1962), laying an early foundation for process orientation.

Hammer and Champy (1993) added to this work by introducing process orientation as a new paradigm of how enterprises conduct their business, also regarding achievements in information technology. While their approach to business process reengineering postulates a radical redesign, in many cases evolutionary approaches that regard organizational, human, and sociological factors prove more appropriate. Taylorism as an organizing principle for organizations is introduced by Taylor (1967). Smith and Fingar (2006) takes a business-oriented view on business process management by investigating strategic decisions made by enterprises, such as mergers and acquisitions, and by discussing the role of business process management in coping with the resulting challenges.

Schmelzer and Sesselmann (2010) looks at business process management from a business administration and practical point of view. The identification of business processes, the organizational settings in which business processes are enacted and controlled, and the introduction of business processes in large organization is described.

Becker et al. (2011) investigates mainly organizational aspects of business process management by looking at process modelling, analysis, and optimization from a practical business perspective. In the business-focused business process management literature, information technology in general and software systems in particular do not play an important role. A volume on different aspects of process-aware information systems is provided by Dumas et al. (2005). Dumas et al. (2018) give an overview of the main organizational and technical aspects in business process management.

Major principles in computer science that are also realized by the information systems architectures are separation of concerns, introduced by Dijkstra (1982), and information hiding identified by Parnas (1972).

There are excellent books on the subsystems discussed in the evolution of information systems. Textbooks on operating systems include Tanenbaum (2007), Silberschatz and Galvin (2008), and Stallings (2004). Ramakrishnan and Gehrke (2002), O'Neil and O'Neil (2000), and Weikum and Vossen (2001) provide a thorough explanation of database technology.

Georgakopoulos et al. (1995) provide an overview of workflow management. Workflow management from the perspective of a commercial workflow product is introduced by Leymann and Roller (1999); in particular, the term production workflow was coined in this book as a highly repetitive and automated realization of a core business process.

Wil van der Aalst et al. (2003a) provide a survey of business process management including the business process lifecycle discussed above. In the last decade, process mining has emerged as an important field of research that investigates different types of relationships between process models and process execution information. This book does not address process mining; instead we recommend the excellent text book by van der Aalst (2016), who presents the current state of the art in all aspects related to process mining. The ProM framework on process mining and analysis is also addressed in van der Aalst et al. (2007). Evaluation of business processes from a business perspective is discussed in Schmelzer and Sesselmann (2010).

Burbeck (2000) introduces roles in service-oriented architectures: service provider, service requestor and service broker. Alonso et al. (2009) looks at middleware systems in general and Web services based system integration in particular. Woods and Mattern (2006) discusses developments at the edge of business engineering and software technology in the context of enterprise services architectures. Service-oriented architectures in an enterprise context are also covered in Woods and Mattern (2006). Enterprise service bus is investigated in Chappell (2004). In a community paper by Mendling et al. (2018), challenges related to blockchains as an underlying infrastructure for business processes are discussed. Architectural principles of blockchain applications are reviewed in Xu et al. (2019).

Part II

Business Process Modelling

3

Business Process Modelling Foundation

This chapter introduces the foundation of business process modelling by investigating abstraction concepts and introducing the main subdomains of business process modelling, namely modelling functions, processes, data, organization, and operation.

3.1 Conceptual Model and Terminology

The business process modelling space as laid out in Chapters 1 and 2 is organized using conceptual models. Figure 3.1 introduces a model of the concepts at the core of business process management. While the terms mentioned have been used in the previous chapters informally, the concepts behind these terms and their relationships will now be discussed in more detail, using conceptual models. These models are expressed in the Unified Modeling Language, an object-oriented modelling and design language.

Business processes consist of activities whose coordinated execution realizes some business goal. These activities can be system activities, user interaction activities, or manual activities. Manual activities are not supported by information systems. An example of a manual activity is sending a parcel to a business partner.

User interaction activities go a step further: these are activities that knowledge workers perform, using information systems. There is no physical activity involved. An example of a human interaction activity is entering data on an insurance claim in a call centre environment. Since humans use information systems to perform these activities, applications with appropriate user interfaces need to be in place to allow effective work. These applications need to be connected to back-end application systems that store the entered data and make it available for future use.

Some activities that are conducted during the enactment of a business process are of manual nature, but state changes are entered in a business process management system by means of user interaction activities. For instance, the delivery of a parcel can be monitored by an information system. Typically, the actual delivery of a parcel is acknowledged by the recipient with her signature. The actual delivery is important information in logistics business processes that needs to be represented properly by information systems. There are several types of events during a logistics process. These events are often available to the user as tracking information. While the activities are of manual nature, an information system—the tracking system—receives information on the current status of the process.

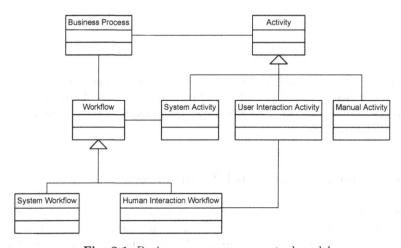

Fig. 3.1. Business processes: conceptual model

System activities do not involve a human user; they are executed by information systems. An example of a system activity is retrieving stock information from a stock broker application or checking the balance of a bank account. It is assumed that the actual parameters required for the invocation are available. If a human user provides this information, then it is a user interaction activity. Both types of activities require access to the respective software systems.

Certain parts of a business process can be enacted by workflow technology. A workflow management system can make sure that the activities of a business process are performed in the order specified, and that the information systems are invoked to realize the business functionality. This relationship between business processes and workflows is represented by an association between the respective classes. We argue that workflow is not a subclass of business process, since a workflow realizes a part of a business process, so a workflow is not in an "is-a" relationship with a business process, but is an association.

With regard to the types of activities mentioned, system activities are associated with workflows, since system activities can participate in any kind of workflow, system workflow or human interaction workflow. User interaction activities and manual activities, however, can only participate in human interaction workflows.

3.2 Abstraction Concepts

To capture the complexity in business process management, different abstraction concepts are introduced. A traditional abstraction concept in computer science is the separation of modelling levels, from instance level to model level to metamodel level, denoted by horizontal abstraction. Horizontal abstraction concepts in business process management are discussed in Section 3.2.1.

Even when using horizontal abstraction, separate subdomains need to be investigated. In order to follow the divide-and-conquer approach, these subdomains need to be represented separately. This abstraction mechanism is called vertical abstraction, and is discussed in Section 3.2.2.

Aggregation can also be used to cope with complexity, motivating another type of abstraction. At a higher level of abstraction, multiple elements of a lower level of abstraction can be grouped and represented by a single artefact. For example, a set of functional activities of small granularity can contribute to a particular business function at a higher level of granularity: a coarse-grained business function "order management" might aggregate many smaller-grained activities, like receiving an incoming order, checking the inventory, and confirming the order. This type of abstraction is called aggregation abstraction, because the coarse-grained business function aggregates activities of smaller granularity.

Aggregation abstraction is different from horizontal abstraction, because all activities (the small-grained and the coarse-grained) are at one horizontal level of abstraction, for example, the instance level. Aggregation abstraction is primarily used in the functional subdomain, where functions of smaller granularity are combined to create functions of larger granularity.

3.2.1 Horizontal Abstraction

Along the lines of the levels of abstraction identified by the Object Management Group, the metamodel level, the model level, and the instance level play important roles in the design and analysis of complex systems in general and software systems in particular. It is instructive to explain these levels in a bottom-up order, starting with the instance level.

The instance level reflects the concrete entities that are involved in business processes. Executed activities, concrete data values, and resources and persons are represented at the instance level.

To organize the complexity of business process scenarios, a set of similar entities at the instance level are identified and classified at the model level.

For instance, a set of similar business process instances are classified and represented by a business process model. In object modelling, a set of similar entities is represented by a class, and in data modelling using the Entity Relationship approach, a set of similar entities is represented by an entity type, and similar relationships between entity types are represented by a relationship type.

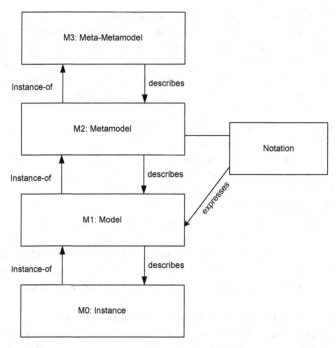

Fig. 3.2. Levels of abstraction

Models are expressed in metamodels that are associated with notations, often of a graphical nature. For instance, the Petri net metamodel defines Petri nets to consist of places and transitions that form a directed bipartite graph. The traditional Petri net notation associates graphical symbols with metamodel elements. For instance, places are represented by circles, transitions by rectangles, and the graph structure by directed edges.

In data modelling, the Entity Relationship metamodel defines entity types, relationship types, and connections between them. Typical graphical notations of the Entity Relationship metamodel are rectangles for entity types and diamonds for relationship types, connected by lines.

While often there is one graphical notation for one approach, a one-to-one correspondence between notation and metamodel is not mandatory. In a Petri net, the concept of a transition could also be represented by another symbol in a graphical notation. There are different notations for representing Petri nets, which differ in the graphical representation of transitions. While some use rectangles, others use solid bars.

Therefore, it is important to distinguish between the concepts of a modelling approach and the graphical notation used to represent these concepts. The complete set of concepts and associations between concepts is called metamodel. A metamodel becomes useful if there is a notation for this metamodel that allows expressing models in a convenient way that allows communication between stakeholders in the modelled real-world situation.

The different levels of abstraction and their relationships are shown in Figure 3.2. A notation associated with a metamodel allows expressing the concepts of that particular metamodel. Each model is described by a metamodel, and is expressed in a notation associated with the metamodel.

3.2.2 Vertical Abstraction

Vertical abstraction in business process modelling is depicted in Figure 3.3, where distinct modelling subdomains are identified. As depicted, process modelling is at the centre of the modelling effort, because it also integrates the modelling efforts that are conducted in the other subdomains.

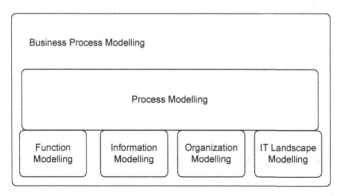

Fig. 3.3. Business process modelling includes multiple modelling domains, integrated by process modelling

Function modelling, data modelling, organization modelling, and modelling of the operational information technology landscape are required to provide a complete picture of a business process. While these subdomains are the most important ones, additional subdomains can be defined if they are relevant.

The functional model investigates the units of work that are being enacted in the context of business processes. The specification of the work can be done at different aggregation levels, from coarse-grained business functions to fine-granular functions at the operational level that are realized by knowledge workers and information systems.

The specification of these functions can be informal, using English text or formal, using syntactic or semantic specifications of functions. While informal descriptions are mostly done at the coarse business level, more precise specifications are required in the software layer when it comes to implementation of certain functions using information systems.

The investigation and proper representation of data in business processes is important, because decisions made during a business process depend on particular data values. Also data dependencies between activities need to be taken into account in process design, to avoid situations in which a function requires certain data not available at that time.

The proper representation of the organizational structure of a company is an important requirement. Activities in the business process can then be associated with particular roles or departments in the organization. Many activities in a business process are performed by or with the assistance of information systems. The operational information technology landscape, that is, the information systems, their relationships, and their programming interfaces, needs to be represented to use the functionality provided by the information systems.

Process modelling defines the glue between the subdomains. A process model relates functions of a business process with execution constraints, so that, for instance, the ordering and conditional execution of functions can be specified. Data aspects are covered because particular process instances may depend on the structure and value of data involved in a particular business process. For example, in a credit approval business process, the type of approval depends on the credit amount requested. In addition, data dependencies between activities need to be taken into account in process model design.

3.3 From Business Functions to Business Processes

As discussed in Section 2.3, value chains provide a high-level organization of the functions that an enterprise performs. To provide a more detailed view, these top-level business functions are broken down to functions of smaller granularity and, ultimately, to activities of operational business processes. Functional decomposition is the technique of choice.

A partial functional decomposition of a value chain is shown in Figure 3.4, where a value system represents the highest level of aggregation. Each value system consists of a number of value chains, characterized by the class diagram on the left hand side in Figure 3.4.

The ordering of the value chains in the value system is not represented in this structure diagram because it does not have any formal meaning. There are complex interactions between these companies, so that, obviously, not all activities in the supplier value chain occur before all activities conducted by enterprise E.

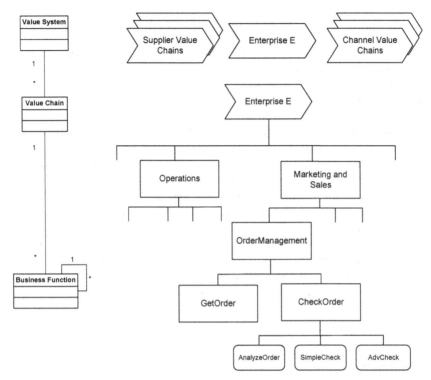

Fig. 3.4. Functional decomposition from value chain to business functions

The functional decomposition of the value chain of enterprise E is exemplified for one particular path of functions in the marketing and sales top-level business function. Among many other functions, marketing and sales includes a business function, *OrderManagement*, that contains functions related to the management of incoming orders. Order management is decomposed further into business functions for getting and checking orders. To check orders, they need to be analyzed, and there are functions for simple and advanced checking of orders.

As shown in Figure 3.4, there are different symbols for business functions and for functions of the finest granularity: business functions are represented by rectangles, while functions of the finest granularity are represented by rectangles with rounded corners. Functions at the leaf level of the functional decomposition are also called activities.

Traditionally, functional decomposition was used to describe enterprises based on the functions they perform. As discussed in Chapter 1, concentrating on the functions an enterprise performs and neglecting their interplay falls short of properly representing how enterprises work. Therefore, functional decomposition is used as first step in the representation of enterprises based on business processes.

Operational business processes relate activities to each other by introducing execution constraints between them. In principle, relating functions to business processes can be applied for different granularities of business functions. In case high-level business functions are considered, a textual specification of the process is used, since concrete execution constraints between their constituents are not relevant in coarse-grained business functions.

Consider, for instance, the business functions incoming logistics and operations. At this very coarse level of functionality, no ordering of these business functions is feasible: both business functions are performed concurrently, and only at a lower level of granularity does a concrete ordering make sense.

For instance, when the operations business function orders additional material, then there are concrete activities that have a concrete ordering. Within operations, an internal order is created and sent to incoming logistics. On arrival of this order, raw material is provided to operations. In case no raw material is available at the manufacturing company, an external order is created and sent to a supplier of the raw material. Therefore, business processes relate fine-grained business functions, typically the leaves of the business function decomposition tree. Figure 2.13 illustrates how high-level business functions can be described.

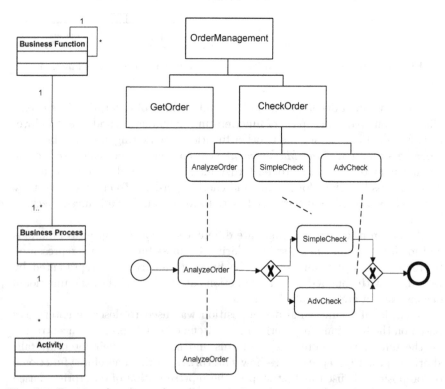

Fig. 3.5. Business functions of small granularity are organized as a business process

In the example shown in Figure 3.5, the activities *AnalyzeOrder*, *SimpleCheck*, and advanced check (*AdvCheck*) are related to each other by execution constraints. The sample business process starts with analyzing the order, and then conducting either a simple check or an advanced check depending on the decision made during process execution. This process has a dedicated start event and a dedicated end event. The business process is started once the start event occurs; when it completes, an end event occurs. Events play a crucial role when interrelationships between business processes are expressed.

A particular business function of higher granularity (*CheckOrder*) consists of fine-grained activities, which are related by execution constraints. However, the check order business function (and the business process that realizes it) is related to other business functions and their respective business processes.

An example showing this situation is displayed in Figure 3.6, where a part of the value chain is shown, in particular, the business functions *Receive Request*, *Request Analysis*, and *Quota Management* are shown. Since there is a strict ordering between these business functions, an execution ordering relation is represented.

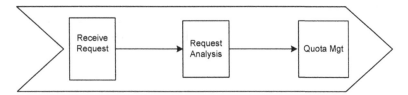

Fig. 3.6. Related business processes, high-level view

After the business process related to receiving the request is processed, it generates its end event. This end event is the signal for starting the second business process, related to request analysis. Finally, the quota is prepared and the business process completes. This discussion shows that business processes at a lower level can be identified, as well as business processes at a higher level, that is, those relating business functions.

The overall organization of these levels is depicted in Figure 3.7. At the left hand side of this figure a UML structure diagram provides a conceptual model of the entities involved. To recapitulate, each enterprise is represented by a value chain, which consists of coarse-grained business functions that are decomposed into smaller-grained business functions, realizing a functional decomposition. Activities are functions of the finest granularity; they are the building blocks of operational business processes.

When a business process is started, the business functions that it contains need to be executed. Therefore, each activity in a business process requires an implementation. The implementation of an activity can be based on functionality provided by information systems, such as registering a new customer or

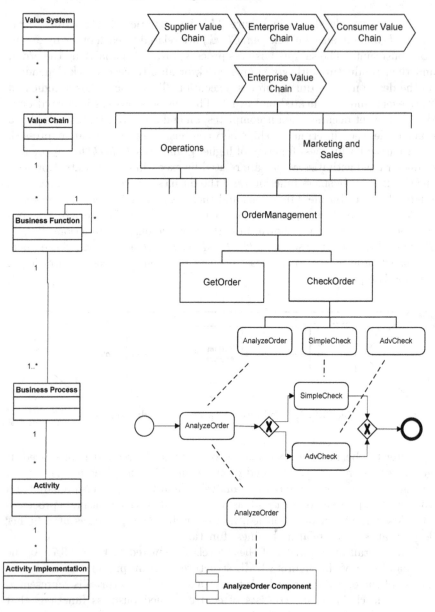

Fig. 3.7. Levels of business process management. From value systems to activity implementations

reserving a flight. However, an activity implementation can also be provided by a knowledge worker without using information systems.

Definition 3.1 A *functional decomposition* of coarse-grained business functions to fine-granular activities defines the *functional perspective* of a business process.   ◇

3.4 Activity Models and Activity Instances

Business functions provide a high-level, coarse-grained representation of the work conducted by enterprises. Activities can be found in the leaves of the functional decomposition. This section investigates how activities can be described. In addition, the actual work conducted during business processes has to be characterized, that is, activity instances have to be characterized. Note that activity models represent the M1 layer of the Meta Object Facility, while the activity instance layer corresponds to M0. Figure 3.8 shows the relationships between business functions, activity models, and activity instances. Notice that there are activity instances for case (Smith, 123212) for all three activity models, even though either a simple check or an advanced check is required. This aspect will be discussed shortly.

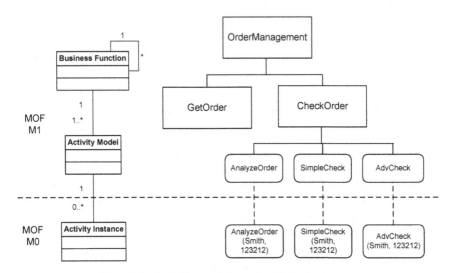

Fig. 3.8. Activity models and activity instances

An activity model describes a set of similar activity instances, analogously to a process model describing a set of process instances with the same structure. While process models are typically expressed in graph-like notations (to be investigated in detail in the next chapter), activity models can be expressed in different forms, for instance, by plain text or by some formal specification or references to software components that implement them.

Activity instances represent the actual work conducted during business processes, the actual units of work. To make this discussion more concrete, assume a process instance that represents the processing of an insurance claim by Clara Smith on the damage amount of US $2000, submitted November 11, 2006. Let EnterClaim(Clara Smith, 2000, 11-11-2006) represent the activity instance responsible for entering the claim in the respective software system of the insurance company. When the company receives the claim, a process instance is started. Within this process instance, the activity instance Enter-Claim(Clara Smith, 2000, 11-11-2006) is started. When the claim is entered in the system, this activity instance terminates.

Each activity instance during its lifetime is in different states. These states and the respective state transitions can be represented by a state transition diagram. A simple state transition diagram for activity instances is shown in Figure 3.9. The states that an activity instance adopts during its lifetime are

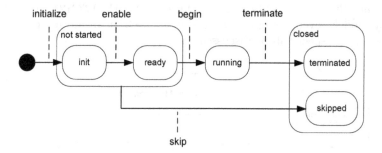

Fig. 3.9. State transition diagram for activity instances

described as follows. When it is created it enters the *init* state; by the *enable* state transition the activity instance can enter the *ready* state.

If a particular activity instance is not required, then the activity instance can be skipped, represented by a *skip* state transition from the *not started* state to the *skipped* state. From the *ready* state, the activity instance can use the *begin* state transition to enter the *running* state. When the activity instance has completed its work, the *terminate* state transition transfers it to the *terminated* state. When an activity instance is in the *terminated* or the *skipped* state, then it is *closed*.

While the state transition diagram shown in Figure 3.9 properly represents the states of most activity instances in business processes, in real-world settings, activity instances are likely to expose a more complex behaviour. Reasons for this complex behaviour include disabling and enabling activities, suspending running activities, and skipping or undoing activities. The respective state transition diagram is shown in Figure 3.10. It provides a more detailed view on the states of activity instances.

The state transition diagram representing the complex behaviour of activity instances is a refinement of the state transition diagram representing their simple behaviour. All state transitions possible in the simple diagram are also possible in the complex state transition diagram. The activity instance is initiated, and it enters the *ready* state before entering the *running* state. If it turns out that an activity instance that is not started is not required then it enters the *skipped* state.

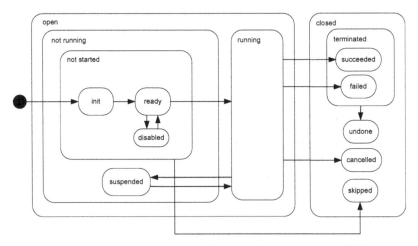

Fig. 3.10. State transition diagram for activity instances, detailed version

But the detailed state transition diagram shown in Figure 3.10 allows more complex behaviour of activity instances. When an activity instance can be activated, it enters the *ready* state. If during the execution of a process instance certain activity instances are currently not available for execution, they can be *disabled*. Activity instances that are in the *init, disabled,* or *ready* state are also in the *not started* state. Once an activity instance is *ready*, it can be started, entering the *running* state. Running activities can be temporarily *suspended,* to be resumed later. An activity instance can terminate either successfully or in failure. Terminated activity instances can be undone, using compensation or transactional recovery techniques.

Based on the description of the behaviour of an activity instance, the question now arises on how to capture the actual behaviour of a concrete activity instance, that is, on how to specify the trace of states and state transitions that the activity instance went through. In this section, events and event orderings are introduced to properly represent the essence of activity instances.

The basic idea of using events for representing activity instances is quite simple: each state transition of an activity instance is represented by an event. These events have a temporal ordering. Based on the state transition diagram for activity instances, each activity instance can be represented by a totally ordered set of events. For the representation of activity instances by events, the simple state transition diagram shown in Figure 3.9 suffices.

Definition 3.2 Let AM be a set of activity models and AI be a set of activity instances. An *activity instance* $i = (E_i, <_i) \in AI$ based on an activity model $I \in AM$ is defined by a totally ordered set of events E_i such that either

- activity instance i is executed, in which case $E_i \subseteq \{i_i, e_i, b_i, t_i\}$, referencing the occurrence of state transitions *initialize, enable, begin,* and *terminate,* respectively, and an event ordering $<_i \subseteq \{(i_i, e_i), (e_i, b_i), (b_i, t_i)\}$, or
- activity instance i is skipped, in which case $E_i \subseteq \{i_i, e_i, s_i\}$, referencing the occurrence of state transitions *initialize, enable,* and *skip,* and an event ordering $<_i \subseteq \{(i_i, s_i), (i_i, e_i), (e_i, s_i)\}$.

The function *model* : $AI \mapsto AM$ maps each activity instance to its activity model, that is, $model(i) = I$ ◇

We define the event set of an activity instance as a subset of the complete event set, $E_i \subseteq \{i_i, e_i, b_i, t_i\}$, since during the execution of an activity instance the events occur one after the other. Therefore, any prefix of the totally ordered event set characterizes a valid state of an activity instance.

If, for instance, an activity instance i has entered the running state, it is characterized by $i = (E_i, <_i)$ such that $E_i = \{i_i, e_i, b_i\}$ and $<_i = \{(i_i, e_i), (e_i, b_i)\}$. In this case, $E_i \subseteq \{i_i, e_i, b_i, t_i\}$ and $<_i \subseteq \{(i_i, e_i), (e_i, b_i), (b_i, t_i)\}$, satisfying the definition.

Note that an activity instance can be skipped if it is in the init or ready state. As a result, the *enable* event might or might not be in the event set of a skipped activity instance.

The causal ordering of events indicated by this definition can be graphically represented by event diagrams. In event diagrams, time proceeds from left to right, and events are shown as bullets. The causal relationships of events are represented by directed arcs.

Due to the nature of event diagrams, they form directed acyclic graphs, where the nodes are events and the edges reflect causal ordering between events. An event diagram for a particular activity instance is shown in Figure 3.11.

In the event diagram shown in part (a) of that figure, an activity instance that is properly executed is shown, while (b) shows the events of a skipped activity instance. To illustrate the relationship between state transition diagrams and event diagrams, each state transition in the state transition diagram is associated with an event in the respective event diagram.

The activity instance starts with a state transition to the init state. This state transition is represented by an *initialize* event in the event diagram. An *enable* state transition brings the activity instance in the *ready* state; this state transition is represented by an *enable* event. An activity instance in the

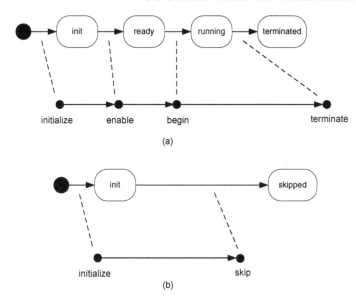

Fig. 3.11. Event diagram for (a) executed activity instance and (b) skipped activity instance

ready state can be started, represented by the *begin* state transition. Finally, the *terminate* state transition completes the activity instance.

Events are points in time, that is, events do not take time. The time interval in which an activity instance is in one state is delimited by two events, the event representing the state transition to enter the state and the event representing the state transition to leave the state. For example, the time interval in which the activity instance is in the running state is delimited by the begin and terminate events.

The ordering of events of multiple activity instances in the context of a business process instance is an important instrument to capturing the execution semantics of business processes, as will be discussed in Chapter 4.

3.5 Process Models and Process Instances

Business processes consist of a set of related activities whose coordinated execution contributes to the realization of a business function in a technical and organizational environment. Business processes are represented by business process models. Since this section concentrates on the execution ordering of activities, disregarding the technical and organizational environment of business processes, the term process model is used.

Figure 3.12 shows the layers of the Meta Object Facility for the process subdomain. In the M0 layer there are process instances that reflect the actual occurrences of a business process. Each process instance is an instance of a

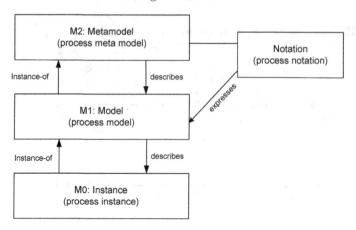

Fig. 3.12. MOF levels of process aspect

process model in the model layer M1. Process models are described by process metamodels, building the M2 layer.

In order to express process models, there needs to be a notation in place that provides notational elements for the conceptual elements of process metamodels. For instance, if the process metamodel has a concept called activity model, then there needs to be a notational element for expressing activity models.

Therefore, in Figure 3.12, a process notation is associated with the process metamodel level and with the process model level; each process model is expressed in a process notation associated with the process metamodel that describes the process model.

3.5.1 Process Models

In this section, a simple process metamodel is introduced. Rather than being on completeness of modelling constructs, the focus of this section is on providing a well-described process metamodel that can be used to illustrate the core components of any process metamodel. Chapter 4 will look at process metamodels of higher complexity.

Any modelling effort starts with identifying the main concepts that need to be represented. In metamodelling, the concepts to be represented are models. The following models are identified as concepts in the metamodel.

- *Process Model*: A process model represents a blue print for a set of process instances with a similar structure. Process models have a two-level hierarchy, so that each process model consists of a set of activity models. Nesting of process models within process models is not represented, because it would introduce complexity that is not required. Each process model consists of nodes and directed edges.

- *Edge*: Directed edges are used to express the relationships between nodes in a process model.
- *Node*: A node in a process model can represent an activity model, an event model, or a gateway model.
  - *Activity Models*: Activity models describe units of work conducted in a business process. Each activity model can appear at most once in a process model. No activity model can appear in multiple process models. This stipulation can be relaxed by qualifying activity model identifiers with process model identifiers; to keep the process metamodel simple, this extension is not covered. Activity model nodes do not act as split or join nodes, that is, each activity model has exactly one incoming edge and exactly one outgoing edge.
  - *Event models*: Event models capture the occurrence of states relevant for a business process. Process instances start and end with events, so process models start and end with event models.
  - *Gateway Models*: Gateways are used to express control flow constructs, including sequences, as well as split and join nodes.

Each process model contains elements at the model level, for instance, activity models. Process instances consist of activity instances. The model level and the instance level do not hold only for activities, but also for events and gateways. For instance, the start event model in a process model rules that each process instance begins with a start event instance. Since events are by definition singular entities, event instances are also called events.

Control flow in process models is represented by gateway models. As with activities and events, gateways are represented in process models by gateway models. This explicit representation allows our considering gateway instances for process instances. This is very useful, since each gateway model can be used multiple times in a given process instance, for instance, if it is part of a loop.

The different occurrences of a given gateway can have different properties. For instance, an *exclusive or* gateway can in one instance select branch 1 while in the next iteration it can use branch 2. This situation can be represented properly if there are multiple gateway instances for a given gateway model in the context of a given process model. In the example discussed, the first gateway instance would select branch 1, while the second gateway instance would select branch 2.

The next step in modelling concerns the identification and formalization of the relationships between these concepts. Figure 3.13 provides a representation of the concepts and their relationships by a structure diagram, defining a process metamodel.

Each process model consists of nodes and edges. The nodes represent activity models, event models and gateway models, while the edges represent control flow between nodes. Each edge is associated with exactly two nodes, relating them in a particular order.

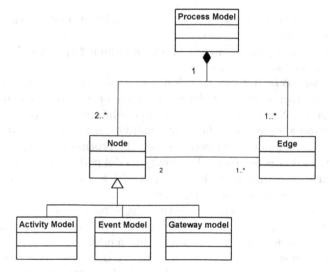

Fig. 3.13. Model for process models: process metamodel, MOF level M2

Each node is associated with at least one edge. The different types of nodes are represented by the generalization relation. Activity models reflect the work units to be performed, event models represent the occurrence of states relevant for the business process, and gateway models represent execution constraints of activities, such as split and join nodes.

While the association between nodes and edges are defined at the node level, the cardinality of the association between special types of nodes (activity models, event models, and gateway models) differs. Each activity model has exactly one incoming and one outgoing edge.

Each process starts with exactly one event, the initial event, and ends with exactly one event, the final event. Therefore, certain events can have no incoming edges (initial event) or no outgoing edges (final event). Gateway models represent control flow. Therefore, they can act as either split nodes or join nodes, but not both. Hence, each gateway model can have multiple outgoing edges (split gateway node) or multiple incoming edges (join gateway node).

Figure 3.14 shows a process model based on the process metamodel introduced. The notation used to express this process model is taken from the Business Process Model and Notation:

- Event model nodes are represented by circles; the final event model is represented by a bold circle.
- Activity models are represented by rectangles with rounded edges.
- Gateway models are represented by diamonds.
- Edges are represented by directed edges between nodes.

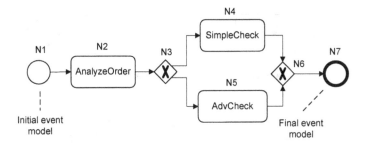

Fig. 3.14. Process notation used to express concepts from process meta model

To ease discussion of this example, nodes are marked with identifiers. The process model represents the checking of an order. The process starts with an initial event model node $N1$, represented by a circle. This event model represents the occurrence of a state relevant for the business process.

In the example, an order has been received, which now needs to be checked. Once this event occurs, the order needs to be analyzed, represented by activity model *AnalyzeOrder* and the edge connecting event node $N1$ to *AnalyzeOrder*. After the order is analyzed, a gateway node is used to decide whether a simple or an advanced check is required. When the chosen checking activity is completed, the gateway model $N6$ is activated and the process completes with the final event model $N7$.

Before the process instance level is addressed, a formalization of the process metamodel shown in Figure 3.13 is introduced.

Definition 3.3 Let C be a set of control flow constructs. $P = (N, E, type)$ is a *process model* if it consists of a set N of nodes, and a set E of edges.

- $N = N_A \cup N_E \cup N_G$, where N_A is a set of activity models, N_E is a set of event models, and N_G is a set of gateway models. These sets are mutually disjoint.
- E is a set of directed edges between nodes, such that $E \subseteq N \times N$, representing control flow.
- $type : N_G \mapsto C$ assigns to each gateway model a control flow construct.

◇

Figure 3.15 shows in part (a) a process model with an explicit representation of a sequence gateway. The set of control flow constructs includes sequential execution, that is, $Seq \in C$. The process model is defined by $P = (N, E, type)$, such that

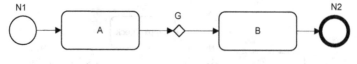

(a) Sequence Flow with Sequence Gateway

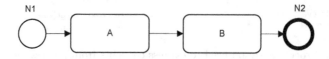

(b) Sequence Flow, Simplified Notation

Fig. 3.15. Alternative representations of sequence gateway

$$N_A = \{A, B\}$$
$$N_E = \{N1, N2\}$$
$$N_G = \{G\}$$
$$E = \{(N1, A), (A, G), (G, B), (B, N2)\}$$
$$type(G) = Seq \in C$$

Whenever there is a direct control flow edge connecting two activity models in a process model, the gateway node G with $type(G) = Seq$ representing the sequence flow can be omitted, as shown in part (b) of that figure. This stipulation simplifies process model representations without introducing ambiguity.

3.5.2 Process Instances

Process models define restrictions on process instances that belong to the process model. Therefore, it is essential to properly define not only process models but also process instances. Modelling process instances is not an easy task, because of their intangible nature. A process instance is started, and it lives for a limited time period before it ceases to exist, similarly to activity instances.

A process instance consists of a number of activity instances as well as event and gateway instances. The ordering relationships of activity instances in a process instance is defined by the relationships of the activity models in the process model.

For instance, if a process model defines an execution ordering constraint between activity models A and B, then for each particular process instance, the activity instance that belongs to activity model A must have terminated before the activity instance for B can be started.

An extension of the process metamodel discussed above is presented in Figure 3.16. There are additional classes for process instances and node instances

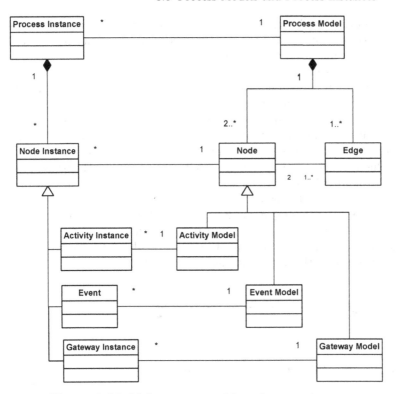

Fig. 3.16. Model for process models and process instances

that are a generalization of activity instances, events, and gateway instances. There are one-to-many relationships between the respective concepts at the model level and at the instance level, as shown in the metamodel.

Each process instance is associated with exactly one process model, and each process model is associated with an arbitrary number of process instances. Each process instance is composed of an arbitrary number of activity instances. Each activity instance is associated with exactly one activity model. The same holds for events and gateways.

Note that each activity model is associated with an arbitrary number of activity instances. In the case of loops, an activity model is associated with multiple activity instances. An activity model that lies on a branch that is not taken during a particular process instance is not associated with any activity instance, explaining the cardinality of the association * that allows zero occurrences of the association, that is, there might be activity models in a process model for which no activity instances are required for a particular process instance.

After introducing events and event orderings to represent activity instances, this section looks at events and event orderings that occur during the enactment of process instances. Process models restrict for a process instance the events and event orderings of its activity instances by imposing execution constraints, such as sequential execution of activity instances. Execution constraints need to be satisfied by all process instances based on a particular process model.

The execution constraints can be precisely specified by events and their ordering. For example, the execution constraint $A \to B$ dictates that the start event of the activity instance corresponding to B can only happen after the termination event of the activity instance corresponding to A. This is the basic idea of characterizing the execution semantics of process instances.

To illustrate these concepts, a process instance based on the process model shown in Figure 3.14 on page 89 is investigated. Each process instance based on this process model starts with an analyze order activity. Depending on a decision, either the simple check activity or the advanced check activity is enacted. This process model makes room for different process instances. Depending on the decision made at the gateway node, either the simple check activity instance or the advanced check activity is executed.

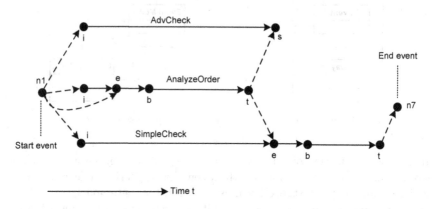

Fig. 3.17. Event diagram of sample process instance (subscripts of *init*, *enable*, *terminate* and *skip* events omitted)

Event diagrams are also useful for capturing process instances. The event diagram of a particular process instance is shown in Figure 3.17, where a process instance is shown during which the simple check activity instance is selected.

When the process starts, activity instances for all three activity models are generated. In event diagrams, the subscripts of the *init*, *enable*, *terminate*, and *skip* events can be omitted, if the activity instance to which the event belongs is clear.

The start event is represented by the event node $N1$ in the process model. The occurrence of this event is represented in the event diagram by event $n1$. Once this event has occurred, the *AnalyzeOrder* activity instance can start, that is, it can enter the ready state, represented by an enable event.

When the *Analyze Order* activity instance terminates, (1) the *AdvCheck* activity instance is no longer required, so that a skip event occurs for this activity instance, and (2) the *SimpleCheck* activity instance is enabled, so that it can start. When this activity completes, the final event $n7$ of the process instance occurs.

Observe that the event diagram shown in Figure 3.17 does not represent the initial or final event of the process or the events related to gateway instances. A complete picture of the events that occur is shown in Figure 3.18.

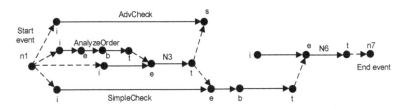

Fig. 3.18. Event diagram of sample process instance, with initial and final events and gateway events

Definition 3.4 Let PI be a set of process instances. A *process instance* $i = (E_i, <_i) \in PI$ based on a process model $P = (N, E, type)$ is defined by a partially ordered set of events E_i such that

• E_i consists of events for all activity instances $j \in AI$ for which $model(j) \in N$

• $<_i$ is an event ordering in E_i that satisfies the ordering of events in each activity instance and in each gateway instance, and the ordering of events between activities satisfies the execution constraints as defined by the process model.

⋄

Note that different types of nodes can create different types of events. Nodes that represent activity models and nodes that represent gateway models can create events for initializing, enabling, beginning, terminating and skipping the respective instance, while nodes that represent events can just occur. This means an event in a process model can occur during the enactment of a process instance based on the model. The event can potentially occur multiple times, if, for instance, the event is part of loop in the process model.

If process instances are discussed that feature multiple activity models, the detailed presentation of event diagrams becomes cumbersome and hard to follow. Therefore, an abstraction is introduced that reduces the events of an activity instance by a line that is delimited by its enable and terminate or skip events. Activity instances that are skipped are represented by a dotted line; activity instances that are executed are represented by a solid line.

The abstraction from the event diagram shown in Figure 3.18 is shown in Figure 3.19

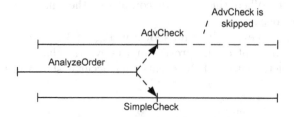

Fig. 3.19. Compact representation of event diagrams

3.6 Process Interactions

Business processes reside in single organizations. Since enterprises cooperate with each other, it is essential to consider the interaction between enterprises. Since all activities that an enterprise conducts are part of some business process, the interaction between enterprises can be described by the interaction of business processes of these enterprises. These interactions typically occur in a peer-to-peer style, following an agreed-upon process choreography.

An example of interacting processes is shown in Figure 3.20. A buyer orders some products from a reselling company. These enterprises are reflected by the respective value chains. Within these value chains are business functions realized by business processes.

The buyer value chain contains an order product business function, and the reseller value chain contains an order management business function. The business process models that realize these business functions are shown in Figure 3.20.

The business process of the buyer starts by his placing an order. This placing of an order is realized by a message to the reseller; the task place order is responsible for sending this message. On the reseller side, this message triggers a receive order event. The processes continue as specified. Since the message flow occurs between multiple activities in both directions, the value chain level representation of the interacting business processes—from buyer to reseller—is not complete in the sense that it does not hold all possible orders of interaction.

Interacting process instances can be visualized adequately by event diagrams. The distributed nature of interacting processes is represented by introducing a horizontal line for each participant, on which the events of that participant appear in an ordered fashion. Participants communicate by sending and receiving messages. In event diagrams, a one-way message interaction

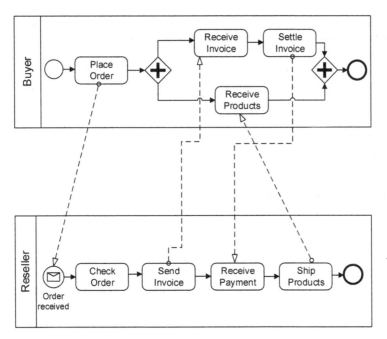

Fig. 3.20. Interacting business processes involving buyer and reseller

is represented by a send event, a corresponding receive event, and an arc connecting the two events. Participants can communicate only by sending and receiving messages.

In order to illustrate these concepts, Figure 3.21 shows the event diagram of one particular process interaction based on the interacting process models shown in Figure 3.20.

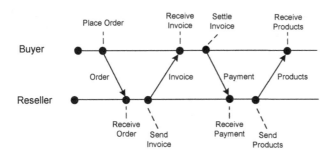

Fig. 3.21. Event diagram of interacting processes shown in Figure 3.20

The diagram shows the timelines of the buyer and the reseller. It abstracts from events regarding the initiating, enabling, starting, and terminating of activities. Instead, it concentrates on message events. Each message send event is marked by the activity instance during which the send occurs, and each receive event is marked by the activity instance during which the receive occurs. It is valid to assume that messages are sent on termination of the respective activity instance and an arrival of a message triggers the enable event for the receiving activity instance.

Interacting processes are formalized as process choreographies, which will be discussed in detail in Chapter 6, where also properties of process choreographies are investigated.

3.7 Further Modelling Dimensions

When defining business processes in Definition 1.1, we stressed that business processes are executed in technical and organizational environments. In this section, modelling techniques are introduced that allow us to capture additional dimensions of business processes. The resulting models provide important information to embed a business process in its technical and organizational environment.

3.7.1 Modelling Process Data

Business processes operate on data. Explicitly representing data, data types, and data dependencies between activities of a business process puts a business process management system in a position to control the transfer of relevant data as generated and processed during processes enactment.

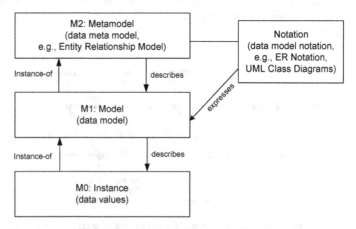

Fig. 3.22. MOF levels of modelling data

Data modelling is at the core of database design. The Entity Relationship approach is used to classify and organize data in a given application domain.

Entity Relationship modelling belongs to the metamodel level, as depicted in Figure 3.22, because it provides the required concepts to express data models. Data modelling will be illustrated by a sample application domain, namely by order management.

In a modelling effort, the most important entities are identified and classified. Entities are identifiable things or concepts in the real world that are important to the modelling goal. In the sample scenario, orders, customers, and products are among the entities of the real world that need to be represented in the data model.

Entities are classified as entity types if they have the same or similar properties. Therefore, orders are classified by an entity type called *Orders*. Since each order has an order number, a date, a quantity, and an amount, all order entities can be represented by this entity type. Properties of entities are represented by attributes of the respective entity types.

The entities classified in an entity type need to have similar, but not identical structure, because attributes can be optional. If the application domain allows, for instance, for an order to have or not to have a discount, then the amount attribute is optional. This means that two orders are classified in entity type order even if one has a discount attribute while another does not.

Entity types in the Entity Relationship metamodel need to be represented in a notation by a particular symbol. While there are variants of Entity Relationship notations, entity types are often represented by rectangles, marked with the name of the entity type. Figure 3.23 shows an entity type *Orders* at the centre of the diagram. Other entity types in the sample application domain are customers and products. The attributes are represented as ellipsoids attached to entity types.

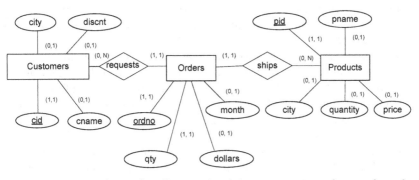

Fig. 3.23. Entity relationship diagram involving customers, orders, and products, O'Neil and O'Neil (2000)

Entities are associated with each other by relationships. For instance, a customer "Miller" requests an order with the order number 42. These types of links between entities are called relationships. Just as there are many customer entities and many order entities, there are many customer-order relationships. To represent these relationships, a relationship type *requests* classifies them all. In Entity Relationship diagrams, relationship types are typically represented by diamond symbols, connected to the respective entity types by edges.

The complex nature of data in a given application domain can be well represented by Entity Relationship Diagrams. These diagrams can be used to create relational database tables, using transformation rules. Once the respective database tables have been created in a relational database, application data can be stored persistently. The data can be retrieved efficiently using declarative query languages, for instance Structured Query Language.

While this discussion focuses on data modelling in the context of database applications, the same data modelling method can be used to represent data structures in business process management. Based on these data structures, data dependencies between activities in business processes can be captured precisely.

Data modelling is also the basis for the integration of heterogeneous data. In the enterprise application integration scenarios discussed above, one of the main issues was the integration of data from heterogeneous data sources. Once data models are available for these data sources, the data integration problem can be addressed. There are advanced data integration techniques that also take into account data at the instance level, but explicit data models in general are essential to addressing data integration.

Data integration can then be realized by a mapping between the data types. For instance, there might be applications on top of database systems A and B, such that these systems have tables CustomerA and CustomerB, respectively, that differ. For instance, while CName is the attribute of the CustomerA table, referring to the name of the customer, CustN might be the respective attribute in the CustomerB table. In order to integrate both tables, the attributes need to be mapped. In this case, CustomerA.CName is mapped to CustomerB.CustN.

In data integration projects, complex integration problems are likely to emerge. There might be attributes that cannot be mapped, but there might also be attributes that need to be mapped to different tables, often by our using transformation rules. The hardest set of problems, however, stem from semantic heterogeneity. There are assumptions on the data that are not explicit in the data model or in the actual data stored in the database. These semantic differences can only be taken into account when investigating the meaning of the attributes in detail, often during interviews with the persons involved in the data modelling and database design of the systems to integrate.

Semantic specification of data can be used to solve these data integration problems. However, complete semantic specification of data requires considerable resources, and the completeness of the semantic specification cannot be proven automatically. Therefore, further research is required to evaluate the possibilities of semantics-based data integration.

In graph-based approaches to business process modelling, data dependencies are represented by data flow between activities. Each process activity is assigned a set of input and a set of output parameters. Upon its start, an activity reads its input parameters, and upon its termination it writes data it generated to its output parameters. These parameters can be used by followup activities in the business process.

The transfer of data between activities is known as data flow. By providing graphical constructs to represent data flow between activities, the data perspective can be visualized and used to validate and optimize business processes. These aspects are covered in more detail in Section 4.6, which introduces graph-based process languages.

To organize data-related issues in business process management, workflow data patterns have been introduced. Workflow data patterns formulate characteristics on how to handle data in business processes. They are organized according to the dimensions data visibility, data interaction, data transfer, and data-based routing.

Data visibility is very similar to the concept of scope in programming languages because it characterizes the area in which a certain data object is available for access. The most important workflow data patterns regarding data visibility are as follows.

- *Task data*: The data object is local to a particular activity; it is not visible to other activities of the same process or to other processes.
- *Block data*: The data object is visible to all activities of a given subprocess.
- *Workflow data*: The data object is visible to all activities of a given business process, but access is restricted by the business process management system, as defined in the business process model.
- *Environment data*: The data object is part of the business process execution environment; it can be accessed by process activities during process enactment.

Data interaction patterns describe how data objects can be passed between activities and processes. Data objects can be communicated between activities of the same business process, between activities and subprocesses of the same business process, and also between activities of different business processes. Data can also be communicated between the business process and the business process management system.

Data transfer is the next dimension to consider. Data transfer can be performed by passing values of data objects and by passing references to data objects. These data transfer patterns are very similar to call-by-value and call-by-reference, concepts used in programming languages to invoke procedures and functions.

In data-based routing, data can have different implications on process enactment. In the simplest case, the presence of a data object can enable a process activity. Data objects can also be used to evaluate conditions in business process models, for instance, to decide on the particular branch to take in a split node.

Workflow data patterns are an appropriate means to organize aspects of business processes related to the handling of data.

3.7.2 Modelling Organization

An important task of a business process management system is the coordination of work among the personnel of an enterprise. To fulfill this, the system has to be provided with information on the organizational structures in which the business process will execute.

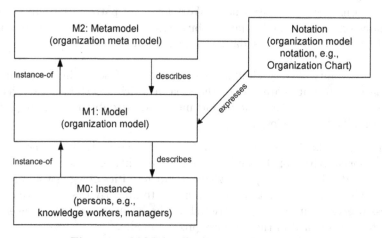

Fig. 3.24. MOF levels of organization aspect

The levels of abstraction in organization modelling are shown in Figure 3.24. As in process modelling and data modelling, the metamodel level provides the means to express models, in this case organizational models. Concepts at this level are positions, roles, teams, and relationships between positions like supervisor. In organization modelling, there are a few formal rules on how to express organizational structures, as well as notations to express them.

The general principle behind organization modelling is the resource, an entity that can perform work for the enterprise. The general concept of resource subsumes humans and other resources, such as trucks, warehouses, and other equipment a company requires to fulfill its goals.

Persons are part of an organization, typically a business organization. The persons in these organizations work to fulfill the business goals of the enterprise. Each person typically occupies some position, and the duties and privileges of that person come with the position, not with the person. This allows filling positions according to an overall organizational plan. In addition, the company can cope better with changes in personnel. Organizational units are permanent groupings of persons based on their positions. Organizational teams or project teams are specific organizational units without a permanent nature. They are conceptualized in the object model shown in Figure 3.25.

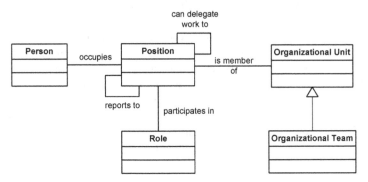

Fig. 3.25. Organization metamodel

Figure 3.26 shows an organizational chart of a fictive enterprise. In order for us to not overload that figure, it contains positions only at the top levels, the chief executive level and the department level. Departments are organizational units with a set of member positions.

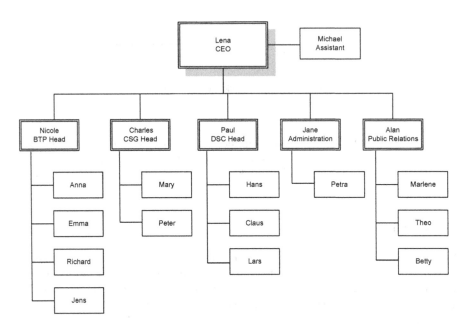

Fig. 3.26. Sample organizational chart

The link between the organizational structure of an enterprise and the business processes is accomplished by work items. Work items represent activity instances to be performed, and work items are associated with knowledge workers to facilitate their selection by knowledge workers. In particular, when the business process management system determines that a certain activity instance enters the ready state, a work item is offered to a set of knowledge workers.

Each work item is associated with exactly one activity instance. The selection of the process participants is subject to resource allocation mechanisms, which will be discussed below. When a knowledge worker completes the activity instance, the business process management system is informed, so that the process instance can be continued accordingly.

In order to discuss the resource allocation principles, a state transition diagram of work items is considered, and a relationship of activity instances to the respective state transitions is provided. The state transition diagram of work items is shown in Figure 3.27.

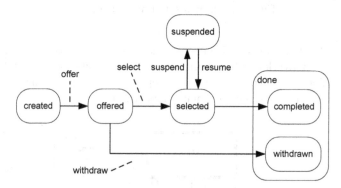

Fig. 3.27. State transition diagram of work items, representing activity instances in human interaction workflows

The assignment of process participants to activities in a business process can be classified by resource patterns. A rich set of resource patterns have recently been introduced; in this book, the most relevant resource patterns are discussed.

Direct Allocation

In direct allocation, an individual person, rather than a position in an organization, is allocated to all activity instances of a particular activity model. This resource allocation is useful in cases where there is exactly one person who is suitable for performing these activities, such as the chairperson of a company, who has to finally decide on investments exceeding a certain threshold.

Direct allocation can always be simulated by role-based allocation, discussed next, simply by providing a role with one member, in our example the company owner. However, if this property of the organization will remain stable over a long period of time, introducing a separate role (owner) is not required, so direct allocation can be used. The limitations of direct allocation will be discussed in the context of role-based allocation.

Role-Based Allocation

Role-based allocation is the standard way of allocating work to the members of organizations. It is based on the understanding that all members of a certain role are somehow functionally equivalent, so that any member of the role can perform a given unit of work.

To each activity model in a business process model, a role is assigned, indicating that all members of the role are capable of performing the respective activity instances. The mapping of role information to specific knowledge workers is called role resolution. Current information on the availability of the knowledge worker is used during role resolution.

There are two ways of realizing role-based allocation. In the first way, when an activity instance enters the ready state, the work item is communicated to the members of the group. Once one member of the group selects a work item, the work items associated with the other group members are deleted. In the second way, only one person is selected to perform the activity instance, so only one work item is created.

Role-based allocation provides a set of interesting advantages with respect to direct allocation, all of which are related to enhancing the flexibility of business processes. Firstly, the business process model does not need to be changed when there are changes in the personnel, that is, employees retire and new employees are hired. When using direct allocation, any change in the personnel related to the directly allocated persons would result in a change in the business process model.

Secondly, by role resolution at run time of the business process, only available persons are selected to perform activities. This approach avoids situations in which persons are selected to perform activity instances that are currently not available, for instance, due to meetings or absence. In direct role resolution, when the person is not available, there is no way of continuing the business process.

Deferred Allocation

In deferred allocation, the decision about who performs an activity instance is only made at run time of the business process. To this end, there is no distinction between deferred allocation and role-based allocation. However, in deferred allocation, rather than using the role information defined during design time, the allocation is performed as an explicit step in the business process, and not influenced by role information.

Authorization

Authorization allocates persons to activity instances based on their positions. So, a list of positions is enumerated that specifies the persons who can perform the activity instance. This could also be achieved by adding a new role that captures the authorization. A specific type of authorization that uses capabilities of the knowledge worker to perform allocation is also possible.

Separation of Duties

The separation of duties allocation scheme relates different allocations within one business process. For instance, a document needs to be signed and countersigned by two employees with a common role. In role-based allocation, these activities could be performed by the same employee. Separation of duties allows relating allocations in a way that this is ruled out, so that each document is signed by two different employees.

Case Handling

In the case handling allocation scheme, certain activities in a business process require an understanding of the overall case. In these environments, it is useful that the same knowledge worker deals with all activities of one business process instance. This avoids errors and reduces processing time, because the knowledge worker already knows the case, and so can solve the issues at hand more efficiently than a colleague to whom the case is not known. This is a key concept in case handling, which is discussed in more detail in Section 8.4. The "retain familiar" allocation scheme is very similar to case handling; however, not all activity instances of a case are allocated to one specific knowledge worker, but rather only a subset of them.

History-Based Allocation

The idea of history-based allocation is that a person is allocated to an activity instance based on what this person worked on previously, that is, on the history of the activity instance that he or she completed. This includes other business process instances. The goal is to allocate work to persons according to their personal experiences and expertise that is not represented in the role information. While this is not part of a role specification, this information needs to be represented in the business process management system so that it can decide on the allocation based on the history and personal experiences. This allocation scheme is useful for realizing a "one face to the customer" strategy, in which for each customer there is a dedicated individual responsible for all aspects of communication with it.

Organizational Allocation

If organizational allocation is used, not roles but the positions within the overall organization are used to allocate activity instances. For instance, to authorize expenditure, the manager of the organizational unit that requested the expenditure needs to approve. Depending on the particular language used to express organizational allocation, complex allocation rules can be realized, all of which take advantage of the organizational structure of the company.

3.7.3 Modelling Operation

While business process management organizes the work that a company performs by focusing on organizational and functional aspects, the realization of business process activities also needs to be taken into account. Activities can be distinguished depending on the level of software system support. The terms system workflows and human interaction workflows were introduced to characterize the different kinds of business process enactment.

A classification of activities in business processes was introduced in Figure 3.1, consisting of system activities, user interaction activities, and manual activities. To recapitulate, system activities are performed by software systems without user interaction, user interaction activities require the involvement of human users and manual activities do not involve the use of information systems.

During the enactment of human interaction workflows, knowledge workers perform activity instances. When a knowledge worker starts working on a specific activity, the respective application program is started, and the input data as specified in the process model is transferred to that application program. When the knowledge worker completes that activity, the output data generated is collected in the output parameters. These parameter values can then be stored in the application program. They can also be transferred by the business process management system to the next activity, as specified in the business process model.

Business process modelling aims at mapping high-level and domain-specific features of the application process; the technical details—the main components of the operational perspective—are taken into account in the configuration phase of the business process management lifecycle. The heterogeneous nature of information technology landscapes led to various kinds of interface definitions, most of which did not prove to be compatible. With the advent of service-oriented computing, the operational aspects of business processes are represented by services, providing the required uniformity.

This section discusses how activities realized by software functionality can be modelled. Conceptually, the same levels of abstraction apply to modelling the operational perspective as to modelling the other perspectives: at the metamodel level, interface definition languages reside. They describe specific interface definitions at the model level. At the instance level executing software code is categorized.

This approach fits the modelling of activity instances (and, therefore, also to process instances) well, because activity instances can be realized by executing software code. It also fits the organizational perspective in which persons reside at the instance level. Persons are—at least in human interaction workflows—responsible for performing activity instances.

In order to automatically invoke this software functionality, business process management systems require concepts and technology to access these systems. The operational perspective of business process modelling provides the information that equips a business process management system with information required to invoke the functionality of external application systems.

The operational perspective includes the invocation environment of application programs, the definition of the input and output parameters of the application program, and their mapping to input and output parameters of business process activities. Therefore, functional requirements need to be detailed in order for us to evaluate whether a certain software system provides the required functionality in the context of a business process.

This perspective is not limited to functional requirements. Non-functional requirements also need to be represented, for instance, security properties and quality of service properties of the invoked applications or services, such as execution time and uptime constraints. In service-oriented architectures, these properties are typically specified in service-level agreements between collaborating business partners. These service-level agreements are part of a legal contract that the parties sign.

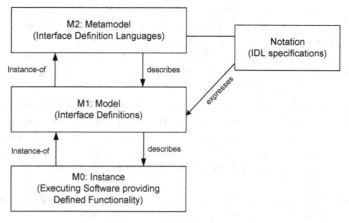

Fig. 3.28. MOF levels of operational perspective

Interface definition languages are used to specify the usage of procedures and functions, implemented by software system. They are also essential to connect software systems that have been developed independently from each other. Therefore, they are essential for middleware systems. Middleware based on service-oriented architectures play an increasingly important part as realization platforms for enacting business processes. The remainder of this section discusses aspects of service-oriented architectures that are relevant for business process management.

The creation of service wrappers that encapsulate business-relevant functionality of existing information systems is called service-enabling. While there are environments in which one service is realized by one information system, the typical case is where business functionality is realized by the interplay of multiple existing application systems, making service-enabling a costly and complex matter.

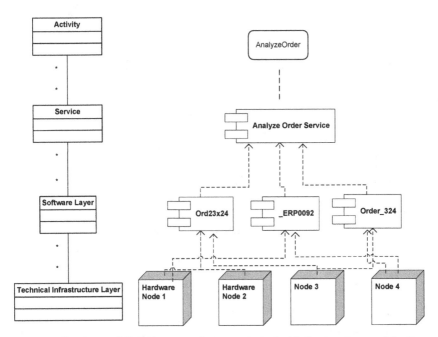

Fig. 3.29. Service-enabling closes gap between technical infrastructure and business processes

Service-enabling closes the gap between business process activities and the technical infrastructure for realizing them. This situation is depicted in Figure 3.29, where the business process activity *AnalyzeOrder* is realized by a service called *Analyze Order Service* which combines the functionality of three underlying software systems that run on a technical infrastructure. While the definition and realization of the *Analyze Order Service* is a complex and challenging task, this book assumes that dedicated business functionality is available and can be used to realize activities in business processes.

Service-oriented computing also facilitates the dynamic binding of services to particular business process activities. This situation is represented in the conceptual model of these layers by a many-to-many relationship between activity and service. This means that a given activity can be realized by multiple services. Advanced concepts in service engineering facilitate the dynamic binding of a business process activity to a service at run time, providing the potential to increase fault tolerance by selecting from a set of possible services a service that is currently operational.

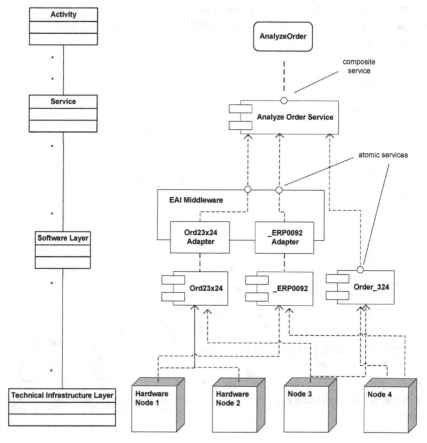

Fig. 3.30. Detailed view on service-enabling, with atomic services and composed services

A more detailed picture is provided in Figure 3.30, where enterprise application integration middleware is explicitly shown. Two legacy systems provide their functionality via enterprise application integration middleware. For each of these systems, an adapter is realized that hides the heterogeneity of the legacy systems from higher levels. But there can also be existing software systems that do not require the enterprise application integration middleware layer.

In the example shown in Figure 3.30, the software component *Order_324* does not require the enterprise application integration middleware. This is the case if the system exposes an interface with a suitable and well-documented interface, such as a Web services interface.

Different types of services are also shown in Figure 3.30: Atomic services provided by individual legacy systems via service-enabling or via enterprise application integration middleware subsystems and composed services, which are built on top of atomic services.

These composed services provide a high-level abstraction layer to be used in the business process layer. In particular, the *AnalyzeOrder* business process activity is realized by the *Analyze Order Service*, a composed service that uses atomic services provided either by enterprise application integration middleware or by a service-enabled software system.

As the current realization of service-oriented architectures, Web services are discussed in Chapter 8, including service composition, which is the technique to define and enact system workflows in service-oriented environments.

3.8 Business Process Flexibility

The quest for flexibility can be regarded as the main driving force behind business process management, both at an organizational level, where strategic business processes are investigated, and at an operational level, where human interaction workflows and system workflows are important concepts for realizing business processes.

According to Wikipedia, flexibility refers to the "ability to easily bend an object or the ability to adapt to different circumstances."

In todays dynamic market environments, "different circumstances" are induced by changes in the market environment of the company. Business processes are objects that need to adapt easily to changes. Since products that companies provide to the market are generated by business processes, flexible business processes are an important asset for coping with market changes in an effective manner.

Different aspects have to be taken into account when considering flexibility. First of all, flexibility is provided by explicit representation of business processes, because adaptations of explicit, graphically specified business processes is much easier than adaptation of written organizational procedures or business policies buried in software code. Flexibility through explicit process representation will be discussed in Section 3.8.

Enactment platforms, such as workflow management systems, provide powerful mechanisms for enacting business processes in diverse technical and organizational environments. One area specific to human interaction workflows is the assignment of knowledge workers to process activities. These organizational aspects will be discussed in more detail in Section 3.8.

In typical workflow environments, such as system workflows and human interaction workflows, information systems are required for enacting workflow activities. The interfaces to these systems might be hardcoded in the adapters of the workflow management system. In dynamic software landscapes, where functionality is provided through standardized interfaces, the ability to change the binding of particular software to workflow activities is another source of flexibility. Flexibility at the operational level where interfacing to information systems is addressed is considered in Section 3.8.

Explicit Process Representations

Business process management systems are created to narrow the gap between business goals and their realization by means of information technology. The main way to provide this flexibility is based on explicit representations of business processes at different levels. While organizational business processes have a coarse-grained structure and are typically specified textually by forms, operational business processes consist of process activities, and execution constraints that relate them.

Graphical notations, such as the ones discussed in Chapters 4 and 6, are well equipped to support communication about these operational business processes between different stakeholders involved in the design and realization of business processes.

Explicit process representations provide flexibility, since changes to the current process can be discussed and agreed upon by the different stakeholders involved in the design of the business process. In this context, flexibility is achieved by changes at the business process model level that are immediately translated to actual business process instances.

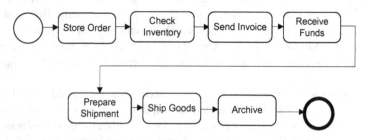

Fig. 3.31. Sample business process model

A simple ordering process is shown in Figure 3.31, illustrating the concepts introduced. This process features a sequence of activities, where the first activity to store the order is preceded by a start event. After the order is stored, the inventory is checked. This version of the business process rules that the shipment is prepared only after the invoice is sent and the funds are received. Finally, the goods are shipped and the process terminates.

Due to the somewhat cautious policy realized by the business process— prepare shipment only after receiving the funds—business process instances based on this process model might suffer from long processing times, resulting in insufficient customer satisfaction.

In order to solve this problem, the process owner starts a review of this business process by inviting process participants and process consultants to a joint workshop. The business process model is used as a communication platform for these stakeholders at this workshop.

Discussing the problem of the process instances, the stakeholders find out that concurrency can be exploited within the process. If activities can be executed concurrently, their order of execution is irrelevant. For instance, the preparation of the invoice can be started before the shipment is handled. The new and improved version of the business process is shown in Figure 3.32.

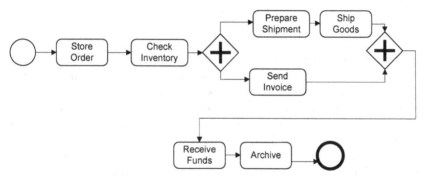

Fig. 3.32. Sample business process model, improved version with concurrency

Although in this example the deficits of the business process are obvious, the improvement of the process by introducing concurrency shows quite well how an explicit process model can foster response to change.

The translation of the business process model to the actual operational environment can be realized in different ways. If the business process is realized by a human interaction workflow, then the modified business process model needs to be deployed in the workflow management system. Deployment typically includes enrichment of the business process model with information to make the process executable.

In particular, there needs to be a translation from the graphical model to an executable format that is specified in a particular workflow language or— in case the system workflow is realized in a service-oriented environment— in a service composition language. In any of these realizations, the explicit representation of business process models provides the flexibility to change the process and to finally enact the modified process.

New process instances would then follow the new, improved business process model. If, on the other hand, business processes are enacted without any system support, then the business process model is translated manually to a consistent set of procedures and policies that the knowledge workers need to follow.

Organizational Modelling

The modelling of organizational aspects also provides flexibility in business process management. In this section, role resolution in an intra-company setting is discussed, in which different approaches are investigated to associate knowledge workers with business process activities. This section uses concepts introduced in Section 3.7.2 in the context of resource patterns.

In the case of human interaction workflows, the enactment environment of the business process has to take into account the organizational structure of the company that runs the business process. Flexibility in organizational modelling is achieved by assigning roles to process activities, and not to specific individuals.

By associating roles with activity models at design time and mapping roles to personnel that is skilled, competent, and available to perform the activity at run time, flexibility is improved, because changes in the personnel structure of the organization do not affect the business processes.

For instance, absent knowledge workers are not with associated with specific activity instances, as are persons who are currently available. Thereby, the dynamic aspect in the organization—knowledge workers might be temporarily absent or there might be changes in the work force—can be represented at the model level. Consequently, changes in the personnel are hidden from the process, as long as the roles defined in the model can actually be filled by persons in the organization.

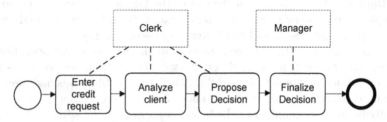

Fig. 3.33. Simple business process model with role information

Consider a business process with a set of activities that need to be executed sequentially. An example of such a business process in a banking environment is in shown in Figure 3.33. These activities involve entering a credit request (*Enter Credit Request*), gathering information on the financial situation of the client (*Analyze client*), proposing a decision on the credit request, and reviewing and submitting the decision.

A subset of these activities is assigned the same role. In the example, a clerk is responsible for the first three activities, whereas the clerk's boss finally decides and submits the decision. This situation can be represented in a business process model by associating the role *Clerk* and the role *Boss* with their respective activities.

For each process instance by role resolution, the system offers these activities to knowledge workers who can fulfill the respective role. Figure 3.34 shows a situation in which three different knowledge workers with the role *Clerk* are associated with the activity instances of that role.

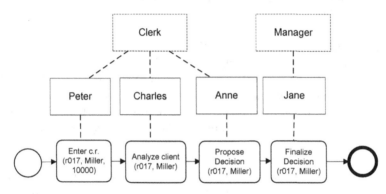

Fig. 3.34. Simple business process instance with knowledge workers associated with activities

While this role resolution is correct from a formal point of view, this situation is undesirable in most cases because each clerk needs to understand the context of the case, which leads to longer process durations and potentially incorrect decisions.

In the example, the hand-over of work from Peter to Charles and from Charles to Anne leads to delays in process executions and should therefore be avoided. In addition, Charles needs to get familiar with the case entered by Peter, and Anne needs to get familiar with the case that Charles analyzed beforehand.

This figure also shows that at the business process instance level, knowledge workers are associated with activity instances, while at the business process model level, roles are associated with activity models.

To provide adequate support through role resolution, the business process model needs to contain the information that whoever conducted the first clerk activity also has to conduct the other two clerk activities. In this case, all clerk activities are associated with Charles, who then can perform them much quicker than the three persons in the previous setting. This beneficial role

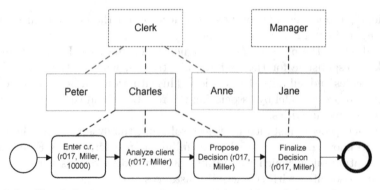

Fig. 3.35. Simple business process instance with one knowledge worker associated with clerk activities

resolution is shown in Figure 3.35. It is realized by the case handing resource pattern, discussed in Section 3.7.2.

This advanced role resolution works well if the same knowledge worker is available during the whole business process instance—or at least during the steps that the person conducts. But there are cases where a person has started on a process instance by conducting the first activity, but then becomes unavailable.

In this case, a decision needs to be made: either the process is delayed until the person returns to work or the case is transferred to another clerk. This clerk needs to understand the overall context of the case before he can start processing the activity. This decision is influenced by multiple factors, such as the type of business process, the expected delay, and the effect of the delay, and therefore cannot be performed automatically in general.

Selection of Business Partners in Process Choreographies

The modelling of organizational aspects in business process management can be extended to business partners, which is important in the context of business-to-business processes.

Consider a business process choreography with multiple business partners, each of which plays a specific role in the choreography. If there is a role *Shipper* specified according to the requirements for shipping goods, it can be bound to specific enterprises that can perform the work. Additional flexibility is gained because the organizations participating in a choreography are not hardwired, but represented at the model level.

There are different options for selecting a particular shipper. The selection can be done before a particular process instance starts. This alternative is useful if sufficient information on the goods to be shipped is available before the process starts.

In scenarios where only during run time of the process instance are the goods and the sender and receiver determined, the dynamic selection of a shipper is useful. Based on the information on the shipment and on its additional properties—such as dangerous goods—an appropriate shipper can be selected at run time.

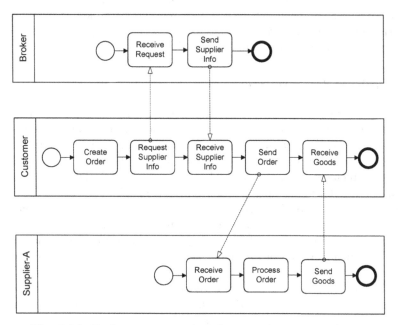

Fig. 3.36. Business partner selected at run time, using a broker

An example involving a customer, a broker, and a set of suppliers is shown in Figure 3.36. In this example, a customer uses a broker to select a supplier. Before the process choreography can be realized, the broker requires information on the suppliers available. This information is gathered by the broker in a separate process choreography, whose message flow is not shown in the figure.

The process choreography starts with the creating of an order by the customer. Then, the customer sends a *Request Supplier Info* message to the broker. The broker receives this message and uses local information to find the supplier most suitable for fulfilling the order. In the *Send Supplier Info* message, the broker informs the customer about this supplier.

The customer receives this message and uses the information received to send an order to the selected supplier, *Supplier-A* in this case. When the supplier has processed the order, the supplier sends the goods to the customer, and the process completes.

In the example shown, the selection is performed using a third party, the broker. While this is a valid option in scenarios where a broker has rich information on a set of business partners, the selection can also be done locally, that is, without the involvement of a third party.

In this case, the actual selection can be performed as a manual activity, using information on suppliers available and capable of fulfilling the order.

Role resolution in this case is not performed by the business process management system, but by a knowledge worker. This task also matches the service-oriented approach, where a service requestor (the knowledge worker) uses the broker to select from among a set of services (supplier services) the one that is suited best for the task at hand.

Standardized Software Interfaces

Standardized interfaces to existing software systems are another means of flexibility in business process management. A variety of techniques to specify software interfaces are known from software engineering and software architectures. It is a key concept to decouple the use of a software component from its implementation, that is, to hide implementation details from usage information, following the information hiding principle.

In the context of business process management, standardized software interfaces are of crucial importance in system workflows, and also in human interaction workflows, since the overall process structure can be decoupled from the implementation of particular activities realized by software components.

A flexible association of process activities with software systems allows us to change the implementation of specific process activities without changing the overall business process. There are two variations: the software system realizing a particular activity can be defined at design time of the process or at run time of the process instances. The first variant is discussed in this section; the dynamic binding of software services to activity instances is discussed in Section 8.3.

An example of changes in the implementation of business process activities is represented in Figure 3.37. In the original implementation, an inventory management system is used to realize the *Check Inventory* activity, and an order management system is used to realize the *Store Order* and the *Prepare Invoice* activities.

This situation is depicted in Figure 3.37 by dotted lines between the business process activities and the information systems that realize them. We assume that an ERP system is deployed to provide the functionality of the order management system and of the inventory management system in an integrated, robust, and scalable manner.

By standardized software interfaces, the business process activities can use the functionality of the new system without changing the business process. This enhances the flexibility of the business process implementation, because the realization of particular process activities can be changed without modifying the business process.

This discussion describes an ideal setting, in which activity implementations can easily be exchanged. However, specific properties of legacy systems

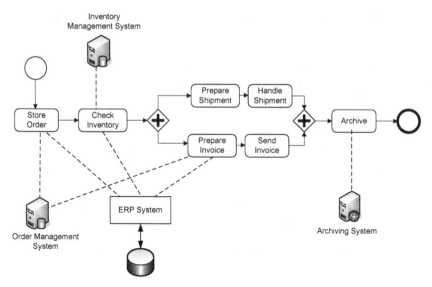

Fig. 3.37. Business process uses ERP systems functionality to realize process activities, while the business process remains unchanged

make the definition of clean, standardized interfaces cumbersome, because legacy systems offer their functionality typically by proprietary and often not well documented interfaces.

This technological problem is also addressed by enterprise application integration systems, where adapter technology is in place to cope with this issue, as discussed in Chapter 2.

In addition, the granularity with which legacy systems provide functionality often does not match the granularity required by the business process. In particular, legacy systems often realize complex subprocesses rather than individual activities in a business process. Sometimes, the processes realized by legacy systems and the modelled business processes are not immediately comparable. These issues have to be taken into account when software interfaces to existing information systems are developed.

One option to solving this problem is developing software interfaces that make available the functionality provided by legacy systems with a granularity that allows reuse of functionality at a finer level of granularity. The granularity should match the granularity required at the business process level.

Depending on the legacy system, its complexity, software architecture, and documentation, as well as the availability of knowledgeable personnel, the required effort can be very high. If the need for finer-grained granularity and efficient reuse of functionality is sufficiently high, then partial or complete reimplementation can be an option.

3.9 Architecture of Process Execution Environments

So far, this chapter has discussed the modelling of different aspects of a business process. This section looks into the representation of a business process management system capable of controlling the enactment of business processes based on business process models.

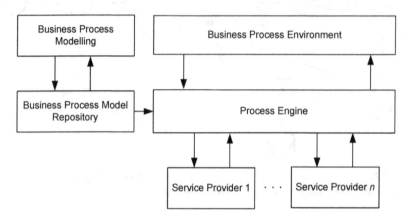

Fig. 3.38. Business process management systems architecture model

Figure 3.38 shows a high-level business process management systems architecture model consisting of components and relationships. The architecture model contains the *Business Process Environment*, a *Business Process Modelling* subsystem, a *Business Process Model Repository*, a *Process Engine*, and a set of *Service Providers*. The roles of these constituents of the architecture model are characterized as follows.

- *Business Process Modelling*: The business process modelling subsystem is used for creating business process models, containing information on activities, their operations, and the structure of the business process. This architecture subsystem can be realized by business process modelling tools.
- *Business Process Environment*: The business process environment triggers the instantiation and enactment of process instances based on process models.
- *Business Process Model Repository*: The business process model repository holds business process models that are created by the business process modelling component.
- *Process Engine*: The process engine is responsible for instantiating and controlling the execution of business processes. It is the core component of a business process management system. This component is triggered by the business process environment. It uses process models to instantiate and control the enactment of process instances. To execute a particular activity

instance, it calls entities that act as providers of the required functionality. In a service-oriented architecture, service providers are called to execute individual services that realize business process activities.

- *Service Providers*: Service providers host application services that realize business process activities. In the architecture model, service providers represent an abstract entity that subsumes not only Web service providers but also knowledge workers that realize particular activities in business processes. The organizational and technical information that the process engine needs in order to determine and access the service provider is also stored in the business process model repository.

These components of the architectural model control the enactment of process instances. To capture the distributed nature of business process executions, the components and the service providers are represented by agents that communicate by sending and receiving messages, that is, the agents do not share memory, but are distributed. These messages are sent along the arcs shown in Figure 3.38.

Gateways are nodes in a process model that are used to guide the process flow. Therefore, for each gateway node the process engine needs to perform some action. This work that the process engine conducts is represented by a gateway instance, just as the work defined by an activity model is represented by an activity instance. A property of gateway instances is that the process engine executes them, whereas activity instances are executed by service providers, requiring nonlocal communication.

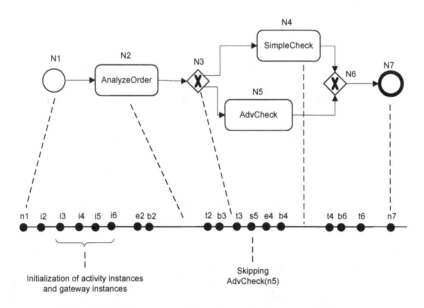

Fig. 3.39. Process model and events of process instance

The events that occur within a process engine during the enactment of a process instance are shown in Figure 3.39. The first event that occurs represents the occurrence of the start event in the process model. Let $n1$ be this event.

The process engine detects that there is a process model deployed for this event. Therefore, a process instance is instantiated. For each activity model in the process model, an activity instance is instantiated; for each gateway node, a gateway instance is created, represented by events $i2$ through $i6$. When the instances are initiated, the *AnalyzeOrder* activity instance can be started, resulting in event $b2$. After the termination of this activity instance in event $t2$, the gateway instance is started, represented by event $b3$.

After the gateway instance terminates in event $t3$, the process engine can decide which path to take. In the process instance shown, the advanced check activity instance is disregarded and the simple check path is taken. Therefore, the *AdvCheck* activity instance is skipped, represented by event $s5$. The *SimpleCheck* activity instance is started (event $b4$) and later terminates in event $t4$. Finally, the execution of the gateway instance and the occurrence of the final event $n7$ terminate the process instance.

The event diagrams introduced are extended to capture agents involved in the enactment of process instances. Each agent is represented by a horizontal line, on which the events that occur in this agent are drawn. Time proceeds from left to right. In addition to the events directly associated with the execution of activity instances, the begin and end of a computation and the sending and receipt of a message are also represented by events. Message events of agents represented by directed arcs connecting the send event with the corresponding receive event.

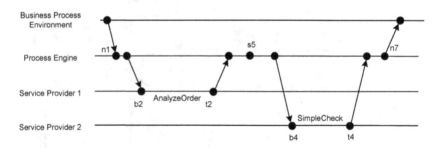

Fig. 3.40. Event diagram of business process execution environment

The business process environment, the process engine, and two service providers are the agents represented in the event diagram. Since the operation of the business process modelling component is not the focus of attention, these components of the architecture model are not represented as agents in the event diagram.

An event diagram of a process instance involving the agents of a business process execution environment is shown in Figure 3.40. To ease presentation, initialization events and events associated with gateway instances are omitted in that figure.

When the initial event of the process model occurs in the business process environment, the process engine instantiates a process instance, including its activity instances. Then, the process engine determines the first activity instance to be executed. A service provider is determined for executing this activity, in the example, *Service Provider 1*.

The service provider receives this message and starts an *AnalyzeOrder* activity instance, marked by event $b2$. Once that activity instance is completed ($t2$), the service provider returns a message to the process engine. This message typically contains the return value of that invocation. Using this information and possibly other information, the process engine can evaluate the condition associated with the gateway node. Based on the decision made by the process engine on behalf of the gateway, the *AdvCheck* activity instance is skipped (skip event $s5$) and the *SimpleCheck* activity is started.

In order to realize this process instance, the process engine sends an invocation message to the service provider responsible for executing the simple check service. *Service Provider 2* receives this message and starts the *SimpleCheck* activity, marked by event $b4$.

Once this activity instance completes in event $t4$, the service provider returns a message to the process engine, which then executes the join gateway node (events omitted). The process instance completes with the final event and by sending the respective message to the business process environment, informing it about the termination of the process instance.

As will be detailed in the next chapter for more complex workflow patterns, control flow patterns restrict the ordering of execution events for activities involved in a business process. For instance, an *AnalyzeOrder* activity can only be started after the initial event has occurred, and a *SimpleCheck* activity can only be started after the *exclusive or* gateway has completed, and so on. The execution semantics of a process instance based on a process model is described by restrictions on the events and their ordering during the execution of process instances.

Bibliographical Notes

The business process modelling foundation is based on conceptual modelling techniques that are an important basis of computer science. To structure the field, object-oriented design techniques are used, most prominently structure diagrams and state transition diagrams of the Unified Modeling Language, introduced in Booch et al. (2005). Event diagrams to illustrate and reason about distributed systems were introduced in Lamport (1978).

Functional breakdown of business functions from top-level functions to operational activities was developed in Porter (1998) in the context of value chains. Based on the early foundation of business process management and the functional breakdown of enterprises, Michael Hammer and James Champy brought process orientation to the agenda, introducing a radical approach to business process reengineering in Hammer and Champy (1993). Davenport focuses specifically on the role of information technology in reengineering work procedures in enterprises, as detailed in Davenport (1992).

In this textbook, we have assumed that the relationships between processes at different levels of abstraction are always hierarchical. This is a simplifying assumption which is useful for the purpose of this textbook. However, in real-world process model collections we also see non-hierarchical relationships that include, for instance, overlaps that do violate the hierarchical structure. The reader interested in behavioural relationships between process models on different levels of abstraction is referred to Weidlich (2011) and Weidlich et al. (2011).

In the design of software systems, it is tradition to investigate different aspects independently of each other. This approach is also taken in work-flow management, where different workflow modelling perspectives have been identified in Jablonski (1997). A conceptual model of the core entities in work-flow management is introduced in Weske (2000). Data modelling in relational database systems is based on the Entity Relationship approach introduced by Peter Chen in Chen (1976). Data modelling techniques are also discussed in database design, as, for instance, in Ramakrishnan and Gehrke (2002) and O'Neil and O'Neil (2000).

Organizational modelling in the context of business process management was addressed by Russell et al. (2005) in the context of resource patterns. Interfaces to software systems are discussed in textbooks on middleware technology, including Henning and Vinoski (1999), where the Interface Definition Language of the Common Request Broker Architecture is discussed. Reijers (2005) discusses trade-offs between generalization and specialization in resource allocation.

4

Process Orchestrations

Business process models specify the activities, with their relationships, that are performed within a single organization, that is, they specify process orchestrations. A process engine acts as a centralized agent to control process orchestrations. Process orchestrations provide a detailed view on the activities of processes and their execution constraints. This chapter is organized as follows.

Section 4.1 introduces control flow patterns, a yardstick in process control flow structures. The patterns will be described both textually and more formally using the event-based approach introduced in the previous chapter. Section 4.2 provides a compact introduction to Petri nets. Different Petri net classes are introduced, including condition event nets, predicate transition nets and, coloured Petri nets. An informal perspective on business process modelling is taken in Section 4.3, where event-driven process chains are discussed. This approach is widely used in the business domain to model business processes from a pragmatic, application-oriented point of view.

Workflow nets are an important Petri net class tailored towards expressing business process models; workflow nets are discussed in Section 4.4. While workflow nets are well suited to modelling business processes and analyzing some of their structural properties, workflow nets exhibit a number of limitations. These limitations have led to the development of a new process modelling language, called Yet Another Workflow Language, introduced in Section 4.5. Graph-based workflow languages that also take into account data dependencies between process activities are investigated in Section 4.6.

In the context of service-oriented architectures and service composition, the Business Process Model and Notation has been proposed as a graphical notation to combine the advantages of a simple and convenient notation and clear semantics. The Business Process Model and Notation is introduced in Section 4.7.

© Springer-Verlag GmbH Germany, part of Springer Nature 2019
M. Weske, *Business Process Management*,
https://doi.org/10.1007/978-3-662-59432-2_4

4.1 Control Flow Patterns

Control flow patterns provide a yardstick for expressing process orchestrations. Control flow patterns are independent of concrete process languages, so that each pattern can be expressed in different process languages. Control flow patterns can also be used to compare the expressiveness of process languages.

Basic control flow patterns include *sequence*, *and* split, and *and* join, as well as *exclusive or* split and *exclusive or* join. These control flow patterns are supported by virtually any process metamodel. Control flow patterns are defined at the process model level. Their execution semantics, however, applies to process instances.

In this section, the semantics of control flow patterns will be investigated on the basis of the events and event orderings they imply on process instances. Due to its simplicity, the sequence pattern is well suited to explaining the general approach.

Consider a process model $P = (N, E, type)$ according to Definition 3.3 with activity models A and B and a sequence flow $A \rightarrow B$. This process model defines an ordering on the activity instances associated with A and B in the context of a single process instance: for each process instance, the activity instance associated with B can only start after the activity instance associated with A has terminated.

As a result, the process model restricts the ordering of events that occur during process instances. In the example, the termination event of the activity instance associated with activity model A must occur before the begin event of the activity instance associated with activity model B.

Each control flow construct is represented in the process model by a gateway. As with activity instances, there are instances for gateways, for example, an instance of a sequence flow ordering the execution of two activity instances. Each gateway instance has a begin event and a termination event. For a uniform treatment of control flow structures, sequences are also considered as gateways, as discussed above.

Activity models are denoted by capital letters, $A, B, C, \ldots$, while the associated activity instances are denoted by $a, b, c, \ldots$. In case multiple activity instances are associated with an activity model in the context of a given process model, subscripts are used, for instance, $a_1, a_2, \ldots$. Gateways are typically denoted by G, and g is an instance of a gateway. Let P be a process model and p a process instance based on this model with an event set $\mathcal{E}_p$.

Because of the strong link between events of process instances and states of activity instances, the state transition diagram already discussed in Section 3.4 is shown again in Figure 4.1.

Sequence

The sequence pattern defines that an activity instance b in a process instance p is enabled after the completion of activity instance a in p, with process model

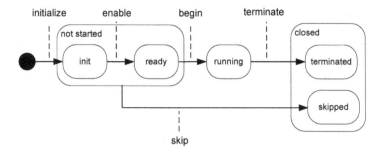

Fig. 4.1. State transition diagram for activity instances

$P = (N, E, type)$ containing activity models A, B, and a gateway model G such that $A, B \in N_A$, $G \in N_G$, $E \supseteq \{(A, G), (G, B)\}$, and $type(G) = Sequence$.

The application of the sequence pattern in $A \to B$ induces an event ordering between the termination event of a (and the activity instance of activity model A) and b, such that b can only be enabled after a has terminated. This approach relates the control flow patterns directly to the state transitions of activity instances.

In particular, the state transition from *init* to *ready* of an activity instance b can only be done after the state transition from *running* of a to *terminated* of a has occurred. Note that *running* and *terminated* are states that activity instances can assume, as represented in Figure 4.1.

In process instance p, for a termination event $t_a \in \mathcal{E}_p$ of an activity instance a, there is an enable event $e_b \in \mathcal{E}_p$ of an activity instance b, such that $t_a < e_b$. The events and their ordering as induced by the sequence pattern are shown in Figure 4.2.

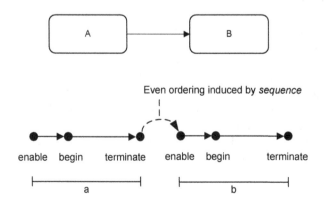

Fig. 4.2. Sequence pattern, with event diagram of process instance

The discussion captures well the case of a single activity instance per activity model. However, if the activity models are part of a loop, then there might be multiple activity instances based on activity models A and B.

Therefore, the execution semantics of the sequence control flow pattern needs to be refined so that eventually *for each* termination event of some activity instance $a1, a2, \ldots$ there is an enable event of an activity instance $b1, b2, \ldots$.

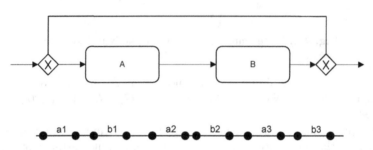

Fig. 4.3. Sequence pattern as part of a loop and event diagram showing three loop iterations

A fragment of a process model where A and B are part of a loop is shown in Figure 4.3; to realize this loop, an *exclusive split* gateway, an *exclusive or* join gateway, and a set of sequence flows are added.

A process instance based on this process model is shown in the lower part of that figure. The loop is iterated three times, resulting in activity instances $a1, b1, \ldots, a3, b3$. Rather than showing all events of these activity instances, just the enable and termination events are displayed. As can be seen in the event diagram, in each iteration of the loop, the activity instance ai terminates before bi can start, for $i \in \{1, 2, 3\}$.

However, the ordering "first a then b" can be violated if a and b belong to different iterations of the loop. For instance, the termination event of $b1$ occurs *before* the start event of $a2$. In order to capture loops properly, it is necessary to define that *for each* termination event of a there is an enable event of b such that $t_a < b_b$. This condition is satisfied by the process instance: for $t_{a1} < e_{b1}$, $t_{a2} < e_{b2}$, and $t_{a3} < e_{b3}$.

These event orderings relate termination events to enable events and not directly to begin events. Since begin events can only occur after the respective enable events have occurred, it is guaranteed that the termination event of ai occurs before the begin event of bi.

And Split

An *and* split or *parallel* split is a point in a process model where a single thread of control splits into multiple threads of control which are executed concurrently. Consider a process model with activity models A, B, and C and a gateway G such that $E \supseteq \{(A, G), (G, B), (G, C)\}$ and $type(G) = AndSplit$.

Since thereby the process model $P = (N, E, type)$ is well defined, we refrain from providing the formal definition of P with the subsets of N.

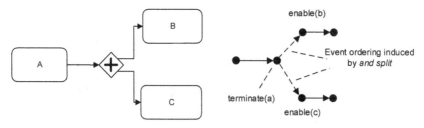

Fig. 4.4. *And* split pattern

An *and* split determines that for each termination of an activity instance a there are enable events of activity instances b and c, and these events occur after the termination event of a. Therefore, for each $t_a \in \mathcal{E}_p$ there exist $e_b, e_c \in \mathcal{E}_p$ such that $t_a < e_b \wedge t_a < e_c$.

And Join

An *and* join is a point in a process model where multiple concurrent threads converge into one single thread of control. It is an assumption of this pattern that each incoming branch is executed exactly once.

Consider a process model with activity models B, C, and D, and a gateway G such that $E \supseteq \{(B, G), (C, G), (G, D)\}$ and $type(G) = AndJoin$. For each

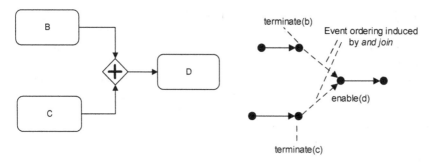

Fig. 4.5. *And* join pattern

enable event of an activity instance d, there are termination events of activity instances b and c, such that the termination events occur before the enable event. Therefore, for each $e_d \in \mathcal{E}_p \, \exists t_b, t_c \in \mathcal{E}_p$ such that $t_b < e_d \wedge t_c < e_d$.

Xor Split

An *xor* split or *exclusive or* split is a point in a process model where one of several branches is chosen. A process model with activity models A, B, and C and a gateway G such that $E \supseteq \{(A,G),(G,B),(G,C)\}$ and $type(G) = XorSplit$ is shown in Figure 4.6.

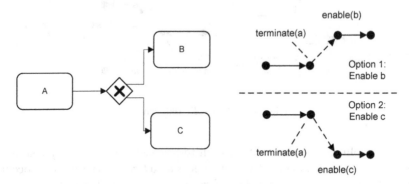

Fig. 4.6. *Xor* split pattern

The execution semantics of an *exclusive or* split determines that for each termination of an activity instance a associated with activity model A there is either an enable event of activity instance b or an enable event of an activity instance c, but not both: for each $t_a \in \mathcal{E}_p$: $e_b \in \mathcal{E}_p \Leftrightarrow e_c \notin \mathcal{E}_p$, such that either $t_a < e_b$ or $t_a < e_c$.

Xor Join

An *xor* join or *exclusive or* join is a point in a process model where two or more alternative threads come together without synchronization. It is an assumption of this pattern that exactly one of the alternative branches is executed.

Consider a process model with activity models B, C, and D, and a gateway G such that $E \supseteq \{(B,G),(C,G),(G,D)\}$ and $type(G) = XorJoin$.

For each termination event of an activity instance b or c there is one and only one enable event of an activity instance d. Therefore, for each $t_i \in \mathcal{E}_p$, such that $i \in \{b,c\}$ there is an event $e_d \in \mathcal{E}_p$ such that $t_i < e_d$.

While it is an assumption of this pattern that the branches are alternative and none of them are ever executed in parallel, the branches can be part of a loop. But even in this case, for each iteration of a loop, the branches are alternative and have *exclusive or* semantics.

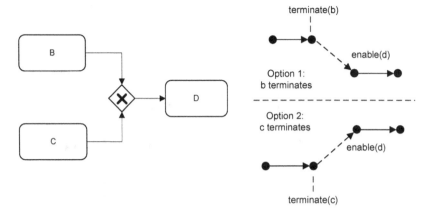

Fig. 4.7. *Xor* join pattern

Or Split

An *or* split is a point in a process model where at least one branch from a set of branches is chosen. Therefore, the selection of any nonempty subset of branches is a proper behaviour of an *or* split. Figure 4.8 shows a process model with activity models A, B, and C and a gateway G such that $E \supseteq \{(A, G), (G, B), (G, C)\}$ and $type(G) = OrSplit$.

An *or* split restricts the events of related activity instances as follows: for each termination event of a there is a subset of enable events of b and c. In general, for each termination event of a there can be enable events for any subset of activity instances on the outgoing branches of the split.

In the example, the respective enable events are $e_b, e_c \in \mathcal{E}_p$, and any subset of this event set reflects an acceptable behaviour of the *or* split, as long as $t_a < e_b$ and $t_a < e_c$ are satisfied (if both branches are selected).

The three kinds of proper behaviour of the *or* split with two outgoing edges are shown in Figure 4.8. In the general case where the *or* split has n outgoing edges, $2^n - 1$ options are possible: all nonempty subsets that can be created out of n activities.

Or Join

An *or* join is a point in a process model where multiple threads of control converge into one single thread. It is an assumption of this pattern that a branch that has already been activated cannot be activated again while the merge is still waiting for other branches to complete.

A process model with activity models B, C, and D, and a gateway G such that $E \supseteq \{(B, G), (C, G), (G, D)\}$ and $type(G) = OrJoin$ is shown in Figure 4.9. Once all active branching paths are completed and the respective end

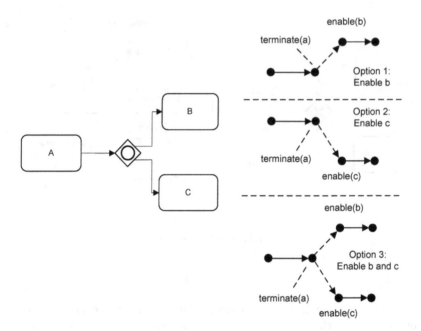

Fig. 4.8. *Or* split pattern

events of the final activities in these paths have occurred, the synchronization takes place.

In Figure 4.9, there are three behavioural options for the join. Either only the upper thread is taken and only activity instance *b* is enabled, or only the lower thread is taken and *c* is enabled, or both threads are performed and *b* and *c* both are enabled. In general, any nonempty subset of the threads are valid options, so that $2^n - 1$ options are allowed for *n* incoming edges of the *or* join.

The *or* join is a problematic control flow pattern. The problem is that the join cannot locally decide how long to wait for its activation. Even from the simple process model fragment shown in Figure 4.9, this problem can be explained: once one incoming branch is triggered, for instance, by termination of *b*, how should the *or* join react? There are two options:

- *Wait*: The *or* join waits before the activity instance *d* is triggered, because the other incoming path—which completes in activity instance *c*—can still be executed.
- *Trigger*: The *or* join triggers *d* immediately after the termination of *b*.

The problem is that we cannot decide which of these alternatives the correct one is. After the first incoming branch has terminated, how long should the *or* join wait for the other branch to complete?

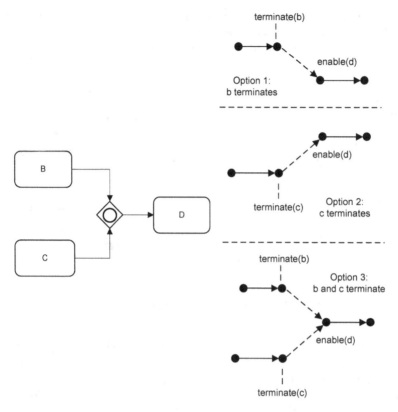

Fig. 4.9. *Or* join pattern

If no additional knowledge is available, there is no way of deciding whether
c will eventually terminate for the particular process instance. Since there is
no upper bound on the waiting time, realizing the waiting alternative leads
to a deadlock situation if the second thread is never activated.

If the *or* join triggers d after one incoming branch is activated, a situation
might occur in which c terminates after d has already started! This behaviour
contradicts the semantics of the *or* join, since in this case it has to wait until
both branches complete. In this book, the *or* join semantics is revisited in
Sections 4.6 and 7.5.

Multiple Merge

A *multiple merge* or *multi-merge* is a point in a process model where two or
more concurrent threads join without synchronization. The activity following
the merge is started for every activation of every incoming branch.

The *multi-merge* is functionally equivalent with the *exclusive or* join; the only difference is that the latter assumes that only one of its incoming branches gets activated. This assumption is not in place for the *multi-merge* pattern.

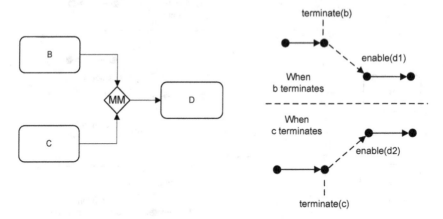

Fig. 4.10. Multi-merge pattern

A process model with activity models B, C, and D, and a gateway G such that $E \supseteq \{(B,G),(C,G),(G,D)\}$ and $type(G) = MultiMerge$ is shown in Figure 4.10. For each terminating activity instance b and c, one activity instance associated with activity model D is started. This means that for each termination event $t_i \in \mathcal{E}_p$, where $i \in \{b,c\}$, there is an enable event e_d that occurs after the respective termination event, that is, $t_i < e_d$, $i \in \{b,c\}$.

The *multiple merge* pattern spawns off new threads of control. These threads need to be identified so that future joins can be realized properly. These aspects are illustrated in an example shown in Figure 4.11, where a process model with an *and* split followed by a *multi-merge* is shown. As a result, any of the threads induced by the *and split* will survive the *multiple merge* and spawn a new instance for activity model D and of the activity models following D in the process model.

Each of the threads of control spawned off by the *multi-merge* is subject to the *and* split/join construct shown in the process model. The *and* join requires information on the identity of the threads that come in; otherwise, situations could arise in which activity instances that belong to different threads of control are synchronized. These issues can be illustrated by the event diagram shown in Figure 4.12. This diagram can be considered an abstract form of an event diagram in which the lifetime of each activity instance is shown as a line with borders marking the enabling and terminating of the activity instance.

The process starts with activity instance a, followed by the concurrent execution of b and c. Assuming b terminates before c does, the *multi-merge*

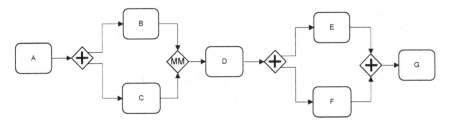

Fig. 4.11. Multi-merge example might lead to incorrect synchronization of branches

spawns off a new thread of control, called thread 1 in Figure 4.11. The first activity instance of this thread is $d1$.

While $d1$ is still running, c terminates, and the *multi-merge* spawns off thread 2, starting with $d2$. When $d1$ completes, the *and* split occurs, and concurrent threads are created, realized by activity instances $e1$ and $f1$.

After $d2$ terminates, $e2$ and $f2$ are created. Assuming that $f1$ and $e2$ terminate, the *and* join faces a situation in which there are termination events of activity instances on its incoming edges. Knowing that these belong to different threads of control ($f1$ belongs to thread 1, while $e2$ belongs to thread 2), the *and* join can "decide" that these threads cannot be synchronized, although they belong to the same process instance.

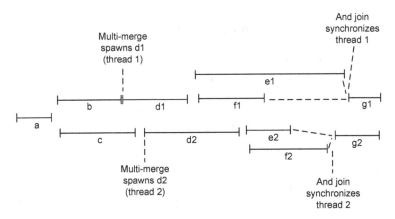

Fig. 4.12. Event diagram of a process instance based on the process model shown in Figure 4.11

Discriminator

The *discriminator* is a point in a process model that waits for one of the incoming branches to complete before activating the subsequent activity. From that moment on it waits for all remaining branches to complete and "ignores" them. Once all incoming branches have been triggered, it resets itself so that it can be triggered again. This allows a discriminator to be used in the context of a loop.

If gathering the ignored branches were not part of the functional behaviour of the discriminator pattern, there would be no way to distinguish a second iteration of a loop from a late branch of its first iteration.

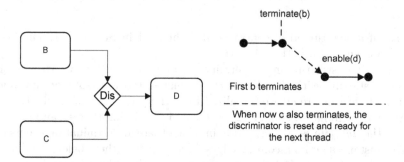

Fig. 4.13. Discriminator pattern

A process model with activity models B, C, and D, and a gateway G such that $E \supseteq \{(B, G), (C, G), (G, D)\}$ and $type(G) = Discriminator$ is shown in Figure 4.13. To discuss the execution semantics of the discriminator, assume that activity instance b terminates while c is still active. If this is the case, d is triggered, and the *discriminator* continues to wait for the termination of c. When c terminates, the discriminator is again ready for the next thread.

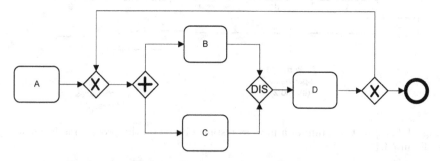

Fig. 4.14. Discriminator example

An example involving the discriminator pattern is shown in Figure 4.14. The process starts with activity instance a before an *and* split occurs that spawns activity instances $b1$ and $c1$. Assuming $b1$ terminates first, the discriminator fires and enables $d1$. When $d1$ terminates, assuming a new iteration of the loop is required, new activity instances based on B and C are created. These activity instances are $b2$ and $c2$. What is remarkable in this example is that there are two instances of activity model C active concurrently, assuming $c1$ has not yet terminated.

Even if $c2$ terminates before $c1$, the semantics of the *discriminator* makes sure that it can only fire and enable $d2$ after the first iteration has completed, that is, only after the remaining activity instance $c1$ has terminated. If this is the case, the *discriminator* can fire a second time, to enable $d2$. The event diagram of this process instance is shown in Figure 4.15.

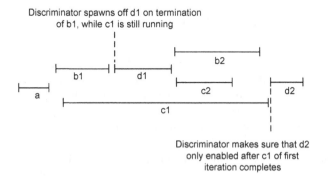

Fig. 4.15. Event diagram of discriminator example

Formally, for each enable event of d there are termination events of b and c, and (at least) one of these termination events occurs prior to the enabling event of d, that is, $\forall e_d \; \exists t_b, t_c \in \mathcal{E}_p$, such that $t_b < e_d \lor t_c < e_d$.

In addition, the discriminator can become active only after the termination events of all incoming edges that belong to the thread that has spawned the current activities have occurred. In the example, $d2$ can only be enabled after the termination operation of $c1$ has occurred.

N-out-of-M Join

The *N-out-of-M join* is a generalization of the *discriminator*. It is a point in a process model where M parallel paths converge into one. The subsequent activity is initiated after $N \leq M$ paths have completed and the respective termination events have occurred. All activities on the $M - N$ remaining paths can proceed unharmed, but their outcome is ignored.

As with the *discriminator*, once all incoming branches have fired, the join resets itself so that it can be performed again. The *N-out-of-M join* is illustrated in Figure 4.16.

A concrete example of the *N-out-of-M join* is a request for quotation process, in which quotations are invited from five companies, although the process

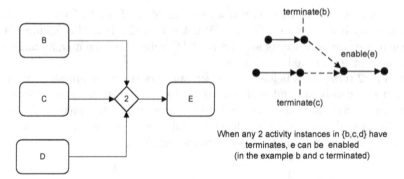

Fig. 4.16. N-out-of-M join pattern

can continue after receiving three quotations. Without a dedicated *N-out-of-M join*, this business rule would be complex to model, because at design time it is not known which of the companies will respond to the request in time.

There are variations on this control flow pattern with respect to the time when the number N of sufficient threads is determined: it can be determined at design time or at run time. The run time specification of N needs to be done in an activity instance that is executed before the join.

There might be additional variations in the design time specification of the *N-out-of-M join* if it is part of a loop. Design time specification of N could therefore be taken within the loop, so that different iterations of the loop use different values N for the number of sufficient threads to complete.

The *N-out-of-M join* degenerates to an *and* join if $N = M$. For $N = 1$, however, it does not realize an *exclusive or* join, because the assumption of the *exclusive or* join is not met (only one thread will be activated).

Nor does it realize a *multi-merge*, because in the *multi-merge* the completion of the second and following threads would enable additional instances of follow-up activities, while the *1-out-of-M join* ignores them. The *1-out-of-M join*, however, realizes the *discriminator* pattern.

Arbitrary Cycles

An *arbitrary cycle* is a point in a process model where one or more activities can be executed repeatedly.

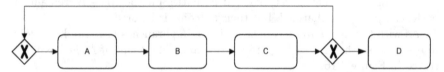

Fig. 4.17. Graphical representation of arbitrary cycles pattern

An arbitrary cycle is graphically depicted in Figure 4.17. In this example, a sequence consisting of activity models A, B, and C is iterated. The iteration is represented by an *exclusive or* split that decides whether to iterate the cycle or whether to leave it and continue with activity instance d, associated with activity model D. In case the loop is iterated, the *exclusive or* join triggers another instance associated with activity model A.

As this example shows, arbitrary cycles are expressed with other control flow patterns, for instance, *exclusive or* split and *exclusive or* join. Since these control flow patterns have been specified already, no additional definitions are required in order to define the arbitrary cycles pattern.

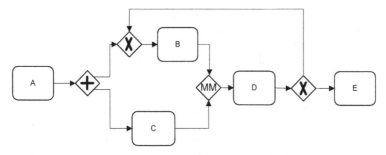

Fig. 4.18. Arbitrary cycles example, using multiple merge pattern

A more complex example of a cycle involving the *multi-merge* pattern is shown in Figure 4.18. In this example, the cycle enters one of two concurrent branches of an *and* split whose branches are joined by a *multi-merge*.

The process starts by activity instance a, followed by the concurrent execution of $b1$ and $c1$. When $c1$ completes, the first firing of the multi-merge spawns off $d2$. We assume that the loop is not taken, so that $e2$ is started, before this thread terminates.

When $b1$ terminates, the multi-merge creates another instance of activity model D, namely $d3$. If the loop is iterated, the second instance of activity model B is created, that is, $b3$ (it holds the same thread identifier than the previous activity instance). When $b3$ terminates, $d4$ is started, and the loop can be entered again by spawning off $b4$. At some point, the loop will be left and the process will terminate.

This example shows that the multi merge is a quite powerful construct, since it allows loops being part of a concurrent branch. However, this process design might lead to situations, where threads overtake each other in the process flow. This happens, for instance, if $b2$ in the first iteration of the loop gets delayed and $b3$ is executed quickly in the second iteration of the loop. This is a valid behaviour of the process model shown, but modelling experts need to be aware of this execution semantics.

There is also an issue with the termination of this process. Actually, the end of the process is signalled twice, since each firing of the *multi-merge* creates a new thread, each of which finally terminates after executing an activity instance of activity model E. This behaviour is not desired, as will be discussed in the context of the soundness property in Chapter 7.

Notice that an *and* join gateway instead of the *multi-merge* would lead to a deadlock situation, once the loop is entered for the first time. Also, the parallel branches are synchronized, so that $d2$ can only be started once both $b1$ and $c1$ have completed.

Implicit Termination

The *implicit termination* pattern is defined as follows: a given process instance should be terminated when there is nothing else to be done. This means, there is no activity instance in the process instance in the *init, ready,* or *running* state and—as a result—no activity instance can be become enabled.

While implicit termination is defined as one of the control flow patterns, its role differs with respect to the other patterns. It does not relate activity instances with each other, such as, for instance, the *sequence* pattern or the split and join patterns discussed. It represents a termination condition of an overall process.

In several process languages, termination is explicit, because there is exactly one state in the process that marks its termination. If there are many states in which the process can terminate, then termination is implicit.

Multiple Instances Without Synchronization

More important than implicit termination are the patterns involving multiple activity instances. These activity instances are based on a single activity model in the context of a business process.

There are many situations that can be expressed properly by multiple instances patterns. For instance, assume an order process in which an incoming order contains a number of order lines. For each of these order lines, a check activity needs to be executed. This means that only at run time can the business process management system decide how many activities actually need to be instantiated in order to perform the required checking activities.

The *multiple instances without synchronization* pattern is defined as follows. In the context of a single process instance, multiple activity instances of one activity model can be created. No synchronization of these activity instances takes place.

An example of the *multiple instances without synchronization* pattern is shown in Figure 4.19. In the process model shown, activity model B uses the pattern. After the termination of activity instance a, a number of activity instances are initiated and enabled for activity model B. In the event diagram, activity instances $b1, b2$, and $b3$ are shown. These instances are enabled and can be started.

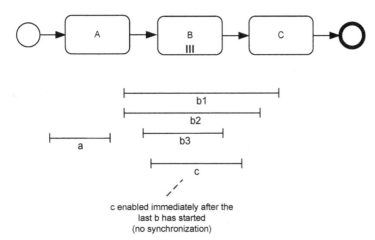

Fig. 4.19. Example for *multiple instances without synchronization*

The term "without synchronization" in the context of this example means that the follow-up activity instance *c* can be enabled immediately after the instances for *B* have been enabled. Since there are no assumptions on the execution times of activity instances, *c* can terminate while activity instances of the multiple instances activity are still running. In the event diagram shown, *b1* and *b2* are still running when *c* has already completed.

This behaviour of the pattern has some consequences. First of all the control flow between activity models *B* and *C* does not—strictly speaking—have the semantics of a *sequence* pattern, since an instance of *C* can be enabled while instances of *B* are still active. As a result, the *sequence* pattern is somehow violated by the multiple instances without synchronization pattern.

This pattern causes problems not only with the sequence flow, but also with the termination of the overall process. Since the activity instances are not synchronized, it cannot be guaranteed that these activity instances have terminated when the end of the process is reached. This means that certain execution guarantees related to soundness properties (which will be discussed in Chapter 7) cannot be satisfied.

Multiple instances patterns can be distinguished for the point in time when the actual number of instances is determined. The *multiple instances without synchronization* pattern does not make any assumptions on whether the number of instances is defined at design time or at run time. This is subject of the control flow patterns discussed next.

Multiple Instances With A Priori Design Time Knowledge

In the *multiple instances with a priori design time knowledge* pattern, the number of activity instances of an activity model is known at design time.

These activity instances are synchronized, so that once all activity instances have completed, the follow-up activity is enabled.

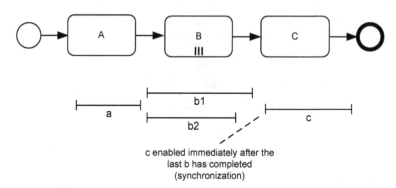

Fig. 4.20. Example for multiple instances with a priori design time knowledge

Figure 4.20 shows an example of the *multiple instances with a priori design time knowledge* pattern. Two things are remarkable in the event diagram.

The follow-up activity c can only be enabled after the last activity instance of B has completed, in this case $b1$. This property is shared by all multiple instances patterns that are "synchronized."

The specific property of the pattern at hand is that the number $n = 2$ of activity instances of B is defined at design time, that is, as part of the process model. Depending on the process language used, there can be an attribute of the activity model B that states, for instance, NrOfInstances = 2;.

Multiple Instances With A Priori Run Time Knowledge

In the *multiple instances with a priori run time knowledge* pattern, the number of instances of a given activity model depends on the characteristics of the case or the availability of resources. Therefore, it is only known at some stage during run time of the process instance, but before the instances of the multiple instances activity are created. This pattern also assumes synchronization of the activity instances before the next activities can be enabled.

Using the process model already shown in Figure 4.20, this pattern is distinguished from the *multiple instances with a priori design time knowledge* pattern by the specification of the number of activity instances.

Rather than specifying the number of activity instances directly, we define an expression. This expression is evaluated during run time to compute the number of activity instances for a specific process instance. This computation occurs before the activity instances of the multiple instances activity are created.

A process language might provide a functional representation of the number of instances to create, so that, for instance,

NrOfInstances = GetNoOfLineitems(order);

might be a valid term. Here, the number of activity instances is computed by a function that takes the current order and returns the number of line items in it. An individual activity instance is then performed for each line item.

Multiple Instances Without A Priori Run Time Knowledge

In the *multiple instances without a priori run time knowledge* pattern, the number of instances of a given activity is not known during design time; nor is it known at any stage during run time before the instances of that activity are enabled.

The difference with the previous pattern is that even while some of the instances are being executed or have already completed, new activity instances can still be created.

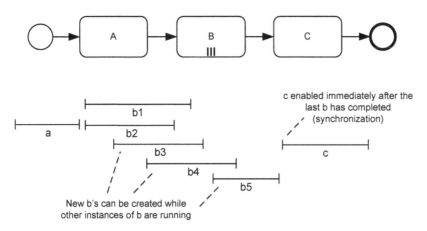

Fig. 4.21. Example for multiple instances without a priori run time knowledge pattern

Figure 4.21 shows that, first, two instances of *B* are created. During the execution of these activity instances, new activity instances are created. When all instances of *B* have terminated—in the example, *b5* is the last activity instance to complete—the next activity instance in the process can be enabled.

In order to realize this pattern in a process language and in a process engine, there need to be additional assumptions in place. The main question in this context is, until what point in time is it possible to create new activity instances of *B*?

One choice would be to indicate that while *bs* are running, new instances of the multiple instances activity can be created. While this is a valid choice, realization of this might not be practical, because it would assume that the activity instances would include the creation of new instances, thereby inter-twining process management tasks (start new process instance) and doing the actual work.

An alternative solution is to install a management activity related to the multiple instances activity. This management activity explicitly defines the end of the multiple instances activity. It is also responsible for creating new instances of the multiple instances activity. It can even create new instances after all instances have terminated. This is a valid approach, since in dynamic settings, there might be an explicit decision about whether additional activity instances are required to achieve the business goal related to the multiple instances activity.

In the first alternative—if the follow-up activity is automatically enabled after the current instances of the multiple instances activity have completed—there are no options to create new instances of the multiple activity task once all instances have completed.

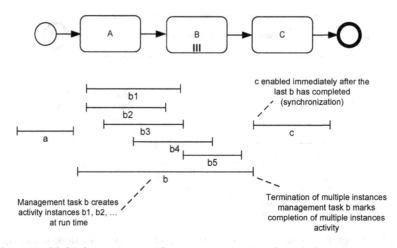

Fig. 4.22. Multiple instances without a priori run time knowledge pattern, including management task

The second alternative, with a dedicated management task for the multiple instances activity, is illustrated in Figure 4.22. In the event diagram, the management task is denoted by b. When the management task completes, the follow-up activity instance can be enabled.

Deferred Choice

Deferred choice is a state-based pattern. State-based patterns capture the im-plicit behaviour of processes that is based not on the current case but rather on the environment or other parts of the process. Some of the following patterns require the existence of an external process that represents the environment. This process is used as a source for external events.

A *deferred choice* is a point in a process model where one of several branches is chosen. In contrast to the *exclusive or* split, the choice is not made explicitly—for example, based on data values or a user decision—but several alternatives are offered to the environment.

The environment activates one of the alternatives, and the other branches are then withdrawn. Because the choice is delayed until one of the alternative branches has actually been started, the moment of choice is deferred to a point in time that is as late as possible.

Regarding the states of activity instances, each of the alternative branches is represented by one activity instance in the init state. The state transition from init to enabled is triggered by the environment, for instance, by sending a message. After the state transition has occurred, the activity instances that were not chosen enter the skipped state.

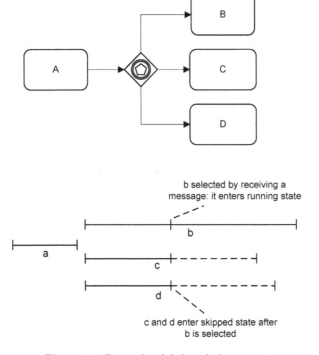

Fig. 4.23. Example of deferred choice pattern

Figure 4.23 shows an example of a deferred choice. In that example, after *a* terminates, activity instances *b, c*, and *d* are created. Assuming that *b* is selected by receiving a message, b enters the enabled state, while c and d are no longer required. Therefore, these activity instances are skipped.

Sequential Execution without A Priori Design Time Knowledge

The *sequential execution without a prior design time knowledge* pattern is described as follows: a set of activity instances is executed sequentially in an order that is decided at run time. No two activity instances of this set are active at the same point in time.

Originally this pattern was called *interleaved parallel routing*; however, this was somewhat misleading: The activity instances do not interleave, and they are not executed in parallel. They are executed sequentially in an order that is defined while the process instance runs. Therefore, in this book the term *sequential execution without a prior design time knowledge* refers to this pattern.

An example of this pattern is shown in Figure 4.24[1] Activity models B, C, and D are part of this pattern, so any sequential execution of activity instances b, c and d are valid. This pattern is very useful in situations in which several activities need to be executed sequentially and in any order. Since for any n elements there are $n!$ permutations, each of which corresponds to a sequential execution ordering of n activity instances, modelling these explicitly is not feasible.

The pattern can even be extended so that the execution ordering is not defined before the first activity instance of the pattern has started. The sequence can be defined also during the execution of the activity instances. A concrete example is as follows: three persons need to work on a file, and each person works on a separate part, so that the order in which the work is conducted is not relevant. In this setting, after completing the first activity instance, one person selects the next person to do his or her work.

The sequential execution in this case is induced by the single resource—the file—that cannot be shared by the persons. Therefore, current allocation of work to persons can be taken into account when deciding at run time on the actual sequence in which the activities are executed.

Milestone

The *milestone* pattern can be used to define that an activity is only enabled if a certain milestone has been reached that has not expired yet.

This pattern is illustrated by an example. Consider a process model with activity models A, B, and C. With a *milestone* pattern, the process designer can determine that activity instance a is enabled only if b has been executed

---

[1]The diagram uses BPMN to illustrate this pattern, even though the BPMN execution semantics would allow concurrency between A, B, and C.

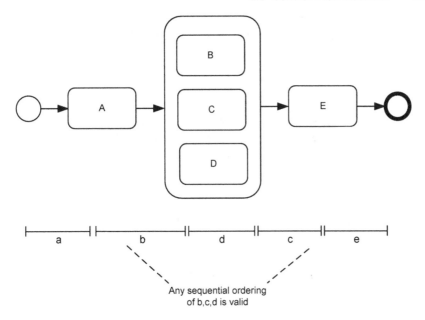

Fig. 4.24. Sequential execution without a priori design time knowledge; any sequential execution ordering of B, C, and D is possible

and c has not been completed. As a result a is not enabled before the execution of b and after the execution of c.

The example is illustrated in Figure 4.25. Since the informal process modelling notation that served well in presenting the patterns so far does not provide an explicit notation for state, Petri nets are used to express the milestone pattern (Petri nets will be introduced in the next section in detail).

The milestone indicates that the execution of an activity a is possible only after activity b is executed and before activity c is started. The execution of a does not change the state of the process, that is, after executing a, the upper process is still in a state where a token is at $p1$. There can also be multiple instances $a1, a2, \ldots$ of activity model A, as long as c has not started and as long as there are token available in $p2$. These options are shown in the lower part of Figure 4.25.

Run Time Patterns

In addition to the patterns introduced above, there are run time patterns defined that are—strictly speaking—not part of a process model. They, rather, characterize the functionality provided by a business process management system.

The first of these patterns is the *cancel activity* pattern. When an activity instance is cancelled, it enters the *cancelled* state. The *cancelled* state is

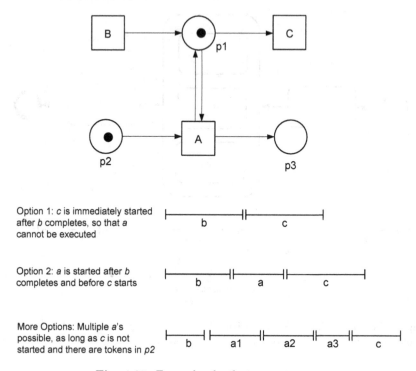

Fig. 4.25. Example of milestone pattern

represented in the advanced state transition diagram for activity instances, shown in Figure 3.10 on page 83.

The second run time pattern is the *cancel case* pattern, in which all activity instances of a process instance are cancelled so that the process instance comes to a halt. To cancel an activity instance, there are different options that depend on the environment in which the activity instance is being executed. If it is a manual activity, then the knowledge worker needs to be informed about the cancellation, so that the person ceases working on the case. She could also perform some cleanup activities, if need be.

If the functionality to execute the activity instance is provided by an information system, then the realization of the *cancel activity* pattern depends on the type of information system used. If the information system is realized by a database application, then terminating the application is a valid option.

If the database application runs—at least the parts that realize the activity instance to be cancelled—in a single database transaction, then cancellation can be realized by aborting the transaction. The database management system guarantees that the database is restored to the state before the execution of the activity instance.

If on the other hand the information system is not based on a transactional information system, cancelling an activity can be much harder. There might be certain parts that are already stored in some kind of non-transactional data store. Identifying these parts and manually undoing the effects of the partial activity instance is a cumbersome and in some cases infeasible task.

Also in manual activities, actions might already have been performed that cannot be undone easily, such as sending an email message. In this case, the cancellation of an activity instance involves manual activities, such as sending another email message withdrawing the former, or making a phone call.

To summarize, it is easy to indicate the behaviour of the cancel activity and cancel case patterns; however, the realization of these patterns in real-world business process management systems is far from that.

4.2 Petri Nets

Petri nets are one of the best known techniques for specifying business processes in a formal and abstract way and, as such, Petri nets are an important basis for process languages. "Formal" means that the semantics of process instances resulting from process models specified in Petri nets is well defined and not ambiguous. Petri nets are "abstract", because they disregard the execution environment of a business process, so that all aspects other than the functional and process perspectives are not covered. The functional perspective in itself is treated in an abstract way, as will be explained below.

In this section, Petri nets are introduced in a pragmatic manner. A large body of literature is available in the Petri net area; the main references relevant to business process management are discussed in the bibliographical notes.

In his Ph.D. thesis, Carl Adam Petri generalizes automata theory by concurrency. He introduces a new modelling approach that has a graphical representation as well as an equivalent mathematical formalization. Petri nets can be used to model dynamic systems with a static structure. The static structure is represented by a Petri net, and the dynamic behaviour is captured by the token play of the Petri net.

Petri nets consist of places, transitions, and directed arcs connecting places and transitions. They are bipartite graphs, so that arcs never connect two places or two transitions. In graphical notations, places are represented by circles, transitions by rectangles, and connectors by directed arcs. Transitions have input and output places. The input places of a transition are the places at the sources of its incoming arcs. Accordingly, a transition's output places are located at the end of its outgoing arcs.

The dynamics of the system represented by a Petri net is modelled by tokens that reside on places. While the structure of Petri nets is fixed, the tokens may change their position according to firing rules. The current distribution of the tokens among the places determines the state of the Petri net and, thus, of the system modelled by it.

A transition may fire if it is enabled. A transition is enabled if there is a token in each of its input places. If the transitions fires, one token is removed from each input place and one token is added to each output place. Different classes of Petri nets exhibit different restrictions on the tokens in a Petri net; this will be discussed later in this section.

The movement of the tokens in the Petri net according to firing rules is called token play. The token play is often considered to be a flow of tokens, although this is not exactly true, since tokens are removed from input places and added to output places; they do not flow from input places to output places.

Because transitions can change the state of a Petri net, they are considered active components, which typically represent events, operations, transformations, or transportations. A place is a passive component, that stands for a medium, a buffer, a state, or a condition. Tokens are used to represent physical objects or information objects. In the context of business processes, transitions represent activities and places containing tokens represent states of the process instances.

Since Petri nets describe the structure of a system, a Petri net represents a business process model, and its transitions represent activity models. The instance level is captured by tokens. This means that the firing of a transition represents an activity instance. Each process instance is represented by at least one token; due to split and join nodes, the number of tokens that collectively characterize one process instance may vary during the lifetime of the process instance.

Since there can be multiple process instances of one process model, the tokens in a Petri net may belong to different process instances. This will be discussed in more detail in Section 4.4, where workflow nets, a Petri net class specifically tailored towards representing business processes, are discussed.

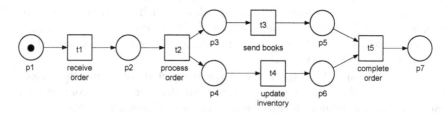

Fig. 4.26. Sample Petri net representing single process instance

A Petri net characterizing a business process model is shown in Figure 4.26. The transitions in this Petri net correspond to activities, while the places and the arcs characterize the execution constraints of the activities. The process starts when a token is put on place $p1$. The token is represented by a black dot in that place. Since there is a token on all input places of the *receive order* transition, this transition is enabled, and it can fire.

Once the *receive order* transition fires, a token is removed from $p1$ and a token is put on $p2$, representing the execution of the *receive order* activity instance. The execution time of this activity instance is not represented; in Petri nets, transitions fire instantly without consuming time.

After the *process order* transition has fired, concurrent branches are opened, since the firing of the *process order* transition puts tokens on both $p3$ and $p4$, enabling the *send books* and *update inventory* transitions. The complete *order transition* is enabled only when both of these transitions have fired. When the process completes there is one token in $p7$.

To summarize, the Petri net represents the process model, while the tokens represent process instances. Since tokens in classical Petri nets cannot be distinguished from each other, classical Petri nets can only host a single process instance.

After informally discussing the basic structure of Petri nets and the dynamic behaviour of the systems represented, we give a formal definition:

Definition 4.1 A *Petri net* is a tuple (P, T, F) with

- a finite set P of places,
- a finite set T of transitions such that $T \cap P = \emptyset$, and
- a flow relation $F \subseteq (P \times T) \cup (T \times P)$.
- A place $p \in P$ is an input place of a transition $t \in T$ if and only if there exists a directed arc from p to t, that is, if and only if $(p, t) \in F$. The set of input places for a transition t is denoted $\bullet t$.
- A place p is an output place of a transition t if and only if there exists a directed arc from t to p, that is, if and only if $(t, p) \in F$. The set of output places for a transition t is denoted $t\bullet$.
- $p\bullet$ and $\bullet p$ denote the sets of transitions that share p as input places and output places, respectively.

$\diamond$

Graphical representations of Petri nets can be mapped onto a tuple (P, T, F), and vice versa. For instance, the Petri net shown in Figure 4.26 can be represented by (P, T, F) such that

- $P = \{p1, p2, p3, p4, p5, p6, p7\}$,
- $T = \{t1, t2, t3, t4, t5\}$,
- $F = \{(p1, t1), (t1, p2), (p2, t2), (t2, p3), (t2, p4), (p3, t3), (p4, t4), (t3, p5),$
  $(t4, p6), (p5, t5), (p6, t5), (t5, p7)\}$.

The state of the Petri net is characterized by the distribution of tokens on the places of the net. The dynamic behaviour of a system is represented by state changes, which are subject to firing rules. As detailed below, there are different firing rules for different classes of Petri nets.

Definition 4.2 The *marking* (or *state*) of a Petri (P, T, F) net is defined by a function $M : P \to \mathbb{N}$ mapping the set of places onto the natural numbers, where $\mathbb{N}$ is the set of natural numbers including 0. $\diamond$

The marking of a Petri net represents its state. The state of the Petri net shown in Figure 4.27 is represented by $M(p1) = M(p2) = M(p3) = M(p6) = 1$ and $M(p4) = M(p5) = M(p7) = 0$. If the places are totally ordered by their identifier (as, for instance, in $p1, p2, \ldots, p7$), the marking can be expressed by an array. In the example, $M = [1, 1, 1, 0, 0, 1, 0]$.

We can also express the state of a Petri net by a list of places that have exactly one token, that is, a place p is in the list representing marking M, if $M(p) = 1$. The marking of the Petri net shown in Figure 4.27 can therefore also be represented by $[p1, p2, p3, p6]$.

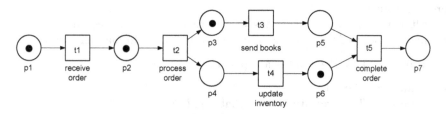

Fig. 4.27. Sample Petri net representing multiple process instances

After having discussed the structure of a Petri net and its state, the dynamic behaviour of a Petri net is addressed.

Definition 4.3 Let (P, T, F) be a Petri net and M a marking. The firing of a transition is represented by a state change of the Petri net.

- $M \xrightarrow{t} M'$ indicates that by firing t, the state of the Petri net changes from M to M'.
- $M \rightarrow M'$ indicates that there is a transition t such that $M \xrightarrow{t} M'$.
- $M_1 \xrightarrow{*} M_n$ means that there is a sequence of transitions $t_1, t_2, \ldots t_{n-1}$ such that $M_i \xrightarrow{t_i} M_{i+1}$, for $1 \le i < n$.
- A state M' is *reachable* from a state M if and only if $M \xrightarrow{*} M'$.

◇

Based on these fundamental definitions, a number of Petri net classes are introduced that differ with respect to their firing behaviour and the structure of their tokens.

4.2.1 Condition Event Nets

Condition event nets are the fundamental class of Petri nets. In condition event nets, at each point in time, each place can have at most one token. Tokens are unstructured; they have no identity and can therefore not be distinguished from one another. The rationale for the denomination of this Petri net class is as follows. If a token is on a place p, then the *condition* p is met. When a transition fires, an *event* occurs and changes the state of the condition event net.

Definition 4.4 A Petri net (P, T, F) is a *condition event net* if $M(p) \leq 1$ for all places $p \in P$ and for all states M.

- A transition t is *enabled* in a state M, if and only if $M(p) = 1$ for all input places p of t and $M(q) = 0$ for all output places q of t that are not input places at the same time.
- The firing of a transition t in a state M results in state M', where

$$(\forall p \in \bullet t)M'(p) = M(p) - 1 \wedge (\forall p \in t\bullet)M'(p) = M(p) + 1.$$

$\diamond$

Since, by definition, $M(p) = 1$ for all input places p of t and $M(q) = 0$ for all output places q of t, it follows for the state M' reached by this firing (assuming output places and input places are disjoint),

$$(\forall p \in \bullet t)M'(p) = 0 \wedge (\forall p \in t\bullet)M'(p) = 1.$$

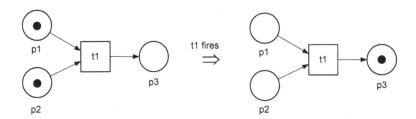

(a) Conditions p1 and p2 met, and condition for p3 not met: t1 is enabled

(b) Firing of t1 withdraws tokens from input places and puts token to output place.

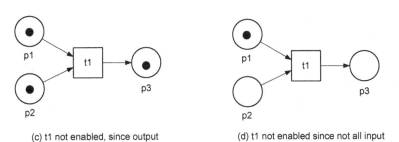

(c) t1 not enabled, since output condition is met

(d) t1 not enabled since not all input conditions are met

Fig. 4.28. Firing behaviour of condition event net

Figure 4.28 shows the firing behaviour of condition event nets. Transition $t1$ is enabled if and only if all input places have one token and all output places have no tokens (a). This means that the conditions represented by the input places of the transition are met and the conditions reflected by the output places of the transition are not met.

The firing of $t1$ withdraws a token from each input place and puts a token on each output place (b). Transition $t1$ is not enabled if there is a token in one of its output places (c) or if not all input places of $t1$ have a token (d).

Since tokens in condition event nets are un-typed and cannot be distinguished from each other, and due to the fact that the number of tokens are limited to one in each place, condition event nets are not well suited to modelling business processes. The reason for this is discussed in the context of place transition nets that face the same problem.

4.2.2 Place Transition Nets

Place transition nets are an extension of condition event nets, because in any state of the Petri net an arbitrary number of tokens can reside in any place. Therefore, places can, for instance, serve as counters. However, tokens are still unstructured objects that can not be distinguished from one another.

To account for multiple tokens in each place, transition enabling needs to be reconsidered. In addition, multiple tokens can be consumed and withdrawn from an input place when a transition fires, and multiple tokens can be produced when a transition fires, according to the weights associated with the arcs connected to the transition. This extension can be represented graphically by multiple arcs from an input place to a transition or by arcs labelled with natural numbers marking their weight.

Definition 4.5 (P, T, F, ω) is a *place transition net* if (P, T, F) is a Petri net and $\omega : F \to \mathbb{N}$ is a weighting function that assigns a natural number to each arc, the *weight* of the arc.

The dynamic behaviour of a place transition net is defined as follows:

- A transition t of a place transition net is *enabled*, if and only if each input place p of t contains at least the number of tokens defined as the weight of the connecting arc, that is, if $M(p) \geq \omega((p, t))$.
- When a transition t fires, the number of tokens withdrawn from its input places and the number of tokens added to its output places are determined by the weights of the respective arcs. From each input place p of t, $\omega((p, t))$ tokens are withdrawn, and $\omega((t, q))$ tokens are added to each output place q of t.
- The firing of a transition t in a state M results in a state M', where

$$(\forall p \in \bullet t) M'(p) = M(p) - \omega((p, t)) \land (\forall p \in t\bullet) M'(p) = M(p) + \omega((t, p))$$

$\diamond$

The definition of the marking of a Petri net is still valid for place transition nets, since we can express, for instance, the fact that there are three tokens on a place p by $M(p) = 3$. The shorthand notation for expressing markings using lists, however, needs to be refined. We do so by attaching superscripts to place identifiers that indicate the number of tokens on that particular place. In the example, the state of a place transition net with three tokens on place p and one token on place q is expressed by $[p^3, q^1]$, or simply $[p^3, q]$.

Assuming that the Petri net shown in Figure 4.27 is a place transition net, in addition to $t3$ (which is also enabled if the Petri net is a condition event net), the transitions $t1$ and $t2$ are enabled. The firing of $t1$ consumes the token from $p1$ and adds a token to $p2$, so that two tokens reside in $p2$. Notice, however, that $t5$ is not enabled, since $p5$ does not contain a token. In the example, each arc has weight one.

While place transition nets allow multiple tokens in each place, they are still not very useful for representing business processes, since the tokens cannot be distinguished from each other. The reason for this problem can be illustrated using the example shown in Figure 4.27, where multiple process instances are represented in the Petri net by multiple tokens. By closely looking at the Petri net and its token distribution, one can detect which tokens belong to which process instances.

There are three process instances active. One process instance is represented by a token in place $p1$, while the second process instance has already performed the *receive order* activity and is therefore represented by the token in $p2$. The *process order* activity spawns two concurrent threads. Therefore, the tokens in $p3$ and $p6$ must belong to the same process instance. When the *send books* activity has been completed, a token is put in $p5$, and the *complete order* activity can be performed, completing the third process instance.

While this discussion indicates that an external observer can in some cases identify the tokens that belong to one process instance, this is not possible in all cases. Consider Figure 4.29, which describes the same system at some later point in time when marking $[p3^2, p4, p5, p6^2]$ is reached. At this point, the first and second process instances have both entered the concurrent branches.

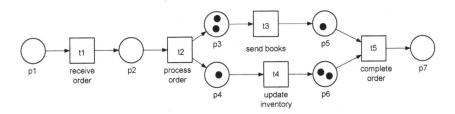

Fig. 4.29. Place transition net with multiple process instances

In this case it is far from clear which tokens belong to the specific process instance. The firing rule of place transition nets defines that the *complete order* transition can fire as soon as there is a token in place $p5$ and a token in place $p6$.

This is a severe problem, because the complete order activity could potentially be conducted for two different process instances! If the first process instance orders books A and B while the second process instance orders books C and D, then a situation could occur in which the sending of books A and B and the update of the inventory for books C and D could be joined, clearly an unacceptable behaviour.

Therefore, the tokens need to carry values, so that in each state of the Petri net it is clear which token belong to which process instance. This limitation of condition event nets and of place transition nets will be lifted by coloured Petri nets, discussed next.

4.2.3 Coloured Petri Nets

In event condition nets and place transition nets it is impossible to distinguish tokens from one another. This shortcoming in simple types of Petri nets is addressed by the colour feature, which allows tokens to have values.

Like variables in programming languages, tokens have typed values. The data type of a token defines the domain of values and the operations that are valid on the data. In the context of coloured Petri nets, data types are also called colour sets, with the understanding that a colour set of a token represents the set of values that the token can possibly have.

In coloured Petri nets, the enabling of a transition is determined not only by number of tokens in the input places of the transition, but also by the values of these tokens. Whether the precondition of a transition is met or not depends on the presence and values of the tokens to be consumed. This behaviour is realized by attaching expressions to transitions that are evaluated to decide whether a transition is enabled.

Similarly, the values of the tokens produced by a transition firing may depend on values of the tokens consumed. This also means that not all of the output places receive tokens upon the firing of a transition, realizing a choice of branches of the net based on the values of the token consumed and the conditions attached to the transition. The specific firing behaviour of a transition is specified in the postcondition of the transition.

As a result, the graphical representation of coloured Petri nets is not complete, since expressions that denote preconditions and postconditions, as well as values of tokens, are not shown.

While there are several variants of coloured Petri nets, the remainder of this section introduces them as developed by Kurt Jensen. The behaviour of transitions is guided by tokens in the input places, in guards attached to transitions, and in expressions attached to arcs, the arc expressions.

Arc expressions are used to determine whether a transition is enabled. Arc expressions evaluate to multi-sets, where multi-sets can contain multiple identical elements. These multi-sets determine the tokens removed from the input places and added to the output places of a transition when it fires.

Definition 4.6 A *coloured Petri net* is a tuple $(\Sigma, P, T, A, N, C, G, E, I)$ such that

- Σ is a nonempty finite set of types, called colour sets
- P is a finite set of places
- T is a finite set of transitions
- A is a finite set of arc identifiers, such that $P \cap T = P \cap A = T \cap A = \emptyset$
- $N : A \to (P \times T) \cup (T \times P)$ is a node function that maps each arc identifier to a pair (start node, end node) of the arc
- $C : P \to \Sigma$ is a colour function that associates each place with a colour set
- $G : T \to BooleanExpr$ is a guard function that maps each transition to a predicate
- $E : A \to Expr$ is an arc expression that evaluates to a multi-set over the colour set of the place
- I is an initial marking of the coloured Petri net

$\diamond$

Bindings are used to associate data values to variables, that is, colours to tokens. For instance, the value "Paula" can be bound to a variable "name." In coloured Petri nets, the enabling of a transition depends on a binding. A transition t is enabled in a binding b if its input places contain tokens that satisfy the arc expressions under binding b and if in addition, the guard function of the transition evaluates to true.

If a transition is enabled, it can fire. Depending on the evaluation of the arc expressions, the respective tokens are removed from the input places. Guided by the arc expressions of the outgoing edges, the respective tokens are added to the output places. For a formal treatment of coloured Petri nets, the reader is referred to the bibliographical notes at the end of this chapter.

To illustrate coloured Petri nets, we provide an example. Figure 4.30 shows a coloured Petri net of a business process for credit request approval. This example illustrates the definition of the static and dynamic aspects of coloured Petri nets.

The coloured Petri net has associated a colour set consisting of [*Customer, Amount*] pairs of values, where *Customer* is a string and *Amount* is an integer value. Coloured tokens represent specific [*Customer, Amount*] value pairs.

Initially, there are three tokens in the *Credit Request* place $p1$, representing the credit requests by Paula, Mary, and Peter and their respective credit amounts. The *AssessRisk* transition is enabled, because there is a token in its input place and there is no additional guard function associated with that transition.

The *AssessRisk* transition is enabled under binding $c = Paula$, $a = 15000$, because there is a token [*Paula,15000*] at $p1$ that satisfies the arc expression. Since there is no additional guard expression associated with that transition, it is enabled, and it can fire.

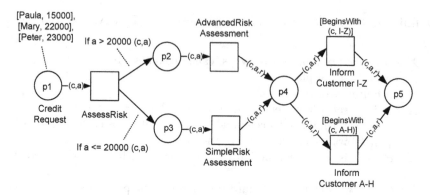

Fig. 4.30. Sample coloured Petri net

When it fires, the *AssessRisk* transition decides on which of its output places a token should be put. This behaviour of the coloured Petri net is due to the arc expressions associated with the outgoing edges of the transition. When the transition fires, the arc expressions of both outgoing edges are evaluated. Since the requested amount is below 20,000, only the arc expression *if a <=20000 (c,a)* is evaluated to true, so that a token is put on $p3$, and no token is put on $p2$.

When the *SimpleRiskAssessment* transition fires, a token is put on $p4$. The token also includes a value assessing the risk of the credit requested, indicated by the arc expression (c, a, r), where r stands for a variable that carries the assessed risk. Assuming there are two risk levels—represented by values l for low and h for high—and Paula gets a low risk assessment, the token $[Paula, 15000, l]$ is put on $p4$.

Depending on the first letter of the credit requester's name, the respective inform customer transition is enabled. This decision is ruled by guard functions, which are represented by functions placed on top of transitions. In the example, the *BeginsWith(name, interval)* returns true if and only if *name* begins with a letter in *interval*. Since the token for Paula is in $p4$, the transition *Inform Customer I-Z* is enabled. After the customer is informed, the process completes.

To summarize, the behaviour of a transition in a coloured Petri net is defined by a guard function, by the tokens that reside in its input places, and by arc expressions. Hence, transition firing in coloured Petri nets exhibits a complex and highly customizable behaviour.

Therefore, it is valid to say that each transition in a coloured Petri net has its own transition behaviour, which provides a high expressive power for this class of Petri nets. At the same time, the graphical representation is no longer sufficient to capture and understand the semantics of the Petri net.

When a transition fires, any number of tokens with any values can be put on the output places of the transition, determined by arc expressions. Because coloured Petri nets provide this expressive power and can handle data as well, they are well suited to representing business process models. They form the basis for workflow nets that will be discussed in Section 4.4.

4.3 Event-driven Process Chains

Event-driven process chains are an important notation to model the domain aspects of business processes. The main focus of this rather informal notation is on representing domain concepts and processes rather than their formal aspects or their technical realization. Event-driven process chains are part of a holistic modelling approach, called the ARIS framework; ARIS stands for Architecture of Integrated Information Systems, and it was developed by August-Wilhelm Scheer.

This approach is often denoted as the ARIS house with three pillars and a roof, as shown in Figure 4.31. The pillars reflect data, control and function, while the roof reflects the overall organization. In each area, three levels of abstraction are identified: a concept level, an architecture level, and an implementation level, characterized by the terms *Requirements Definition*, *Design Specification*, and *Implementation Description*, respectively.

The concept level is the highest level of abstraction in which data, control and function are modelled. This level looks at nontechnical requirements of business processes and their execution environment. Business goals and functions are typical artefacts in the function view at this level. The data view is expressed by data modelling techniques using Entity Relationship diagrams.

In the control view, business processes are described by event-driven process chains, which are also used to integrate the different views. The organizational view at the concept level deals with the organizational structures of a company, described by organizational diagrams. The architecture level is the intermediate level, and it aims at bridging the gap between the concept level and the implementation level. At the implementation level, steps towards concrete realization of the business process are addressed.

This framework is specified by a set of metamodels that describe various views, similar to the business process perspectives introduced in Chapter 3. The main views are as follows.

- *Functional View*: The functional view represents the goals and subgoals of the enterprise and their relationships. In general, one subgoal might contribute to a number of goals at the higher level. For instance, the subgoal "reduce business process execution time" contributes to the goals "increase customer satisfaction" and "reduce overall cost."

  At a lower level of abstraction, each subgoal is associated with a set of functions that contribute to goals and subgoals. Functions are then hierarchically decomposed until the desired granularity of functions is achieved, similarly to functional decomposition in value chains.

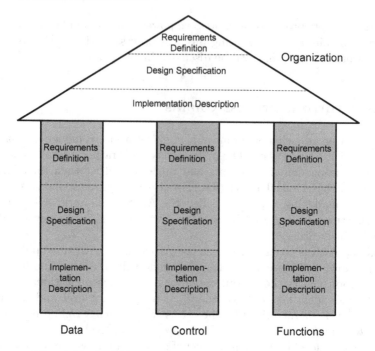

Fig. 4.31. ARIS business process framework, Scheer (2000)

- *Organizational View*: The organizational view describes the organizational structure of an enterprise at a type level and at an instance level. There are detailed specifications of organizational entities, including their relationships and positions, roles, skills, and individuals associated with them. Administration information such as the address of an organizational entity can be represented. The organizational view also includes organizational aspects of information technology of the enterprise, including its main operational information systems, its storage facilities, and its network infrastructure.
- *Data View*: The data view characterizes business relevant data objects that are manipulated by functions during business process execution. Entity Relationship diagrams are used for data modelling.
- *Business Value View or Output View*: The business value view describes the outcome of business processes, that is, the products and services the enterprise generates. These can be physical goods like automobiles or electronic devices, as well as intangible goods, such as a processed order or a flight booking.

These views are integrated in a control view. This control view provides linkage between the artefacts in the different views. Functions, for instance, are associated with the organizations that are responsible for conducting these functions. Analogously, data and business value artefacts are associated with functions, data, and organization, providing an integrated view of the business processes of an enterprise.

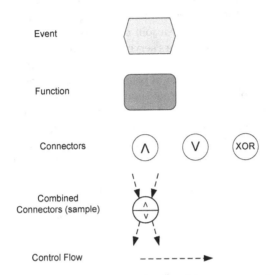

Event

Function

Connectors

Combined
Connectors (sample)

Control Flow

Fig. 4.32. Building blocks of event-driven process chains

Process modelling uses event-driven process chains. The main building blocks of event-driven process chains are events, functions, connectors, and control flow edges, as shown in Figure 4.32.

The entering of a business-relevant state is represented by an event in an event-driven process chain. Examples of events are the receipt of an order, the completion of processing an order, and the completion of shipping a product.

In event-driven process chains, events are represented by hexagons. Events are marked by a string, often of the type *order is received*, indicating a business relevant object (order) and the state change that has occurred to this object (is received). Events are passive elements in the sense that they do not provide decisions.

Functions represent units of work. The granularity of these functions depends on the modelling purpose. In general, functions in event-driven process chains are at a rather low level of granularity; their contribution to functions at higher levels of granularity or to business goals is specified in the functional view.

Unlike events, functions are active elements that take input and transform it to output. Input and output can be information products or physical products. Functions can also make decisions that influence the behaviour of the process through connector nodes associated with the function. Functions are triggered by events, and on the completion of a function, an event occurs. In event-driven process chains, functions are represented by rounded rectangles.

Connectors are used to model causal ordering relations, that is, to represent the process logic. There are three types of connectors, for logical *and*, *or*, and *exclusive or* (*xor*). These connectors serve both as split nodes and as join nodes. Depending on the number of incoming edges, it can be determined if a connector is a split connector or a join connector.

It is also possible that connectors serve at the same time as split connector and join connector. In case split and join realize the same semantics (for instance, both have *and* semantics), a connector with an *and* symbol suffices. In case the split and join have different semantics, the connector can be divided into an upper and a lower part, each of which holds a notational symbol. An example of a combined connector is shown in Figure 4.32, where the upper part shows an *and* join and the lower part shows an *or* split. Other combinations are also possible. Edges are used to provide the glue between events, functions, and connectors.

Event-driven process chains are defined as follows.

Definition 4.7 A tuple $A = (E, F, V, m, C)$ is an *event-driven process chain*, if

- E is a nonempty set of events
- F is a nonempty set of functions
- V is a set of connectors
- $m : V \mapsto \{and, or, xor\}$ is a mapping that assigns to each connector a connector type, representing *and*, *or*, and *exclusive or* semantics.
- Let $K = E \cup F \cup V$. $C \subseteq K \times K$ is a set of edges connecting events, functions, and connectors such that the following conditions hold:
  - (K, C) is a connected graph
  - Each function has exactly one incoming edge and exactly one outgoing edge.
  - There is at least one start event and at least one end event. Each start event has exactly one outgoing edge and no incoming edge. Each end event has exactly one incoming edge and no outgoing edge. There is at least one start event and one end event. All other events have exactly one incoming edge and one outgoing edge.
  - Each event can only be followed (possibly via connectors) by functions, and each function can only be followed (possibly via connectors) by events.
  - There is no cycle in an event-driven process chain that consists of connectors only.
  - No event is followed by a decision node, that is, an *or* split node or an *exclusive or* split node.

◇

The definition of event-driven process chains is illustrated by Figures 4.33 and 4.34. Figure 4.33 shows how connectors can link multiple events to one function. The figure uses two events per function, but any number of events is possible. In the upper part of Figure 4.33, the occurrence of events triggers a function.

Depending on the connector used, the occurrence of one event (*exclusive or* join connector), the occurrence of two events (*and* join connector), or the occurrence of any nonempty subset of events (*or* join connector) triggers a function F. There is no surprise with respect to the semantics of the connectors: an *exclusive or* connector triggers F after either $E1$ or $E2$ has occurred; for the *and* connector to trigger the function, both events must occur, and the or connector triggers F after any nonempty subset of events $E1$ and $E2$ has occurred.

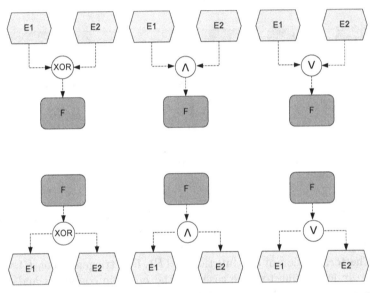

Fig. 4.33. Syntax rules on event-driven process chains: multiple events, single function

In the lower part of Figure 4.33, a connector links a function F to multiple events. The execution semantics of the split connectors follows the traditional way: an *exclusive or* split connector represents the business logic that after F, either event $E1$ or event $E2$ occurs. The decision about which event actually occurs during a particular process instance is made by function F. Analogous considerations hold for the *or* split connector, where any nonempty subset of events $\{E1, E2\}$ can occur after F. The *and* split connector determines that after function F, both events $E1$ and $E2$ occur.

Figure 4.34 shows how one event can be linked to multiple functions. In event-driven process chains, events are passive elements that occur—events are not active entities that can make decisions. Therefore, any combination of one event followed by a decision involving multiple functions is disallowed, as shown in Figure 4.34.

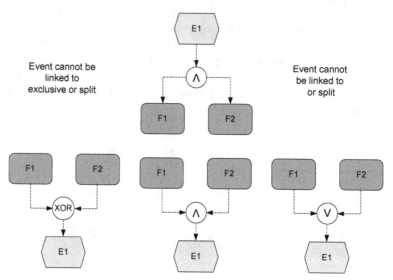

Fig. 4.34. Syntax rules on event-driven process chains: multiple functions, single event

Notice that an event can precede an *and* split connector, since all branches are taken, so that no decision needs to be made by the event. In the lower part of Figure 4.34, the occurrence of functions triggers the occurrence of an event. The termination of one function in $\{F1, F2\}$ triggers event $E1$ via an *exclusive or* join connector; the cases for the *and* join connector and the *or* join connector can also be seen in that figure.

Having defined event-driven process chains and their structural constraints, we illustrate the definitions with an example. The following process is represented by an event-driven process chain in Figure 4.35.

The process starts with the receipt of a customer order. This receipt of a customer order realizes a state change of the enterprise that is relevant for the business process. Therefore, it is represented by an event. Event-driven process chains start with events (never with functions), since a function is always a consequence of an event and cannot therefore be performed without the state change represented by the event.

When an order is received, it is analyzed and either accepted or rejected. When it is accepted, the stock is checked for availability of the ordered products. If all products are in stock, then the products are shipped and the bill is sent. In case there are additional bills open, the payment will need to include these open bills. The other parts of the event-driven process chains deal with the manufacturing of products if the ordered products are not in stock.

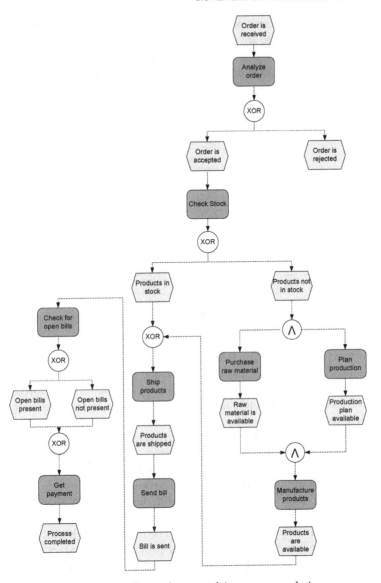

Fig. 4.35. Example event-driven process chain

While most constructs of event-driven process chains can be explained in this example, the process is a severe simplification of real-world ordering processes.

While the process aspect in terms of the functions and events that occur in business processes is well captured by event-driven process chains, there are other types of diagrams that abstract from the relatively fine-granular level of event-driven process chains.

Interaction flow diagrams provide a high-level view on the organizational entities that participate in a business process, as well as their interactions. An interaction flow diagram is a directed graph, whose nodes correspond to organizational entities and whose edges represent interactions between the organizations. An interaction flow diagram of the event-driven process chain discussed above is shown in Figure 4.36.

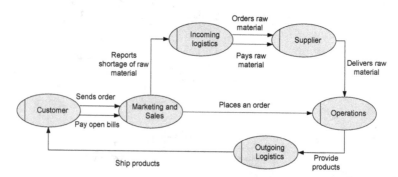

Fig. 4.36. Sample interaction flow diagram, adapted from Scheer et al. (2005)

The interaction flow diagram shown describes at a high level of abstraction a business process in which a customer sends an order to the marketing and sales department, which triggers the purchase of raw material, before operations manufactures the products and finally ships them to the customer, who pays for ordered products.

While the overall interactions are properly represented in interaction flow diagrams, the ordering in which these interactions actually occur is not in the scope of interaction flow diagrams. For instance, the two interactions between customer and sales are not ordered in the diagram.

However, the reader of an interaction diagram might be able to deduce the ordering of interactions by common sense. For instance, placing an order is done before paying for the ordered item. The diagram itself abstracts from these ordering relationships and, therefore, provides an abstract, high-level representation of the organizational entities involved in a business process and their relationships through interactions.

Function flow diagrams are a refinement of interaction flow diagrams in the sense that they (i) represent the ordering of interactions and (ii) provide coarse-grained functions for representing these interactions. Figure 4.37 shows the mapping of an interaction flow between the customer and the marketing and sales department to a function flow. The latter includes functions and an ordering relationship between these functions, indicating that the entering of the order precedes the processing of the order by the marketing and sales department.

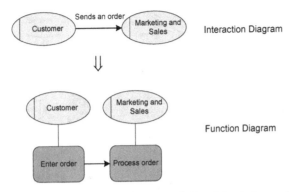

Fig. 4.37. Mapping interactions to relationships between functions

The complete picture of function flow in this example is shown in Figure 4.38. In addition to the functions and their ordering, split and join nodes are introduced. Function flow diagrams provide information on the coarse grained functions involved in a business process, as well as the organizational entities that perform them. In addition, the ordering of these functions is also represented in function flow diagrams.

In the sample function flow diagram it is clarified that planning the manufacturing and purchasing of material are performed concurrently, but the item is only manufactured after the supplier has processed the order and manufacturing has received the material. The function flow diagram also models the fact that payment of the received material is performed concurrently to manufacturing the item.

To summarize, function flow diagrams provide high-level information on the functions in a business process and on the organizational entities that perform them and their ordering. Events of the business process are not covered by function flow diagrams.

Additional views are represented by enhancing event-driven process chains with notational symbols for data involved as well as for process paths and process groups. Data and material are represented by rectangles, associated with functions by solid arrows. The direction of the arrows indicates whether the data is used for input or output (or both). Process groups hold a collection of processes, and process paths indicate where the process continues.

A part of an extended event-driven process chain is shown in Figure 4.39. This part consists of a single function to analyze an order and its environment. When the order arrives, the function is triggered, represented by the respective event. In order to check the order, the order document and the stock status are used as input data.

We assume the function is performed by the operations department. When the function completes, the result is recorded in the check result data object. The function is also responsible for creating the respective event: either the

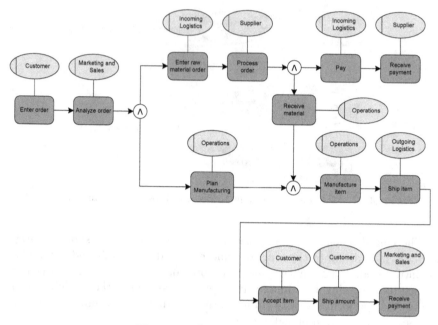

Fig. 4.38. Sample function flow

products are in stock or the products are not in stock and need to be manufactured.

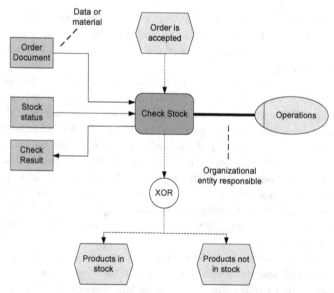

Fig. 4.39. Example of extended event-driven process chain

Event-driven process chains allow us to model business processes from a business perspective. The explicit representation of the occurrence of relevant situations by events and the bipartite structure, in which events and functions alternate, lead to verbose and often actually quite complex process representations.

Due to their semiformal nature, business engineers and process designers enjoy a fair degree of freedom when expressing business processes. When it comes to implemented business processes, process designers and systems engineers need to make explicit what was intended by the event-driven process chain.

The *or* join is an important control flow construct in EPCs, which is used quite often, because it allows us to represent any type of join behaviour. We have already discussed the problematic semantics of the *or* join in Section 4.1. Due to the nonlocal semantics, the decision on when the join needs to be performed cannot be taken without nonlocal knowledge.

Since event-driven process chains are primarily used to model business processes at a business level, typically humans interpret event-driven process chains. Since humans, when assessing an EPC, have nonlocal knowledge, the semantics of the *or* join is clear to them.

The problems start when an EPC needs to be translated into an executable format, for instance, to serve as input for a workflow management system to control the enactment of business processes. There are approaches in handling the *or* join semantics, based on global state transition systems; for details, the reader is referred to the bibliographical notes.

Section 7.5 introduces a technique to translate event-driven process chains to workflow nets; this technique facilitates the evaluation of properties of EPCs with respect to deadlocks and proper termination of the business processes represented.

4.4 Workflow Nets

Event-driven process chains provide an informal notation for representing business processes and their environment. To precisely specify and reason about business processes, more formal approaches need to be investigated, such as, Petri nets.

While Petri nets are very useful for representing simple types of processes, complex processes such as business processes require advanced modelling mechanisms. In particular, tokens need to carry information at least about the process instance they belong to.

Workflow nets are an approach to enhance traditional Petri nets with concepts and notations that ease the representation of business processes. At the same time, workflow nets introduce structural restrictions that prove useful for business processes.

The reasons for using Petri nets in general and workflow nets in particular for business process modelling are as follows.

- *Formal Semantics*: Business processes can be defined in a formal manner. This observation holds in particular for the control flow aspect of Petri nets.
- *Graphical Representation*: Activities in a business process and their execution constraints are expressed graphically in a Petri net, which eases communication about business processes with the different stakeholders involved (although some stakeholders prefer semiformal techniques like event-driven process chains).
- *Analysis of Process Properties*: The formal semantics of business processes expressed in Petri nets allows for the analysis of process properties.
- *Tool Independence*: Although several business process management tools are based on Petri nets, the formalism itself is vendor independent.

4.4.1 Definitions

The main concepts in workflow nets are illustrated in Figure 4.40. Like Petri nets, workflow nets focus on the control flow behaviour of a process. Places represent conditions and tokens represent process instances. Activities of a business process are represented by transitions in the workflow net.

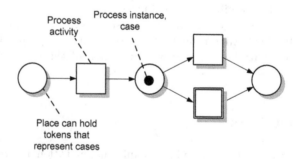

Fig. 4.40. Sample workflow net

Because tokens represent business process instances, tokens hold application data including process instance identifiers, that is, the tokens are coloured. However, in workflow nets, the colouring of tokens is not represented explicitly, as will be discussed in more detail below.

Workflow nets can be hierarchically structured. In the sample workflow net shown in Figure 4.40, there is a complex business process activity represented by a transition with a double border. The internal structure of a complex activity is realized by another dedicated workflow net. Hierarchical structuring of workflow nets is not investigated in detail; in the context of the

YAWL process language, hierarchical structuring is investigated. Based on these considerations, workflow nets can be defined as Petri nets with specific structural restrictions.

Definition 4.8 A Petri net $PN = (P, T, F)$ is called *workflow net* if and only if the following conditions hold.

- There is a distinguished place $i \in P$ (called initial place) that has no incoming edge, that is, $\bullet i = \emptyset$.
- There is a distinguished place $o \in P$ (called final place) that has no outgoing edge, that is, $o \bullet = \emptyset$.
- Every place and every transition is located on a path from the initial place to the final place.

$\diamond$

The rationale of this definition is as follows: a token in the initial place i represents a process instance that has not yet started; a token in place o represents a finished process instance. Each place and each transition in a workflow net can participate in a process instance; therefore, each place and each transition needs to be located on a path from i to o.

As a consequence of these structural properties of workflow nets, the initial place i is the only place without incoming edges, and the final place is the only place without any outgoing edges.

If there was another place $i' \neq i \in P$ without incoming edges, then i' could not be located on a path from i to o, contradicting the definition of workflow nets. And if there was a place $o' \neq o \in P$ without outgoing edges, then o' could not be on a path from i to o. Therefore, places with the properties of i' and o' cannot exist in workflow nets.

A sample workflow net is shown in Figure 4.41. It represents a simple claim management process in which, initially, the claim is recorded and, concurrently, a witness report is created and the client status is checked. After the results have been gathered, an assessment of the claim is performed. In the case of a positive assessment, the damage is compensated. In the case of a negative assessment, the claim is rejected. Finally the claim is filed and the process completes.

4.4.2 Control Flow in Workflow Nets

The ability to represent control flow structures in workflow nets is investigated. As with any other process modelling language, the sequence pattern can easily be expressed in workflow nets. In Figure 4.42, the sequential execution of A and B is realized by a place p and the associated arcs. As indicated above, the execution of a business process activity is represented by the firing of a transition.

The firing rule of Petri nets makes sure that A puts a token on p only after its termination. Hence, B is enabled only after there is a token in p.

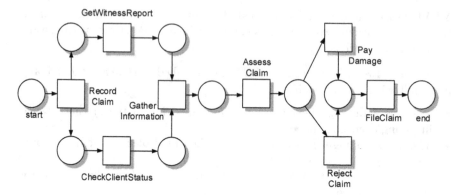

Fig. 4.41. Sample workflow net

Since only enabled transitions can fire, we have the following sequence of events: A fires and puts a token in p enabling B, which can now start its execution. Therefore, by transitivity of the ordering relation, B can only start after A has terminated.

Observe that colouring information is not regarded when discussing control flow in workflow nets. For the sequence pattern, the colouring of the tokens can be disregarded. However, if transitions need to make decisions when they fire, the colouring of the tokens needs to be taken into account; this will be discussed in more detail below.

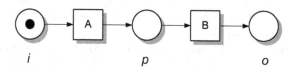

Fig. 4.42. Sequence pattern in workflow net

And split and *and* join control flow constructs can also be expressed in workflow nets conveniently. Again, standard Petri net firing behaviour suffices. Figure 4.43 shows a workflow net in which there is a transition A that puts tokens in its output places $p1$ and $p2$, enabling B and C, respectively. As a result, transition A realizes an *and* split. After B and C have terminated, there are tokens in $p3$ and $p4$, enabling the *and* join transition D.

The *exclusive or* split and *exclusive or* join patterns can also be expressed in standard Petri nets. As shown in Figure 4.44, an *exclusive or* split can be realized by a place with multiple outgoing edges leading to multiple transitions. These transitions are enabled at the same time. This type of *exclusive or* split is called implicit exclusive split, because its behaviour depends on the behaviour of the transitions involved, in this case, A and B.

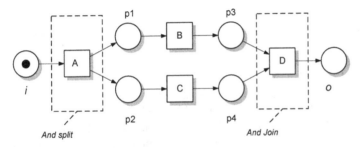

Fig. 4.43. *And* split and *and* join patterns in workflow nets

Although both transitions are enabled—in the example, A and B—only one transition can fire, withdrawing the token from $p1$ and adding a token to $p2$. The *exclusive or* join is realized by a place that receives a token from either A or B.

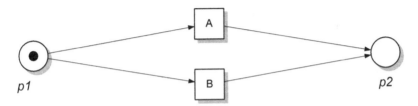

Fig. 4.44. *Implicit exclusive or* split also known as *deferred choice*

In the scenario shown in Figure 4.44, the transitions involved decide by their firing behaviour about the branch of the workflow net that the process instance takes. Since the decision is deferred to the latest point in time, this pattern is also called *deferred choice*.

There is a second type of *exclusive or* split in workflow nets, in which the decision on which path to take is made explicitly by a transition. This feature takes advantage of coloured Petri nets, in which transitions can implement decision rules, which are evaluated at run time to decide which of its output places to put tokens on.

This also means that the behaviour of classical Petri nets is no longer valid for workflow nets. As a consequence, as in coloured Petri nets, the graphical representation of the workflow net does not fully specify the behaviour of the process instance controlled by the workflow net.

The workflow net shown in Figure 4.45 illustrates these observations. Transition A implements a decision rule by associating conditions with each of its outgoing edges. An *exclusive or* semantics of this decision can be realized in different ways (workflow nets do not prescribe any of them).

The first way to realize an *exclusive or* semantics is to make sure that the conditions are chosen in a way that always one and only one condition evaluates to true. The second way is to evaluate conditions of outgoing edges in order. As soon as one condition evaluates to true, the respective edge is chosen, and the token is put on the respective place.

The problem with this strategy is that there might be situations in which no condition evaluates to true. If no additional measures are taken, then the case gets stuck at this point. This problem can be tackled by defining a default branch which is taken if none of the (expressions of the) other branches evaluates to true.

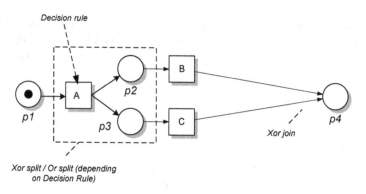

Fig. 4.45. Decision rule based split, can realize *or* split, *exclusive or* split, and *and* split

To express the particular split and join behaviour of transitions in work-flow nets, the transitions are labelled with specific symbols. This labelling of transitions is called syntactic sugaring; it is shown in Figure 4.46.

It is the responsibility of the modeller of the workflow net to make sure that the decisions associated with the transitions match their symbols. The *and* split and *and* join markers indicate that the traditional Petri net firing behaviour of transitions is in place. If a transition is marked with an *and* split symbol, the reader of the workflow net knows that the transition puts a token on all its output places, while the *xor* split marker models an exclusive decision when the transition fires.

Workflow nets represent business processes, focusing on activities and their execution constraints. To enhance the representation of business processes and to provide a means to represent in more detail the environment in which these processes are enacted, triggers have been introduced. In the context of workflow nets, triggers are annotations to transitions that provide information on who or what is responsible for an enabled transition to fire.

Situations in real-world business processes that can be represented by triggers are the receipt of an electronic message or a time-out of a timer to remind

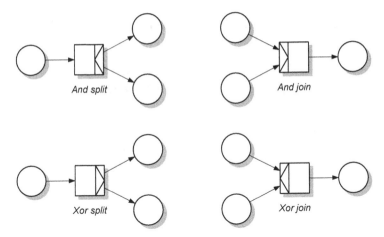

Fig. 4.46. Syntactic sugaring of transitions in workflow nets

an employee of an upcoming deadline. Generally, a business process management system is a reactive system. It reacts to events in its environment by enabling an activity. Triggers play an important role in informing the system about events in the process environment that are relevant for the process.

Figure 4.47 shows the types of triggers used in workflow nets. Transitions that can fire immediately after they have been enabled are not marked with a trigger; triggering is therefore *automatic*. For example, automatic triggers are used for transitions that are realized by invoking a software system, where no user interaction is required.

A *user trigger* is attached to transitions that require human interaction. By marking a transition with a user trigger, the process modeller expresses the fact that a human user takes the initiative to start the activity represented by the transition. This trigger is relevant in human interaction workflows, where work items are used to communicate with human users.

A work item list of a particular user contains items, each of which represents an activity (more precisely, an activity instance) that is enabled and that can be executed by that user. Whenever a transition with a user trigger enters the enabled state, a work item representing this activity is sent to the work item lists of the users who can perform it. Role information is used to determine the knowledge workers. When a user selects a particular work item, the activity is started and the work items reflecting it can be deleted from the work item list.

Modelling organizational aspects like users or roles is not supported by workflow nets. A transition marked with a user trigger indicates that the activity represented by that transition requires a human to start it. Organizational aspects need to be covered by tools that employ workflow nets for process modelling and other techniques for modelling organizations. The same applies for representing data, which is also not covered by workflow nets.

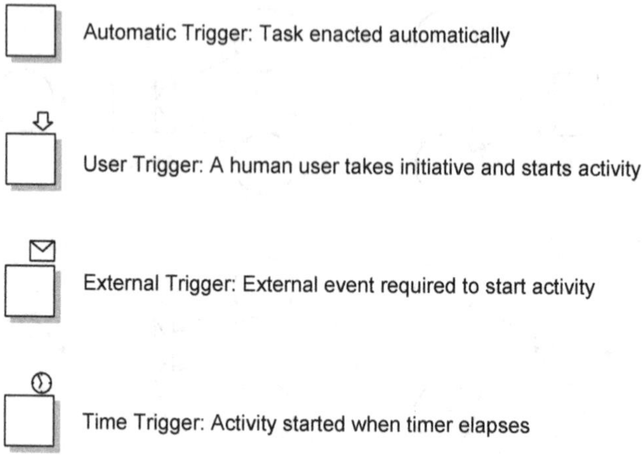

Automatic Trigger: Task enacted automatically

User Trigger: A human user takes initiative and starts activity

External Trigger: External event required to start activity

Time Trigger: Activity started when timer elapses

Fig. 4.47. Triggers in workflow nets

An external trigger is the main instrument for reacting to external events like an incoming message. When the transition that carries an external trigger enters the enabled state, it listens for this event. When the event occurs, for instance, when an order arrives, the transition fires and the activity starts execution.

Time triggers are used to specify situations where the start of an activity depends on temporal aspects. Time triggers can be assigned a time-out value. The timer is started when the transition enters the enabled state. When the timer runs out, the enabled transition fires. If the transition is no longer enabled, the timer is stopped.

Figure 4.48 shows a workflow net with a typical usage of triggers. In this process, a request is sent, represented by the *Send Request* transition. The workflow net implements an *implicit exclusive or* split that concurrently enables (transitions that represent) activities to collect the response to the request and to send a reminder.

The *Collect Response* activity is marked by an external trigger, so that it is started once the response comes in. A reminder should be sent if after a defined time interval, for instance, 14 days, no response is received. This business logic can be implemented in a workflow net by attaching a timer trigger to the *Send Reminder* transition.

The timer is started when the transition enters the enabled state, that is, after the request is sent. If the response is received within the timer interval, then the *Collect Response* transition fires. In this case, the *Send Reminder* transition is no longer enabled, so that the timer can be stopped.

Triggers can also illustrate very well the difference between an *explicit exclusive or* split and an *implicit exclusive or* split, as shown in Figure 4.49. In an *explicit exclusive or* split (a), the decision on which branch to activate is made by a decision transition, so that either transition A or transition B

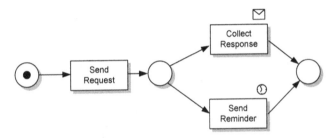

Fig. 4.48. Sample workflow net with external trigger and time trigger

is enabled. In this setting, the desired functionality is not realized, because if
A is enabled, the timer will not be started, and if B is activated, there is no
way for the user to start working on activity A.

The desired functionality is provided if both transitions are enabled concurrently, as shown in part (b) of Figure 4.49. The timer is started, and the
user trigger is available. If the user starts the activity on time, that is, before the timer expires, then the timer is stopped. If the user fails to start the
activity on time, activity B is started to cater to this situation.

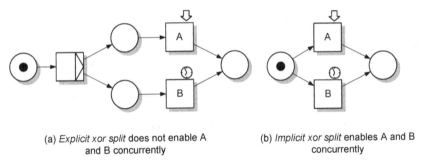

(a) *Explicit xor split* does not enable A   (b) *Implicit xor split* enables A and B
           and B concurrently   concurrently

Fig. 4.49. Sample workflow nets illustrate the difference between *explicit xor* split
(a) and *implicit xor* split (b)

Trigger activities can formally be represented by places with an arc to the
respective transition. For instance, a user trigger of a transition A is represented by a place p such that $p \in P$ and $(p, A) \in F$, as shown in Figure 4.50.
The behaviour of the user is represented as follows. If and when the user selects this activity, a token is put in place p, enabling transition A. In this case,
A can fire, representing the execution of that activity.

While the behaviour of the user trigger is specified well using the additional
place and the additional arc, there is an issue to cope with: the Petri net
resulting from expanding the user trigger by a place and an arc is no longer a
Workflow net! This is due to the fact that p is not on a path from the initial
place i to the final place o. In the context of business processes involving

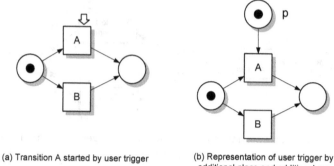

(a) Transition A started by user trigger   (b) Representation of user trigger by
                                                  additional place and additional arc

Fig. 4.50. Representation of triggers

multiple parties, however, these trigger places are very useful to interconnect the processes involved.

While workflow nets have been primarily developed to represent business processes within organizations, workflow nets can also be used for processes spanning multiple organizions, as shown in Figure 4.51. The diagram shows a business process involving a customer and a bookstore, and it contains activities for the ordering of books by the customer and the processing of the order by the bookstore.

All activities in this scenario are represented by transitions of one workflow net. In order to satisfy the structural properties of workflow nets, the process starts in the initial place i at the customer, and it ends in the final place o at the customer. Later, in the context of business process choreographies, more elaborate techniques will be introduced that separate an externally observable behaviour of a business process from its internal realization. However, in the current example, the workflow spans multiple parties.

The process starts with the customer browsing the online catalogue of a bookstore and selecting books. If books are found, an order is assembled and sent, represented by the send order transition. This transition spawns off two concurrent threads, as shown by the *and* split symbol.

In one thread, the message is sent to the bookstore. The sending of the order is represented by a token in the input place of the receive order transition. When the order is received in the bookstore, the order is processed. If the order is okay, the books are sent; otherwise, a message is sent to the customer that informs him that not all books are available.

This means that the bookstore sends one of two possible messages for each case. On the customer side, this situation is handled by an *implicit exclusive or* split. In this split, two transitions can be enabled at the same time. If the bookstore sends the books, the receive books transition of the customer is enabled and will fire.

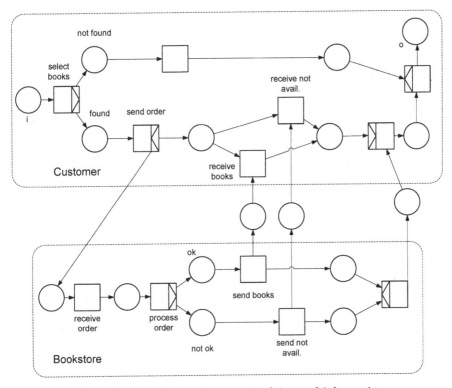

Fig. 4.51. Sample workflow net involving multiple parties

If, on the other hand, the information message is sent, the respective transition on the customer side is enabled. Observe that the alternative branches in the bookstore need to be joined, and the join transition is connected to the customer side. This is required in workflow nets, because otherwise there would be places in the workflow net (*send books* and *send not available*) that are not on a path from the initial place to the final place.

4.4.3 Representing Process Instances

Workflow nets cover the model level in process modelling and—by tokens—the process instance level as well. This means that for each business process model represented by a workflow net there can be multiple process instances following this model. Each process instance is represented by a set of tokens in the workflow net.

A sample workflow net with a set of tokens belonging to different process instances is shown in Figure 4.52. The workflow net represents a business process in which claims are processed; the details of this process are not relevant to introducing how process instances are represented in workflow nets. The tokens are coloured; they contain values. If we abstract from any application

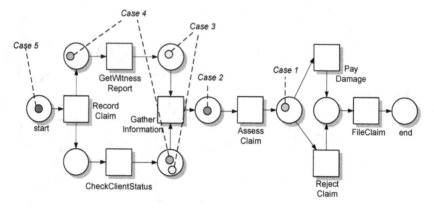

Fig. 4.52. Sample workflow net with coloured tokens representing process instances

data that might be represented by tokens, each token carries at least a process instance identifier.

The workflow net shown in Figure 4.52 holds tokens that represent a set of cases that are concurrently executed. Case 5 has a token is in the initial place; the case is not yet started. Case 4 is reflected by two tokens, because it is currently on a parallel branch of the net. The same holds for Case 3, but for Case 3 the *GetWitnessReport* transition has already been conducted. Case 2 has already completed the parallel branch, so that the two parallel branches have already been joined, and the two tokens of Case 2 have been merged into a single token, as shown in Figure 4.52.

4.4.4 Discussion

Workflow nets are a well-known technique to model business processes in an abstract and formal way. In order to provide a formal background, especially in the context of soundness properties which will be investigated in Chapter 7, several restrictions were introduced. Without these restrictions, formal analysis of workflow nets would not be feasible.

Data and Conditions

Data is not explicitly represented in workflow nets. Data is only handled in an abstract way, by denoting that tokens can be coloured, but the usage of these data structures in the process is not investigated.

While the workflow net represents the structure of a set of similar process instances (that is, the process model), the individual cases are represented by tokens. Each case is represented by at least one token. In general, when the case starts, there is one token in the source place i, and when the case completes, there is one token in the sink place o.

The workflow management system that controls the enactment of cases requires differentiating between the tokens that belong to different cases. A transition t with incoming edges from places p and p' realizes an *and* join. This means that t can only be enabled when there are tokens in p and p', and these tokens need to belong to the same case.

Therefore, tokens need to be typed. Tokens need (at least) to include a process instance identifier, so that t can synchronize the branches represented by p and p' only, if these places have tokens that belong to the same case. As a simplification often made in the context of workflow nets, each workflow net contains tokens that belong to a single case. In this case, the tokens do not need to be typed.

Decision transitions that realize *or* splits and *exclusive or* splits require expressions that are evaluated for each process instance to decide which branch to take. These decision expressions are also disregarded in workflow nets.

Decisions are abstracted from in the following way: wherever there is a decision transition, each of the alternative branches will be taken eventually. This assumption mirrors the non-determination of firing in traditional Petri nets: multiple enabled transitions that share a common input place will fire in a non deterministic fashion.

The same assumption is now in place for decision nodes in workflow nets: each expression in a decision transition will eventually evaluate to true. When analyzing workflow nets, this assumption is in place to detect structural errors in workflow nets. Errors that result from erroneous conditions associated with decision transitions, however, are not considered.

Temporal Aspects

Activities in workflow nets are represented by transitions. When a transition fires, it withdraws tokens from its input places and puts tokens in its output places, depending on the decision made by the transition. These steps (withdrawing tokens, determining where to put tokens, and finally putting the tokens) in Petri nets are represented by the firing of the transition, which does not consume time. This assumption is in contradiction with activity instances, which do take time. The processing of an insurance claim, the preparation of a quote, and the checking of a warehouse inventory are activities that take time.

The fact that activities take time is also reflected by the state transition diagram of activities. In state transition diagrams, state transitions are triggered by events. For instance, the completion of an enter customer order activity enables a check inventory activity. This means that activity instances have lifecycles that consist of a number of steps, from their instantiation, their enabling, and their execution to their termination. In workflow nets, these steps are not represented, because firing puts an activity from the enabled state immediately into the terminated state.

This contradiction is partly solved in workflow management systems using Petri nets. Assume that a business activity represented by a transition is realized by invoking a piece of software. The invocation of the software is often represented by the firing of the transition. However, software procedures also take time. In addition, the follow-up activities should not be enabled when the previous activity is started, but when it completes. If an activity is implemented in software, then the follow-up activities should not be enabled when the software is invoked, but after it has completed.

The timeliness of activity instances represented by workflow nets also implies that no events can occur during an activity instance. In real-world business processes, however, this is not true. Many things do happen during the execution of a business process activity. For instance, while an inventory is being checked, new items may enter the warehouse. These issues are not covered by workflow nets; it is the responsibility of business process management tools to solve issues that might result from these abstractions in workflow nets.

4.5 Yet Another Workflow Language

The motivation for the development of Yet Another Workflow Language (YAWL) was the lack of a process language that directly supported all control flow patterns. While it uses workflow nets as a major ingredient, the execution semantics of process instances is specified by state transition systems and not by Petri nets. In this section, YAWL and its support for control flow patterns, as well as its execution semantics, are investigated.

While Petri nets provide a sound formalism for expressing most control flow patterns, the following deficiencies have been identified that hamper the expression of the full set of control flow patterns.

- *Multiple Instances*: Multiple instances patterns describe business processes with multiple instances of specific activities. The number of activity instances of one particular activity model might not be known at design time. Petri nets do not provide adequate means to describe multiple instances tasks.
- *Advanced Synchronization Patterns*: Petri nets can directly express *and* split/join and *exclusive or* split/join using places, transitions and firing rules of traditional Petri nets. Advanced synchronization patterns such as, for instance, *or* split and *or* join and *discriminator* patterns, however, cannot be conveniently expressed in Petri nets.
- *Nonlocal Firing Behaviour*: The enabling of activities in a business process is based on local knowledge only. In the context of Petri nets, the presence of tokens in the input places of a transition indicates activation of that transition. In business processes, there are situations in which nonlocal parts of the process are affected by a decision. For instance, the cancellation pattern somehow vacuum-cleans defined parts of the Petri net when being

activated. If used to cancel a customer order, different activities in different parts of the Petri net need to be cancelled in order to cancel the overall customer order.

4.5.1 Definitions

Notation wise, YAWL is based on a variant of workflow nets, called YAWL nets, which are building blocks for YAWL specifications. YAWL nets enhance traditional workflow nets with direct arcs between transitions, explicit split and join behaviour that can be attached to transitions, nonlocal behaviour (on the firing of a transition, parts of the YAWL net are cleansed of tokens), and the handling of multiple instances tasks.

Since this book concentrates on the conceptual aspects of process languages and not on technical aspects, a simplified version of YAWL nets is introduced. The interested reader is referred to the bibliographical notes of this chapter for further reading on YAWL, including detailed technical information and the YAWL system.

Because YAWL specifications contain a set of YAWL nets, YAWL nets are defined first.

Definition 4.9 A *YAWL net* is a tuple $(C, i, o, T, F, split, join, rem, nofi)$, such that

- C is a set of conditions
- $i \in C$ is the initial condition, and $o \in C$ is the final condition
- T is a set of tasks, such that C and T are disjoint
- $F \subseteq (C - \{o\} \times T) \cup (T \times C - \{i\}) \cup (T \times T)$ is a flow relation, such that every node in $C \cup T$ is on a directed path from i to o
- $split : T \nrightarrow \{And, Xor, Or\}$ is a partial mapping that assigns the split behaviour of a task
- $join : T \nrightarrow \{And, Xor, Or\}$ is a partial mapping that specifies the join behaviour of a task
- $rem : T \nrightarrow \mathcal{P}(T \cup C - \{i, o\})$ specifies the subnet of the YAWL net that is cleansed when the task is executed, where $\mathcal{P}(\mathcal{S})$ denotes the power set of $\mathcal{S}$
- $nofi : T \nrightarrow \mathbb{N} \times \mathbb{N}^{inf} \times \mathbb{N}^{inf} \times \{dynamic, static\}$ is a partial function that specifies the number of instances of each task (min, max, threshold for continuation, and dynamic/static creation of instances), where $\mathbb{N}^{inf}$ indicates the set of natural numbers plus an infinite value symbol.

◇

YAWL nets, also definition wise, are an extension of workflow nets. If $(C, i, o, T, F, split, join, rem, nofi)$ is YAWL net, (C, T, F) is a workflow net, except for the fact that the flow relation in YAWL nets allows direct arcs between tasks. As discussed below, this is a shorthand notation for a more

Petri-net-like flavour, in which there is always a condition between the transitions, representing the tasks.

In workflow nets, labels of transitions mark the split and join behaviour. These labels are not part of the formal definition of workflow nets. In contrast, the annotation of transitions with specific split and join behaviour is part of the definition of YAWL nets.

For each task a cancellation region can be defined. When a task with a cancellation region is executed, all tokens are removed from the cancellation region. The removal function *rem* defines parts of the YAWL net that need to be cleansed from tokens when the task is executed. In this way, nonlocal behaviour can be expressed.

There are also differences with respect to handling tokens. In Petri nets, firing of a transition removes tokens from its input places and adds tokens to its output places. In Petri nets, tokens are never on transitions. In YAWL nets, however, tokens *reside at transitions* while the transition is being executed. This also means that the execution of a transition takes time, another fundamental difference to Petri nets (and also to workflow nets), in which the firing of transitions does not consume time.

The number-of-instances function *nofi* can be used to assign information about multiple instances to tasks. In an entry $(min, max, threshold, d/s)$ associated with a task t,

- *min*: Minimum number of instances of task t for one case
- *max*: Maximum number of instances of t for one case
- *threshold*: If the threshold is reached, then all active instances of that task are cancelled and the task completes
- *d/s*: The letter d stands for dynamic and s stands for static creation of new instances. In the dynamic case, new task instances can be created while instances of this task are already running. Static means that all instances are created up front, and no additional instances can be created at run time of the task.

YAWL specifications use YAWL nets as building blocks, and multiple YAWL nets involved in a workflow specification can be connected to each other by composite tasks.

Definition 4.10 A *YAWL specification* S is a tuple $(Q, top, T^\diamond, map)$, such that

- Q is a set of YAWL nets
- $top \in Q$ is the top level YAWL net
- $T^\diamond = \bigcup_{N \in Q} T_N$ is the set of all tasks. Conditions and tasks of all YAWL nets are disjoint, that is,
  $N_1 \neq N_2 \implies (C_{N_1} \cup T_{N_1}) \cap (C_{N_2} \cup T_{N_2}) = \emptyset, \forall N_1, N_2 \in Q.$
- $map : T^\diamond \nrightarrow Q - \{top\}$ is a function that maps each composite task onto a YAWL net. Hence, each task $t \in T^\diamond$ for which $map(t)$ is defined is a composite task.

For each YAWL net, except the top-level net, there exists a task that maps to it, and for each YAWL net there exists at most one task that maps to it.

◇

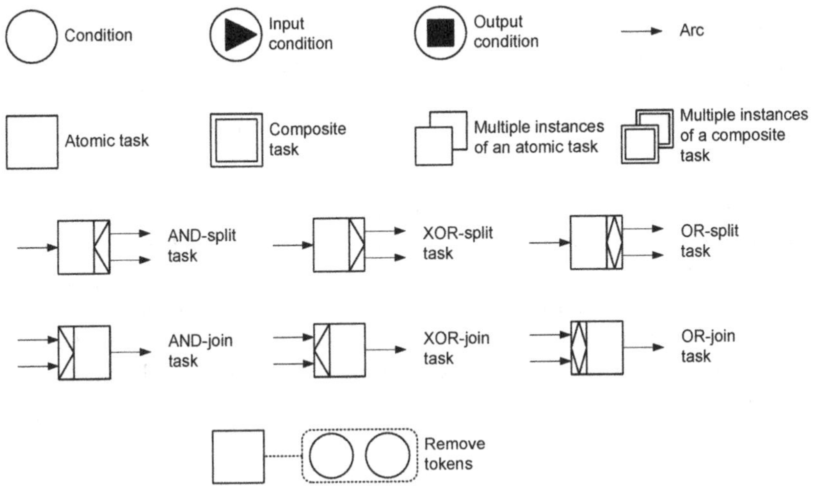

Fig. 4.53. Notational elements of YAWL, van der Aalst and ter Hofstede (2005)

The notational elements of Yet Another Workflow Language are shown in Figure 4.53. The notation borrows most elements of workflow nets, so that conditions are represented by circles and tasks are represented by rectangles. The initial condition and the final condition of a YAWL net are labelled with specific symbols.

There are several notational extensions for tasks. Composite tasks have a double border to indicate that they map to a YAWL net. Tasks with multiple instances are represented by double rectangles, as shown in Figure 4.53. Composite tasks can also have multiple instances; in this case, the notational symbols are combined.

The graphical representation of the split and join behaviour of a task is equivalent to that in workflow nets. Finally, the set of tokens that are removed when a task is executed is shown by a dotted line. This graphical representation might become cumbersome if the tasks and conditions are spread across a large YAWL specification and if multiple tasks remove tokens.

4.5.2 Simple Control Flow Patterns

We now discuss how YAWL supports control flow patterns. It is obvious that the basic control flow patterns are directly supported. The sequence pattern is shown in Figure 4.54, where two alternative representations are shown: in YAWL nets, the control flow edge can directly connect A and B, so that the condition place can be dropped. Notice that these two representations are equivalent, that is, any YAWL net with conditions connecting two tasks can be transformed to an equivalent YAWL net with direct connections, and vice versa.

Fig. 4.54. Representations of sequence pattern in YAWL

And split and *and* join patterns are shown in part (a) of Figure 4.55. On completion of the split task A $(split(A) = and)$, tasks B, C, and D are enabled, and the three tasks can be executed concurrently. The join task E $(join(E) = and)$ is enabled only if B, C, and D have been completed. The *exclusive or* split shown in part (b) of that figure selects exactly one alternative, so that E can start if exactly one branch is completed. In this case, $split(A) = join(E) = Xor$.

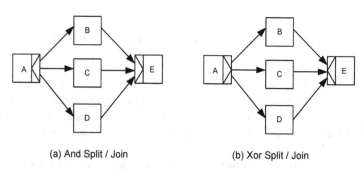

(a) And Split / Join   (b) Xor Split / Join

Fig. 4.55. *And* split/join and *xor* split/join patterns

YAWL specifications require additional information that allows evaluating conditions to decide, for instance, which path in an *exclusive or* split to take. These conditions, however, are not part of the formal specification.

Figure 4.56 shows the inclusive *or* split. From a notation point of view, the *or* split and the *or* join can be defined similarly to the other control flow structures. However, the decision on when the *or* join is activated is complex. These aspects will be discussed in more detail when the execution semantics of YAWL is investigated.

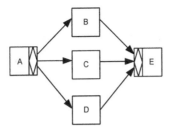

Fig. 4.56. *Inclusive or* split and *inclusive or* join patterns

4.5.3 Execution Semantics

The execution semantics in YAWL is defined by state transition systems. Each YAWL specification has a corresponding state transition system that describes the execution semantics of process instances based on that specification. The rules implemented in this state transition system are of a generic nature, so that they can be applied to any YAWL specification.

The overall idea for expressing the execution semantics is that each task is represented by an individual state transition diagram. A state transition diagram of a task specifies its current state. The state of the process instance is then represented by the combined state of all tasks involved in the process instance plus conditions that are currently met at the process level.

Task Instances

State transition diagrams consist of conditions represented by circles and transitions represented by rectangles. Since multiple instances tasks can take more states than single instance tasks, single instance tasks are investigated first. The state transition diagram for single instance tasks is shown in Figure 4.57. In this section, task instances are investigated before state transition diagrams at the process level are investigated. To stay in line with terminology in YAWL, this section uses the term task instance, which describes the same concept as the term activity instance we have used so far.

The following conditions are available for a task instance:

- *enabled*: Task instance is enabled, but not yet executing
- *exec*: Task instance is currently executing
- *completed*: Task instance is completed
- *active*: Task instance is currently active

The execution semantics of a task instance is specified by the state transition diagram shown in Figure 4.57. Despite the fact that transitions do not use Petri net transition semantics, it is appropriate to discuss the basic operation of state transition diagrams with Petri net terminology.

When the task instance is entered, a token is put on the active and enabled conditions. An enabled task instance can start. Once the start transition fires,

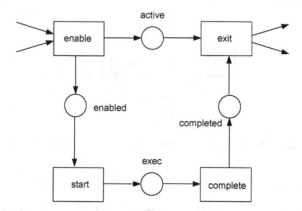

Fig. 4.57. State transition diagram for YAWL tasks with static number of instances

the task instance enters the exec condition. When the task instance completes, it enters the completed condition; finally, the task instance is terminated by firing the exit transition. Note that the active condition and the exit transition are somewhat artificial for single instance tasks; their role will become clear when multiple instances tasks are addressed.

To summarize, the state transitions for a task t have the following semantics. The state transition enable checks the join condition of t; t might be a join node of type *And, Xor,* or *Or,* as specified by $join(t)$. When the enable transition occurs, the input tokens as defined by the join condition are removed from the input conditions of the task.

In case of a single instance task, one token is put in the active condition and one token is put in the enabled condition. When the start transition occurs, one token is removed from the enabled condition and one token is added to the exec condition. The task instance is now executing. The termination of a task instance is represented by the completed transition in the state transition diagram. In this case, one token is removed from the exec condition and one token is added to the completed condition.

The exit transition is specifically relevant for multiple instances tasks, because it fires if the termination condition of a multiple instances task is met. In case there is a cancellation region defined for task t, the exit transition also removes tokens from the cancellation region of the workflow specification, as defined by $rem(t)$. Finally, the exit state transition generates tokens depending on its split behaviour, defined by $split(t)$

The state transition diagram for multiple instances tasks is shown in Figure 4.58. There is an additional state transition, *add*, that spawns new task instances. Arcs drawn in bold indicate that multiple tokens can flow along these arcs.

To discuss the execution semantics of a multiple instances task, the static case is considered first. In this case, all task instances are created up front,

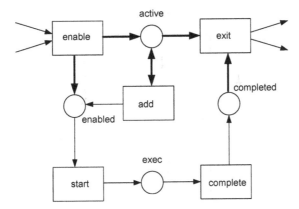

Fig. 4.58. State transition diagram for multiple instances tasks with dynamic creation of new instances

and no task instances can be added while instances of the task run. Consider a multiple instances task with $[4, 6, 4, s]$: four to six task instances are created, and the multiple instances task terminates when the threshold of four instances that have completed is reached.

Consider a process instance in which the enable transition creates five task instances by putting five tokens in the active condition and five tokens in the enabled condition. For each token in the enabled condition, the start transition can fire.

The termination of the overall task (completion of the required task instances) is realized by the exit transition. Exit can fire if the threshold number of tokens are in the completed condition, indicating the completion of a sufficient number of task instances. Assuming four task instances have been completed, the threshold value is reached, and the exit transition removes four tokens from the completed condition and four tokens from the active condition.

However, since five task instances have been started, there is one additional task instance present. This task instance is represented by one token in the active condition and one token in either the enabled or the exec condition. This task instance might also have already entered the completed condition. In the example shown in Figure 4.59, the task instance is still executing.

To implement a proper completion of the task, the exit transition needs to delete all remaining tokens from the state transition system of the task. In this case, two tokens that collectively represent the fifth (and not required) task instance are removed, completing the task and all its task instances, of which four have been performed completely.

In the example discussed, the number of task instances was statically defined, so that the dynamic creation of new task instances was not possible. In the following example, additional task instances can be created at run time. Let $[3, 10, 8, d]$ define the multiple instances property of the task. This means

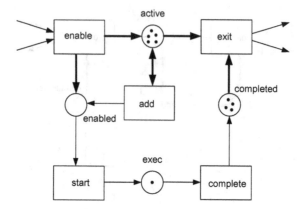

Fig. 4.59. State transition diagram for multiple instances task with five instances, four of which have completed

that there are at least three instances, at most ten instances, and the threshold is eight completed task instances.

Assume that three task instances are started up front. In this case, the enable transition puts three tokens in the active condition and three tokens in the enabled condition. The enabled task instances can start.

The dynamic creation of new task instances is represented by the state transition *add*. As soon as there is one task instance in the active condition, the add transition can fire. When it fires, an additional token is put in the enabled and active conditions, representing the creation of a new task instance at run time. In this way, *add* realizes the dynamic creation of task instances at run time. Using this feature, YAWL directly supports the *multiple instances without a priori run time knowledge* control flow pattern, introduced in Section 4.1.

The other parts of the state transition system remain unchanged, so that the originally created task instances and the dynamically created task instances are handled equivalently: the exit transition can fire if there are a sufficient number of completed task instances available, in this case, eight.

The actual trigger for creating new task instances is not in the scope of the state transition system. It is assumed that the user or a software system spawns new task instances as desired. The state transition system is capable of monitoring the state of a task, including the states of its task instances.

Process Instances

The discussion of state transition diagrams is extended from a localized view of individual tasks to a process view. In order to do this, a number of definitions are required. The first definition extends the compact representation of YAWL nets in a way that it syntactically complies with the workflow net definition:

wherever there is an arc connecting two tasks in a YAWL net, a new condition is added and the arcs are modified accordingly.

Definition 4.11 Let $N = (C, i, o, T, F, split, join, rem, nofi)$ be a YAWL net.

- C_N^{ext} is an *extended condition set*, such that

$$C_N^{ext} = C \cup \{c_{ij} | (t_i, t_j) \in F \cap T \times T\}$$

- $F_N^{ext} \subseteq C_N^{ext} \times T \cup T \times C_N^{ext}$ is an *extended flow relation set*, such that

$$F_N^{ext} = F - T \times T \cup \{(t_i, c_{ij}), (c_{ij}, t_j) | (t_i, t_j) \in F \cap T \times T\}$$

$\diamond$

This definition is illustrated by an example, shown in Figure 4.60, which exhibits a YAWL net

$$W_1 = (C_1, i_1, o_1, T_1, F_1, split, join, rem, nofi),$$

such that $C_1 = \{i_1, o_1\}$, $T_1 = \{A, B, C, D, E, F, G\}$, $split(C) = Xor$, and $join(G) = Xor$. The flow relation F_1 is given by the arrows in Figure 4.60. Observe that task F is a composite task, referencing a YAWL net W_2, with $C_2 = \{i_2, o_2\}$, $T_2 = \{H, I\}$, and $F_2 = \{(i_2, H), (H, I), (I, o_2)\}$. For the time being, the multiple instances tasks are not defined in detail. The respective workflow specification is a tuple $(Q, top, T^\diamond, map)$, such that $Q = \{W_1, W_2\}$, $top = W_1$, $T^\diamond = \{A, \ldots I\}$, and $map(F) = W_2$.

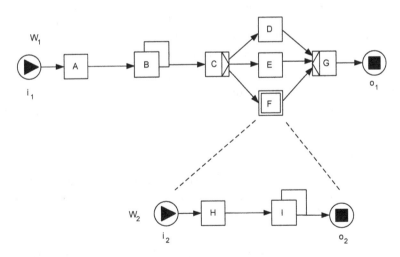

Fig. 4.60. YAWL specification

The extended condition set and the extended flow relation are shown in Figure 4.61. Observe that for each direct connection between tasks in the original YAWL net, one condition and the respective arcs are added: $C_1^{ext} = \{i_1, c_{AB}, c_{BC}, c_{CD}, c_{CE}, c_{CF}, c_{DG}, c_{EG}, c_{FG}, o_1\}$.

The extended flow relation F_1^{ext} is given by the arrows in Figure 4.61. Analogously, the extended condition set and the extended flow relation for W_2 are given by $C_2^{ext} = \{i_2, c_{HI}, o_2\}$ and $F^{ext} = \{(i_2, H), (H, c_{HI}), (c_{HI}, I), (I, o_2)\}$.

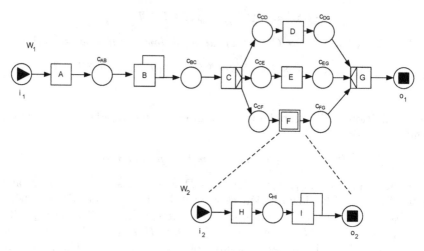

Fig. 4.61. YAWL specification with extended condition set C^{ext}

Since there are multiple process instances for which tasks are being executed, the identity of these cases needs to be taken into account when describing the state of tasks and their task instances. Therefore, the following assumptions concerning process identifiers are made.

- Each process instance has a unique case identifier.
- Each task instance has a unique task instance identifier.
- Identifiers are structured to allow for child/parent relationships. This means that each task instance identifier can be associated with its process instance or case.
- I denotes the set of identifiers.

Based on case identifiers and the state transition system discussed above, a workflow state can be characterized as a bag of tokens, where each token has a condition and a case identifier.

Definition 4.12 Let $S = (Q, top, T^\diamond, map)$ be a YAWL specification, and let $C^\diamond = \bigcup_{N \in Q} C_N^{ext}$ be an extended condition set. A workflow state s of a process instance associated with workflow specification S is a multiset over $Q^\diamond \times I$, where $Q^\diamond$ is the set of conditions of all tasks in the process instance, that is,

$$Q^\diamond = C^\diamond \cup (\bigcup_{T \in T^\diamond} \{exec_t, active_t, enabled_t, completed_t\})$$

$\diamond$

A workflow state is characterized by a state transition diagram. This state transition diagram is composed of state transition diagrams for all its tasks. These individual diagrams are linked to each other by conditions at the process level as specified by the extended condition set.

To illustrate workflow states, consider a process instance based on the workflow specification shown in Figure 4.61. Assume that two instances of task B are currently active, such that one is still executing and one has already completed. The workflow state is sketched in Figure 4.62, zooming into the state transition system for task B.

The enable transition of task B has exactly one incoming arc, which originates from the c_{AB} condition in the extended condition set. Since B is not a join node, enable can fire if there is a token in c_{AB}. Assuming two instances of B are required, two tokens are put in the active state and two tokens are put in the enabled state.

The state transition diagram represents a state, in which one task instance has completed and one task instance is still executing. When the second task instance of B is also completed, the exit transition can fire, terminating task B. A token is put on condition c_{BC}, which is then used to enable task C. Note that each task $A, \ldots, I$ is represented by a state transition diagram linked to the state transition diagram of the process.

Nested Processes

The approach of defining the execution semantics of process instances by state transition diagrams can be extended conveniently to nested processes. Figure 4.63 shows the extended state transition diagrams for composite tasks.

When an instance of a composite task is started, one token is put on the *exec* state, indicating that the task instance is now running. The detailed status of the subprocess is shown in the lower part of Figure 4.63. Starting the task also puts a token in the initial condition of the subprocess, marked by i_{map}.

The ellipsis summarizes the state transition diagram of the subprocess (without the initial and the final condition, of course). When the subprocess terminates, the condition o_{map} is reached, and the complete transition can fire, completing an instance of the subprocess.

The extension of the state transition diagram to composite tasks is orthogonal to multiple instances tasks, so that by adding an *add* transition, multiple instances of composite tasks, and therefore also multiple instances of subprocesses, can be represented properly.

The example discussed above is used to investigate the execution of composite task F realized by the YAWL net W_2, shown in Figure 4.61. A partial

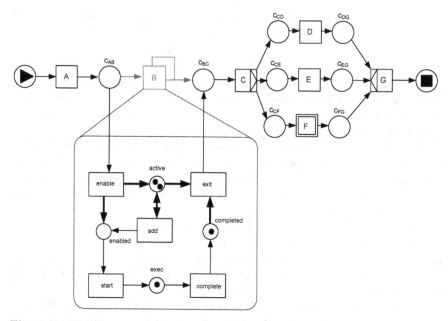

Fig. 4.62. Workflow state with two task instances of B active, one is executing and one has completed

state transition diagram focusing on the state of the composite task is shown in Figure 4.64.

When an instance of the composite task F is executed, a token is put on the exec state of the state transition diagram of that task. In addition, the subprocess needs to be started, represented by a token in the start condition of the YAWL net that F maps to; since $map(F) = W_2$, a token is put on i_2, the start condition of W_2.

The token at i_2 enables the subprocess. The first task to execute is H. The lower part of Figure 4.64 shows the state during the execution of the subprocess where task H is currently executing. When H terminates, a token is put on state c_{HI}, so that the execution of the subprocess can continue with the multiple instances task I. This example shows quite well the recursive application of state transition diagrams for composite tasks.

4.5.4 Advanced Control Flow Patterns

Having discussed how the execution semantics is specified, we can investigate advanced control flow patterns.

Discriminator

The discriminator is a specific type of join node that uses the first signal it receives for triggering the outgoing task. The other signals are ignored. When

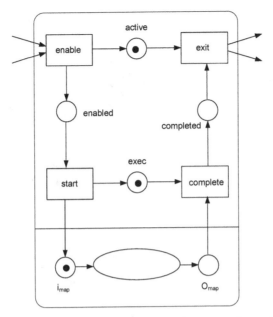

Fig. 4.63. State transition system for composite tasks

signals have been received from all incoming branches, the discriminator resets itself. The authors of Yet Another Workflow Language propose to simulate this behaviour of the *discriminator* pattern by an *exclusive or* join in combination with a cancellation region in the way shown in Figure 4.65.

In this example, assume that tasks B, C, and D are active concurrently, following the *and* split task A. Assuming that B completes first, the *discriminator* fires, and E is triggered. Since E is an *exclusive or* join task, it can be executed. Since a cancellation region is defined for E, E deletes all tokens from the region. In this case, tokens are withdrawn from tasks C and D.

This simulation of the *discriminator* pattern with *exclusive or* join and cancellation region is now evaluated with respect to the semantics of the discriminator. The simulation exhibits significant semantic differences with the specification of the discriminator. First of all, the discriminator does not cancel running activities.

All activities on the incoming branches of the *discriminator* can complete without disturbances; only their termination will be ignored. Secondly, the cancellation of the activities takes place on the termination of the task instance E. So the activities are cancelled not before E starts, but after E terminates. As a result, the proposed representation of the discriminator pattern in YAWL is not completely satisfying.

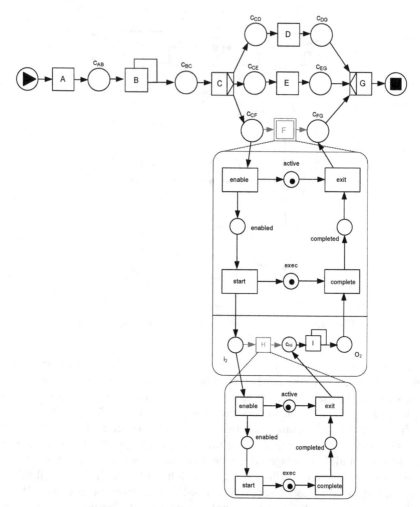

Fig. 4.64. Workflow state, where composite task F is currently active

N-out-of-M Join

The *N-out-of-M join* has M incoming branches, and the follow-up activity is triggered once N branches have completed. This behaviour can in part be expressed in YAWL by multiple instances, as shown in Figure 4.66. The idea is to start M instances and to define a threshold of N instances, so once N instances have completed, the multiple instances task completes.

While multiple instances can be used to represent an *N-out-of-M join* with identical activities, this approach falls short of representing concurrent branches comprised of different activities. Therefore, only a very specific type of *N-out-of-M join* can be realized in YAWL using multiple instances. Hence,

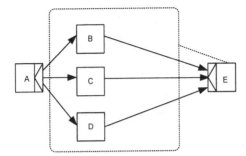

Fig. 4.65. Discriminator in YAWL using cancellation

the *N-out-of-M join* is not completely expressed, since it should be able to synchronize different branches of a process and not only multiple instances of a given task.

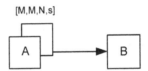

Fig. 4.66. *N-out-of-M join* using multiple instances

Multiple Instances Tasks

Yet Another Workflow Language is tailored towards supporting multiple instances patterns. The *multiple instances without synchronization pattern* is shown in Figure 4.67. In this example, A spawns two concurrent branches, consisting of multiple instances of task B and a single instance of task C.

The multiple instances of task B are not synchronized, which means that B cannot have outgoing edges, because outgoing edges would indicate that the follow-up activity can only be started if the task instances of task B have completed.

The *multiple instances with a priori design time knowledge* is shown in Figure 4.68. In this pattern, the number of instances of task B is known at design time. Therefore, the multiple instances attributes of task B can be set accordingly.

By setting the minimum number of instances and the maximum number of instances to n, where n is the number of required instances of task B, this pattern can be realized. Notice that the threshold is set to infinity (inf), so that no threshold will keep all instances from completing. The control flow edge from B to C indicates that C can only start when all instances of task B have completed.

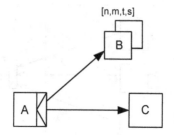

Fig. 4.67. Multiple instances without synchronization

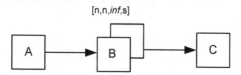

Fig. 4.68. Multiple instances with a priori design time knowledge

If the number of instances is known only at run time, but before the first instance of B starts, a function is required to determine the number of instances of B, as shown in Figure 4.69. This difference with the previous pattern is reflected by using q for the number of instances, where q is determined at run time of the process instance, but before the start of multiple instances task B. For example, the number of line items in an order can be determined at run time. In the example, q reflects this number, so that exactly q instances of task B are performed.

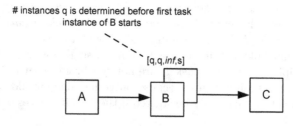

Fig. 4.69. Multiple instances with a priori run time knowledge

Figure 4.70 shows multiple instances without a priori run time knowledge. In this pattern, the number of instances of B becomes available only while instances of task B run. This means that new instances of B can be created dynamically. This behaviour of the multiple instances task in YAWL is described by the fourth parameter d. We still might define a minimum, a maximum, and a threshold value. But these can also be set to *inf*, providing maximum flexibility of a multiple instances task.

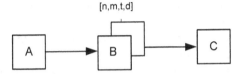

Fig. 4.70. Multiple instances without a priori run time knowledge

4.5.5 Discussion

Yet Another Workflow Language has a number of advantages, but also some drawbacks. The graphical representation of process models is closely related to workflow nets, so that people familiar with workflow nets can use YAWL immediately.

The execution semantics of YAWL is well-specified by state transition systems. The representation of executing tasks by state transition systems combines state transition diagrams—to describe the dynamic behaviour of process activities, as shown in Figure 3.9—with Petri net markings.

One of the conceptual issues when representing business process activities by Petri nets is the timeliness of the transition firing. Business process activities take time, they have a start, they are active for a time interval, before they complete. In contrast to Petri nets, the durations of process activities are well captured by state transition systems in YAWL. At the same time, process instances are represented by tokens, similar to markings in Petri nets.

YAWL has excellent support for multiple instances patterns. The specification of multiple instances actually goes one step ahead of the control flow patterns in that it allows us to define a threshold of completed task instances. The construct to model multiple instances tasks in YAWL is very useful and has many applications in real-world business processes.

The semantics of multiple instances tasks is handled very well by state transition systems in YAWL. The *add* transition allows the dynamic creation of new task instances while task instances are active; the *exit* transition can realize the threshold semantics by cancelling all remaining task instances when the threshold number of completed instances has been reached.

The state transition systems also capture in a very elegant way composite tasks. By recursively applying the concept, subprocesses can easily be attached to composite tasks. The multiple-instances property is orthogonal to tasks being composite, so that any composite task can at the same time have multiple instances.

The remove function *rem* associated to tasks allows us defining regions of the workflow specification from where to withdraw tokens when the task completes. Conceptually it is rather simple to "remove tokens" from process instances to cancel tasks. It becomes much harder, however, when we look at the concrete realization of these tasks.

In real-world business processes, many tasks are realized by software systems. Removing a token from a task means to cancel the invocation of the system. If the software system has transactional capabilities then the transaction can be aborted, rolling back the software system to a consistent state. Not all software systems used in business processes are, however, are transactional. In this case, the software might have already performed its work partially at the time, the token is removed. In such situations, it is unclear, how the business process management system should behave. In many cases, human involvement is required to solve the resulting problems manually.

We have already discussed in some detail the weaknesses of YAWL in representing some advanced control flow patterns, including the discriminator and the M-out-of-N join. Despite these drawbacks, YAWL is a well-designed process modelling language that also comes with prototypical implementations for modelling and enactment.

For further information about the fundamentals of YAWL and the YAWL system, the reader is referred to ter Hofstede et al. (2010), a comprehensive book that explains the complete conceptual basis of YAWL. This also includes the handling of data. For each YAWL net, a data passing model specifies the data flow dependencies between its tasks. Resources are defined in an organizational model, featuring hierarchical decomposition. The distribution of work is defined in a worklist distribution model, which uses the organizational model. Hence, not only the execution semantics is defined on a conceptual level, but also other aspect that are important for designing and implementing a workflow management system.

4.6 Graph-Based Workflow Language

In this section, a graph-based workflow language is introduced. This language was developed in the context of a commercial workflow management system. It exhibits a series of interesting concepts that are not addressed by the other process languages discussed in this chapter, including the explicit representation of data dependencies between activities and dead path elimination as a technique to describe the execution semantics of business processes.

4.6.1 Process Metamodel

To illustrate this modelling language, an example of a credit request process is shown in Figure 4.71. The activities are shown as nodes of the graph, control flow is represented by solid arcs, and dotted arrows indicate data flow. Data flow, for instance, between activities *Collect CreditInfo* and *Assess Risk* indicates that *Assess Risk* requires data that has been created or modified by *Collect CreditInfo*.

The process starts with collecting credit information, followed by an assessment of the credit risk. Then, either the credit is accepted or a request

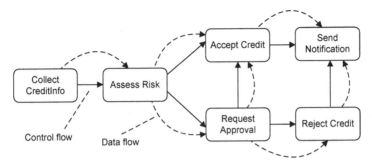

Fig. 4.71. Credit request process model, expressed in graph-based workflow language

approval activity is started. The request approval activity determines the final decision on the credit request; it either approves the credit or rejects it. In any case, the requestor is informed by a notification message.

Data is covered by parameters of activities; each parameter has an associated data type. Each activity has a set of input parameters and a set of output parameters (might be empty). Whenever the output parameter of one activity is used as an input parameter of another activity, a data flow occurs. Transitive data flow is often not shown in process models.

Each control flow edge has an associated condition. This condition is evaluated after the activity from which the control flow originates has terminated. If the condition is evaluated to true, the edge is signalled, and the follow-up activity can be started.

The execution semantics of process graphs is based on the signalling of edges. There are two ways of signalling: true signalling and false signalling. When an activity terminates, the conditions of its outgoing edges are evaluated. For each edge that evaluates to true, the follow-up activity is signalled true. For each edge that evaluates to false, the edge is signalled false.

When all incoming edges of an activity are signalled—that is, each edge is signalled true or false—the start condition of that activity is evaluated. The start condition realizes the join behaviour of that node. If the start condition of an activity evaluates to true, the activity enters the enabled state. If it evaluates to false, the activity is not enabled. In this case, the activity is skipped and all its outgoing edges are signalled false.

By using true and false signalling, the *or* join problem is solved, because each incoming edge will be signalled eventually. This technique is called *dead path elimination*, because paths not taken in the execution of a process are marked with the false signal; they are therefore somehow eliminated. Unfortunately, dead path elimination only works in the absence of loops in process models, but the iteration of activities guided by an exit condition is supported.

Each activity is associated with a start condition. As indicated above, this start condition is evaluated if all incoming control flow edges have been

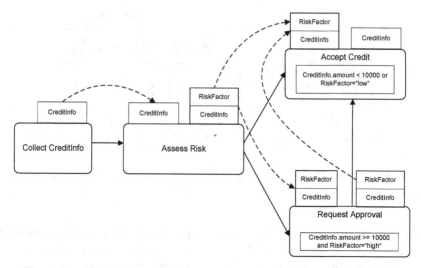

Fig. 4.72. Detailed view on parameters and conditions (partial process)

signalled (either true or false). The start condition uses this information as well as input parameters received from previous activities to decide on the state transition. If the start condition is evaluated to true, then the activity is enabled. If it is evaluated to false, the activity is skipped and false signals are sent to each of its outgoing edges, regardless of the conditions attached to these edges.

To illustrate these concepts, Figure 4.72 shows a refined version of the process model shown above, which includes parameters, start conditions, and data flow between process activities.

The *Collect CreditInfo* activity is responsible for providing information about the credit, including customer information and the amount requested. This information is stored in the output parameter *CreditInfo* of the *Collect CreditInfo* activity. The *Assess Risk* activity takes the credit information as input parameter and assesses the risk of granting the credit. The result of this activity is stored in an output parameter *RiskFactor* that is made available to the follow-up activities *Accept Credit* and *Request Approval*.

The use of start conditions can be illustrated in this example: the *Request Approval* activity can be started if the credit amount is at least 10,000 Euros and the risk factor is high. This start condition takes as input the risk factor and the credit amount, both of which are provided to the *Request Approval* activity by the output parameters of the *Assess Risk* activity.

The start condition of the *AcceptCredit* activity makes sure that it can only be started if the credit amount is below 10,000 Euros or the risk factor is low. The credit can also be accepted if the credit was approved by the *Request Approval* activity. This information is made available to the *Accept Credit* activity by the output parameter *RiskFactor* of *Request Approval*.

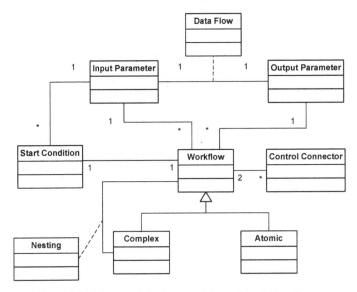

Fig. 4.73. Metamodel of a graph-based workflow language

Depending on the particular implementation used to enact this process, either data can be transferred between activities by the business process management system, or references to data objects can be subject to data flow, so that the system is not burdened with large amounts of data if complex data needs to be transferred between process activities.

To organize these concepts, a workflow metamodel is shown in Figure 4.73.

The workflow class is the central class in the metamodel; it contains workflow objects that can be either atomic or complex, and atomic workflows can be executed either automatically or manually. This property of workflows is reflected in the metamodel by complex and atomic as subclasses of the workflow class. The workflow hierarchy is represented by the nesting class, an association class that defines the relationship between a complex workflow and a workflow, which can be complex or atomic. Atomic workflows are also called activities.

The process model shown in Figure 4.72 can be represented properly in this metamodel: there are atomic workflows, *Collect CreditInfo*, *Assess Risk*, *Request Approval*, and *Accept Credit*, that are linked by control connectors, as shown in the figure. Each control connector is associated with exactly two workflows. Note that atomic workflows are also workflows, due to the generalization relationship between the respective classes.

Each atomic workflow is associated with a set of input parameters and a set of output parameters. These sets might be empty, as is the input parameter set of the *Collect CreditInfo* activity. Input and output parameters can be involved in a data flow. Each data flow connects an output parameter to an input parameter. The data types of parameters connected by data flow need to be compatible.

Observe that each parameter can be involved in multiple data flows. The start condition of a workflow is used to evaluate at run time if the workflow has to be executed. Information passed by data flow can be used for this evaluation.

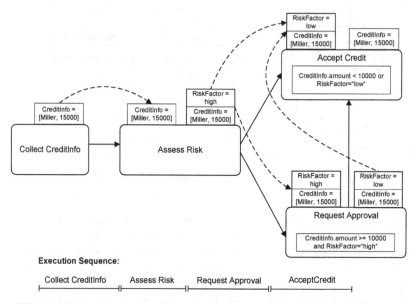

Fig. 4.74. Process instance based on process model shown in Figure 4.72

4.6.2 Process Instances

The enactment of workflows based on these specifications is addressed using the process instance shown in Figure 4.74. Dead path elimination is used to describe the execution semantics of process instances that are represented in graph-based languages.

The *Accept Credit* activity can only be enabled after request approval has signalled its outgoing edge. If *Request Approval* is executed, then the signalling is true; otherwise, the edge is signalled false. Therefore, after the *Assess Risk* activity has provided a high risk factor as output value, *Accept Credit* cannot be started, at least not immediately after *Assess Risk* terminates.

Since in the particular process instance, the risk is assessed to be high, the request approval activity needs to be executed, and the start condition of the *Request Approval* activity is evaluated to true. This activity is started and approves the credit request; this approval is represented by changing the value of the risk factor from *high* to *low*. When the edge to the *Accept Credit* activity is signalled, the start condition of that activity is evaluated to true, and the credit is granted.

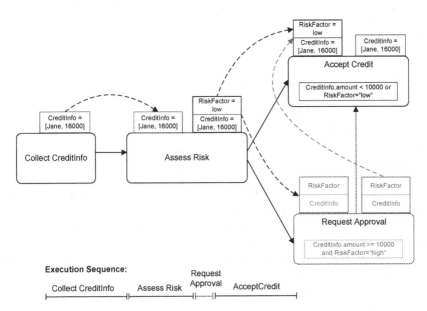

Fig. 4.75. Process instance where request approval activity is not required

A second process instance is shown in Figure 4.75. In the case shown, Jane requests a credit amount of 16000 Euros. *Assess Risk* determines a low risk factor, so *Request Approval* is not required. In this case, the edge from *Assess Risk* to *Request Approval* is signalled, but the start condition of *Request Approval* is evaluated to false, since this activity is not required.

Request Approval then relays a false signal to its outgoing edge, in this case, to the *Accept Credit* activity. Now all incoming edges of the *Accept Credit* activity have been signalled, so that the start condition can be evaluated. Since the risk factor is low, the start condition is evaluated to true, so that the credit can be granted.

4.6.3 Discussion

Graph-based workflow languages are useful for implementing business processes, in which process activities are realized by software systems. Just as procedures realized by software systems read input parameters on their start and write output parameters on their termination, so do process activities in graph-based workflow languages.

Data flow can be expressed well by relating output parameters of process activities to input parameters of follow-up activities. Since control flow is defined by edges between activities and start conditions of activities, basic control flow patterns, such as sequence, splits, and joins can be expressed.

Graph-based workflow languages do not support arbitrary cycles, because in cyclic process models, dead path elimination causes problems. Advanced control flow patterns, such as multiple instances patterns or discriminator pattern, are also not supported by graph-based workflow languages.

4.7 Business Process Model and Notation

This section introduces the *Business Process Model and Notation (BPMN)*, developed under the coordination of the Object Management Group. Version 2 of this international standard introduces a series of modifications, including a new extension of the acronym. BPMN used to stand for *Business Process Modeling Notation*. In Version 2, the standard also defines a meta-model, so that *Business Process Meta Model and Notation* would have been a valid choice. Unfortunately, the term *meta* was dropped, resulting in the rather imprecise official extension we now see in this section's heading. In the remainder of this book, we will mostly use the acronym.

The intent of the BPMN for business process modelling is very similar to the intent of the Unified Modeling Language for object-oriented design and analysis. To identify the best practices of existing approaches and to combine them into a new, widely accepted language. The set of ancestors of BPMN includes graph-based and Petri-net-based process modelling languages, such as UML activity diagrams and event-driven process chains.

While these modelling languages focus on different levels of abstraction, ranging from a business level to a more technical level, the BPMN aims at supporting the complete range of abstraction levels, from a business level to a technical implementation level. This goal is also laid out in the standards document, which states that "The primary goal of BPMN is to provide a notation that is readily understandable by all business users, from the business analysts that create the initial drafts of the processes, to the technical developers responsible for implementing the technology that will perform those processes, and finally, to the business people who will manage and monitor those processes. Thus, BPMN creates a standardized bridge for the gap between the business process design and process implementation."

The BPMN defines several diagram types for specifying both process orchestrations and process choreographies. Since this chapter focuses on orchestrations, only business process diagrams and collaboration diagrams are discussed in this section. Diagram types regarding process choreographies, that is, choreography diagrams, will be discussed in the next chapter.

To classify the level of support that a particular BPMN software tool provides, the standard introduces so-called conformance classes.

- *Process Modelling Conformance*: The process modelling conformance class includes the BPMN core elements, process diagrams, collaboration diagrams and conversation diagrams. Subclasses are defined that contain a limited set of visual modelling elements (*Descriptive* subclass), an extended set of modelling elements (*Analytical* subclass) and modelling elements that are required to represent executable processes (*Common Executable* subclass), respectively.
- *Process Execution Conformance*: The process execution conformance class requires a software tool to support the operational semantics of BPMN. If, in addition, the mapping from BPMN to WS-BPEL as defined in the standard is implemented, the tool satisfies *WS-BPEL Process Execution Conformance*. WS-BPEL and the mapping from BPMN to this XML language is addressed in Chapter 8.
- *Choreography Modelling Conformance*: The choreography modelling conformance class includes the BPMN core elements, collaboration and choreography diagrams. Choreography modelling will be discussed in Chapter 6.

4.7.1 Principles

The BPMN standard defines a notation and a meta model that organizes the concepts used in the notation. While much more complex, the BPMN meta model is similar to the meta model discussed in Section 3.5. To avoid redundancy and to provide a solid basis, the standard is organized in layers.

The BPMN Core Structure is the foundation of the standard, which defines generic concepts like BaseElement, which is the abstract super class for most BPMN elements. These concepts are refined subsequently in packages related to processes, choreographies, collaborations, and conversations. The reader interested in the BPMN meta model is referred to the BPMN standard, referenced in the bibliographical notes at the end of this chapter. This text concentrates on the language constructs and their execution semantics rather than on the organization of the standard.

The basic BPMN modelling elements allow expressing simple structures in business processes, while expressive power is added by the complete element set. The basic elements are easy to comprehend, so that process designers and practitioners can use the language without extensive training. When process designers become familiar with the language, more elaborate language elements can be added.

The graphical notation of a business process is complemented with a set of attributes. These attributes can be associated with the complete process diagram and with particular elements. Some attribute values have implications on the visual appearance of the symbols used in process diagrams. For instance, whenever a gateway activates a single outgoing edge from a set of outgoing edges, the gateway is marked with the X symbol to indicate its *exclusive or* split semantics.

The BPMN has the flavour of a framework rather than of a concrete language, because some aspects, for instance, expressions, are not covered by the standard, and left to the process designer. Expressions are used, for example, to decide which branch to follow in the case of an *exclusive or* split. During business process modelling projects, the persons responsible can use a language of their choice. However, within one business process diagram, only one expression language can be used.

In case a high-level business process is modelled, informal textual expressions might be useful. An example would be "if the credit amount exceeds 5000 Euros, then the monthly income of the client needs to be checked". In this case, the language to formulate expressions would be plain English text. If business processes need to be represented at a technical implementation level, formal languages with an operational semantics, such as programming languages, are required.

Organizational aspects are represented in the BPMN by pools and swimlanes, similar to those in UML activity diagrams. There is a hierarchy of swimlanes within a given pool: lanes, and arbitrarily nested sub-lanes. Lanes represent organizational entities such as departments in organizations. Sublanes can be used to define organizational entities within departments. Nesting of arbitrary depth is permitted, but process diagrams might get cluttered in case of extensive nesting. By drawing flow objects in swimlanes, the organizational entity responsible for performing the specific objects can be represented graphically.

Each pool may specify a concrete organization, but it may also represent a placeholder for a specific organization, that is, a role. Examples of roles in a supply chain scenario are "supplier", "manufacturer", and "customer". When it comes to enacting business processes, concrete organizations are bound to these roles, so that one concrete supplier interacts with a specific manufacturer, which interacts with a specific set of customers.

Each process resides in a single pool. As a consequence, each process is performed by a single organization. Business processes can interact with business processes enacted by other organizations in order to realize business-to-business scenarios. These assumptions of the BPMN regarding pools and the scope of business processes are in line with Definition 1.1.

4.7.2 Business Process Diagrams

The notational elements in business process diagrams are divided into four basic categories, each of which consists of a set of elements, shown in Figure 4.76.

Flow objects are the building blocks of business processes; they include events, activities, and gateways. The occurrence of states in the real world that are relevant for business processes and, more generally, anything relevant that happens, can be represented by events. Activities represent units of work performed during business processes. Gateways are used to represent the split and join behaviour of the flow of control between activities, events, and gateways.

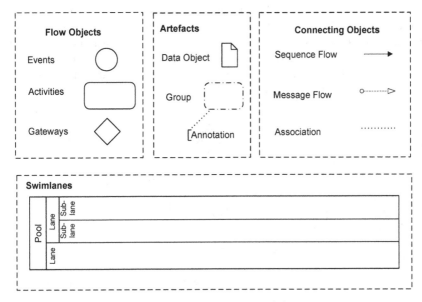

Fig. 4.76. BPMN: categories of elements

Artefacts are used to show additional information about a business process that is "not directly relevant for sequence flow or message flow of the process", as the standard mentions. Data objects, groups, and annotations are supported artefacts. Each artefact can be associated with flow elements. Artefacts serve only information purposes, so that the execution semantics of a process is not influenced by them.

Data objects are represented simply by a name; the internal structure of data objects cannot be defined in BPMN. The main purpose of data object artefacts is documentation of the data used in the process. By directed association edges, the modeller can represent the fact that a data object is read or written by a process activity. Paper documents, electronic information, as well as physical artefacts, like shipped products, can be represented by data objects.

Text annotations document specific aspects of the business process in textual form. The text is graphically associated with the object in the business process diagram that the text explains. Group objects are artefacts that are used to group elements of a process. Groups do not have a formal meaning; they just serve documentation purposes. Groups may span lanes and even pools.

Connecting objects connect flow objects, swimlanes, or artefacts. Sequence flow is used to specify the ordering of flow objects, while message flow describes the flow of messages between business partners represented by pools. Association is a specific type of connecting object that is used to link artefacts to elements in business process diagrams.

Figure 4.77 shows a BPMN business process diagram, representing an ordering process. The example introduces the main elements of the language: events, activities, gateways, and sequence flow. The process model starts with an event. A sequence of activities to analyze the order and to check the stock are performed, before an *exclusive or* split is done. The latter is represented by a gateway with the respective marker.

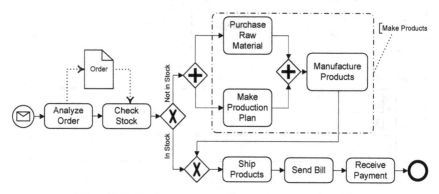

Fig. 4.77. Business process diagram expressed in BPMN

If the ordered products are in stock, then the lower branch is selected. Otherwise the product has to be manufactured first, so that the upper branch needs to be chosen. The expression language used in this process diagram is plain English text (*In stock*, *Not in Stock*), so that humans can easily understand the conditions. The manufacturing part of the process can be seen as a detour, since both branches converge in the exclusive join gateway before the products are shipped, the bill is sent, and the payment is received.

This process diagram also contains events that mark the start and end of the process. The start event is marked with an envelope symbol, indicating that the process starts on receiving a message. There are many different event types and markers for events, the most widely used of which will be discussed shortly.

Data in processes plays an increasingly important role. The example represents the order processed as a data object. Data objects can be associated with flow elements, indicating a relationship. In the example shown in Figure 4.77, there is a data object *Order*, which is associated to activities *Analyze Order* and *Check Stock*. The orientation of the association edge indicates the type of relationship. In our process diagram, *Analyze Order* writes the data object, while *Check Stock* reads it.

Grouping of activities using the group artefact can increase the understanding of the process model by humans. This is exemplified by a group annotated by *Make Products*. In this example it is rather obvious that the three activities are responsible for making the product in case the ordered products are not in stock. However, in larger process models grouping is a convenient way of expressing additional information for humans that can not conveniently be provided by the more formal modelling elements of the BPMN.

The roles involved in this process have not been represented in the process diagram. If the roles are important for the modelling purpose, for example, if responsibilities in the organization have to be defined or hand-overs between departments need to be investigated, roles must be represented in process diagrams. Figure 4.78 shows a process diagram of the ordering process introduced above, enriched with role information.

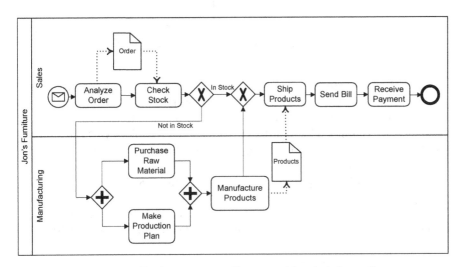

Fig. 4.78. Business process diagram with role information

There are two departments of the company modelled, *Manufacturing* and *Sales*. Receiving and analyzing the order as well as checking the stock and deciding about manufacturing the products is also decided by the sales department. Obviously, producing the ordered items is performed by the manufacturing department. Since hand-over between organizational entities is important, the model also contains a data object *Product*. This illustrates that also physical products can be represented by data objects in BPMN. In this case, the write edge from *Manufacture Products* to *Products* can be interpreted as the production of the physical goods. The read edge from *Products* to *Ship Products* refers to the use of the physical products during the shipment activity.

Activities

Activities are units of work. They are the major ingredients of business processes. The BPMN provides powerful means for expressing different types of activities. Figure 4.79 shows the activity types that the BPMN supports.

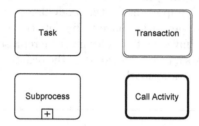

Fig. 4.79. Activity types in the BPMN

Activities characterize units of work. Activities which are not further refined are called atomic activities or tasks. Activities might also have an internal structure, in which case they are called subprocesses. Rather than showing the structure, the modeller can decide to hide the complexity of the subprocess, using the plus symbol. But subprocesses can also be expanded, exposing their internal structure.

An example of a subprocess is shown in Figure 4.80. In that figure, the collapsed subprocess is marked with the subprocess marker, and the expanded subprocess exhibits its internal process structure. The link between the representations is established by the unique identifier *Evaluate Credit Risk*.

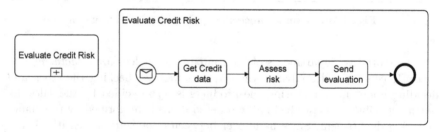

Fig. 4.80. Collapsed and expanded subprocess

Call activities can be used to refer to globally defined process diagrams, or tasks, facilitating reuse of activities. An example of a call activity involving a globally defined process diagram is shown in Figure 4.81. In the upper part of that figure, a simple process containing a sequence of activities is shown. The first activity is an embedded subprocess with activities to set up a project team and to create a marketing campaign. After these activities have been completed, the embedded subprocess terminates. Then the *Update Web Site* activity is performed.

This call activity references the global process diagram shown in the lower part of that figure, reusing it. This design allows to define certain processes or tasks once to be used several times. In the example, each update of the web site could be realized by a call activity, reducing maintenance effort in large process repositories.

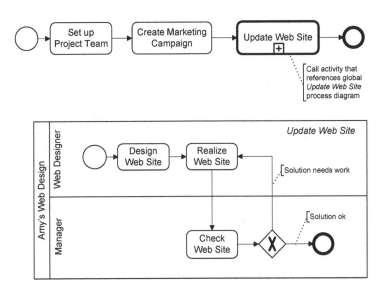

Fig. 4.81. Process diagram with a call activity that references a global process diagram; the reference is maintained in the respective attribute of the call activity

Activities can be marked with symbols that refine their execution semantics; activity markers are shown in Figure 4.82. We have already used the subprocess marker. Notice that transactions will be discussed later in this section after the required events have been introduced.

The loop marker is used to indicate that an activity is iterated during process execution. If the activity has the LoopCharacteristics attribute set, with attribute class StandardLoopCharacteristics, then the activity represents a *while* loop or a *repeat-until* loop. Whether the loop activity realizes a *while* loop or a *repeat-until* loop is guided by the testTime attribute. Setting it to Before realizes a *while* loop, while setting it to After realizes a *repeat-until* loop. The different types of loops can not be distinguished by the visual appearances of the respective loop activities in process models.

Multiple instances tasks have the LoopCharacteristics attribute set, with attribute class MultiInstanceLoopCharacteristics. The multiple instances of an activity can be executed sequentially or in parallel. The number

Fig. 4.82. Activity markers refine the behaviour of activities

of instances is either specified by an expression that returns an integer value or by the cardinality of a list data object, discussed below.

The markers for sequential and parallel multiple instances activities are shown Figure 4.82. A *for* loop with n iterations can be realized by a sequential multiple instances activity, whose expression evaluates to n.

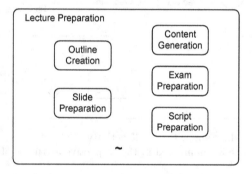

Fig. 4.83. Sample adhoc process

A subprocess that is marked with an adhoc marker consists of a set of tasks that are not related to each other by sequence flow. The execution of tasks of the adhoc subprocess is not restricted. Each activity can be executed an arbitrary number of times. This means that adhoc activities are not embedded in sequence flow; they can be invoked without a specific trigger or event.

An adhoc subprocess is marked with a tilde symbol at the bottom of the rounded rectangle. Adhoc activities are very useful for unstructured parts of processes. Using `AdHocOrdering`, the modeller can define whether the activities in an adhoc subprocess can be executed in parallel or whether they are executed sequentially. An adhoc subprocess completes, if its `CompletionCondition` evaluates to true. An example of an adhoc subprocess that represents the preparation of a lecture is shown in Figure 4.83.

Send Task

Receive Task

User Task

Manual Task

Business Rule Task

Service Task

Script Task

Fig. 4.84. Task types specify the kind of task that is represented

In BPMN, tasks can be decorated with task types which makes it easier for human readers to understand the specific type the task represents. Figure 4.84 lists the task types of the BPMN.

User tasks represent traditional workflow tasks that involve user interaction. When the process comes to a point where a specific task is to be performed by a user, the user is informed, for instance, by the appearance of a new work item in his or her inbox.

When selecting the work item, an application is started that the user works with in order to perform the task. To facilitate role resolution, role and skill information are typically associated with a user task. Integration with organizational modelling is required to facilitate role resolution, because the BPMN does not support the modelling of detailed organizational aspects.

Manual tasks are performed without the support of software systems. Sending a printed letter or transferring goods in a logistics environment are examples of manual activities. While the actual execution of these activities is outside the scope of an information system, the business process management system needs to be informed about the completion of a manual activity.

The completion information typically includes a return code, so that the system is aware of a successful or unsuccessful completion of the manual task. This information can be important for the remaining parts of the business process, so that in the case of unsuccessful completion, the business process can take compensating actions for the failed manual activity.

Business rules are logical rules to be interpreted by a rules engine. In BPMN we can model a task that triggers a business rule by marking it with a business rule marker and adding the appropriate information. When the *business rule task* task is executed, the business rule is invoked. The actual representation of business rules and their enactment using rules engines is not in the scope of the BPMN.

A *service task* is implemented by a piece of software, either using a Web services interface or an application programming interface to a software system. A *script task* is a task that uses some scripting language expression in order to be performed. Script tasks are used to represent simple functionality, for which no dedicated software system is required. The particular scripting language used and the interaction platform for script expressions depend on the tool support available. When the script completes execution, the script task completes.

There are also task types related to sending and receiving messages. Since these task types rely on events, we will introduce events first and return to send and receive tasks only when we have done so.

A *compensation task* is invoked to compensate for activities that need to be undone. The compensation concept is strongly connected to transactions, which will be discussed in the context of compensation events in the next section.

Events

Events play a central role in business process management, since they are the glue between situations in the real world and processes that will react to these events or trigger them. Events in a business process can be partitioned into three types, based on their position in the business process: start events are used to trigger processes, intermediate events can delay processes or they can be triggered during process executions. End events signal the termination of processes. There are obvious connection rules associated with these events. Start events have no incoming edges, end events have no outgoing edges, and intermediate events have both an incoming and an outgoing edge.

This book covers the most common event types, shown in Figure 4.85. The rows contain the event types, the columns the position (start, intermediate, end) and the nature of the event, discussed shortly. There are also intermediate events that are attached to boundaries of activities rather than having an incoming sequence flow.

The simplest type of event is the blanco event that has no marker. (The standard calls this event *none event*. Since blanco events are in fact events, we stick to the former terminology and use the term *blanco event*.) This event type is used whenever the cause of the event is either not known or is irrelevant for the current modelling purpose. Blanco events can be used as start events or as end events.

Events play two major roles, and each event in a process model plays exactly one of those. These roles are referred to by *catching* and *throwing*. An event is of catching nature, if the process listens and waits for the event to happen. Whenever the respective event happens, the process catches it and reacts accordingly. All start events are catching events.

An event is of throwing nature, if it is actively triggered by the process during process execution. Sending a message to a business partner is an example of a throwing event. All end events are throwing events, because the end event is actively triggered by the process.

Intermediate events can be either catching or throwing. A good example is the intermediate message event, which comes in two flavors. As throwing

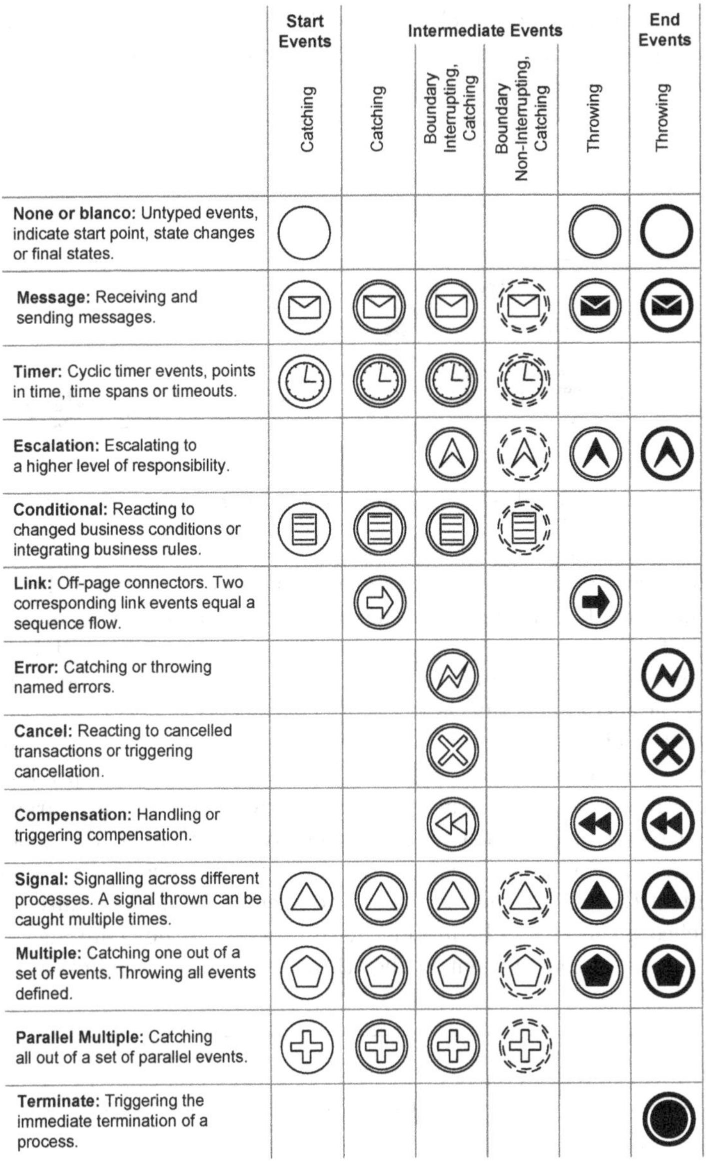

	Start Events	Intermediate Events					End Events
	Catching	Catching	Boundary Interrupting, Catching	Boundary Non-Interrupting, Catching	Throwing		Throwing
None or blanco: Untyped events, indicate start point, state changes or final states.	◯					◯	◯
Message: Receiving and sending messages.	◉	◉	◉	◉	◉		◉
Timer: Cyclic timer events, points in time, time spans or timeouts.	◷	◷	◷	◷			
Escalation: Escalating to a higher level of responsibility.		◭	◭	◭	◭		◭
Conditional: Reacting to changed business conditions or integrating business rules.	▤	▤	▤	▤			
Link: Off-page connectors. Two corresponding link events equal a sequence flow.		⮕			⮕		
Error: Catching or throwing named errors.		◎					◉
Cancel: Reacting to cancelled transactions or triggering cancellation.		⊗					⊗
Compensation: Handling or triggering compensation.		◁◁			◀◀		◀◀
Signal: Signalling across different processes. A signal thrown can be caught multiple times.	△	△	△	△	▲		▲
Multiple: Catching one out of a set of events. Throwing all events defined.	⬠	⬠	⬠	⬠	⬟		⬟
Parallel Multiple: Catching all out of a set of parallel events.	⊕	⊕	⊕	⊕			
Terminate: Triggering the immediate termination of a process.							⬤

Fig. 4.85. Common event types in the BPMN, adapted from the BPMN Poster, BPM Offensive Berlin (2011)

event, the intermediate message event sends a message to a business partner. As catching event, the process waits for a message to come in, that is, it waits for the event to happen.

This example shows quite clearly the difference. Catching events wait for things to happen , while throwing events actively trigger events.

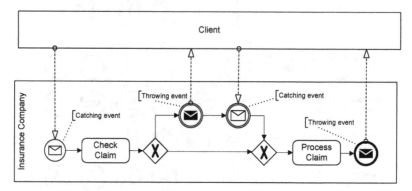

Fig. 4.86. Throwing and catching events

Throwing and catching events are further illustrated in Figure 4.86, which shows a claim handling process of an insurance company involving interactions with a client. The process starts with the start message event "catching" the claim message. (More precisely, with the start event catching the event that represents the incoming claim message.)

In case the claim is incomplete, the insurance company sends a request for clarification to the client. This sending of a message is represented by a throwing intermediate message event. The event symbol is marked with a black envelope to show this throwing behaviour, that is, the sending of the message. At this point, the process waits for the event that represents the receipt of the answer message from the client. The intermediate message event catches this event and continues with processing the claim and sending the response letter to the client in the (throwing) message end event.

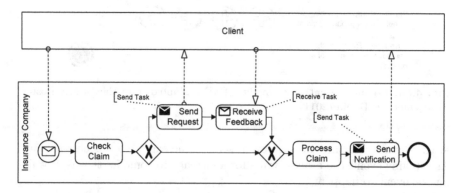

Fig. 4.87. Using markers to identify send tasks and receive tasks

Task types, introduced above, also provide options of expressing certain real-world situations, for instance, related to sending and receiving messages. Instead of send events, we can also use send tasks, that is, tasks that are marked with task type send. Like with sending and receiving events, a dark envelope represents send tasks, while the light envelope shows that a task receives a message. Figure 4.87 shows a process diagram using send and receive tasks. BPMN also supports a specific type of receive task that can be used to instantiate a process, but a receive event is much more appropriate in most cases.

Returning to blanco events, blanco start events are of catching nature, while blanco end events are of throwing nature. Since there is no way of marking blanco intermediate events as either catching or throwing events, by convention, all blanco intermediate events are—by definition—of throwing nature.

Message events are among the most often used events in BPMN. We have already seen in Figure 4.86 message start events, message end events, and intermediate message events of catching and throwing nature. We now look at intermediate events on the boundary of activities, called boundary intermediate events, or attached intermediate events.

Each intermediate event of this kind is associated with an event context, used to determine whether the event has occurred. In particular, the intermediate event will be triggered only, if the activity that the intermediate event is attached to is still active when the event occurs.

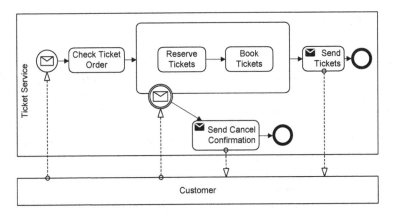

Fig. 4.88. Process diagram with interrupting boundary event

An example of a process model containing a boundary event is given in Figure 4.88. The process starts by a customer sending a ticket order to a ticket service. After receiving the message and checking the order, a subprocess is entered. In the subprocess, the tickets are reserved and finally booked. Notice that processes and subprocesses do not require start and end events. While it is good practice to use start and end events on the process level, they might be dropped for simple subprocesses. The boundary event represents the option of the customer to cancel the order.

If the cancellation message is received while the subprocess is still active, the subprocess is cancelled, and the confirmation of the cancellation is sent. If no cancellation message is received while the subprocess runs, the subprocess completes and the tickets are sent.

In this example we have discussed a boundary event that interrupts the subprocess it is attached to. But boundary events might also be of non-interrupting nature.

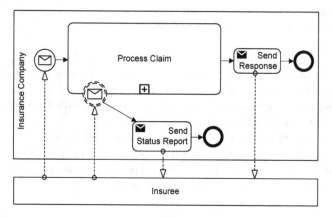

Fig. 4.89. Process diagram with non-interrupting boundary event

An example of a non-interrupting boundary event is shown in Figure 4.89. In this process, an insuree sends a claim report to an insurance company. The complex processing of the claim is hidden in the subprocess *Process Claim*. While this subprocess is active, the insuree can ask, even multiple times, for the current status of the claim handling. The respective incoming message is caught by the boundary event, and a status report is sent. Since the processing of the claim should not be interrupted by this request, the boundary event is non-interrupting, indicated by its dashed outline.

Timer events are used frequently in process diagrams. They are quite versatile, since they can represent time intervals, points in time, and timers, similar to count down watches.

Figure 4.90 shows a process diagram involving several types of timer events. The process starts with a start timer event. By the annotation we learn that the process is instantiated every first Monday in October. When this event is caught, a strategy meeting is announced. Then the process pauses for 14 days, represented by the intermediate timer event.

The execution semantics of intermediate timer events is as follows. When the previous activity is completed, the timer is started. This is like starting a

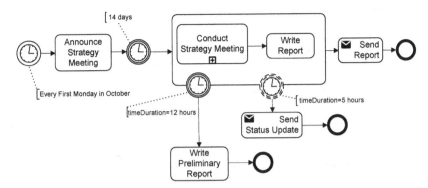

Fig. 4.90. Process diagram with interrupting and non-interrupting boundary timer events

count down watch with the value set to 14 days in this case. In Figure 4.90, we used an annotation to show the time period.

In BPMN, timer events have attributes that are used to represent timer values in a structured fashion. In particular, the attribute `timeDuration` holds an expression that defines the time duration the timer waits for. Attributes `timeDate` and `timeCycle` are used to specify points in time and recurring timers, respectively.

After the duration has elapsed, the subprocess and thereby the strategy meeting can be started. When this happens, two additional timers are started for the boundary events. Timer 1 with duration 12 hours for the interrupting timer event and Timer 2 with duration 5 hours for the non-interrupting timer event.

Assuming the subprocess is still active after 5 hours, Timer 2 is triggered, and a status update is sent. This event does not interrupt the subprocess. After being triggered, this timer is immediately reset, so that it can trigger the sending of the next status update after another 5 hours, if the meeting is still ongoing at that time. This example shows that non-interrupting boundary events can occur multiple times while the subprocess is active.

If the subprocess is not completed after 12 hours, Timer 1 elapses, and the subprocess is interrupted. A preliminary report is written, and the process terminates.

Link events are quite specific, since they—unlike all other events—do not represent something that happens in the real world. Rather, they are a means to layout large process diagrams that span multiple pages or screens. A part of the process ends with a link event of throwing nature, while the next part of the process starts with a link event of catching nature. Consequently, link events are intermediate events, even though they have no outgoing (throwing link event) or no incoming edge (catching link event).

Regarding the execution semantics, two matching link events are equivalent to a sequence flow. It is important to stress that link events do not connect

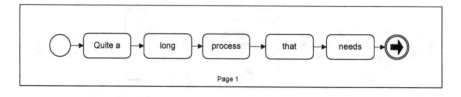

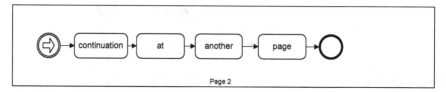

Fig. 4.91. Link events connect different parts of one process

multiple processes, but just parts of one process. Link events are illustrated in Figure 4.91.

Error events also come in two flavours. A throwing error event indicates the occurrence of an error in a certain scope, for instance, in a subprocess. Catching error events are always on the boundaries of subprocesses. They catch the error and interrupt the subprocess, in case certain parts of the subprocess are still active. After catching an error, typically error handling activities are performed.

An example involving error events is shown in Figure 4.92. A subprocess for planning a workshop consists of planning the workshop followed by concurrent activities involving the registration of attendees and reserving a venue. If too few attendees register for the workshop, an error is thrown, and the workshop has to be cancelled. The cancellation is facilitated by a boundary error event that catches the occurrence of the error within the subprocess. In this example, error handling is done by the *Cancel Workshop* activity.

Notice that once the error event is thrown, any running activity in the subprocess will be interrupted. In the example, *Reserve Venue* might be still running at that point in time. If this is the case, it is interrupted immediately, since no venue needs to be reserved when the workshop is cancelled.

Compensation events are strongly connected to transactions. Transactions are specific subprocesses, whose activities have transaction semantics, specified by a transaction protocol. Probably the most widely used transaction protocol is the ACID model, which states that transactions have the following ACID properties:

- *Atomicity*: Either all activities in a transaction are executed successfully or none is.
- *Consistency*: The correct execution of a transaction brings the system from one consistent state in another consistent state.

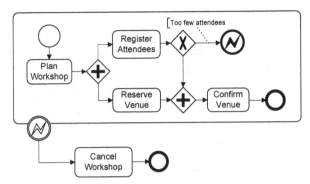

Fig. 4.92. An error is thrown in a subprocess; it is caught by an error boundary event attached to that subprocess

- *Isolation*: The activities of a transaction are executed in isolation from other transactions, that is, transactions do not interfere with each other.
- *Durability*: Effects of transactions survive any system failure that might occur at a later point in time.

Assuming the ACID transaction model, all transactions need to obey the atomicity property: Either all activities of the transaction need to be successfully completed, or none at all. In database systems, this all-or-nothing property of transactions is typically implemented by locking protocols or multiversion concurrency control schemes.

In business processes, the situation is a bit more complex, since we cannot lock large parts of business processes for an extended period of time or create multiple versions of the same data object. In business process management, the typical assumption is that each activity is executed in an atomic fashion. This means, however, that one activity of a transaction can have completed already, when another activity decides to fail. In this case, the first activity needs to be undone, using compensation. An example is used to illustrate this concept.

Figure 4.93 shows a business process diagram that contains a transaction. The transaction involves activities to book a flight and to book a hotel. The all-or-nothing property of this transaction states that either both activities are performed successfully or none will. This property makes sure that the traveller will not end up with a flight booked and no hotel room booked, or vice versa.

Thus, the process needs to rule out that one activity of the transaction succeeds, while the other activity fails. This is done by compensation. Assume that the hotel booking activity is performed successfully, but the booking of the flight fails. In this case, the booking of the hotel room needs to be undone. This is done by cancelling the booking of the hotel room.

When one activity in a transaction subprocess fails, for all activities of the transaction that have been successfully executed already, the compensating

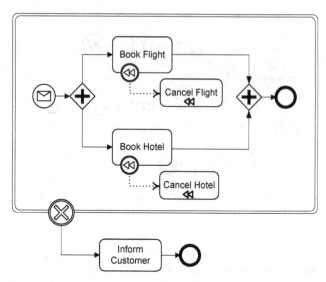

Fig. 4.93. Business process diagram with transaction and compensation elements, adapted from Object Management Group (2011)

activities are started. In this example, after the booking of the flight fails, the *Cancel Hotel* compensating activity of the *Book Hotel* activity is executed. Thereby, the booking of the hotel room is undone, so that the effects of neither of the activities in the transaction are persisted.

The cancellation boundary event catches the unsuccessful completion of the transaction. It can be used to execute activities after the transaction has unsuccessfully completed, like informing the customer in the example.

Signal events communicate certain situations to a wide audience. For each signal throw event, there can be several events that catch the signal. Similar to a flare that can be seen in a wide perimeter, a signal can be caught by different parts of the same process, by other processes within the same process diagram, and even by other process diagrams. Signals are similar to the event publication / event subscription mechanism in distributed computing, where a given signal event can have many subscribers throughout the process landscape.

There are additional types of events that the BPMN supports. For more information about these—less frequently used—events, the reader is referred to the standards document.

Sequence Flow and Gateways

In the BPMN, control flow is called sequence flow. Sequence flow is represented by solid arrows between flow objects, that is, activities, events, and gateways. BPMN supports several types of sequence flow, including normal flow, conditional flow, default flow, and exception flow.

The normal flow of a business process represents expected and desired behaviour of the process. It begins in the start event of a process diagram and continues via a set of flow objects until it reaches an end event.

Exceptional situations are represented by exception flow. With respect to process execution semantics, there is no difference between normal flow and exception flow. The only difference is that exception flow does not define the desired flow of the process, but exceptional situations. Exception flow is created by intermediate events attached to the boundary of an activity, as discussed above in the context of boundary events.

There are two additional types of sequence flow, namely conditional flow and default flow. Since these play important roles in the context of gateways, we introduce gateways first.

Fig. 4.94. Gateway types in the BPMN, Object Management Group (2011)

In BPMN, each gateway acts as a join node or as a split node. Join nodes have at least two incoming edges and exactly one outgoing edge. Split nodes have exactly one incoming edge and at least two outgoing edges. We can also express gateways with multiple incoming and multiple outgoing edges in BPMN. These gateways are called mixed gateways. Since two behaviours— split and join—are expressed by a single concept (for example, *exclusive or*), best practice is not to use mixed gateways but to use a sequence of two gateways with the respective split and join behaviour instead.

The gateway types of the BPMN are shown in Figure 4.94, that is, the *exclusive*, the *parallel*, the *inclusive*, the *event-based*, the *complex* and two instantiation gateway types, which are discussed later in this section.

As shown in that figure, there are two representations of the exclusive gateway, one without a marker and one with a marker. This feature of an unmarked gateway in the BPMN can be considered inconsistent with the definition of an unmarked, that is, blanco event. The *blanco gateway* actually represents a particular kind of gateway, while the *blanco event* does not. To avoid misunderstandings, we recommend to always use gateway markers.

Parallel split and join is supported by virtually any process modelling language. In the BPMN, there is a parallel gateway that can be used to represent *and* split and *and* join behaviour.

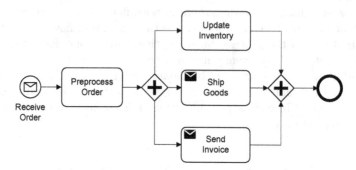

Fig. 4.95. Example involving the parallel gateway

An example is shown in Figure 4.95. This process starts with receiving and preprocessing an order. Then the parallel gateway triggers the execution of three activities. The inventory is updated, the goods are shipped, and the invoice is sent. There are no execution constraints defined between these activities, they can be executed concurrently. When the activities have completed, the *and* join synchronizes the parallel flows, and the process terminates.

Exclusive gateways are also available in any process modelling language. The gateway realizes an "exclusive" behaviour, because exactly one option is chosen from a set of alternatives. An example is shown in Figure 4.96. After the credit risk is evaluated, an exclusive gateway is reached.

This gateway decides which checking activity shall be executed. The credit is granted if the credit risk is low or a certain threshold value is not exceeded. In case of medium credit risk, a subprocess for an advanced credit check is started. If neither of these conditions holds, the credit request is rejected. This behaviour is operationalized by formal conditions, attached to the sequence flows. A sequence flow stores its condition in its `conditionExpression` attribute.

To decide on the branch to select, the exclusive gateway uses these conditions. These sequence flow edges are then specialized to condition flow edges. The standard defines that the conditions are "evaluated in order". The first condition that is evaluated to true is chosen. An exclusive gateways might have a default edge, which does not have a condition attached. It is always evaluated last. This execution semantics makes sure that exactly one outgoing edge will be triggered.

Notice that this property holds even if there are overlapping conditions on the outgoing edges of the gateway. In Figure 4.96, the conditions are overlapping, since both conditions might evaluate to true, for example, if *Risk=medium and Amount=800*. Assuming that the conditions are evaluated

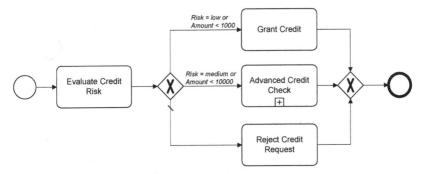

Fig. 4.96. Exclusive gateway with conditions and default flow

from top to bottom, then the first condition evaluates to true, and *Grant Credit* is selected. However, if the other condition appears first in the condition evaluation ordering, then *Advanced Credit Check* is chosen.

If the requested amount exceeds 10,000, none of the conditions evaluates to true, so that the default flow is taken and the request is rejected. In any case, the *exclusive or* split semantics of the gateway is realized.

Since the decision is taken based on data, for instance, the value of the *Risk* and *Amount* data objects, the exclusive gateway is also called data-based exclusive gateway.

Figure 4.97 shows a process diagram with a loop. The loop is represented by two exclusive gateways, a join gateway and a split gateway. It is a characteristic of a loop that the join appears before the split in the process flow. After a document is prepared, it is checked. Depending on the outcome of the checking activity, either the process is continued with archiving the document or the loop is iterated.

Fig. 4.97. Exclusive gateways realizing a loop

In BPMN, the process could also be represented by using a single gateway instead of two gateways. The split gateway that decides whether to iterate the loop needs to be kept. Instead of the join gateway in the beginning of the process, the edge from the split gateway can directly lead to the first activity in the loop. According to the BPMN, activities with multiple incoming edges act as merge nodes. Such an activity gets enabled and can be executed, if one of its incoming edges is triggered. This process is shown in Figure 4.98. It has exactly the same execution semantics as the process shown in Figure 4.97.

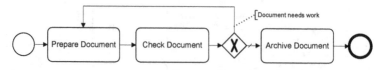

Fig. 4.98. Process diagram with uncontrolled flow

Process activities with multiple outgoing edges are also possible in BPMN. In this case, each of the outgoing edges will be followed. These activities might lead to modelling errors. The reason being that the split behaviour of activities with multiple edges is different from their join behaviour. Activities with multiple outgoing edges represent a parallel split gateway, while activities with multiple incoming edges realize a merge gateway.

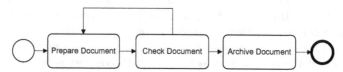

Fig. 4.99. Process diagram with split and join activities, representing a livelock

This fact is illustrated by Figure 4.99, which shows a variant of the previously discussed process with activities acting as split nodes (*Check Document*) and activities acting as join nodes (*Prepare Document*). As a result, for each iteration of the loop, both outgoing edges of the checking activity are triggered. For each iteration of the loop, the document is archived. In addition, the loop will never terminate, resulting in a livelock.

This modelling error could be fixed by attaching conditions to the outgoing edges of the *Check Document* activity, that is, by using conditional flow. However, it is good practice for process activities to have exactly one incoming edge and exactly one outgoing edge. The split and join behaviour of the process should be represented explicitly by gateway nodes rather than implicitly by activities with multiple incoming or multiple outgoing edges.

Just like an exclusive gateway, an *event-based* gateway realizes an exclusive choice. However, rather than deciding itself using process data, the gateway uses the environment to let others decide on how to continue the process. It allows several events to happen, and the environment decides on what actually will happen.

A typical usage of this pattern is shown in Figure 4.100. The process starts with the sending of an invoice by a reseller to one of its customers, followed by an event-based gateway. When the gateway is reached, two things can happen. Either the funds are received or the timer event occurs. Whichever occurs first, decides, that is, the environment decides on how the process continues.

On the completion of the gateway, the *Receive Funds* task is enabled. At the same time, a count down timer for the intermediate timer event is started with a duration of 14 days. If the amount is received within 14 days, the intermediate timer is deactivated and the process completes. If, however, the customer does not pay within 14 days, the timer event occurs, and a reminder is sent. Afterwards, the gateway is reached again, and the customer has another 14 days for paying his invoice.

Notice that only catching intermediate events and receive tasks can occur after event-based gateways. The standard defines that either receive tasks or message intermediate events can occur after a given event-based gateway, not both. In addition to timer intermediate events, like shown in the example, signal events and a few other events are allowed at this position, but message events and timer events occur most frequently.

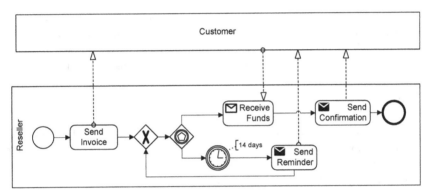

Fig. 4.100. Example of an *event-based* gateway

The semantics of an event-based gateway is fundamentally different from the semantics of a data-based exclusive gateway. In an event-based gateway, multiple activities are enabled and ready for receiving messages at the same time, realizing the *deferred choice* pattern. In the data-based exclusive gateway, the decision is made by the gateway itself—more precisely, by the conditions associated with the condition flow edges leaving the gateway. However, both gateways exhibit an *exclusive or* semantics.

The *inclusive* gateway exposes the most flexible behaviour, since it subsumes and extends both exclusive gateways and parallel gateways. Inclusive gateways can be used in situations where an arbitrary non-empty set of outgoing branches need to be selected. As with the *data-based exclusive or* split, it is the responsibility of the modeller that at least one branch be chosen. An example of an inclusive is shown in Figure 4.101, where a trip is planned and then—depending on the concrete planning of the trip—any subset of flight, hotel, and rental car is booked.

A *complex gateway* allows the definition of combined split and join behaviour. Consider a *complex split gateway* with outgoing sequence flows to A, B, and C. The gateway may define that either A or, jointly, B and C need

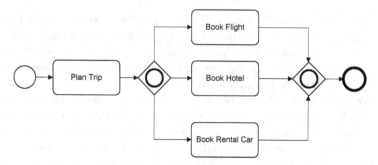

Fig. 4.101. Example of an *inclusive or* gateway

to be executed. It may also define that any pair of sequence flows is valid. The behaviour is specified in the activation condition and an expression of the gateway. The behaviour of the complex gateway is not known from its visual appearance, so that modellers should use this construct with caution.

Handling Data

All business processes deal with information or physical artefacts. To represent information and physical artefacts, BPMN provides data objects. While the term data object seems to indicate digitalized information, it also covers physical objects, such as documents and products.

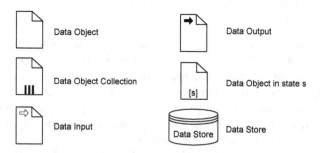

Fig. 4.102. Notational elements regarding data

The notational symbols regarding data in BPMN are shown in Figure 4.102. Often, data objects represent digitalized objects, such as orders in an information system. Since BPMN concentrates on process modelling, there are no data modelling capabilities available. This would also not be appropriate, since the UML provides excellent data and object modelling capabilities, for example, class diagrams.

The relationships between data objects and activities or, more generally, flow objects are specified by data associations. A directed edge from an activity to a data object means that the activity creates or writes the data object. Directed edges in opposite direction indicate read relationships.

Typically processes use data that has been created before the process has started. Examples of this type of data is customer information stored in a customer relationship management system or production information stored in a database. To represent that a process uses these types of data, input data objects can be used. Analogously, if data objects are created as output to be used by other processes, these are marked with a data output marker, as shown in Figure 4.102.

Information systems that store data can be represented in process models as data stores. Since BPMN covers a wide spectrum of application domains, also non-technical stores such as, for instance, warehouses, can be represented by data stores.

The life time of data items that are neither data input nor data output is restricted to the duration of the process instance, that is, data objects are volatile. An association of a data object with a data store, however, indicates that the data object is persistently stored in that data store. Therefore, data stores do not only serve the documentation purpose but also carry a semantics that is important for an implementation of the process.

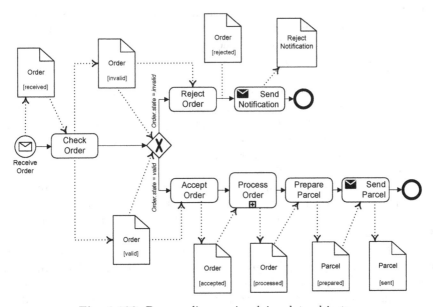

Fig. 4.103. Process diagram involving data objects

A sample business process involving data objects is shown in Figure 4.103. In this order handling process, the start message event occurs when an order is received. This message contains a data object *Order* in state *received*, indicated by the association from the start event to that data object.

The *Check Order* activity might produce different results: either the order is valid or invalid. This behaviour is represented by two data object symbols in the diagram, which have different state markers, reflecting the outcome of the checking activity.

This illustrates that, in general, an association from an activity A to a data object D in state s means that A might change the state of D to s, but it might as well not. Modellers need to make sure that at least one of the data objects an activity is related with in a write association, is actually created as output.

In the example, the order checking activity changes the state of the data object to either *valid* or *invalid*. The current value or state of a data object can be used by expressions, for instance, by expressions that decide which path is taken following an exclusive gateway.

The respective attributes of the conditional flows leaving the exclusive gateway are visualized. If *Order.state=invalid*, the upper branch is chosen and the order is rejected. If *Order.state=valid*, the lower branch is chosen and the order is accepted. In the former case, a rejection message is sent. If, however, the order is accepted, the order is processed, a parcel is prepared and sent.

Notice that the *Prepare Parcel* activity reads an order in state *processed*. This is a typical use of data objects including states; it implements a business policy that a parcel can be prepared only if the respective order is processed. While this situation is obvious for the process shown, the language features provide additional expressiveness regarding data, which proves quite useful in real-world settings.

There is a shorthand notation for a data flow between activities that follow each other directly in sequence flow. Rather than providing two edges from and to, respectively, the activities, the data object can simply be associated with the sequence flow connecting these activities. This language construct is illustrated in Figure 4.103 to show the data flow between the *Reject Order* and *Send Notification* activities.

Data objects also come in collections. A process activity may process a collection of data, such as a list of data, instead of an individual data object. A sample business process involving a collection of data objects is shown in Figure 4.104.

As shown in Figure 4.103, the *Process Order* subprocess reads the order data object in state *accepted* and changes the state of that data object to *processed*. The data objects in these states are also shown in the subprocess refinement in Figure 4.104. Notice that the order in state accepted is a data input of the subprocess, while the order in state processed is data output of the subprocess. This example shows how data objects are communicated from a subprocess activity to its internal process and back.

When the subprocess starts, the order is preprocessed, resulting in a list of order positions and a data object representing the order header. The list of order positions serves as input to the *Process Order Position* activity. As

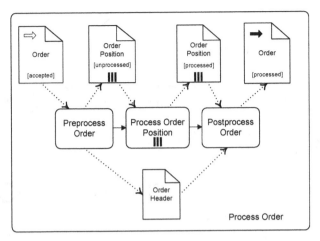

Fig. 4.104. Diagram of the *Process Order* subprocess from Figure 4.103, involving data object collections

shown by the marker of this activity, it is a multiple instance activity. With a data object collection as input, the multiple instance marker indicates that an activity instance is created for each object in the collection. In our example, each order position is processed by an individual instance of the *Process Order Position* activity.

Once all order positions are processed, the respective data object collection is created, and the multiple instances activity terminates. Postprocessing of the order involves assembling the order positions and the order header to create the order, which is now in the processed state. That data object is provided to the follow-up activities on the process level as data output, as shown in Figure 4.103.

Finally, we sketch the execution semantics of data objects in BPMN. Each process activity is associated with input sets, which contain data objects which have to be available when the activity starts. Notice that this set can be empty in case an activity is not associated with any data object. In the example, the activity *Accept Order* in Figure 4.103 has one input set containing just one data object, namely the order data object in the valid state.

In general, however, there might be multiple input sets associated with a given activity. When sequence flow arrives at the activity, the input sets are visited. For each input set, the system checks if the data objects are available in the requested states. The activity can be started, once all data objects for an input set are available, making sure that an activity can deal with alternative input data objects.

This approach is illustrated in Figure 4.105, which shows a variant of the ordering process discussed above. In this variant, a response message is sent in any case. To realize this behaviour, the *Send Response* activity has two

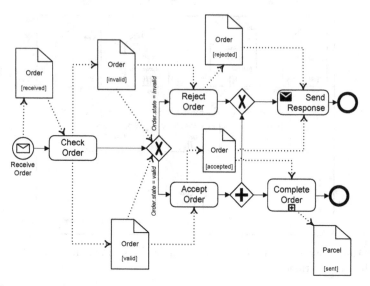

Fig. 4.105. Process diagram involving multiple input sets of an activity

input sets, one of which consists of the order object in state *rejected*. The other consists of the same data object in state *accepted*.

From the discussion of the process it is obvious that these input sets are alternative. Either the response message contains the information that the order is rejected or it sends a message that tells the client that the order is accepted. When control flow enters the *Send Response* activity, either of the input sets is available, realizing the intended process behaviour.

Process Instantiation

So far, most aspects of BPMN process diagrams have been covered. Activities, events, gateways, and sequence flow were introduced and their execution semantics have been discussed. In formal language theory, the semantics of a language or grammar determines the meaning of the words, written in that language. In process languages like the BPMN, the meaning of the process diagrams—the words of that language—is defined by the behaviours that the diagram specifies.

For each language construct covered, its execution semantics was discussed. For example, a sequence flow between two activities restricts their execution ordering, after an exclusive gateway exactly one option will be chosen, etc.

However, so far we have disregarded the question when a process should actually be instantiated. This is an important aspect of the execution semantics of a process language. Luckily, the process diagrams discussed so far always had a single start event. In this case, the instantiation question can trivially be answered: A process should be instantiated if and when the start event occurs.

The case is more complex for process diagrams with multiple start events. The BPMN states that start events are alternative. This means that whenever one start event occurs, a process is instantiated.

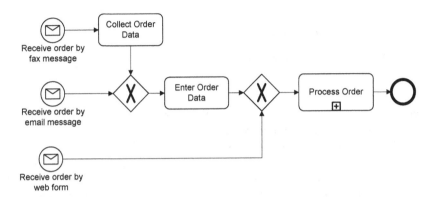

Fig. 4.106. Process diagram with multiple alternative start events

Figure 4.106 shows a process diagram with several start events. These events represent alternative ways of receiving an order. If the order is received by fax message, the data first needs to be digitalized in the *Collect Order Data* activity. Once the data is available in electronic form, it can be entered in the information system of that company, using the *Enter Order Data* activity. Notice that the order can be immediately entered in the information system, if it is received by email message. Finally, the order can be processed immediately after process start, if the order has been issued via a web form.

These alternative ways of receiving an order can be represented by multiple start events. These start events are alternative, and the process is in line with their alternative nature, because all start events are merged by exclusive gateways. Notice that in this example substituting an exclusive gateway with a parallel gateway would result in a deadlock situation.

However, there are situations which do require multiple start events. The BPMN reserves a specific element for these situations, shown in Figure 4.107. In that example, a process is instantiated only if an application is received and a corresponding vacancy is available. Notice that the availability of a vacancy is represented by a condition start event. (For illustration purposes, we use a condition start event here, even though BPMN allows only message start events). We use the parallel event-based gateway to capture this situation. A process is instantiated only if all incoming events have occurred.

This example covers another interesting aspect. When multiple start events are required to start a process, these start events need to be correlated with each other. Correlation is used to tie events to process instances.

In the concrete example, the *Receive application* event needs to reference a vacancy. When there are multiple vacancies and multiple applications re-

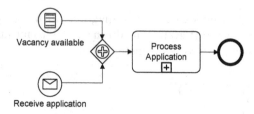

Fig. 4.107. Process diagram with two start events, both of which need to occur to instantiate the process

ceived, a process can only be started if an application is received and the vacancy referenced in the application is actually available.

To illustrate this concept, assume vacancies $V1, V2$, and $V3$. This means that condition start events occur only for these vacancies. If an application is received that references a vacancy that is not available, for example $V4$, then no process instance can be instantiated. If, however, an application is received which references vacancy $V1$, a process is instantiated. This makes sure that a process is instantiated only if there is an open position available for the application received.

4.7.3 Collaborating Processes

Business processes involving multiple organizational entities can interact with each other. The BPMN is not restricted to single-organization business processes, but is ready to express business processes of multiple organizations that collaborate.

As already introduced, pools represent specific process participants or roles, such as role supplier or role customer. Lanes are used to represent organizational entities within participants. Typically, top level divisions within companies are represented by lanes, such as marketing and sales, operations, and logistics; but more fine-grained organizational entities can also be represented by sub-lanes, if required by the process.

Sequence flow is allowed within processes only, that is, between nodes that reside in a single pool. Therefore, sequence flow may cross lane boundaries, but it may never cross a pool boundary. Communication between processes can occur only through message flow.

The rationale behind this stipulation is as follows. Sequence flow defines an execution order of activities in a given process. Within an organization, we can set up procedures and rules, even a workflow engine, that make sure that the activities are executed as specified in the process model.

However, we can not ask for a certain execution ordering of activities in a process of one of our business partners. We can only send a message to our business partner, which will then influence its business processes. Therefore, business-to-business communication is handled exclusively through messages, while intra-company communication can be handled directly through sequence flow.

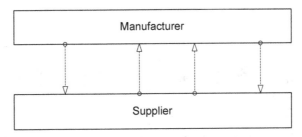

Fig. 4.108. Business processes collaborating through message flow

Collaborating processes can be represented on different levels of abstraction. In the most abstract way, only the roles of the partners are represented and the message flows between them. There is no information about the internal processes available. Also the ordering of message flow edges from left to right does not have any meaning.

Figure 4.108 shows a collaboration diagram involving a supplier and a manufacturer. The diagram does not indicate that first the manufacturer sends a message to the supplier, even though the left most edge has that orientation. We can not even conclude from the diagram that the message flow actually happens. A message send event might be on an optional path, so that not all process instances actually send a message!

Since we cannot look inside these pools, they are called black box pools. Collaboration diagrams involving black box pools provide a high level view by providing roles of participants and message flow that might occur.

An example of a business process with one black box pool and one white box pool is shown in Figure 4.109. A manufacturer sends an order to its supplier, represented by a message flow from the manufacturer pool to the message start event of the supplier. Then an invoice is sent, payment is received, and the material is sent.

In a typical business-to-business collaboration, business partners communicate in a structured way by sending and receiving messages. While the externally visible behaviour of a process that runs in a given organization is essential for the overall communication, the internal process is not relevant. Pools can also be used to provide this form of abstraction. The internal structure of a business process can be abstracted from and, only the externally visible communication behaviour can be shown.

There are two advantages related to expressing only the externally visible behaviour. The first advantage is that the information hiding principle is followed, so that the complexity of internal business processes does not add to the complexity of the overall process.

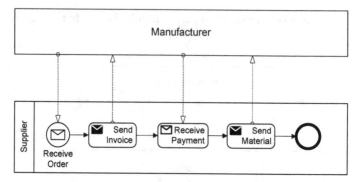

Fig. 4.109. Collaborating business processes with public process of the *Supplier*

The second advantage is based on business considerations. Business processes are a significant asset of a company, so that the company is not willing to expose its internal processes to the outside world. Since only the communication behaviour of a process can be observed from the outside, a process restricted to its communication activities is called *public process*.

We can also provide public processes for both communication partners. In this case, message flows are no longer associated with borders of pools, but with the actual send and receive tasks. This view provides details about the communication activities of both collaborating processes. To illustrate this, Figure 4.110 shows also the communication tasks of the manufacturer and their process flow.

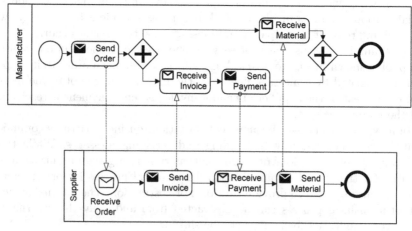

Fig. 4.110. Collaborating business processes with public processes of both partners

The process of the manufacturer starts by sending an order. The process continues with concurrent branches. In one branch the manufacturer waits for the ordered material; in the other branch, it waits for receiving the invoice. After the invoice is received, the payment is sent.

A partner might also choose to expose its complete internal process. This is done by adding activities and potentially also control structures to its public process. The resulting process is called *private process*. A private business process contains all activities that are enacted within a company; it realizes a process orchestration.

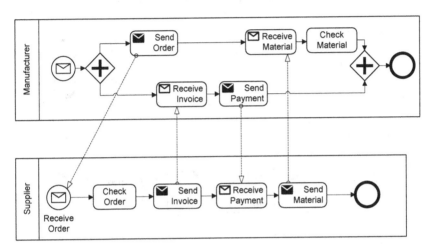

Fig. 4.111. Collaborating business processes with private processes of both partners

A private business process of the manufacturer shown in Figure 4.111 contains an activity *Check Material*, so that the manufacturer can check the material after receiving it. This is a typical example of an activity that is executed in the process orchestration of a partner, but which has no implication on the externally visible behaviour of the process. Therefore, it is part of the private process, but not of its public process.

So far, each pool represented a single organization, for instance a concrete supplier or a a concrete manufacturing company. The BPMN also provides means to express pools that represents multiple organizations that participate in the process collaboration.

An example involving multiple instance pools is given in Figure 4.112, where a credit request process is shown. There are three pools in this collaboration, a customer, a credit agency, and a bank. As indicated by the multiple instances marker in the bank pool, multiple banks participate in this collaboration, while only one customer and only one credit agency participate.

The process starts by the customer filling a credit request and sending it to the credit agency, spawning off a new process instance. The credit agency requests offers from several banks, represented by the multiple instances subprocess. In each instance of the subprocess, one offer message is sent to a concrete bank, and a response is received from that bank. The subprocess instances are created concurrently, so that the requests are sent out concurrently and the respective messages are collected from the banks, as they come in.

The BPMN states that the number of multiple instances of a subprocess matches the number of instances of a multiple instances pool it communicates with. In our example, the number of subprocess instances that send the request messages and receive the response matches the number of banks.

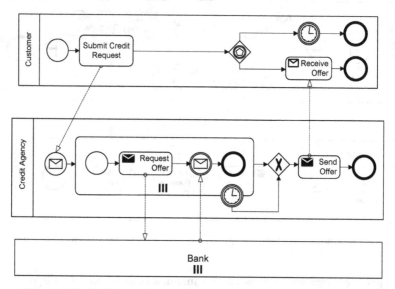

Fig. 4.112. Collaborating processes with a multiple instances pool

The process continues as follows. Once all responses are collected or a timer elapses, an offer is selected and submitted to the customer. If the customer is still patiently waiting to receive this offer, it does so.

While the BPMN can graphically represent the interaction of business processes, there are no formal properties defined on the relationship between a business process and its externally visible behaviour. Correctness criteria for process choreographies that consist of a set of interacting business processes are also not part of the BPMN. These aspects will be discussed in the context of process choreographies in Chapter 6.

4.7.4 Executability and Exchange Format

One of the points of critique regarding earlier versions of the BPMN was the lack of executable processes, which resulted in the need to translate BPMN diagrams to executable languages, like WS-BPEL. In the current version, executability is addressed in BPMN, and first process engines that natively support that standard are available.

Maybe the most important aspect of the BPMN in its current version is the standardization of the exchange format. By providing XML Schema definitions for the standard, tool vendors can provide a serialization format for BPMN diagrams, so that process models can be exported from one tool to be imported in another tool. This is a very important feature, since it allows the automatic transfer of process models between tools that are rather on the domain aspect to tools that are focusing on executable processes.

Bibliographical Notes

Control flow patterns are the building blocks of process orchestrations; they were introduced by van der Aalst et al. (2003c). A revised version was published in Russell et al. (2006). Russell et al. (2016) provide a comprehensive overview of the workflow patterns. Petri nets were introduced by Petri (1962). Girault and Valk (2010) published a textbook on Petri nets that investigated in detail the specification and verification of computer systems.

There are numerous extensions of Petri nets, including the colour extension reported in Jensen and Kristensen (2009), which looks at modelling and validation of concurrent systems. van der Aalst and Stahl (2011) provide a comprehensive approach to modelling processes, based on coloured and hierarchical Petri nets.

Workflow nets are introduced in van der Aalst (1998) and also in van der Aalst and van Hee (2004), where organizational aspects and tools are also addressed. Event-driven process chains are introduced in Scheer (2000). The application of event-driven process chains is reported in Scheer et al. (2004). An investigation of the formal semantics of event-driven process chains is given in Kindler (2004); run time considerations are reported in Cuntz and Kindler (2005). Investigations regarding the semantics of the *or* join are reported in Mendling and van der Aalst (2007) and in Gfeller et al. (2011). Yet Another Workflow Language is introduced in van der Aalst and ter Hofstede (2005); the YAWL system is described in van der Aalst et al. (2004). ter Hofstede et al. (2010) present a comprehensive book about all aspects of the YAWL language, the YAWL system, and related approaches. Graph-based workflow languages are introduced in Leymann and Altenhuber (1994) and Leymann and Roller (1999); workflow applications are considered in Leymann and Roller (1997).

In the context of flexible workflow management, graph-based workflow languages, including their technical aspects like handling of application data, are introduced in Weske (2000). A graph-based workflow language with block structuring is proposed by Reichert and Dadam (1998). In the context of the Unified Modeling Language, Activity Diagrams can be used to represent business processes, as shown in Booch et al. (2005). An early overview of workflow languages is given in Forst et al. (1995); Weske et al. (2005) devote a chapter to workflow language, also discussing service composition languages.

Instantiation of process models is discussed in Decker and Mendling (2009), where BPMN and other process languages are investigated with respect to their instantiation semantics.

The BPMN specification is available by the Object Management Group (2011). A poster explains the key concept of the BPMN in a concise way; more information can be found in BPM Offensive Berlin (2011). A workshop series is devoted to the Business Process Model and Notation; workshop proceedings are available as Mendling et al. (2011) and Dijkman et al. (2011). This notation is also in the centre of Silver (2011), where practical aspects of BPMN are discussed.

5

Business Decision Modelling

It is an interesting observation that business process management in general and business process modelling in particular traditionally have neglected decisions. This might come as a surprise, because basically any business process contains decisions. It should not come as a surprise that decision modelling and execution came into the focus of business process management recently.

In this chapter, we extend the scope of business processes with decisions. In particular, Decision Model and Notation (DMN) is discussed, which complements BPMN with decision modelling.

5.1 Motivation

The previous chapter discussed key concepts of business processes and the most prominent business process modelling languages to express them. The primary focus was on activities and their causal ordering. In fact, these are the only aspects covered by Petri-net-based process modelling languages. The industry standard BPMN has added further concepts like events, data objects, and organizational roles, as discussed in Section 4.7.

While traditional business process modelling provides an important cornerstone to facilitate analysis, improvement, and enactment of business processes, it fails to support one important aspect that nearly every business process has: decisions.

To illustrate the role of decisions in business processes, the BPMN process diagram shown in Figure 5.1 is investigated. This figure shows a business process from finance, which starts when a credit card application is received. After recording the application information, the process has to decide on the basic credit card eligibility of the applicant.

This decision is represented in BPMN by a business rule task *Determine Basic Credit Card Eligibility*; in the remainder of this chapter, we will refer to business rule tasks also as decision tasks. The decision taken by that task is used to guide the process flow. If the applicant is not eligible for the credit

© Springer-Verlag GmbH Germany, part of Springer Nature 2019
M. Weske, *Business Process Management*,
https://doi.org/10.1007/978-3-662-59432-2_5

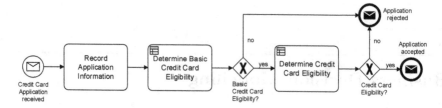

Fig. 5.1. Business process with decision tasks

card, her application is rejected. Otherwise, a second decision is taken to ultimately decide on the application. A second *exclusive or* gateway is used to either send a rejection letter or to send an acceptance letter of the credit card application.

This example shows that decisions are—to some extent—represented in BPMN already, as decision tasks and as different outgoing edges of an *exclusive or* gateway. The decision logic, however, cannot be defined in BPMN. Still, business processes have to take decisions, as illustrated by the credit card example.

To discuss the role of decision taking during process executions, the architecture of process oriented information systems shown in Figure 3.38 on page 118 has to be revisited. During process execution, the process engine keeps track of the execution semantics of the business process. For each activity, the engine invokes the respective service, as defined in the implemented process model.

In general, there are two general approaches for decision making in business processes, automated decision making by a software service and human decision making. In the business process shown in Figure 5.1, we focus on the first decision, i.e., the decision task *Determine Basic Credit Card Eligibility*. When this task is executed, the process engine invokes a service provider. Depending on the configuration of the system, this can be either a software service or a human employee who takes the decision based on the data available and her personal experience.

The decision taking by a software service is illustrated in Figure 5.2(a). When the decision task needs to be executed, the process engine invokes the software service with the parameters provided by the credit card application. After completion, the software service provides a return value, in this case either *yes* or *no*. This output is used by the process engine to decide on the continuation of the process: Either the *no* branch of the *exclusive or* gateway is followed and a rejection message is sent or the *yes* branch is followed and the full eligibility check is conducted to ultimately decide on the credit card application.

Due to increasing auditing requirements that companies face today, it is important to document any decision making activity properly. To this end,

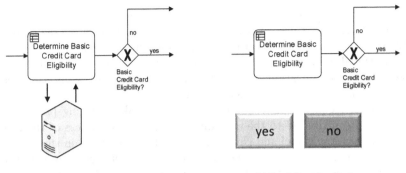

(a) Decision taken by software service   (b) Decision taken by human

Fig. 5.2. Alternative ways to take decisions in business processes

for any decision that is taken during the execution of a business process, the following questions have to be answered.

1. How exactly is a decision taken?
2. What data is used to take the decision?
3. What policies are taken into account?
4. Who is responsible for taking a decision?

In the credit card application example, these questions are not completely answered. The first question looks at how exactly the decision was taken. In the first implementation scenario, the decision was determined by the software code that implements the software service. While we can say that it is clear how the decision was taken on a software code level, software code is typically too low-level to communicate decision making to a potential auditor in a comprehensible way.

Similar considerations apply to the second question, which data was used? This question can be answered on a technical level that mentions database tables and the respective queries to access them, but this might also not be suited for an auditor. Additional policies can be regarded as input to a software engineering project, which subsumes a variety of software requirements and software design documents. Ultimately it will be very hard to trace back the software code to the particular policies that govern decision making.

The last question relates to the person responsible for the decision taken. If the decision is taken by a software service, no person is even involved during process execution. However, a set of persons might be candidates for being responsible, including requirements engineers of the software development project and software developers that actually coded the service. In any case, the information to answer these questions is disparate and can only be traced back with significant effort, if this is at all possible.

In many cases, decisions are taken by humans, which is illustrated in Figure 5.2(b) by buttons *yes* and *no*. Returning to the questions of decision making, in human decision taking, we can easily identify the person responsible for the decision. However, we do not know in detail, how the decision was taken or which policy was used by that person. Since knowledge workers can use additional information that might not even be stored in the information systems of the organization, we cannot confidently answer the question about the data being used during decision taking.

These shortcomings in documenting decision taking during process execution have contributed to the development and to the success of the recent standard Decision Model and Notation that will be discussed in the next section. Based on the design principles and the language elements, we will return to the questions on decision taking and the role of DMN in answering them.

5.2 Decision Model and Notation Overview

DMN is a sibling standard to the well-known and widely used BPMN standard. Its goal is to provide the expressive means to model decisions, both the structure of decisions and the concrete decision logic. In Section 5.2.1, we introduce the DMN by investigating decision requirements diagrams, which we can use to provide a structuring of decisions and related artefacts, such as data input and organizational policies. Decision logic is in the centre of Section 5.2.2, where the main focus is on decision tables, the most widely used technique to represent decision logic.

Before the modelling elements of the DMN are introduced, a characterization of the types of decisions that can be expressed in DMN is appropriate.

In the daily business of an organization, many decisions are taken. These decisions are of different nature, ranging from operational decisions to strategic decisions. An example of an operational decision is whether or not a credit card can be granted; this example was introduced earlier in this chapter. Operational decisions are characterized by a quite narrow scope, so that the data required and the decision logic is known before the decision is taken.

An example of a strategic decision is to which market an insurance company should expand over the next five years. This decision is of strategic nature, and it is much broader and more complex than the operational decision discussed above. We will probably not be able to provide a concrete logic formula for the strategic decision; there will always be factors that are unknown. In the business world, these decisions are typically taken by the management, typically based on the experience of the acting management.

To provide accountability of decision making and a basis for decision automation, DMN is designed to represent operational decisions, i.e., those decisions for which we know the required data input and how the decision output depends on the input, i.e., the decision logic.

5.2.1 Decision Requirements Diagram

DMN provides decision requirements diagrams that allow us to model the structure of decisions and the artefacts involved. These diagrams are graphs that consist of nodes and edges of the types shown in Figure 5.3.

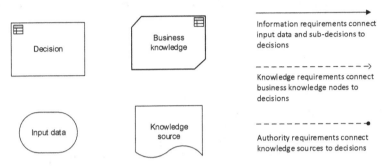

Fig. 5.3. Modelling elements of DMN decision requirements diagrams

- *Decision*: Decisions are the core elements of decision requirements diagrams; decisions use input data and decision logic to compute output values.
- *Input data*: Input data represents data objects that are used by the decision as input.
- *Business knowledge*: A business knowledge node provides decision logic that can be reused by different decisions in decision requirements diagrams, using an invocation mechanism. This concept is useful if decision logic is shared by several decisions.
- *Knowledge source*: Knowledge sources are important to document the reasons for a specific decision logic. These will not directly be used during decision taking, but knowledge sources are important to provide transparency in decision management, which is an essential aspect of auditing requirements.

Nodes of these types can be connected in DMN decision requirements diagrams by edges of different types:

- *Information requirements*: Information requirements connect input data nodes to decisions, defining that the input data is used as an input to the decision. Edges of this type can also relate a sub-decision to a decision, meaning that the output of the sub-decision serves as an input to the decision.
- *Knowledge requirements*: Knowledge requirements connect business knowledges to decisions, meaning that the business knowledge is used to take the decision.

- *Authority requirements*: Authority requirements connect knowledge sources to decisions and to business knowledge nodes, indicating any policy or legal regulation that guides the decision making.

These modelling elements are illustrated by an example shown in Figure 5.4. This diagram provides a high-level view of the decision that lies behind the decision task *Determine Basic Credit Card Eligibility*, which was introduced in Figure 5.1.

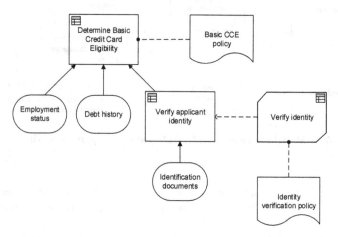

Fig. 5.4. Example of a decision requirements diagram

The diagram shows that the employment status of the applicant and her debt history are input parameters to determine the basic credit card eligibility. This decision also requires the output of the *Verify applicant identity* decision, which—due to its relative position—serves as a sub-decision. This sub-decision requires identification documents, as shown by its input data and the information requirements edge.

The example also allows us to discuss business knowledge and knowledge sources. *Verify identity* is an example of a business knowledge node, which provides the decision logic to evaluate the *Verify applicant identity* decision. When this decision has to be taken, its input data are used as input parameters to the business knowledge, which evaluates the decision and returns an output value to the *Verify applicant identity* decision. This value travels along the information requirements edge to the top-level decision. It provides the third input value that the top-level decision requires.

Knowledge sources provide documentation information about the decision logic, not the decision logic itself. In the example, the *Basic CCE policy* guides the top-level decision, while the *Identity verification policy* defines the rules that are used by the business knowledge *Verify identity*. While knowledge sources do not define decision logic directly, they provide important means to answer some of the questions that were introduced earlier in this section.

Decision requirements diagrams allow us to answer some of the questions raised above. By showing the relationships between decisions and subdecisions and input data used by these, we can answer question (2), related to the data to be used during decision taking. By investigating the knowledge sources in a decision requirements diagram, we can also answer question (3), which is related to the reasoning behind a certain decision and the respective policies.

Question (4) about the responsibility of decision taking can also be answered by decision requirements diagrams. Just like BPMN, DMN allows us to define various attributes for modelling elements. In particular, each decision in a decision requirements diagram features attributes to characterize roles that are involved in decision making.

- `decisionMaker`: The decision maker attribute allows us to define one or more roles or organizational units that are responsible for making the decision. An example of a decision maker in the credit card example is a member of the credit card application department.
- `decisionOwner`: The decision owner attribute defines the organizational role that is responsible for decision taking. In the example, the head of the credit card application department is the owner of the *Determine Basic Credit Card Eligibility* decision.

To summarize, decision requirements diagrams allow us to answer questions (2), (3), and (4). To address question (1) on how decisions are actually taken, different ways to define decision logic in DMN will be covered in the next section.

5.2.2 Decision Logic

Decision logic describes how the output of a decision is derived from its input. In general, so-called value expressions are used to define decision logic. The DMN standard distinguishes between different types of value expressions.

- *Literal expression*: One form of literal expression is defining decision logic by text. Literal expressions can also be used to define decision logic formally precise, for instance, through program code.
- *Decision Table*: Decision tables are widely used to define decision logic. Decision tables will be covered in Section 5.3.
- *Invocation*: Invocations are a mechanism to use existing decision logic, provided by a business knowledge node.

Despite the fact that DMN mainly targets operational decisions that can be executed automatically, the language also allows us to define decision logic in an informal, imprecise manner, using English text as literal expression.

In an apartment rental scenario, the landlord might define her decision logic as follows.

I will accept an applicant if he or she has a good employment history and a good credit rating. The applicant must not have any pets. All supporting documents must be authentic. And, on top, the applicant must be a nice person.

Since we cannot operationally formalize the precise meaning of having a *good employment history* or of being a *nice person*, this decision can only be taken by the landlord using her personal opinion and taste. This decision cannot be taken automatically.

Despite the formal imprecision of the decision logic, DMN can still be used to define the decision, using English text. We can also define in a decision requirements diagram the input data that is required for taking the decision, including the required documents by the applicant. As a consequence, both formally precise and imprecise decisions are covered by DMN.

Literal expressions can also be defined in a formal manner. DMN provides a dedicated language, called Friendly Enough Expression Language, or FEEL. An example using FEEL expressions is shown in Figure 5.5, which contains a decision requirements diagram to determine the net income from the gross income and the legal status of a tax payer. For convenience, the expressions are associated with the respective decision in the diagram; formally, decision logic is not part of decision requirements diagrams.

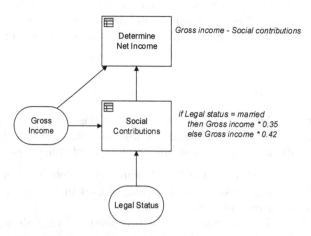

Fig. 5.5. Decision logic expressed by literal expressions

The decision requirements diagram shows a decision *Determine Net Income*, with a sub-decision *Social Contributions* that calculates an output value based on its input values *Legal Status* and *Gross Income*. The decision logic is defined by an expression, using an *if-clause*. If the legal status of the tax payer is *married*, then the social contributions amount to 35% of her gross income, otherwise to 42% of her gross income. Notice that the value of the expression is not explicitly assigned to some variables; it is just passed as the output to the decision that determines the net income, which is done by subtracting the social contributions from the gross income.

This example also shows that a decision can also be considered as a computation. Again, the computation is well documented by the decision requirements diagram.

5.3 Decision Tables

Due to their ability to provide decision logic in a compact and formal, yet readable form, decision tables are widely used to define decision logic in decision models.

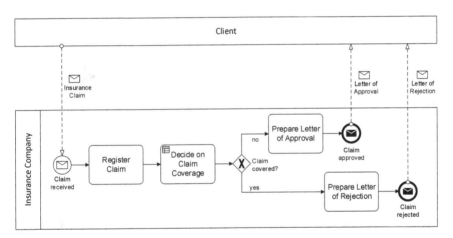

Fig. 5.6. Business process collaboration to handle an insurance claim

Figure 5.6 shows a process collaboration that involves a client and an insurance company. The collaboration starts when the client sends an insurance claim. The insurance company receives the claim and registers it, before the decision is taken whether or not to cover the claim. This decision is represented by the *Decide on Claim Coverage* decision task. Depending on the decision taken, either a letter of approval or a letter of rejection is prepared and sent.

Before the decision logic can be discussed in detail, the process model needs to be enhanced with data objects. While this is not strictly required, it allows us to provide an association between data objects in the process model and input data used during decision taking.

The business process of the insurance company including data objects is shown in Figure 5.7. It contains two data objects, representing the claim and the customer contract, respectively. The decision task reads both data objects, as defined by the arcs between the respective data objects and the decision task.

From a process modelling perspective, data objects do not have any internal structure. In the example, we do not know the structure of the claim, neither do we know the attributes in the customer contract. Since decision logic uses specific attributes of data objects, in general, data objects in processes cannot be directly used as input to decisions. In the example, we only know that information about the claim and information about the customer contract are required to take the decision on claim coverage. We do not know which attributes contain the required information. During the definition of the decision logic, this information has to be retrieved from the information systems that store and maintain the data objects.

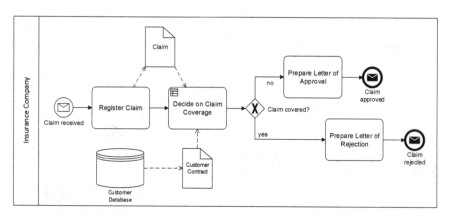

Fig. 5.7. Insurance claim handling process with decision task and data objects

To illustrate these concepts in a concrete scenario, we assume that the process covers bike thefts. In this setting, the claim data object contains an attribute *Value* that refers to the value of the stolen bike; an attribute *Theft-Time* contains the time of day when the bike was stolen. The *Customer Contract* data object contains attributes for name and address of the customer, and also the type of contract. The latter is represented by an attribute *Type*.

The information stored in the attributes of the data objects can be used in decision requirements diagrams. Figure 5.8 shows the resulting diagram, defining that the *Decide on Claim Coverage* decision has *Claim.Value*, *Claim.TheftTime*, and *CustomerContract.Type* as input data.

After discussing the structure of input data objects, the structure of decision tables is addressed. The columns in a decision table refer to data input and also the output of the decision. While the DMN standard allows multiple

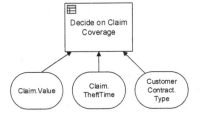

Fig. 5.8. Decision requirements diagram of *Decide on Claim Coverage* decision

output columns, we will concentrate on decision tables with a single output. The rightmost column of a decision table refers to the output of the decision.

The decision table of the *Decide on Claim Coverage* decision is shown in Figure 5.9. We can observe that the data input shown in the decision requirements diagram can be found in the decision table as well. Decision taking depends on the value of the claim, on the theft time of the bike, and on the customer contract type.

Decide on Claim Coverage				
F	*Claim.Value*	*Claim.TheftTime*	*CustomerContract.Type*	*Claim covered*
	[0€;2000€]	*[0;24]*	*{Gold, Silver, Bronze}*	*{yes, no}*
1	[0€;200€]	-	-	yes
2	[201€;500€]	-	Gold	yes
3	[201€;500€]	[6;22]	Silver	yes
4	[201€;500€]	[8;18]	Bronze	yes
5	[501€;1000€]	[6;22]	Gold	yes
6	[501€;1000€]	[8;18]	Silver	yes
7	-	-	-	no

Fig. 5.9. Decision table of *decide on claim coverage* decision

The rows of the table define the decision logic. DMN allows us to define different hit policies that tell us exactly how to interpret the rows in a decision table. In the example, the letter *F* represents the *First* hit policy. This hit policy defines that the rows are evaluated in order, and the first row that matches the input values will be selected, and the output value will be returned. Other hit policies provided by the DMN will be covered in the next section.

In general, each row in a decision can be considered as a conjunction of conditions. Each input column refers to a condition, and all conditions have to be met for a row to be selected. The fields of input columns can contain values, intervals and other types of expressions. The hyphen symbol in a field of an input column means that any value for the respective input data is allowed.

To illustrate the evaluation of decision tables, a case of a silver customer with claim value 850€ and theft time 18 (6 o'clock in the afternoon) is considered. Starting in row 1, we evaluate if the claim value is between 0 and 200; since this is not true, the first row cannot be selected, and we can move to the second row. Again, the claim value does not match the interval for that row. We have to move on until row 5 to satisfy the first condition relating to the claim value. Since the bike was stolen at 6 o'clock in the evening, also the theft time condition is satisfied by row 5. However, the customer type condition is violated, because this option is available only for gold customers. Moving on to row 6, all conditions are met for our case, so that the decision returns *yes* and the claim can be covered.

The process model shown in Figure 5.7 takes the return value *yes* of the decision task and uses it to decide on the outcome of the data-based *exclusive or* split. Finally, the letter of approval is prepared, and the claim is approved. This example shows the interaction between business processes and decisions.

The decision table specifies the decision logic in a concise and comprehensible way. All thefts until a claim value of 200€ are covered. Claims with theft value between 200€ and 500€ are covered for gold customers. Claims of this value range for silver customers are only covered if they occurred between 6 o'clock in the morning and 10 o'clock in the evening. Claims in that value range are covered for bronze customers in a narrower theft time window. Claims up to 1,000€ are only covered for silver and gold customers, where the theft time window of silver customers is again narrower than that of gold customers. No claims exceeding 1,000€ are covered.

5.4 Hit Policies

The motivating example discussed in the previous section illustrates how decision logic can be expressed in decision tables. The rows of the decision table were evaluated in order, the first row that matched was selected, and the corresponding output value was returned. Therefore, this policy of evaluating decision tables is called the *First* hit policy. DMN provides a rich set of hit policies, which are discussed next.

The hit policies can be distinguished into single hit policies and multi-hit policies. In single hit policies, for each possible combination of input values, there is at most a single row that is selected. Even if a given input combination matches multiple rows, a single hit policy makes sure that only one row is selected. We assume that for each input combination, at least one row matches. This is a valid assumption, because otherwise input combinations would exist for which the decision could not provide an output value. Decision tables with this property are called *complete*.

5.4.1 Single Hit Policies

To provide a precise understanding of the hit policies, we assume a decision table with n input columns $I_1, I_2, \ldots, I_n$ and one output column O. Each input combination i is an element of the Cartesian product of the input columns, i.e., $i \in I_1 \times I_2 \times \ldots \times I_n$. In other words, i is an n-tuple that consists of one value for each input column. The decision table has m rows $R_1, R_2, \ldots R_m$. Let $matches(R_i)$ be the set of input combinations that match the row R_i, and let $out(R_i)$ be the output value of R_i.

These definitions are applied to the decision table shown in Figure 5.9. Since there are three input columns, $n = 3$, such that $I_1 = Claim.Value, I_2 = Claim.TheftTime$, and $I_3 = CustomerContract.Type$. Since there are seven rows in the decision table, $m = 7$.

A claim by a silver customer with claim value 850€ and theft time 18 is one possible input combination. Formally, the claim can be represented by a tuple $i = (850€, 18, silver) \in Claim.Value \times Claim.TheftTime \times CustomerContract.Type$.

We now investigate which rows this tuple matches. Since the claim value exceeds 200, the tuple does not match the first row. As a consequence, $i \notin matches(R_1)$. The same holds for rows 2 through 5. The first row that matches is row 6, i.e., $i \in matches(R_6)$. As a result, the output value $out(R_6) = yes$ of row 6 is returned for the input combination i.

Based on these notions, the single hit policies are characterized as follows. Let $i, j \in I_1 \times I_2 \times \ldots \times I_n$ be input combinations, and let $R_1, R_2, \ldots R_m$ be the rows of the decision table.

- *Unique (U)*: In the *Unique* hit policy, for each input combination, exactly one row matches, i.e., $i \in matches(R_k) \Leftrightarrow i \notin matches(R_l), 1 \leq k \neq l \leq m$.
- *Any (A)*: The *Any* hit policy allows several matches for a given input combination; however, these matches need to agree on the output value, so that 'any' match can be selected to derive the output value: $i \in matches(R_k) \cap matches(R_l) \implies out(R_k) = out(R_l), 1 \leq k, l \leq m$.
- *Priority (P)*: The *Priority* hit policy allows several rows to match for a given input combination, and these do not need to agree on the output value. The output value to be returned is determined by the ordering of output values in the output domain.
- *First (F)*: The *First* hit policy shares the assumptions with the previous hit policy. However, the output is based on the ordering of the rows, so that the first row that matches determines the output of the decision.

Based on these characterizations of hit policies, we can check for a given decision table if the respective hit policy is satisfied. Since the *First* and *Priority* hit policies do not restrict matching in decision tables, all decision tables can be combined with these hit policies. However, the other hit policies might be violated by a decision table.

The *Unique* hit policy imposes the strongest requirements on a decision table, since each input combination matches exactly one row. A decision table with this property also satisfies the *Any* hit policy. The reverse is not true, because the *Any* hit policy allows multiple rows to match for a given input combination, which *Unique* forbids.

The decision table in Figure 5.9 satisfies the *First* hit policy. However, it does not satisfy the *Unique* hit policy, because there exist input combinations which match multiple rows. Due to the last row in the table, actually, many input combinations have multiple matches. This applies, for instance, to the case of the silver customer with claim value 850€ and theft time 18 which matches rows 6 and 7.

The *Any* hit policy allows an input combination to match several rows. However, this hit policy is also violated, since rows 6 and 7 have different output values (*yes, no*), so that we cannot use any of them to compute the output of the decision.

To solve this problem, row 7 can be changed to claim values in excess of 1,000€. The resulting table is shown in Figure 5.10. With this modifica-

Decide on Claim Coverage				
U	*Claim.Value*	*Claim.TheftTime*	*CustomerContract.Type*	*Claim covered*
	[0€;2000€]	*[0;24]*	*{Gold, Silver, Bronze}*	*{yes, no}*
1	[0€;200€]	-	-	yes
2	[201€;500€]	-	Gold	yes
3	[201€;500€]	[6;22]	Silver	yes
4	[201€;500€]	[8;18]	Bronze	yes
5	[501€;1000€]	[6;22]	Gold	yes
6	[501€;1000€]	[8;18]	Silver	yes
7	> 1000€	-	-	no

Fig. 5.10. Decision table that satisfies the *Unique* hit policy; but it is not complete

tion, the table satisfies the *Unique* hit policy and, thereby, also the *Any* hit policy. Unfortunately, the table is no longer complete, since there are input combinations which do not match any row. An example is the case of a silver customer whose 850€-bike was stolen at 8 o'clock in the evening, at theft time 20. This input combination neither matches row 6 (because theft time 20 is not covered) nor the modified row 7 (claim value does not exceed 1,000€).

In order to provide a decision table that satisfies the *Unique* hit policy and that is complete, several rows have to be added. These rows reflect the decision outcome *no* for the different value intervals.

To cover all cases of silver customers with claim value between 501€ and 1,000€ that are outside of the covering theft time interval, a dedicated row ([501€;1000€],]18;8[, silver, no) has to be added. Notice that expressions of the form]*l*; *u*[denote the open interval of all values *v* such that $l < v < u$. When considering time of day,]18; 8[defines all thefts that occur after 6 o'clock in the evening and before 8 o'clock in the morning.

Notice that row 10 of that decision table also covers the case of a claim with value 850€, theft time 20 for a silver customer, which was not covered in

	Decide on Claim Coverage			
U	Claim.Value	Claim.TheftTime	CustomerContract.Type	Claim covered
	[0€;2000€]	[0;24]	{Gold, Silver, Bronze}	{yes, no}
1	[0€;200€]	-	-	yes
2	[201€;500€]	-	Gold	yes
3	[201€;500€]	[6;22]	Silver	yes
4	[201€;500€]	]22;6[	Silver	no
5	[201€;500€]	[8;18]	Bronze	yes
6	[201€;500€]	]18;8[	Bronze	no
7	[501€;1000€]	[6;22]	Gold	yes
8	[501€;1000€]	]22;6[	Gold	no
9	[501€;1000€]	[8;18]	Silver	yes
10	[501€;1000€]	]18;8[	Silver	no
11	[501€;1000€]	-	Bronze	no
12	> 1000€	-	-	no

Fig. 5.11. Decision table that satisfies the *Unique* hit policy and is complete

the previous version of the decision table shown in Figure 5.10. The resulting decision table is shown in Figure 5.11.

5.4.2 Multi-Hit Policies

The DMN standard also allows us to define multi-hit policies for decision tables. As the name suggests, there can be multiple matching rows for a given input combination, i.e., multiple 'hits'. All these rows are used to compute the output of the decision. While most decision tables use a single hit policy, there are situations in which a multi-hit policy allows us to define the decision logic in a more concise way.

The DMN standard provides the following multi-hit policies.

- *Output order (O):* In the *Output order* hit policy, the output of the decision is an ordered list consisting of the output values of all matching rows. The order is defined by the order of the output values in the output value domain. This is analogous to the single hit policy *Priority* that uses the ordering of values in the output domain to derive the output value.
- *Rule order (R):* In the *Rule order* hit policy, the order of the output values is determined by the order of the matching rules.
- *Collect (C):* The *Collect* hit policy returns an unordered list of output values; it can be extended with an aggregation operator that is applied on the output values. The hit policy C+ returns the sum of the values as decision output, C< the minimum value, C> the maximum value, and C# the number of values, i.e., the number of matching rows.

An example of a decision table with the C+ multi-hit policy is given in Figure 5.12. The table decides on the number of annual leave days for employees. The output of the decision depends on the age of the employee and the years of service. The table reads as follows.

C+	Decide on Leave Days		
	Age	Years of Service	LeaveDays
	Number	Number	Number
1	-	-	26
2	> 30	-	2
3	> 60	-	3
4	-	> 10	2
5	-	> 20	3
6	-	> 30	4

Fig. 5.12. Decision table with multi-hit policy *Collect* and summation aggregation

- Row 1: Any employee gets 26 days of annual leave.
- Row 2: If an employee is older than 30 years of age, regardless of the number of years in service, he or she receives another 2 days of annual leave.
- Row 3: Once an employee turns older than 60 years, 3 additional days of annual leave are granted.
- Rows 4–6: Depending on the years of service, up to 4 additional days of annual leave are granted.

Using a multi-hit policy, the decision table defines in a concise way the number of annual leave days. Depending on the input combination, up to all six rows can match. This holds, for example, for Anna, a 62 year old employee who has been in service for 31 years. In this case, the C+ hit policy returns the sum of output values of all rows, i.e., 40. The employee Berta, aged 24 who served for 3 years, would receive just 26 days of annual leave. Chris is 44 years old, and he served for 12 years for the company; he would receive 30 days of annual leave.

To illustrate the other multi-hit policies, the cases of Anna, Berta, and Chris are revisited. Anna (62, 31) matches rows 1–6, resulting in Output order O: (2, 2, 3, 3, 4, 26), Rule order R: (26, 2, 3, 2, 3, 4), Collect summation C+: 40, Collect minimum C<: 2, Collect maximum C>: 26, and Collect count C#: 6. Berta (24, 3) matches only row 1, so that O: (26), R: (26), C+: 26, C<: 26, C>: 26, and C#: 1. Chris (44, 12) matches rows 1, 2, and 4. As a result, O: (2, 2, 26), R: (26, 2, 2), C+: 30, C<: 2, C>: 26, and C#: 3.

While multi-hit policies provide a powerful mechanism to define decision logic in a concise manner, understandability might be hampered. Therefore it should be a conscious modelling decision if decision logic is defined using a single hit policy or a multiple hit policy. In many cases, the *Unique* single hit policy provides a high degree of understandability, while defining the logic of a decision precisely.

It is worth mentioning that multi-hit policies do not add expressive power to decision tables. In fact, any decision table can be transformed to a decision table that can be evaluated using the *Unique* single hit policy. For details, the reader is referred to the bibliographical nodes at the end of this chapter.

Bibliographical Notes

The Decision Model and Notation standard was published in Object Management Group (2018). Taylor and Purchase (2016) provide an introduction to decision modelling, focusing on different application scenarios of DMN. An introduction to DMN from a practical angle that also looks at decision execution can be found in Silver and Tirelli (2018).

Decision tables have been addressed in the literature since many years. Early works on decision tables includes the work by Schumacher and Sevcik (1976) that looks at a mapping from decision tables to program code. Over the years, decision tables have been used in different application domains and disciplines, for instance in management, as shown by a credit-risk evaluation scenario by Baesens et al. (2003).

In one of the earliest works combining decision logic with business processes, Batoulis et al. (2015) introduce an approach to derive decision logic from business processes. A method to translate decision tables into unique decision tables was introduced in Batoulis and Weske (2018b). Algorithms to find overlapping rules and missing rules in decision tables can be found in Calvanese et al. (2018). Haarmann et al. (2018) introduce an approach to map DMN decision models to Ethereum smart contract code, to be executed on a blockchain.

6

Process Choreographies

The previous chapter discussed how execution constraints between activities of a given business process can be captured in process orchestrations. However, dependencies do not exist only between activities of the same process orchestration, but also between activities of different process orchestrations. This is the case if they participate in a business-to-business collaboration. To realize these collaborations, process orchestrations interact with each other, typically by sending and receiving messages.

Choreographies have a central role in ensuring interoperability between process orchestrations, each of which is performed by a participant in a business-to-business collaboration. Several industry initiatives are in place for establishing standardized choreographies in particular domains. Examples include RosettaNet for the supply chain domain, SWIFTNet for financial services, and Health Level Seven (HL7) for health care services. They all define rules for the collaboration that companies need to comply with in order to collaborate with each other.

By introducing collaboration rules, costs for the individual companies are reduced: interaction behaviour does not need to be agreed upon by every business partner, but, rather, industry-wide standards serve as reference for the intended collaboration. New companies can join the market more easily, since they know the rules of that domain.

These collaboration rules are specified by process choreographies. While domain-specific process choreography standards are important in their particular fields, they lack the flexibility to define new types of business-to-business collaborations that are important for supporting cooperation between companies in today's dynamic market environments. Therefore, new approaches for the definition and implementation of process choreographies are required.

The goal of this chapter is introducing a common understanding of the concepts used in process choreography design and implementation and on the steps that are required to develop choreographies. This chapter is organized as follows. Section 6.1 looks at the motivation for process choreographies and introduces terminology. Choreography design phases are investigated in

© Springer-Verlag GmbH Germany, part of Springer Nature 2019
M. Weske, *Business Process Management*,
https://doi.org/10.1007/978-3-662-59432-2_6

Section 6.2. The actual design of process choreographies is addressed in Section 6.3, while their implementation is discussed in Section 6.4.

Process choreographies are composed of sets of individual interactions. Service interaction patterns have been introduced to provide a set of recurring interaction types. These important building blocks for process choreographies are studied in Section 6.5. A particular process choreography language is introduced in Section 6.6.

6.1 Motivation and Terminology

In today's business scenarios, companies increasingly join forces to combine their services and products to provide added-value products to the market. These products are typically realized by business processes, which in many cases take advantage of the existing software infrastructures of the participating companies.

Because business-to-business collaborations are quite complex, and any failure in the collaboration might have an immediate effect on the operational business of the company, the cooperation between companies should be designed very carefully. Process choreographies can be used for this endeavour.

The requirements of process choreography development depend on the number of interacting partners and the desired level of automation. In business environments, where the cooperation of business partners is realized through traditional means like fax messages being sent and read and understood by humans, where humans can pick up the phone and settle any ambiguities, detailed and formal process choreographies are not essential.

However, if the cooperation is to be realized—at least in part—by information systems, so that a high level of automation is achieved, there need to be unambiguous models that specify in detail the nature of the collaboration of business partners in the context of a process choreography. These considerations are illustrated by an example.

Consider a bidding scenario in which the owner of a car uses an auctioning service to sell his car to the highest bidder. Potentially, thousands of people can participate in the auction and place their bids. Such scenarios require agreement on how the participants need to interact with each other in order to avoid problems that could appear as the result of wrong interaction.

To illustrate the problems that could arise from erroneous interaction, consider a collaboration involving process orchestrations run by two companies. The process orchestrations, including the interaction by message flow, are depicted in Figure 6.1.

The business process of *Company 1* can only be initiated by the receipt of a message. This message can only be sent by activity *B2* of the business process of *Company 2*. *B2* in turn can only be performed after *A2* is completed. However, *A2* waits to receive a message from activity *C1* to be sent by *Company 1*. As a result, both process orchestrations cannot proceed: they are

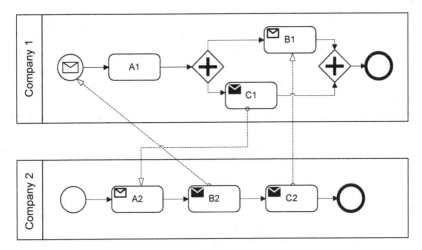

Fig. 6.1. Deadlock of interacting process orchestrations

stuck in a permanent deadlock situation. To avoid these kinds of problems, the partners involved in a process choreography need to agree on the process choreography.

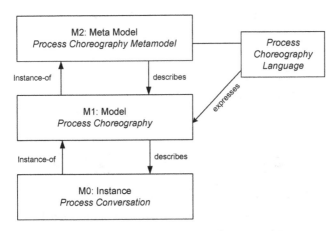

Fig. 6.2. MOF levels of process choreographies

Each of the process orchestrations shown in Figure 6.1 exposes a valid behaviour if considered on its own. The behaviours are valid because each process instance will perform a set of activity instances before it completes. Deadlock situations, infinite loops, and other types of undesired behaviour cannot appear.

The problem encountered is due to links between send and receive activities in the process orchestrations. As the example illustrates, the viewpoint of an individual process orchestration does not suffice for reasoning about the interaction between process orchestrations; a global view on the interactions between process orchestrations is required.

The levels of abstraction found in process choreographies are shown in Figure 6.2, where the Meta Object Facility levels are shown with the respective artefacts. At the metamodel level, the *Process Choreography Metamodel* is shown which provides the concepts to express *Process Choreographies* at the model level.

Concrete instances of process choreographies are called *Process Conversations*, which appear at the instance level. A *Process Choreography Language* provides constructs to express process choreographies based on a process choreography metamodel.

While Figure 6.2 shows the overall organization of the artefacts in process choreographies, a detailed investigation of the artefacts and their relationships is required. The core artefacts involved in process choreographies and their relationships are shown in Figure 6.3. This figure is similar to the process metamodel shown in Figure 3.16 on page 91, because it represents the model level and the instance level.

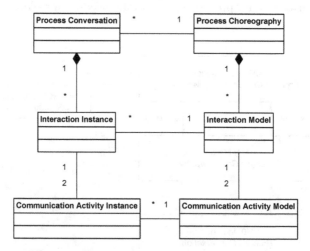

Fig. 6.3. Process choreography conceptual model

In the conceptual model of process choreographies shown in Figure 6.3, on the right-hand side the concepts at the model level are shown: each *Process Choreography* is composed of a set of *Interaction Models*.

Each interaction model is associated with two objects of the class *Communication Activity Model*. Communication activity models are activity models in process orchestrations that exhibit a communication behaviour by sending or receiving messages. For the time being we focus on simple interactions involving two activities.

As with process orchestrations, we can distinguish between models and instances. The instance level is shown on the left-hand side in Figure 6.3, covering the concrete message exchange between interacting process instances.

The term *Process Conversation* refers to the concrete messages that are exchanged as specified in a given process choreography. Therefore, process choreographies serve as conversation models. Each process conversation consists of a set of *Interaction Instances*, each of which is the concrete realization of a message exchange as specified by the associated interaction model. Each interaction instance is associated with *Communication Activity Instances*, which are the concrete activity instances that send and receive messages.

6.2 Development Phases

This section introduces the development of process choreographies, guided by phases. The main goal of this section is to provide an understanding of the concepts and artefacts involved in the design of process choreographies, rather than on providing a reference methodology for choreography design.

The phases involved in the development of process choreographies are depicted in Figure 6.4. These phases are organized into design phases and implementation phases, shown in the upper and lower part of that figure, respectively. There are three associated roles that represent the stakeholders involved in choreography design and implementation. Based on the discussion of these roles in Section 1.2, their specific responsibilities in the context of process choreographies are highlighted.

Business engineers are mainly involved in the choreography design phases, including *scenario modelling, domain scoping, milestone definition*, and *participant identification*. Business engineers are responsible for business-related aspects of the process choreography; they need to make sure that the collaboration contributes to the goals of the enterprise, similarly to organizational business processes.

System architects are responsible for the architectural aspects of the implemented process choreography. System architects are at the border of design and implementation, as sketched in Figure 6.4. This means that they are involved in the design of process choreographies as well as in their implementation. In particular, they are involved in the specification of the behavioural interfaces, discussed later in this chapter.

Once the process choreography design is completed, *developers* are responsible for realizing the process orchestrations in a way that the overall business-to-business collaboration as specified in the process choreography is realized. Behavioural interfaces are important artefacts for designing the individual process orchestrations.

Based on this discussion of the stakeholders in process choreography design and implementation, the phases are sketched.

Scenario modelling is at the heart of choreography design: scenarios describe the overall setting and goals of the process choreography. They are also useful for integrating the results of the other design phases. To model a particular scenario, a domain in which the cooperation will take place needs to be specified. This is performed during the *domain scoping* phase by business engineers.

Formal notations are not required in scenario modelling and domain scoping, so that the scenario and the domain can be described in a language that allows expressing the relevant concepts. Depending on the specific setting of the project, plain English text enriched with informally specified graphical diagrams can be used.

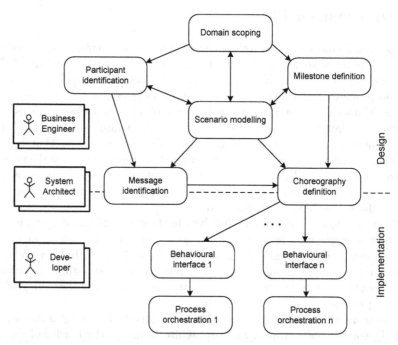

Fig. 6.4. Phases during choreography design and implementation

The *participant identification* phase is devoted to defining different roles of choreography participants. There are two options for doing this. These roles are specified in a way that allows for the selecting of concrete process participants on the basis of their properties as laid out in the participant roles.

In the context of process choreographies, the term process participant refers to an organization, rather than to an individual. For instance, the role shipper can be played by multiple shipping companies, all of which are appropriate for participation in the process choreography.

In the *milestone definition* phase, the participants define certain states of the choreography in which the cooperation has achieved certain results, typically characterized by intermediate products. These states are called *milestones*. Milestones and their ordering describe behavioural aspects of the choreography from a high level of abstraction.

In the *message identification* phase, the interactions in the scenario are used to identify and design messages that realize the various interactions. This phase has business aspects as well as technical aspects; it is therefore located on the border of the design and implementation of process choreographies. The design aspects include the business content of the messages, while the implementation aspects include the technical realization of these messages and concrete message formats.

Finally, the *choreography definition* phase combines the *message identification* and the *milestone definition* phases of the modelled scenario. The result of this phase is a detailed specification of the interactions between the participants, the messages to realize the interactions, and the milestones that are reached during the resulting conversation in the instance layer.

The *choreography definition* phase, just like the *message identification* phase, includes business aspects as well as technical aspects. Unsuccessful interaction behaviour would arise if, for instance, message formats were used that one or more participants would not understand. To avoid this problem, it is assumed that message formats as well as the semantics of the messages are agreed upon by the participants.

Domain standards, like the ones mentioned above, are in place to provide a common terminology, and, thereby, an understanding of the concepts used. These standards are enhanced with technical information, so that data structures and message formats are available. *Business engineers, system architects*, and *developers* participate in *choreography definition* and *message identification*.

In the lower part of Figure 6.4, the phases during implementation of process choreographies are shown. Based on the choreography definition, *behavioural interfaces* of all roles in the process choreography are defined. Behavioural interfaces serve as blueprints for the design of the individual process orchestrations realized by the participants of the process choreography.

6.3 Process Choreography Design

The design of process choreographies involves a series of activities. In each of these activities, artefacts are developed. These activities are described as follows:

1. *High-level Structure Design*: In high-level choreography design, the participant roles as well as their communication structures are identified. High-level structure design is conducted during the *Participant identification* phase.

2. *High-level Behavioural Design*: High-level behavioural models specify the milestones of the collaboration and the order in which the milestones are reached. High-level behavioural design is done during the *milestone definition* phase.
3. *Collaboration Scenarios*: High-level choreographies are refined by introducing dedicated collaboration scenarios that relate the reaching of milestones to the communication between process participants. Collaboration scenarios are developed during the *choreography definition* phase, based on the scenarios informally specified during *scenario modelling*.
4. *Behavioural Interfaces*: From these collaboration scenarios, for each participant role, a behavioural interface is derived.

6.3.1 High-Level Design

High-level process choreography design involves structure design and behaviour design. In high-level structure design, participant roles of the choreography are defined, as part of the *participant identification* phase. Figure 6.5 shows a high-level structure diagram for participants involved in a bidding scenario. This diagram identifies a seller, an auctioning service, and multiple bidders as participants. It also shows that these participants are pairwise interconnected. Therefore, any participant can interact directly with any other.

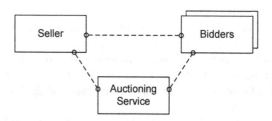

Fig. 6.5. High-level structural model of participants in bidding scenario

High-level behaviour design uses milestones that are achieved during the collaboration; it is therefore part of the *milestone definition* phase. Each milestone represents a state in the overall collaboration that has a business meaning, represented by some business value. Milestones correspond to subgoals reached during the collaboration on the way to reaching its ultimate goal.

For instance, the ultimate goal in the bidding scenario is that the offered goods are sold, paid for, and delivered to the bidder with the highest bid. Several intermediate steps can be distinguished: the initial setup of the auction, the entry of potential bidders into the auction, the actual bidding process, and the delivery and payment.

Each milestone can be identified by an expression that describes the state reached in that milestone. The milestones of (a part of) the bidding scenario are depicted in Figure 6.6, where expressions like *Auction is set up* and

Bidding phase is over are used. These expressions indicate states during the collaboration that have a business meaning.

In that figure, milestones are defined by circles, where the initial milestone has a single border, the intermediate milestones have double borders, and the ultimate goal milestone has a bold border. This notation follows the BPMN, where start events, intermediate events, and end events are drawn in the same manner. Mapping milestones to events is valid, because reaching a milestone effectively realizes an event. For instance, the completion of the bidding phase can be represented by an event *Bidding phase is over*, as shown in Figure 6.6.

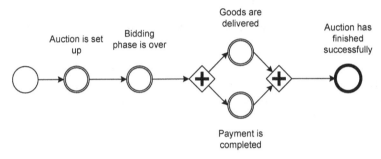

Fig. 6.6. High-level behavioural model for bidding scenario, represented by milestones

Milestones have dependencies with respect to other milestones. For instance, the auction has to be set up before the bidding process can be finished. During the bidding scenario, first the auction is set up, defining the first milestone, *Auction is set up*. The next milestone, *Bidding phase is over*, is reached when the bidding phase completes. Then there is an *and* split gateway, so that the next milestones *Goods are delivered* and *Payment is completed*, can be reached concurrently. If both milestones are reached, the auction can complete, reaching the final milestone, *Auction has finished successfully*.

It might also happen that a milestone is not reached in a certain conversation. This situation occurs in the bidding scenario, for instance, if no single bid is placed during the auction. In this case, delivery and payment cannot occur, and the conversation ends without the final goal being reached. This negative outcome can be modelled by introducing new milestones, reflecting the positive and negative outcome of the bidding phase, respectively. This diagram is shown in Figure 6.7.

6.3.2 Collaboration Scenarios

Having identified the collaboration milestones, collaboration scenarios can be addressed, as part of the *choreography definition* phase. In this phase, the interactions needed to proceed from one milestone to another are specified.

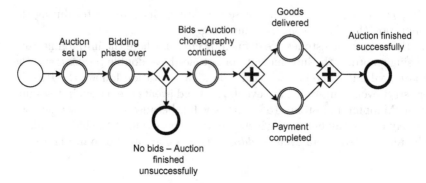

Fig. 6.7. High-level behavioural model for bidding scenario, with different outcomes

One or several collaboration scenarios show the interactions and their dependencies that need to occur between two milestones. To this end, interactions between process participants serve as the building blocks for the resulting collaboration scenarios.

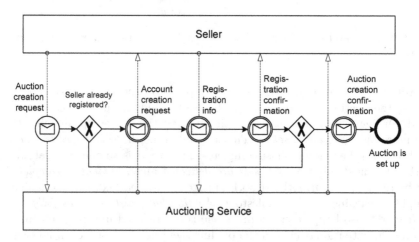

Fig. 6.8. Collaboration scenario: reaching milestones through interactions

Scenarios should be kept small, as it is easier to reach agreement on less complex interaction behaviour. Additional scenario models might be introduced to deal with special cases and exceptions.

Figure 6.8 depicts the initial part of the bidding choreography, where the first intermediary milestone *Auction is set up* is reached. An *Auction creation request* initiates the conversation and, if not registered with the auctioning service yet, the seller needs to be registered. Once the *Auction creation con-*

firmation message is received by the seller, the *Auction is set up* milestone is reached.

Notice that the *Auction is set up* milestone is the final milestone in this collaboration scenario. Therefore, it is drawn in bold in Figure 6.8. However, this milestone is an intermediate milestone in the high-level behavioural model, so that it is drawn with a double border in Figure 6.6.

This example uses control flow patterns to express the relationships between the interaction models. To this end, the interaction models between participants can be represented as a specific kind of process, in which the building blocks are interaction models, rather than business process activities, as in process orchestrations.

Although scenario models define control flow between interactions, the concrete message structures have not been addressed yet. Data interoperability is an important aspect in process choreography projects. Therefore, data models including possible data transformation rules need to be added. Once these aspects are defined in sufficient detail, all artefacts are aggregated in the final process choreography.

While the collaboration scenario depicted in Figure 6.8 shows the milestones and the resulting interactions, as well as their dependencies, the interfaces of the individual participants need to be specified; these specifications are called *behavioural interfaces*. A behavioural interface covers the individual view of one specific participant in the process choreography; the internal aspects of the own process orchestration, as well as the interactions involving only other participants, are disregarded.

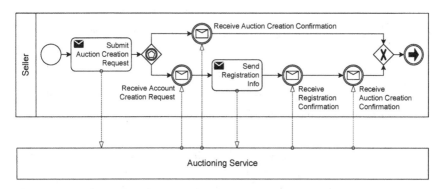

Fig. 6.9. Behavioural interface for seller

Figure 6.9 shows the behavioural interface for the seller in the auctioning scenario. Behavioural interfaces consider parts of process orchestrations that exhibit externally visible behaviour, for instance, communication activities and events that represent the sending or receiving of a message.

6.3.3 Compatibility

Process choreography design needs to ensure that the process orchestrations of the participants play together well in the overall collaboration. Compatibility is the ability of a set of participants to interact successfully according to a given process choreography.

Unsuccessful interaction behaviour could arise, if, for instance, different message formats were used in a collaboration and one participant does not understand the content of a message sent by another participant.

Another source of incompatibility—which this section will focus on—is due to wrong and misaligned interactions. If, for instance, a participant expects a notification at some point in its process before it can proceed, and none of the other participants sends such a notification message, then the process cannot continue, so a deadlock situation emerges. Compatibility of interacting processes aims at avoiding this type of undesired behaviour due to erroneous interactions between process orchestrations.

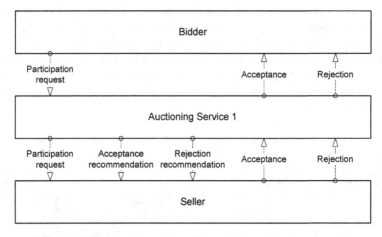

Fig. 6.10. Interactions of participants in auctioning scenario

The bidding example illustrates the different aspects of compatibility introduced in this section. Figure 6.10 shows an auctioning scenario with three participants involved. A potential bidder must be accepted for participation before she can place her bid. Therefore, the bidder first needs to send a *Participation request* to the auctioning service.

As a response, the auctioning service can send an *Acceptance* notification or a *Rejection* notification. In some cases, the seller is requested to make the final decision on whether a bidder can be accepted. In order to perform this interaction, the auctioning service forwards the request of the bidder to the seller. It might also give a recommendation for accepting the bidder. The seller can send a notification about his decision back to the auctioning service.

The auctioning scenario depicted in Figure 6.10 represents the participants by pools that interact by sending and receiving messages. However, the figure does not show any behavioural dependencies between the different message exchanges. Nevertheless, compatibility can be investigated based on this high-level representation of the scenario.

Since only the structure of the interaction is taken into account, we refer to it as *structural compatibility*. This property of a process choreography comes in two flavors. *Strong structural compatibility* is given if, for every message that can be sent there is a participant who can receive it, and if for every message that can be received, there is a participant who can send it. Because each message flow connects exactly two participants in Figure 6.10, strong structural compatibility is satisfied in this example.

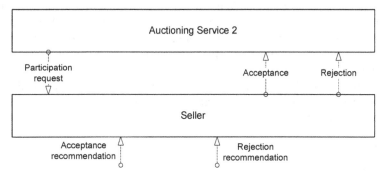

Fig. 6.11. Alternative auctioning service results in weak structural compatibility

Weak structural compatibility is given if all messages sent by participants can be received by other participants. However, it is not required that all messages that participants can ever receive will actually be sent by other participants.

Since the individual process orchestrations have in most cases been developed independently of each other, a complete structural match between participants cannot always be achieved. The occurrence of weak structural compatibility is more likely. In this case, all messages sent can be received, but it is not required that for every message that can be received there be a participant who can actually send such a message.

The rationale behind this definition is that the interaction can take place, even though some participants are able to receive additional messages. It is assumed that these messages are not essential for the overall process choreography. This will be discussed in more detail below.

In an alternative setting, a new auctioning service, for example, always forwards the request by the bidder to the seller without providing recommendations. In this case the seller will never receive any recommendation. However, if these recommendations are not essential for the seller process orchestration, as the example indicates, the cooperation can still be successful. This example is shown in Figure 6.11, disregarding the bidder, who remains unchanged.

Unlike structural compatibility, *behavioural compatibility* considers behavioural dependencies, that is, control flow between interaction instances of a conversation. Therefore, the process orchestrations of the interacting partners are interconnected, and the resulting process structure is analyzed. Such analysis requires a formal, unambiguous representation.

In an approach for checking behavioural compatibility by Martens (2003b), process orchestrations are represented by a specific class of Petri nets, namely *workflow modules*. Workflow modules are basically workflow nets with additional communication places that are used to represent message flow between participants.

Whenever a participant sends a message, the process orchestration of that partner features a transition with an output communication place that can hold messages sent. At the receiver side, the workflow module requires a matching input communication place. This place is an input place of the transition that receives the message.

Each process orchestration is represented by a workflow module that defines its internal behaviour and its external communication behaviour. Workflow modules are defined as follows:

Definition 6.1 A Petri net $PN = (P, T, F)$ is a *workflow module* if and only if the following conditions hold:

- The set of places P is partitioned into sets P^N of internal places, P^I of incoming places, and P^O of outgoing places.
- T is a nonempty set of transitions.
- The flow relation F is partitioned into an internal flow relation $F^N \subseteq (P^N \times T) \cup (T \times P^N)$ and a communication flow relation $F^C \subseteq (P^I \times T) \cup (T \times P^O)$.
- (P^N, T, F^N) is a workflow net.
- There is no transition t connected to both an incoming place and an outgoing place.

◇

Figure 6.12 shows workflow modules for the participants *Auctioning Service 1* and *Seller*. For presentation purposes, the workflow modules represent only a small part of the auctioning and seller process orchestrations.

The process fragment of the auctioning service considered sends a recommendation to either accept or reject the bidder. It is then able to receive either an acceptance or a rejection message. The seller can receive a recommendation message before sending either a rejection message or an acceptance message.

Note that workflow modules are not workflow nets, because in workflow nets each place and each transition is on a path from the initial node to the final node. In workflow modules this is not true, because communication places

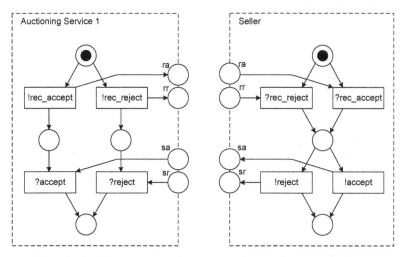

Fig. 6.12. Workflow modules as basis for checking compatibility

by definition have either no incoming edges (places for receiving messages) or
no outgoing edges (places for sending messages).

For instance, place *ra* of the auctioning service in Figure 6.12 has no
outgoing edge and place *ra* of the seller has no incoming edge. Because in
workflow nets only the initial place can have no incoming edge and only the
final place can have no outgoing edge, workflow modules are not workflow
nets.

Interaction activities are represented by transitions in workflow modules.
Sending transitions are marked with an exclamation mark followed by an
identifier of the message sent. For instance, *!rec_accept* marks the transition
that sends a recommendation for accepting the new bidder.

Transitions that model activities that receive tokens are marked by a question mark followed by an identifier of the message received. For instance, receiving an accept recommendation message by the seller is represented by the
transition *?rec_accept*.

The sending of the message is represented by the firing of the transition.
When *!rec_accept* fires, a token is put on the communication place *ra*. This
communication place represents an outgoing message of the auctioning service.

Communication places act just as normal places in Petri nets. A transition
with a communication place as an input place is enabled only if there is a
token in that place. Thereby, message flow can be represented properly. The
receiving transition can only be performed if a message has arrived.

The workflow module approach requires strong structural compatibility of
the workflow modules. Therefore, there need to be corresponding places for
all communication places in each module. In the next step, the corresponding
communication places are merged, and a new initial place and a new final
place are added.

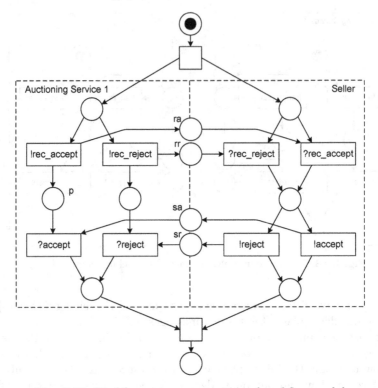

Fig. 6.13. Workflow net as composition of workflow modules

As a result, the workflow modules are merged in such a way that a Petri net results, as shown in Figure 6.13. This Petri net is a workflow net because, following Definition 4.8, there is one dedicated initial place and one final place, and each node is on a path from the initial place to the final place.

Although the resulting structure is a workflow net, the composition of the workflow modules is not satisfactory. Consider a process instance in which the auctioning service recommends accepting the bidder, while the seller decides to reject the bidder. In this case, there is a token in the communication place *sr*, and a token in place *p* of the auctioning service. The process choreography is in a deadlock, because neither the *?accept* transition nor the *?reject* transition of the auctioning service is enabled. The reason for this situation is the structure of the auctioning service.

Figure 6.14 shows that an updated version using *Auctioning Service 1'* does not suffer from this problem.

Figure 6.15 depicts a larger part of the collaboration, where buyers can request permission to the auction. The figure shows the behavioural interfaces of the buyer, the auctioning service, and the seller.

The behavioural interfaces of the roles and their relationships are explained as follows. The buyer places a participation request at the auctioning service,

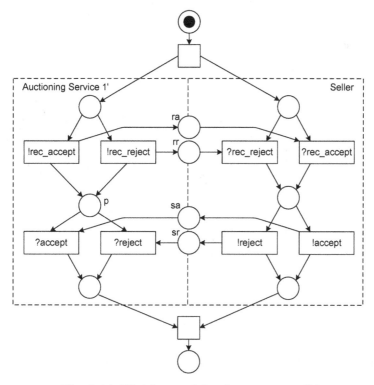

Fig. 6.14. Workflow modules that are compatible

represented by a *!participation_req* transition that puts a token in the communication place *pr* of the buyer. This token represents the actual message sent from a buyer to an auctioning service.

The interactions between the auctioning service and the seller has been discussed above. The auctioning service sends a recommendation to the seller, who receives it. Then the seller decides on accepting the buyer and sends the respective message to the auctioning service, who forwards it to the buyer.

While this specification describes the interaction between the participants of a conversation, it also allows extending the internal processes of the individual participants. The auctioning service could, for instance, look up historical data about the buyer before proposing a recommendation and sending it to the seller. The seller could also have an internal decision making process in place, possibly spanning different organizational units, to accept or reject a buyer request.

No matter how the internal processes of the participants look like, we need to make sure that these internal processes are in line with their behavioural interfaces. Ensuring this is a challenging task when dealing with a large number of participants in an auctioning scenario involving, for instance, hundreds of potential buyers, several auctioning services, and dozens of sellers.

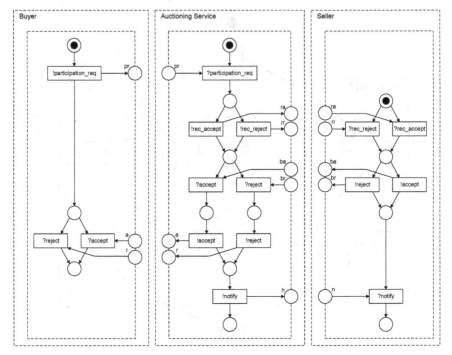

Fig. 6.15. Behavioural interfaces: getting a participation permission

The approach based on workflow modules will be investigated in more detail in Section 7.6.1 in the context of weak soundness, because this specific correctness criterion was established in the context of choreography design. Further approaches are mentioned, with their references in the bibliographical notes at the end of this chapter.

6.4 Process Choreography Implementation

After discussing the design of process choreographies, this section looks at the implementation of choreographies. Behavioural interfaces serve as blueprints for the internal realization of process orchestrations, because each process orchestration needs to expose an externally visible behaviour that was specified as the behavioural interface of the respective participant.

Assume that there is a set of behavioural interfaces compatible with each other. These interfaces can now be refined to local process orchestrations. In local process orchestrations, activities can be added or, in some cases, even reordered, while the observable behaviour has to be preserved.

The relationship between the behavioural interface and the local process orchestration needs to be investigated, so that the correctness of the overall collaboration can be achieved. Each local process orchestration needs to be consistent with the respective behavioural interface definition. This section will introduce consistency criteria using a business-to-business collaboration scenario.

Figure 6.16 provides an overview of the participants in that scenario: a *Buyer*—for instance, a car manufacturer—uses reverse auctioning for procuring specific components. To ease the selection of an appropriate *Seller* and to manage the auction, the buyer outsources these activities to a dedicated *Auctioning Service*. A *Shipper* is selected to transport the ordered goods from the seller to the buyer.

As in the example discussed above, the auction is not public, so that only registered parties can participate. Since it is a reverse auctioning scenario, sellers need to request permission to participate in the auction beforehand. Once the auction has started, sellers can place their bids. When the auction completes, the buyer selects a seller according to the lowest bid or according to some other evaluation criterion. Finally, the goods are shipped and payment is processed.

In this sample scenario, there are two alternatives for selecting a shipper: either the selected seller determines the shipper that would deliver the goods to the buyer, or the seller provides a list of shippers with different transportation costs and quality levels, from which the buyer can choose a shipper.

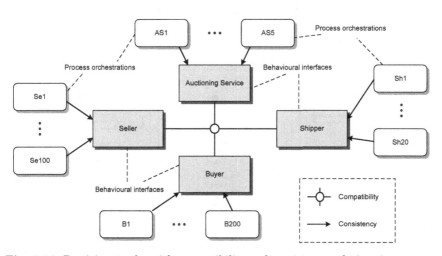

Fig. 6.16. Participant roles with compatibility and consistency relations in a reverse auctioning scenario

As shown in Figure 6.16, there can be several sellers, shippers and—in a generic setting—multiple buyers and auctioning services. In this figure, each participant role is specified by a set of its behavioural interfaces, as discussed in the previous section. These interfaces need to be compatible with each other, so that the collaboration can be successful.

Each participant role can be potentially played by several process participants. Each of these process participants develops a process orchestration. These process orchestrations need to be consistent with the behavioural interface of the participant role. For instance, the process orchestration of seller *Se1* needs to be consistent with the behavioural interface of the *Seller* role.

Using consistency rules, each participant can check locally whether its local business process orchestration fits its behavioural interface. If the behavioural interfaces are compatible with each other and if, in addition, for each participant, the internal business process orchestration is consistent with the respective behavioural interface, then a successful collaboration between the process participants is realized—additional checks involving the internal business process orchestrations of the participants are then not required.

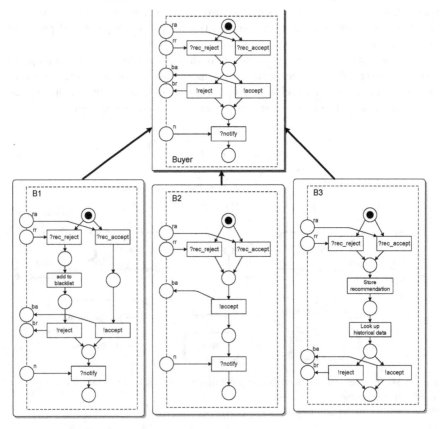

Fig. 6.17. Alternative implementations for buyer role

The behavioural interface of a participant role leaves room for multiple process orchestrations, that is, there are multiple process orchestrations consistent with a given behavioural interface.

In order to illustrate this, Figure 6.17 presents three process orchestrations for the buyer role in the reverse auctioning example, namely *B1*, *B2*, and *B3*. While the structure of the process orchestrations is at first sight similar to the behavioural interface, there are subtle differences between them.

First of all, the process orchestrations for participants *B1* and *B3* contain additional internal activities. In *B1*, the buyer maintains a blacklist, consisting of sellers that have not been recommended for acceptance by an auctioning service. In *B3*, the received recommendation is stored in any case, represented by the *Store recommendation* transition. Before the buyer decides whether to accept a seller, the historical data is consulted, represented by the *Look up historical data* transition.

Buyer *B1* has the same set of communication places as the behavioural interface of the *Buyer* role, but different control flow. *B2* and *B3* have different communication places than the behavioural interface. The question now is whether any of these implementations is consistent with the behavioural interface of the *Buyer* role.

The answer to this question depends on the consistency notion in place. By common sense we can argue that all three local process orchestrations are consistent with the behavioural interface of the buyer: *B1* stores negative recommendations in a blacklist, and it always follows the received recommendations sent by the auctioning service. This realizes a behaviour that is consistent with the interface, although not all possibilities of the buyer interface are realized: *B1* does not decide about accepting a seller on its own but always follows the recommendation received.

Buyer *B2* accepts every seller, so that the recommendations received are discarded. We can argue that the behaviour of *B2* is consistent with the buyer interface, although not all behaviours are possible, that is, *B2* cannot reject a seller.

B3 stores the recommendation received and makes an independent decision about accepting a seller. We can argue that this behaviour is also consistent with the buyer interface, because *B3* can communicate as specified, at least regarding recommendation and decision messages. However, *B3* is not able to receive a notification message. If we assume that this message is not essential then also *B3* is a valid implementation of the buyer interface.

This discussion shows that the decision on whether an implementation is consistent with a behavioural interface is subject to consistency criteria.

Consistency Criterion: Public-to-Private Approach

The public-to-private approach defines a consistency criterion. It is based on Petri nets and uses notions of behavioural inheritance to characterize the relationship between a behavioural interface and a private process orchestration.

While we do not cover the formal details of the approach in this book, we introduce its essence. First, the partners agree on a choreography, which is defined as a Petri net. The net is partitioned among the partners, defining the responsibilities of the partners regarding the overall choreography.

The partition of each partner defines its behavioural interface, that is, the public process of the partner. This public process can be enhanced to implement a private process orchestration. The refinement of a public process to realize a private process can only be done by a set of transformation operations, which are graph operations on the Petri net.

- *Loop*: By adding a loop with start place and end place of the loop being exactly one place in the public process, the process can be transformed.
- *Detour*: An edge in the Petri net can be substituted by a subnet, which implements a detour of the original flow, defined in the public process.
- *Concur*: A concurrent branch can be added by designing a subnet which is spawned concurrently to the original flow, later to be synchronized with the flow.

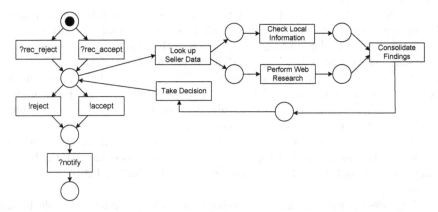

Fig. 6.18. *Loop* transformation operation of the public-to-private approach

It has been shown that applying only these transformation operations does not change the externally visible behaviour of the process. The resulting private process is a specialization of the public process. It has also been shown that combining the private processes of the partners will result in a correct and sound overall process choreography. As a result, all private processes that can be derived from a given public process using only the transformation operations are consistent with the public process.

Technically, the approach is based on branching bisimulation. According to this equivalence notion, two processes are branching bisimilar, if they can mutually simulate each other's behaviour, that is, if one process can do everything that the other process can do and vice versa.

The approach disregards locally added activities of the private process. These activities are called silent activities.

An example of a loop transformation is shown in Figure 6.18, where the loop can be taken after receiving either recommendation. The private process is composed of the public process and the local refinement, generated by the transformation operation. The loop consists of a subprocess containing activities for looking up seller data, checking further information about the seller, consolidating the results and, finally, taking a decision.

The loop has the character of a while loop, since it can be iterated zero or more times. From this example, it is also clear that the behavioural interface of the process is not changed by that operation. All communication operations—those that receive or send messages—and their behavioural constraints are unchanged.

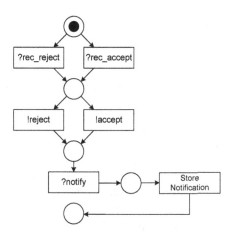

Fig. 6.19. *Detour* transformation operation of the public-to-private approach

Figure 6.19 shows the detour transformation. One edge of the Petri net is exchanged by a detour. In the example shown, the detour consists of a single activity only, an activity for storing the received notification. In general, the detour may consist of a more complex net structure. As for the other transformation operations, the added subnet needs to be sound. This means that there are neither deadlocks nor lack of synchronization. Soundness is investigated in detail in the next chapter.

Figure 6.20 shows the concur transformation operation. The buyer sets up a seller account after sending an acceptance message. In a more general setting, the added parts of the private process can be performed concurrently to other parts of the process, which is indicated by the parallel split behaviour of the *!accept* transition.

The architecture of the public-to-private approach fits nicely to the architecture of behavioural interfaces and local process orchestrations, shown in Figure 6.16. The behavioural interfaces are the public processes of the partners, while the process orchestrations are the private processes of the partners.

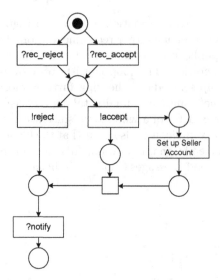

Fig. 6.20. *Concur* transformation operation of the public-to-private approach

For each behavioural interface definition, there can be multiple private processes. In the public-to-private approach, these private processes can only be designed by applying the transformation operations.

To conclude this section, we discuss whether the alternative implementations shown in Figure 6.17 are—according to the public-to-private approach—consistent with the behavioural interface of the buyer.

Using the terminology of the public-to-private approach, the question is answered whether the private processes of buyers $B1$, $B2$, or $B3$ are consistent with the public process of the buyer. For convenience, we denote the public process of the buyer by B.

$B1$ cannot be derived from the public process of the buyer using the transformation operations only. This is not surprising, since $B1$ cannot behave like B can behave. In particular, $B1$ cannot send an acceptance message after receiving a rejection recommendation, although this is a legal behaviour of B. Therefore, $B1$ is not consistent with B.

$B2$ does not even have the same set of transitions that B has. We would need a delete operation to derive $B2$ from B. Since there is no delete operation, $B2$ cannot be derived from B. $B2$ does not expose the complete behaviour of B, since, for example, $B2$ can never send a rejection message. For the same reason, $B3$ is not consistent with the public process of the buyer. $B3$ can not receive a notification message.

This discussion illustrates that the public-to-private approach is based on a strict notion of equivalence, namely branching bisimulation. On the other hand, it makes sure that the combination of the private processes still exposes correct behaviour.

On the other hand, there are quite complex extensions possible with this approach. To illustrate this claim, Figure 6.21 shows the private process of a buyer, with the combined transformation operations applied.

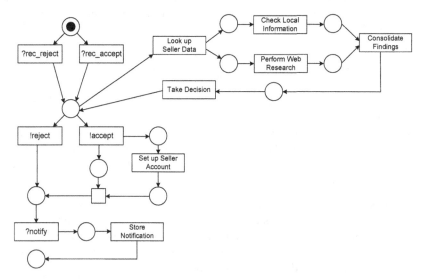

Fig. 6.21. Private process that—according to the public-to-private approach—is consistent with the public process of the buyer

Despite the relative complexity of that private process, we can argue that it exposes exactly the same behaviour as the public process of the buyer role. Notice that branching bisimulation disregards silent activities. The process starts by receiving a recommendation message. Then either a message is sent or a loop is iterated. If an acceptance message is sent, a seller account is set up. In any case, a notification is received, stored, and the process terminates properly.

For further details on consistency in process choreographies in general and the public-to-private approach in particular, the reader is referred to the bibliographical notes of this chapter.

6.5 Service Interaction Patterns

In Chapter 4, control flow patterns have been introduced that describe control flow in process orchestrations. However, there are several differences between process orchestrations and process choreographies that need specific consideration: choreographies are based on message exchange, and potentially many participants interact in a choreography, while orchestrations are based on control flow between the activities of a single process performed by a single organization.

Service interaction patterns aim at filling this gap by proposing small granular types of interactions that can be combined to process choreographies. As with control flow patterns for process orchestrations, service interaction patterns can also be used to benchmark languages for their ability to express advanced conversations. Service interaction patterns can be classified according to the following schemes.

- *Number of participants involved*: Bilateral interactions involve two participants, whereas multilateral interactions involve more than two participants.
- *Number of messages exchanged*: Single transmission versus multi-transmission interactions.
- *Variations in message receiver*: In case of two-way interactions, *round-trip interaction* means that the receiver of the message is necessarily the same as the sender, whereas *routed interaction* means that the receiver of the message in general differs from the sender.

The BPMN is used to provide graphical representations of service interaction patterns. Since this notation is not specifically tailored to the needs of service interaction patterns, the graphical representations of the patterns are not complete. Together with the textual representation of the patterns, the service interaction patterns are described properly.

Send

The send pattern represents a one-way interaction between two participants seen from the perspective of the sender. There are different flavours of this pattern, considering, for instance, the moment when the sender selects the receiver: The receiver is known either at design time of the choreography or only during the execution of a conversation.

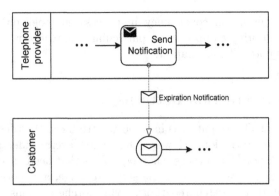

Fig. 6.22. Send pattern

Figure 6.22 illustrates an example where a phone provider notifies a customer that her prepaid credit will expire in 10 days. The participants are represented by pools; the send pattern is realized by a send task. The binding time (design time or run time) is not expressed in this diagram.

Receive

The receive pattern also describes a one-way interaction between two participants, but this time seen from the perspective of the receiver. In terms of message buffering behaviour of the receiver, two cases can be distinguished. Messages that are not expected are either discarded or stored until a later point in time, when they can be consumed.

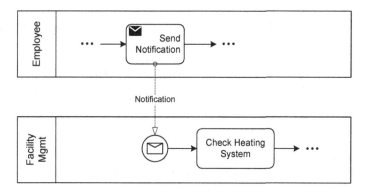

Fig. 6.23. Receive pattern

In the example shown in Figure 6.23 the facility management department of a company receives a notification that the heating system in a building does not work properly. The receipt of the message is represented by a start message event. On occurrence of this event, a process orchestration is started in the facility management that checks the heating system and tries to find the source of the problem.

Send/Receive

In the send/receive pattern, a participant sends a request to another participant who then returns a response message. Both messages belong to the same conversation. Since there could be several send/receive interaction instances happening in parallel, corresponding requests and responses need to be correlated.

If, for instance, a procurement department requests quotes for different items from different suppliers, the different request/response pairs belong to

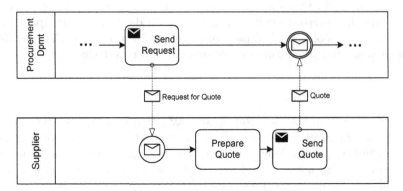

Fig. 6.24. Send/receive pattern

different conversations. In this situation the procurement department must be able to tell which quote belongs to which request.

Therefore, correlation information must be placed inside the messages. For instance, the request could carry a request identifier which is then also contained inside the response message. This example is shown in Figure 6.24.

Racing Incoming Messages

Racing incoming messages are common in business-to-business scenarios; this pattern is described as follows: a participant is waiting for a message to arrive, but other participants have the chance to send a message. These messages by different participants "race" with each other. Only the first message arriving will be processed.

The type of the message sent or the category the sending participant belongs to can be used to determine how the receiver processes the message. The remaining messages may be discarded or kept for later consumption. This aspect is not covered by the racing incoming messages pattern.

Figure 6.25 shows a scenario where a travel agent has reserved a flight for a customer, and now waits for a confirmation or a notification that the flight details are not acceptable. In the case of confirmation the payment is initiated, and in the case of rejection a new flight reservation might be needed.

One-To-Many Send

A participant sends out several messages to other participants in parallel. It might be the case that the list of recipients is already known at design-time of the choreography or, alternatively, the selection of the recipients takes place in the course of the conversation.

An example for this pattern is shown in Figure 6.26: four weeks before the start of a general election of a new a government, all registration offices

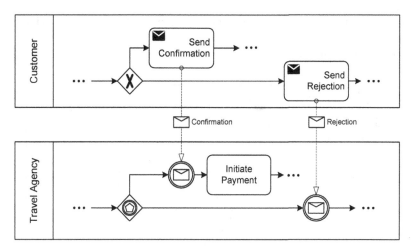

Fig. 6.25. Racing incoming messages pattern

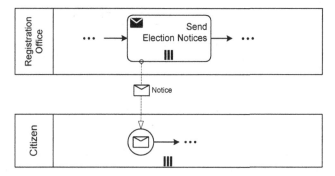

Fig. 6.26. One-to-many send pattern

send out election notices to the registered citizens in their respective area of responsibility.

In the BPMN, this pattern is represented by a multiple instances task that sends election notices to all voting citizens. Citizens are represented by a multiple participant pool, indicated by the marker at the bottom of the citizen pool.

One-From-Many Receive

In the one-from-many receive pattern, messages can be received from many participants. In particular, one participant waits for messages to arrive from other participants, and each of these participants can send exactly one message.

Typically, the receiver does not know the number of messages that will arrive, and stops waiting as soon as a certain number of messages have arrived or a time-out occurs.

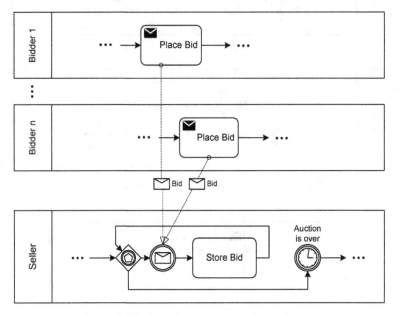

Fig. 6.27. One-from-many receive pattern

Imagine an auctioning scenario in which the bidders bid by sending a message directly to the seller. Each bidder can send exactly one message. The seller accepts these messages until the auction is over, and then decides on the highest bid. This scenario is depicted in Figure 6.27.

One-To-Many Send/Receive

In the one-to-many send/receive pattern, a participant sends out several requests to different other participants and waits for responses. Typically, not all responses need to be waited for. The requester rather waits for a certain amount of time or stops waiting as soon as enough responses have arrived.

A travel agency looks for the best offer for a flight on a certain route. The agent therefore initiates requests and the airlines give their prices and current availability, as illustrated in Figure 6.28.

Multi-Responses

In the multiple responses pattern, a participant sends a request to another participant who sends back multiple messages. An important question in this

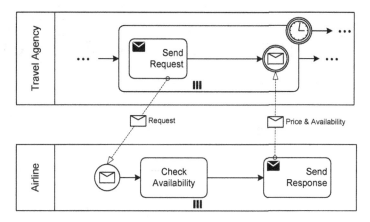

Fig. 6.28. One-to-many send/receive pattern

scenario is how the requester knows that there are no more messages to be expected.

One option would be that the messages contain information about whether there will be more messages or not. Another option could be that the last message is of a special type. Finally, also a time-out could be used to stop waiting for further messages.

Contingent Requests

In the contingent requests pattern, a participant sends a request to another participant. If this participant does not answer within a given time, the request is sent to a second participant. Again, if no response comes back, a third participant is contacted, and so on. Delayed responses, that is, responses arriving after the time-out has already occurred, might or might not be discarded.

Figure 6.29 shows an example where a manager delegates a task to one of his employees. If this employee does not accept the task on time, it is delegated to another employee, and so on.

Atomic Multicast Notification

The atomic multicast notification pattern is explained as follows. A participant sends out notifications to several other participants who have to accept the notification. In specific cases, only one participant is required to accept it; in other cases, a subset of the participants or all participants are required to accept it.

Request With Referral

The request with referral pattern is especially important in service-oriented environments where a registry is in place that allows binding to services at run

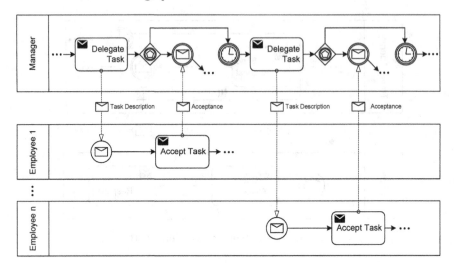

Fig. 6.29. Contingent requests pattern

time. But also simple types of dynamic behaviour can be represented by this pattern, for instance, the transmission of a new collaboration partner during an interaction.

In particular, the request with referral pattern can be used if a participant A sends a message to another participant B containing a reference to participant C. Although B does not need to know C in advance, B can now interact with C. This pattern describes the concept of *link passing mobility*.

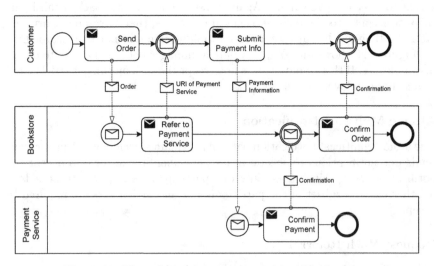

Fig. 6.30. Example involving request with referral pattern

As an example of this pattern, consider a customer who buys a set of books online. The bookstore redirects the customer's Web browser to the Web page of an external payment service. Conceptually, this means that the bookstore refers the payment service to the customer, who can then use the service, although the customer was not aware about this service beforehand. This sample scenario is modelled in Figure 6.30.

Relayed Request

The relayed request pattern is common in emailing collaboration scenarios. A participant A sends a request to another participant B who forwards it to a third participant C who will actually interact with A. However, B always gets copies of the messages exchanged in order to be able to observe the conversation.

6.6 Let's Dance

In the Section 6.4, Petri nets were used to express process choreographies. The main idea was to show the behavioural interfaces for the participants of a process choreography and their interconnection using message flow. As an alternative to modelling behavioural interfaces, languages for expressing interaction models directly have been designed. The main difference to modelling connected behavioural interfaces is that interactions are used as basic building blocks for choreographies, and behavioural dependencies are defined between these interactions.

Let's Dance is a choreography language following this interaction-centric approach. It is based on control flow patterns and service interaction patterns. Control flow specification is the main focus, so the language abstracts from concrete message formats. This section concentrates on the interaction modelling capabilities of Let's Dance rather than on organizational aspects or milestones.

The main focus of Let's Dance is to capture interactions and their behavioural dependencies. Elementary interactions are the building blocks by which complex interaction rules can be defined.

An elementary interaction is a combination of a send activity model and a receive activity model. An actor reference belonging to a role is given for every activity model. This reference indicates which activity instances must be performed by the same participant. Typically, there is only one participant per role involved in a conversation. In these cases, the actor reference can be omitted in the diagrams.

Elementary interactions are shown in Figure 6.31. At the left-hand side in that figure, an interaction between a participant of role *Seller* and a participant of role *Auctioning Service* is defined. It also states that a message of type *Auction creation request* is sent during the interaction.

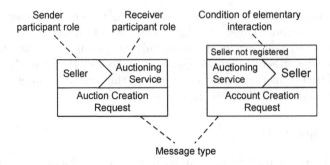

Fig. 6.31. Elementary interaction and conditional elementary interaction

At the right-hand side, a conditional elementary interaction is shown. Conditional elementary interactions are valid only if the condition is met. In the example shown, the *Auctioning Service* sends an *Account creation request* message to the seller only if the seller is not registered.

In this section, the basic execution constraints between elementary interactions are discussed. The graphical representations of these execution constraints are depicted in Figure 6.32.

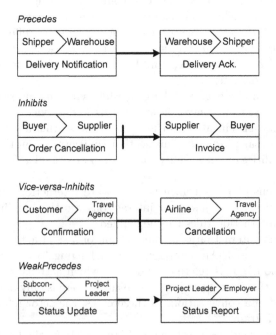

Fig. 6.32. Basic control flow structures relating interactions

As seen in the milestone example, a *precedes* relationship between two interactions means that an instance of the target interaction can occur only if the instance of the source interaction has already occurred. If in a logistics environment a delivery acknowledgment message should be sent only after a delivery notification has been received, a precedes relationship between the respective elementary interactions can be used to represent this business rule.

An *inhibits* relationship indicates that an instance of the target interaction can occur only if no instance of the source interaction has occurred yet. In an example involving an order process, an invoice should not be sent after an order cancellation by the buyer has been received.

Also, scenarios where two interactions inhibit each other, that is, an instance where either one or the other interaction can complete, are very common. Consider, for instance, a travel agency that either receives a confirmation message from the customer or a cancellation message from the airline. To cater to these situations, a specific notational element for *vice-versa-inhibits* is introduced.

A *weak precedes* relationship means that an instance of the target interaction can occur only after the instance of the source interaction has already completed or was skipped. Imagine a project management scenario where the project leader expects status updates from a subcontractor that are merged into a status report for the employer. However, in special cases the project leader and the subcontractors can agree that no status update is needed.

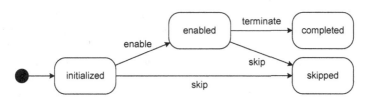

Fig. 6.33. Interaction instance lifecycle

The lifecycle of interaction instances is shown in Figure 6.33. Interaction instances can be in the states *initialized, enabled, completed,* and *skipped*. An interaction instance becomes skipped if any of the inhibiting instances has completed.

An interaction instance becomes enabled if there are no precedes or weak precedes relationships targeting the corresponding interaction or all preceding instances are completed and all weakly preceding instances have been completed or were skipped.

An instance must execute, that is, the actual message exchange occurs, only if it is enabled. After the message exchange, the instance is in the completed state. In the case of skipping, dead path elimination execution semantics is applied, as was discussed in Section 4.6.

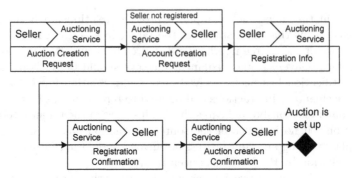

Fig. 6.34. Interaction modelling

Figure 6.34 shows a set or related interactions in the auctioning scenario, from its start until the first milestone, that is, until the auction is set up. The semantics of the modelled interaction is as follows.

The conversation starts with the *Seller* sending an *Auction creation request* message to the *Auctioning service*. The precedes relationship defines that, if this message arrived, an *Account creation request* message can be sent to the *Seller*. Then, the *Seller* sends a *Registration info* message to the *Auctioning service*, which responds with an *Registration confirmation* message.

The weak precedes relationship connecting the last elementary interactions defines that the *Auctioning service* can send an *Auction creation confirmation* to the *Seller* if it has either sent a Registration confirmation message before or if the sending of that message was skipped. The latter is used to cater to situations in which a *Seller* is already registered at the *Auctioning service*.

In addition to the basic control flow constructs, there are advanced control flow constructs in Let's Dance. Several interactions can belong to a composite interaction. None of the contained interaction instances can become enabled before the enclosing composite interaction instance has become enabled, and the composite interaction instance can only complete after all contained interaction instances have completed or been skipped.

Interactions can also be guarded, meaning that at the moment an interaction instance could become enabled, a guard condition must be fulfilled. If this condition is not fulfilled, the instance is skipped. Finally, repetitions and parallel branching with an unbounded number of branches are modelled through repeated interactions. There are four types of repeated interactions, similar to those in programming languages: while, repeat, for each (sequential), and for each (concurrent).

"For each" repetitions have an expression attached that determines a collection over which the repetition is performed. The knowledge about how many instances are to be created for this interaction might be available at design time or might be known only at run time.

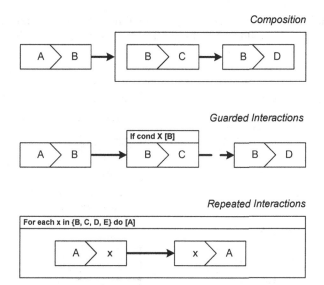

Fig. 6.35. Advanced control flow constructs

Repetitions can have stop conditions attached to them. For instance, a repeated receive interaction should be stopped as soon as answers from ten participants have arrived.

The expressions attached to guarded and repeated interactions can be written in plain English, as Let's Dance is not tied to any specific expression language. However, it must be defined which actor is going to check whether a condition evaluates to true or which collection results from a repetition expression.

Let's Dance and also interaction BPMN (as mentioned in the bibliographical notes of this chapter) have been instrumental in the development of the choreography modelling capabilities of BPMN, since they put interaction modelling in the centre of attention.

6.7 Choreography Modelling in BPMN

The BPMN provides a rich set of language constructs to express process choreographies at different levels of abstraction. This section focuses on choreography diagrams, because we can use them to define the concrete behavioural dependencies between messages exchanged during a collaboration, that is, a choreography. The concepts are illustrated by an auctioning scenario, similar to the one discussed earlier in this chapter.

In Section 6.3, we have investigated interactions between participants in the context of milestones that are reached during a conversation. We return to that example to introduce choreography modelling in BPMN. Before doing so, we will introduce the building blocks of BPMN choreographies in Figure 6.36.

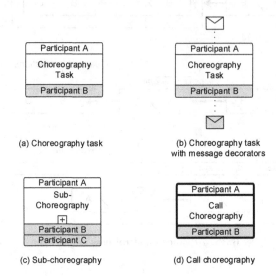

Fig. 6.36. Notational elements used in BPMN choreography diagrams

The main building blocks of choreography diagrams are choreography tasks. Each choreography task represents a message interaction between two participants. A choreography task consists of three parts, one participant that initiates the interaction, one interaction partner, and a choreography task name.

Each message interaction is initiated by exactly one participant, the *initiator*. The initiator is highlighted white, while its interaction partner, the *respondent*, is shown in grey.

In the choreography task shown in Figure 6.36(a), Participant A is the initiator. Notice that the role (initiator, respondent) of a participant is not represented by its position in the choreography task, but by the highlighting of the respective compartment of the task.

Message decorators can be used to represent messages sent during an interaction. Message decorators indicate whether a single message is sent during an interaction or whether an interaction consists of two messages, one sent from the initiator to the respondent and one message sent back. Figure 6.36(b) shows message decorators for both participants, representing the fact that the interaction consists of two messages sent, an initiating message and a response message. Request-reply is a typical message exchange pattern represented by a choreography task. Sending a request-for-quote message from a buyer to a supplier and the quote return message can be collectively represented by one choreography task, with the buyer being the initiator.

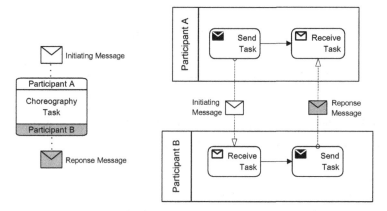

Fig. 6.37. Choreography task and corresponding collaboration diagram

Nodes in choreography diagrams can also represent more complex message exchanges, for instance, message exchanges involving three participants. These interactions are represented by sub-choreographies, as shown in Figure 6.36(c). Analogous to the naming conventions in business process diagrams, choreography task and sub-choreographies are collectively called choreography activities.

Consider a scenario where a buyer sends request-for-quote messages to two suppliers. After receiving the quotes from the suppliers, it chooses one of them and sends an order. This scenario can be represented by a sub-choreography.

If a choreography task occurs several times in a given process choreography, we can use call choreographies, as shown in Figure 6.36(d). The structure and the semantics of call choreographies are identical to that of choreographies; the only difference relates to the possibility to refer to them several times in a given process choreography.

Figure 6.37 shows a choreography task involving two participants and two messages sent. Participant A initiates the interaction by sending an initiating message to B, who sends a response message. In the right-hand side of that figure, a sample process diagram is shown that realizes that choreography. This example illustrates that within one choreography task, several related messages can be sent and received.

Figure 6.38 shows a simplified version of the choreography discussed earlier in the context of Figure 6.8. This version assumes that each seller needs to be registered before the auction can be confirmed. Thereby, the choreography does not need to take a decision. Decisions in choreographies will be discussed later in this section.

Notice that the seller starts the choreography by initiating a message exchange with the auctioning service. Once this message exchange completes, an account needs to be created, and, once the registration information is sent, the auctioning service confirms the auction creation.

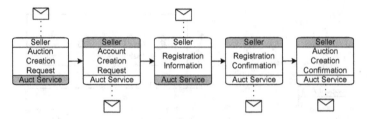

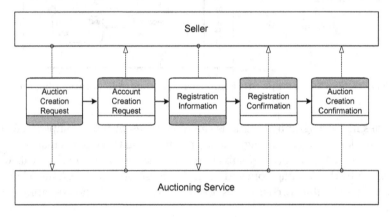

Fig. 6.38. Collaboration scenario, described by BPMN choreography diagrams

Fig. 6.39. Choreography diagram with pools

Choreography diagrams can also use pools and message flow. Since in this case the participants can be derived from the labelling of the pools, participant labels can be omitted from choreography tasks, shown in Figure 6.39.

In this example, each choreography task represents a simple message exchange between two participants. As discussed before, more complex behaviour can be represented by choreographies, for example, if multiple participants are involved. In these settings, a graphical representation of the choreography using pools can become quite complex. As a result, enriching choreography diagrams with pools should only be done when few participants are involved in a choreography.

While choreography diagrams look quite similar to process diagrams—both have task nodes, control flow edges, and gateways—there are important conceptual differences. Consider the choreography diagram shown in Figure 6.40, which shows a sequence of choreography tasks, involving a customer, a reseller, and a payment organization. To explicitly state the start and the end of a choreography, BPMN choreography diagrams provide a limited set of start events and end events.

First, the customer orders products by sending an order message to the reseller. The reseller confirms the order by sending a confirmation message.

In the next step, the customer sends the funds to the payment organization, which confirms the payment.

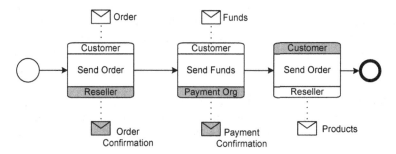

Fig. 6.40. Choreography diagram that is not enforceable, since the reseller cannot know if the customer has already sent the funds

The problems start with the third choreography task, that is, when the reseller should send the products to the customer. The reseller cannot know that the message exchange between the customer and the payment organization has actually materialized. Choreographies with this property are called non-enforceable, since it is not possible to enforce the communication behaviour that is specified in the choreography diagram by the local process orchestrations.

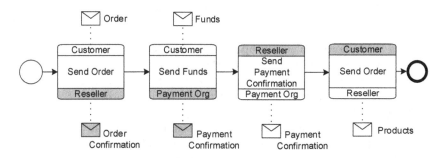

Fig. 6.41. Choreography diagram that is enforceable

The problem is due to the fact that the initiator of one message exchange, the reseller, was not involved in the previous message exchange. BPMN deals with this problem by allowing only choreography diagrams, in which the initiator of a message exchange is involved in the choreography task immediately preceding it, if there is any. Then the participant knows, either as initiator or receiver, that the message exchange is completed. Consequently, the choreography is enforceable.

The problem in the example can be fixed, if the payment organization sends a message to the reseller, informing it about the payment, as shown in Figure 6.41. Then, formally, the initiator of the last task is also involved in the previous task, so that the order of message exchanges defined in the choreography diagram can be enforced by the local process orchestrations.

Control flow using gateways has been discussed extensively in the orchestration chapter, where control flow patterns have been investigated. Control flow is a cornerstone of process orchestrations, and it is also important for process choreographies.

While the semantics of gateway nodes are virtually identical for process orchestrations and process choreographies, their implementation is much more complex for the latter. This is due to the lack of central control and, related to this, the lack of global data.

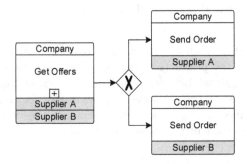

Fig. 6.42. Choreography diagram with exclusive gateway

Figure 6.42 shows a choreography diagram which involves an exclusive gateway. The choreography defines that the company first invites and receives offers from two suppliers. After the company has decided, in an internal process activity, which supplier to select, it either sends an order to *Supplier A* or to *Supplier B*.

The BPMN standard mentions a set of consistency criteria for the exclusive gateway in choreography diagrams. It states that all participants that are affected by a decision share the data that the decision is based on. Only then the suppliers can know whether they will receive an order.

This requirement can be fulfilled by an additional sub-choreography that is performed immediately prior to the exclusive gateway. This sub-choreography informs the receivers of the choreography tasks immediately following the gateway about the decision. The resulting process choreography is shown in Figure 6.43.

Choreography diagrams serve as blue prints to develop process orchestrations for the participants involved. Figure 6.44 details parts of the process orchestrations of the participants that realize the choreography discussed above. This diagram focuses on the realization of the exclusive gateway by the part-

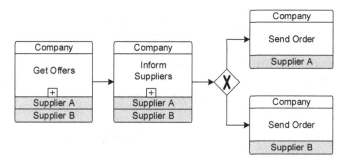

Fig. 6.43. Additional sub-choreography *Inform Suppliers* makes sure that receivers are informed about the decision taken by the exclusive gateway

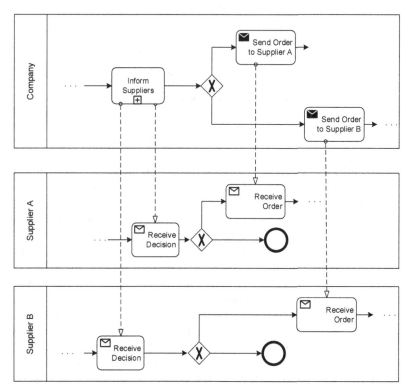

Fig. 6.44. Collaboration diagram with process orchestrations, implementing the choreography defined in Figure 6.43

ners' orchestrations; process activities relating to the invitation and sending of the offer have been discarded.

The company informs the suppliers about its decision by sending the respective messages. After receiving its inform message, each supplier knows whether or not to expect an order. As a result, the exclusive decision on the choreography level is translated to a decision in the process orchestration of each supplier, which realizes the choreography.

We now investigate a choreography design of this scenario using event-based gateways. Just like in process orchestrations, event-based gateways expose the deferred choice behaviour, so that it is not required that the deciding partner informs the other participants of its decision.

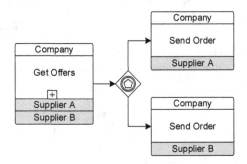

Fig. 6.45. Choreography diagram with event-based gateway

This approach is illustrated in Figure 6.45, which revisits the example introduced above. In this case, the suppliers may or may not receive an order. This choreography can conveniently be implemented using an exclusive gateway in the process orchestration of the company and event-based gateways in the orchestrations of the suppliers.

The choreography can be used to design process orchestrations of the partners, as illustrated in Figure 6.46. The decision by the company is represented by an exclusive gateway. The suppliers are ready to receive the order. It is good practice to limit the time it waits for the order by a timer. When the timer has elapsed and the event is caught, the supplier process terminates.

These examples show the alternative use of the exclusive gateway and the event-based gateway in process choreographies. If the exclusive gateway is used, an additional message exchange might be required to inform participants about the decision taken by one partner. In case of the event-based gateway, this message exchange is not required. Instead partners need to deal with a period of uncertainty, in which they do not know whether or not to expect a message.

The BPMN also supports parallel gateway and inclusive gateway. For both gateways, the initiators of all choreography tasks directly following the gateway must also participate in the task that preceded the gateway. Only then they are aware of the completion of the previous task, so that they can initiate the message exchange following the gateway.

An example of a parallel gateway is shown in Figure 6.47. This choreography shows a simple variant of the example discussed earlier, in which the company sends orders concurrently to both suppliers.

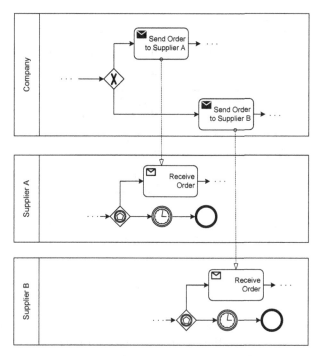

Fig. 6.46. Collaboration diagram with process orchestrations, implementing the choreography defined in Figure 6.45

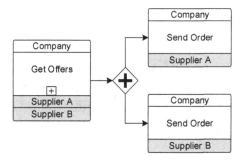

Fig. 6.47. Choreography diagram using parallel gateway

A process diagram implementing the constraints imposed by the choreography diagram is given in Figure 6.48. The parallel gateway on the choreography level is realized by a parallel gateway on the level of process orchestrations.

To conclude this section, we return to the auctioning scenario that was used to motivate choreography diagrams in BPMN earlier in this section. In that scenario, the decision whether a seller needs to register was disregarded. This example is now complemented using an event-based gateway. The resulting choreography is shown in Figure 6.49.

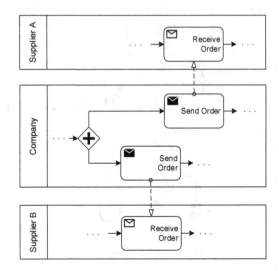

Fig. 6.48. Process diagram realizing parallel gateway of process choreography

The bidder sends an auction creation request, and the auctioning service either responds by a registration request or by confirming the creation of the auction. Through the use of an event-based gateway, there is no need for data exchange or for agreement on a decision, one participant decides and informs the others, that's it.

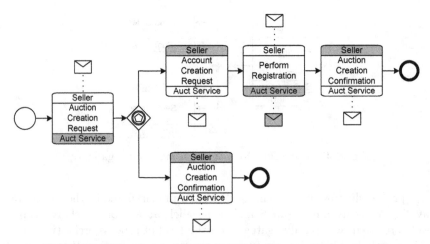

Fig. 6.49. Choreography diagram representing auctioning scenario

While choreography diagrams can capture useful information regarding the collaboration of participants, the implementation of process orchestrations needs to take into account business aspects, legal aspects, and technological aspects as well and combine them with good engineering skills to come up with viable solutions.

Bibliographical Notes

Business process choreographies were introduced as a mechanism to investigate business-to-business collaborations. In this context, domain standards were established that not only specify the message communication between the parties involved in a business-to-business interaction, but also the content of the messages. Domain standards of this kind are RosettaNet for supply chain management, the Society for Worldwide Interbank Financial Transfer in the financial sector, and Health Level Seven in health care. The Organization for the Advancement of Structured Information Standards puts forward the ebXML standard for business collaboration in Dubray et al. (2006).

More recently, service interaction patterns have been introduced in Barros et al. (2005), and the language Let's Dance was introduced in Zaha et al. (2006a). Interaction BPMN was proposed by Decker and Barros (2007). Business process choreographies are also investigated in Decker (2009) and Decker and Weske (2011). The execution semantics of service choreographies is reported in Decker et al. (2006). A unifying framework for compatibility and consistency in business-to-business process integration is introduced in Decker and Weske (2007).

The relationship between a global public process choreography and the realizations of the individual private orchestrations are investigated in van der Aalst and Weske (2001), based on work on process inheritance as introduced in Basten and van der Aalst (2001). The equivalence of process models, using their observable behaviour, is studied in van der Aalst et al. (2006). The relationship between compatibility notions in process choreographies and consistency of process implementations with regard to behavioural interfaces is studied in Decker and Weske (2007).

The operating guidelines approach is related to process choreographies; however, rather than our checking interconnected interface processes, a behavioural interface can be used to generate an operating guideline, which characterizes the valid interaction behaviours; operating guidelines are introduced in Massuthe et al. (2005).

This text book can only introduce a limited set of choreography modelling capabilities of the BPMN. For a complete presentation, there is no substitute for the standards document Object Management Group (2011).

While most research work in the area of process choreographies have traditionally focused on conceptual aspects, recently also technical topics emerged. Nikaj et al. (2015) propose to enrich BPMN choreography diagrams with technical details based on the Representational State Transfer (REST) architectural style, introduced by Fielding (2000). Implementation specific aspects are discussed by Nikaj et al. (2018). Technical platforms are not limited to REST; also blockchains emerged as an implementation platform for business process choreographies, as discussed by García-Bañuelos et al. (2017).

7

Properties of Business Processes

The investigation of properties of business process models is an important aspect of business process management. If a certain property at the business process model level can be shown, then all process instances based on that business process model expose this property. In this chapter, the most important properties for process models are introduced and related to each other.

While structural dependencies of processes are important, dependencies related to data processed during business processes should be taken care of. Data dependencies between activities in business process models are studied in Section 7.1.

Structural properties of process models are at the centre of attention; these properties are neither application specific nor domain specific. Conceptually, the situation is similar to normalization in database theory. If all tables in a relational database schema are, for instance, in third normal form, then certain anomalies can no longer occur during the run time of the database applications.

Structural properties of business processes have been investigated in the context of Petri nets. Based on structural soundness, investigated in Section 7.3, the original soundness criterion introduced in the context of workflow nets is discussed in Section 7.4.

While soundness is an important criterion, it appears to be too strong for particular settings. Consequently, relaxed soundness has been introduced as a less rigid property that is still helpful in analyzing business process models. Section 7.5 looks at relaxed soundness. Further soundness criteria and an overview of soundness criteria are discussed in Section 7.6.

In Section 7.7 we investigate the impact of decisions in general and decision tables in particular on the soundness of business processes. To do so, a dedicated property called decision soundness is introduced and illustrated by examples.

© Springer-Verlag GmbH Germany, part of Springer Nature 2019
M. Weske, *Business Process Management*,
https://doi.org/10.1007/978-3-662-59432-2_7

7.1 Data Dependencies

Application data are an integral part of business processes. Data can be created, modified, and deleted during the execution of business processes. Since business processes consist of a set of activities that are related, these activities operate on an integrated set of application data.

Data in business process models has two aspects, both of which need to be covered:

- Data that activity instances manipulate by invoking applications or services.
- Data dependencies between process activities.

The former issue is dealt with in the operations subdomain. In service-oriented systems architectures, for instance, the parameters of service invocations are specified, so that data can be communicated correctly with software systems at run time.

At the process level, data dependencies between process activities is typically described by data flow. An example of data flow in a business process in the financial sector is given. A credit approval business process contains activities to enter a credit request, to assess the risks of granting the credit, and to inform the customer about the decision made by the financial institution.

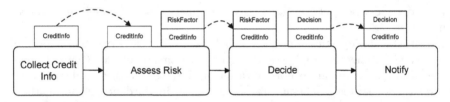

Fig. 7.1. Data dependencies imply activity orderings

The activities of this process model operate on case data, in particular, the credit request. The credit request can be represented by a record data type with fields for the name and address of the credit requester, the amount requested, and other information, such as the risk related to granting the credit.

There are data dependencies between the activities mentioned. The *Collect Credit Info* activity is the first activity performed. Only when this data is available, can the risk be assessed in the *Assess Risk* activity, the final decision be made(*Decide*), and the requestor be notified (*Notify*). Therefore, the ordering of the activities in the business process is strongly related to the data dependencies of the activities.

The process model is illustrated in Figure 7.1, using a graph-based process language that explicitly represents input and output parameters of activities and data dependencies. Observe that the actual data transfer can be performed by passing references to data objects or values of data objects, as described in Section 3.7.1 in the context of workflow data patterns.

This diagram shows that data dependencies have implications on the ordering of activities in the process: the *Assess Risk* activity can be started only when the credit information is available. Since this data object is provided as output parameter *CreditInfo* of the *Collect Credit Info* activity, this activity needs to complete before the risk can be assessed, implying an ordering between these activities.

This example shows that data dependencies between process activities are reflected by data flow. A data flow edge between an output parameter of one activity and an input parameter of another activity represents the fact that the latter activity requires a data value that the former generates. In the example, the *Collect Credit Request* activity generates an output parameter *CreditInfo* that the *Assess Risk* activity requires for its start.

If, as assumed so far, output parameter values are only available when the respective activity terminates, there is a direct implication of data flow on control flow. This property is known as *control flow follows data flow*, and it is explained as follows.

Control flow needs to follow data flow, since otherwise the process instance would come to halt. This observation is illustrated in an example shown in Figure 7.2, where a data dependency from the *Assess Risk* activity to the *Decide* activity is shown, while the control flow constraint exists, for some reason, in the opposite direction.

As a result, neither of these activities can be started, because control flow defines that *Assess Risk* can only start after *Decide* has completed, and *Decide* can only start after *Assess Risk* has generated the risk factor data value.

Because the risk factor value is only available when the activity terminates, both activities are stuck in a permanent waiting condition, and a deadlock situation has occurred. The process model shown in Figure 7.2 results from a modelling mistake, and the *control flow follows data flow* rule can be used to detect these kinds of modelling mistakes.

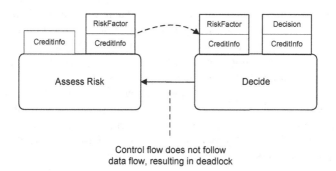

Control flow does not follow
data flow, resulting in deadlock

Fig. 7.2. Data flow violated by control flow, resulting in deadlock

These considerations hold only if it is assumed that an activity instance requires its input parameters at the start. If this constraint is relaxed and input parameters can be consumed *after* an activity instance has started, then in a process with a data flow $A \to B$, B can actually start before A terminates. At some point—when the input values are required—B needs to wait for A to deliver the required data.

This assumption can also be relaxed at the producer side of data. If we allow activities to generate data *while they are running*, then the generated data can be taken by the follow-up activity, so that activities can execute concurrently, realizing a data value stream between them.

While most workflow management systems assume that input data is available up front and that only on completion, does an activity instance write output data values, some approaches, for instance, the BPMN, relax this assumption.

The use of data dependencies for process enactment control will be discussed in more detail in the context of case handling in Section 8.4, where data dependencies—and not the process structures—are the driving force for process control.

7.2 Object Lifecycle Conformance

All business processes generate or manipulate data. An ordering process in a reseller company deals with products, customers, and orders. A claim handling process in an insurance company requires data about the insuree and the claim. Additional data objects might be required, for example, an assessment of the damage or a report by an evaluator.

Object-orientation provides expressive means to organize data objects, with respect to both structure and behaviour. Object structures can be represented by class diagrams, which consist of classes and relationships between them. Classes are containers for objects, so that the relationships between classes define relationships between objects. The Unified Modeling Language is the standard for object-oriented analysis and design.

But not only the structure of objects and their relationships to other objects can be specified, also their behaviour. Behaviour of objects is represented by states and state transitions that objects can perform. State transitions are typically done by executing methods. State transition diagrams are used to capture the behaviour of objects, their object lifecycle.

The object lifecycle of a quote object is shown in Figure 7.3. When a quote object is created, it enters the *initial* state. Then a draft version of the quote is created. At this point, it is ready to be confirmed by a manager.

A typical company policy determines that a quote can only be sent if it is confirmed. The quote object can perform the state transition from *draft* to *confirmed* by executing the confirm method, triggered by the manager. However, there is also the possibility that the manager prepares the quote

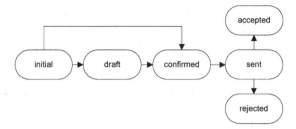

Fig. 7.3. Object lifecycle of quote object

personally, so that the quote is implicitly confirmed, represented by the state transition from the *initial* state to the *confirmed* state. Confirmed quotes can be sent. Then either the quote is accepted or rejected.

All these activities mentioned occur in the context of a business process. When the manager confirms the quote, he enacts a process activity. This activity is part of a business process, with activities preceding it and with activities following it. This means that state transitions of objects are performed by business process activities.

Since business processes define an order of activities and activities induce state changes of data objects, both need to be in line with each other. As a result, for example, the state of a quote object can be changed to *accepted* only if it is in state *sent*, not when it is in the *draft* state. The business policy to send only confirmed quotes can be realized by the process, using the lifecycle of the quote object.

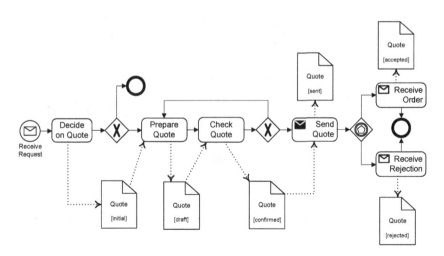

Fig. 7.4. Business process operating on a quote data object

Figure 7.4 shows a business process operating on a quote data object. When a request for quote is received, it decides whether to prepare a quote.

If this is the case, a quote data object is initialized and the quote is prepared. After it is prepared, it enters the draft state. The checking activity can trigger either of two state transitions. If the check is successful, then the quote enters the confirmed state. Otherwise, it remains in the draft state and is refined in the prepare quote task.

Once the quote is confirmed, it can be sent to the customer. Then an event-based gateway is used to react on either message that can be received. If an order is received, the quote is accepted. Otherwise, the quote is rejected. Notice that in BPMN, receive tasks do not change the state of data objects, they just receive messages. Due to space limitations, we permit them to also change the state of the quote object in this example.

This example illustrates that the behaviour of data objects used during business processes and the process itself need to fit to each other. In the example shown, both fit nicely. The process only uses state transitions of the quote object that are defined in the lifecycle of that object. In this case, the business process conforms to the lifecycle of the data object, the process is *object lifecycle conformant.*

The notion of object lifecycle conformance provides a link between a business process and the data objects it operates on. A violation of object lifecycle conformance is a useful hint to correct the models, either the lifecycle of the data object or the process model.

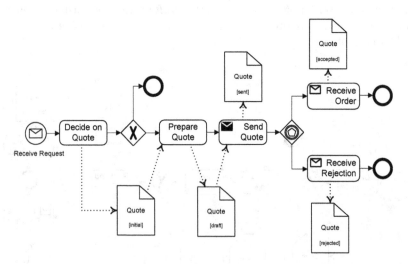

Fig. 7.5. Business process that does not conform to the quote object's lifecycle

A business process that does not conform with the lifecycle of the quote object is shown in Figure 7.5. While on first sight this process looks like a correct process model, the process sends a quote in the draft state. Consulting the object lifecycle of the quote object in Figure 7.3, we see that there is no state transition from *draft* to *sent*, which shows the violation.

This example illustrates the additional means that object lifecycle conformance provides to check the correctness of process models. The problem does not need to be in the process model; the designer of an object lifecycle model might have overlooked certain state transitions that are meaningful from a process perspective.

7.3 Structural Soundness

In this section, the structure of business process models is investigated, and an initial soundness criterion is introduced. While the considerations in this section hold for process models represented in any of the process orchestration languages introduced above, this section uses Petri nets, in most cases, workflow nets, to represent these structural errors. The reasons are not only of historical nature—workflow nets were the first approach for which soundness was investigated—but also practical: the formal foundation of workflow nets allows to formally specify and reason about soundness properties.

The type of structural error discussed in this section can be characterized by dangling transitions or places, that is, transitions without input places or output places. Figure 7.6 shows a Petri net with dangling places and transitions. Notice that this Petri net is not a workflow net, since there are multiple places without incoming edges and not all nodes, for instance, $t5$, are on a path from i to o.

When a token enters the Petri net in place i, transition $t1$ is enabled. Note that there is no way that $t4$ can ever be enabled. When $t2$ fires, $t5$ and $t3$ are enabled. When $t3$ terminates, the output place o is reached, signalling the completion of the case. However, at this point in time, $t5$ could still be running! As a consequence, the token at the output place o does not signal the completion of the case. These types of errors are ruled out by the definition of workflow nets.

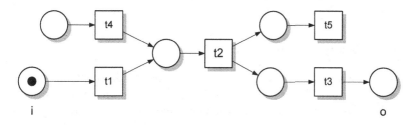

Fig. 7.6. Petri net with dangling places and dangling transitions

This example motivates the development of correctness criteria for process models to prevent the modelling errors discussed. The simplest correctness criterion uses the structure of business process models. It is inspired by the definition of workflow nets and takes advantage of the definition of workflow nets.

Definition 7.1 A process model is *structurally sound* if the following conditions hold:

- There is exactly one initial node, which is the only node without any incoming edges.
- There is exactly one final node, which is the only node without any outgoing edges.
- Each node in the process model is on a path from the initial node to the final node.

◇

Structural soundness also goes well with the definition of business process models, which states that business process models consist of related activities. Structural soundness makes this relationship concrete by defining that each activity is embedded in the context of the process and that no activities are independent of other activities of the same business process.

Many business process languages enforce structural soundness, for instance, event-driven process chains and business process diagrams expressed in the BPMN. However, the process designer has the freedom to use these process languages to design process models that are structurally sound.

7.4 Soundness

The first behavioural soundness criterion for business processes was developed by Wil van der Aalst in the context of workflow nets; but this criterion is also applicable to other process modelling notations. For this, the execution semantics of these languages have to be taken into account. If formal proofs are required, then process languages with a formal execution semantics, such as workflow nets are needed.

7.4.1 Motivation of Soundness

In order to motivate the soundness criterion, a number of workflow nets with errors are discussed. Figure 7.7 shows a workflow net with two transitions which exhibit an *exclusive or* split behaviour and an *and* join behaviour.

The *exclusive or* split transition $t1$ puts a token either in the upper input place of $t2$ or in the lower input place of $t2$, but not in both places. As a consequence, the *and* join transition $t2$ can never be enabled, because not all input places have tokens. Therefore, cases based on the workflow net shown will suffer from deadlock—no case will ever terminate.

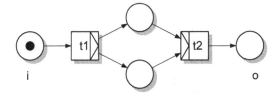

Fig. 7.7. Workflow net with deadlock

While in a deadlock the activities involved can never be executed, in a livelock situation a set of activities are trapped in an infinite loop. Livelock can be the consequence of different types of errors in process models. If a condition to enter a loop is always evaluated to true, then the loop is never left. This type of error cannot be detected on the basis of process models.

Not only can erroneous conditions in decision nodes lead to livelock, but also erroneous process structures, as shown in Figure 7.8. This workflow net suffers from the fact that the loop is entered by an *and* split transition and not by an *exclusive or* split transition. Therefore, the loop is repeatedly iterated, realizing a livelock situation.

In addition to the livelock, this workflow net also suffers from the fact that each time the loop is iterated, one token is put in the output place. Therefore, a token in the output place no longer indicates the completion of the process.

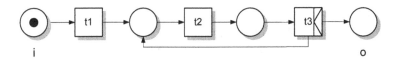

Fig. 7.8. Workflow net with livelock

A workflow net that suffers from different problems is shown in Figure 7.9. Depending on the decision made by the *exclusive or* split transition $t1$, either a deadlock or an improper termination occurs. If $t1$ puts a token on $p1$ and no token on $p2$, then the *and* join transition $t3$ cannot be enabled, since there will not be a token at place $p3$. As a consequence, a deadlock situation will occur.

If, however, $t1$ puts a token in $p2$, then $t2$ can fire, putting a token in the output condition o. At this point, there is still a token in $p3$, showing a situation similar to that in the previous case: the process instance does not terminate properly because the process runs even after a token is put in the final place.

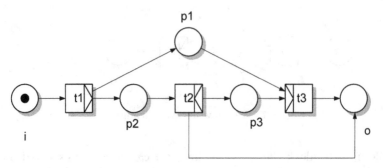

Fig. 7.9. Workflow net with deadlock/remaining tokens

7.4.2 Definition

Based on these observations, soundness in workflow nets is defined. The idea of the soundness criterion is to make sure that all tasks can participate in a process instance; each process instance eventually terminates, and when it terminates there is exactly one token in the final place.

In order to formally specify sound workflow nets, the following definition on the states of a workflow net is useful.

Definition 7.2 Let $PN = (P, T, F)$ be a workflow net, $i \in P$ be its initial place, $o \in P$ its final place, and M, M' markings.

- $[i]$ is the state in which there is exactly one token in place $i \in P$ and no token in any other place of the workflow net
- $[o]$ is the state in which there is exactly one token in place $o \in P$ and no token in any other place of the workflow net
- $M \geq M'$ if and only if $M(p) \geq M'(p), \forall p \in P$
- $M > M'$ if and only if $M \geq M' \wedge \exists p \in P : M(p) > M'(p)$

$\diamond$

Using these definitions, the soundness criterion can be specified in a formal way.

Definition 7.3 A workflow system (PN, i) with a workflow net $PN = (P, T, F)$ is *sound* if and only if

- For every state M reachable from state $[i]$ there exists a firing sequence leading from M to $[o]$, that is,

$$\forall M([i] \xrightarrow{*} M) \implies (M \xrightarrow{*} [o])$$

- State $[o]$ is the only state reachable from state $[i]$ with at least one token in place o, that is,

$$\forall M([i] \xrightarrow{*} M \wedge M \geq [o]) \implies (M = [o])$$

- There are no dead transitions in the workflow net in state $[i]$, that is,

$$(\forall t \in T) \; \exists M, M' : [i] \xrightarrow{*} M \xrightarrow{t} M'$$

◇

Reachability analysis can be used to decide whether a given workflow net is sound. The idea of reachability analysis is that the states and the state changes of process instances are represented explicitly. Reachability graphs are used to represent the different states that a process instance can take.

A reachability graph consists of nodes and labelled edges, where the nodes correspond to states of the workflow net and the edges represent state transitions. State transitions occur by firing transitions. Therefore, each state transition is labelled with the transition that realized this state transition.

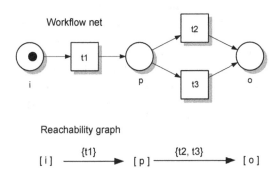

Fig. 7.10. Workflow net and corresponding reachability graph

Definition 7.4 A directed graph $G = (V, E, l)$ is called a *reachability graph* of a workflow net PN if V corresponds to the set of reachable states of the workflow net and $E \subseteq V \times V$ corresponds to state transitions. The mapping $l : E \mapsto \mathcal{P}(T)$ assigns to each edge a set of transitions, such that $(M, M') \in E \Leftrightarrow M \xrightarrow{t} M'$ for each $t \in l(E)$.   ◇

This definition is illustrated by the example shown in Figure 7.10. In the upper part of that figure, a simple workflow net is shown. The reachability graph in the lower part of that figure contains all states that are reachable from the initial state. The graph also shows that $[o]$ can be reached from $[p]$ by either firing transition $t2$ or $t3$.

A workflow net with a loop is shown in Figure 7.11. The *exclusive or split* transition B is used to decide whether or not to iterate the loop. Figure 7.12 shows the corresponding reachability graph. In this case, the loop in the workflow net is reflected by a loop in the reachability graph.

The soundness criteria can be proven based on the reachability graph:

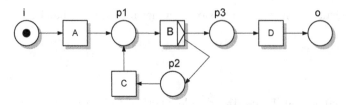

Fig. 7.11. Workflow net with loop

- For every state reachable from [i] there is a continuation to state [o]: this can be shown by following the arcs from the initial state. Any path of maximal length will terminate in state [o].
- It can be concluded from Figure 7.12 that [o] is the only state reachable from the initial state with one token in place o.
- All transitions participate in an execution that starts in state [i] and terminates in state [o]. In order to show this property, for each transition in the workflow net there needs to be a path containing it in the reachability graph that leads to the final state.

  In the example, transitions A, B, and D participate in every sound execution, and C is involved if the loop is performed. Therefore, any transition can participate in a process instance—although obviously not every transition participates in every process instance.

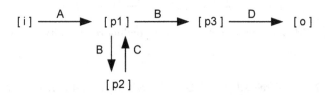

Fig. 7.12. Reachability graph of workflow net shown in Figure 7.11

In real-world settings, the decision that the *exclusive or* split transition B makes might depend on process data, such as a credit amount or the status of a customer. These types of application-specific information are not considered in soundness analysis; they are abstracted from by a simple assumption: in every workflow net, each decision alternative is eventually taken.

As a result of this assumption, the loop is iterated only a limited number of times. Eventually, the *exclusive or* split will decide to leave the loop and to put a token on place p3 so that the process instance can terminate.

This assumption in workflow net analysis does not need to be valid in each process model. There is nothing that prevents the modeller of a workflow net for defining erroneous conditions for the *exclusive or* split, for instance, the

Boolean constants *true* and *false* to decide about whether to take the loop or to leave it.

If *true* is used for entering the loop and *false* for iterating it, then the loop will never be left. As a result, the workflow net never reaches the output condition *o*, although—formally—it is a sound workflow net! These aspects are not covered in workflow net analysis.

The analysis of workflow nets is based on a fairness assumption, which states that whenever there are several options to choose from, eventually any of these options will be chosen. Obviously, this fairness assumption is violated when choices are labelled with the constants *true* and *false*, respectively.

To illustrate the fairness assumption, consider a process to prepare a quote. A clerk prepares a draft quote document, which is then either agreed by a supervisor, or the supervisor asks the clerk for certain changes. In this setting, the fairness assumption states that—possibly after many iterations— eventually the supervisor agrees to the quote. As a result, each possible choice is taken eventually.

7.4.3 Soundness Theorem

Reachability analysis based on reachability graphs is a simple method to characterize the cases that comply with a given workflow net. However, reachability analysis only works well for small examples. The reachability graphs of real world business processes involving dozens of activities suffer from state explosion, which renders reachability graph analysis inappropriate in these settings.

Besides manually creating a reachability graph and checking for the three properties of workflow nets that collectively define soundness, there are computer-supported ways to determine soundness. The first class of approaches creates the reachability graph automatically and checks the soundness property. Due to the state explosion problem, this approach suffers from exponential run time behaviour. As a result, the creation of the reachability graph might not be feasible for real-world applications.

But there are other options that take advantage of the rich set of tools that have been developed by the Petri net community. In the remainder of this section, one of these approaches is discussed. It is based on a theorem that states a formal relationship between sound workflow nets and liveness and boundedness.

The general idea is deriving a Petri net from the workflow net to be checked for soundness, as sketched in Figure 7.13: By adding a transition t^* to a workflow net PN, and linking the final place o to t^* and t^* to the initial place i, a Petri net PN' is created.

We can show that PN' is live and bounded if and only if PN is sound. As a consequence, existing techniques to analyze liveness and boundedness for Petri nets can be used to check a workflow net for the soundness property.

For an important subclass of Petri nets, there are efficient analysis techniques for liveness and boundedness. This renders the check for soundness of workflow nets an efficient task, even for large workflow nets, which can be found in real-world scenarios.

Theorem 7.1 *Let* $PN = (P, T, F)$ *be a workflow net and* $t^* \notin T$. *PN is sound if and only if* (PN', i), *such that* $PN' = (P', T', F')$, $P' = P$, $T' = T \cup \{t^*\}$, *and* $F' = F \cup \{(o, t^*), (t^*, i)\}$, *is live and bounded.* ◇

To prove this theorem, we first show that if PN' is live and bounded, then PN is a sound workflow net. Then, it is shown that from the soundness property of the workflow net, liveness and boundedness properties of the Petri net PN' follow. The proof is illustrated in Figure 7.13.

Since PN' is live, for each transition there is a firing sequence starting in the initial state $[i]$ that activates it. This is especially true for the added transition t^*. Since o is the only input place of t^*, we can conclude that there is a state M reachable from $[i]$ with at least one token in o, that is, $M \geq [o]$.

When t^* fires, a token is put on the initial place i. Again, there is a firing sequence that leads to a state in which there is a token in o. Since PN' is bounded, $M = [o]$, because otherwise tokens would aggregate in a place of the Petri net.

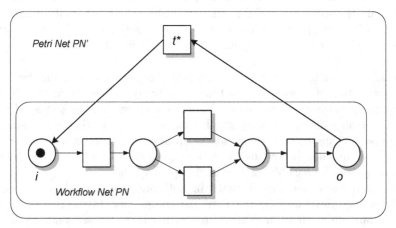

Fig. 7.13. Workflow net PN and Petri net PN', illustrating soundness theorem

Now we show that if PN is sound, PN' is bounded. This is shown by contradiction. Assume that PN is sound, but that PN' is unbounded. Since PN is sound and (by assumption) PN' is unbounded, there exist states M, M' such that $i \xrightarrow{*} M \xrightarrow{*} M'$ and $M' > M$, allowing the aggregation of tokens in a place of PN'.

Since PN is a sound workflow net, there exists a firing sequence σ such that $[i] \xrightarrow{*} M \xrightarrow{\sigma} [o]$. Applying the same firing sequence σ to state M' leads to a state $M'' > [o]$. This means that in M'' there is a token in o; but there is at least one additional token in the net! This is a violation of the soundness property of PN and shows the contradiction.

Finally, we have to show that if PN is sound then PN' is live. Soundness implies that each transition can participate in a firing sequence leading from the initial state $[i]$ to the final state $[o]$. By firing t^*, the initial state $[i]$ can be reached, so that liveness of PN' follows.   ◇

For arbitrary Petri nets, liveness and boundedness are still complex to compute, so that exponential run time behaviour can be expected. However, for an important subclass of Petri nets, liveness and boundedness can be computed in polynomial time. This subclass is free choice nets. Free choice nets have the property that the sets of input places of two transitions are either disjoint or identical.

Definition 7.5 A Petri net (P, T, F) is a free choice net if and only if for $t_1, t_2 \in T$ either $\bullet t_1 = \bullet t_2$ or $\bullet t_1 \cap \bullet t_2 = \emptyset$.   ◇

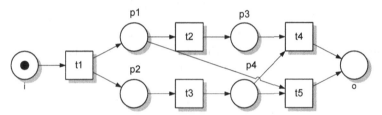

Fig. 7.14. Non-free-choice workflow net

Figure 7.14 shows a non-free-choice workflow net, because $\bullet t4 = \{p3, p4\}$ and $\bullet t5 = \{p1, p4\}$, resulting in $\bullet t4 \cap \bullet t5 \neq \emptyset$, and $\bullet t4 \neq \bullet t5$.

Non-free-choice nets are not very desirable in business process modelling, because the behaviour of the system depends on the ordering in which concurrent transitions fire.

In the example, if $t2$ fires before t_3, then t_5 cannot fire, since the token in $p1$ is no longer available. In this case, $t4$ can fire, terminating the workflow net. If, on the other hand, $t3$ fires before $t2$, then there is the possibility that $t5$ fires. In this case, $t2$ cannot fire, since the firing of $t5$ withdrew the token from $p1$. This means that there is no free choice in firing transitions $t4$ and $t5$, but the choice is predetermined by the firing behaviour of nonlocal transitions, in our case $t2$ and $t3$.

Note that the free choice property is orthogonal to the soundness property. There are non-free-choice workflow nets that are sound and those that are not sound. The workflow net shown in Figure 7.14 is non free choice. Looking at its reachability graph in Figure 7.15, we can show that this is in fact a sound workflow net.

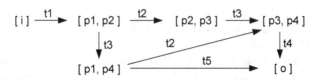

Fig. 7.15. Reachability graph of non-free-choice workflow net in Figure 7.14, showing its soundness

7.5 Relaxed Soundness

For a specific class of business processes that are often the outcome of real-world business process modelling using semiformal modelling techniques, the soundness property appears to be too restrictive. In these settings, the convenient representation of process models is in the centre, rather than formal aspects. Relaxed soundness aims at providing a correctness criterion that accepts these aspects and nevertheless provides a formal property that business processes can be analyzed against.

To illustrate the concepts behind relaxed soundness, a sample event-driven process chain is shown in Figure 7.16. The process represented deals with the handling of incoming goods. The goods are checked, and if they are not okay, a complaint is filed. In any case, the receipt of the goods is documented. If the goods are not okay, this information needs to be recorded in the goods receipt.

The problem with this example is that the *exclusive or* split connector in the upper right part of the event-driven process chain needs to wait until the decision on whether the goods are okay is made. If the goods are not okay, the *exclusive or* split needs to select the left branch, triggering an *and* join connector. The *and* join connector waits for the second incoming edge before the process can continue.

While this event-driven process chain captures the semantics of the business process quite well, it also permits a set of undesired executions:

- If the *exclusive or* split selects the *and* join branch but the goods are okay, the *and* join waits permanently for the filed complaint, which will never appear. As a result, the process is stuck in a deadlock situation.
- If the *exclusive or* split does not select the *and* join branch, but the goods are not okay, the *and* split cannot fire, because just one incoming edge—the filed complaint—is signalled. In this case, the receipt of the goods is registered, but the complaint on the quality of the goods is lost.

The underlying idea of relaxed soundness is that process models are acceptable if they allow desired process instances with certain additional properties, discussed below. However, undesired process instances are not generally disallowed, as in the original soundness property.

To investigate relaxed soundness in more detail and to reason about the formal properties of event-driven process chains, an algorithm to translate an

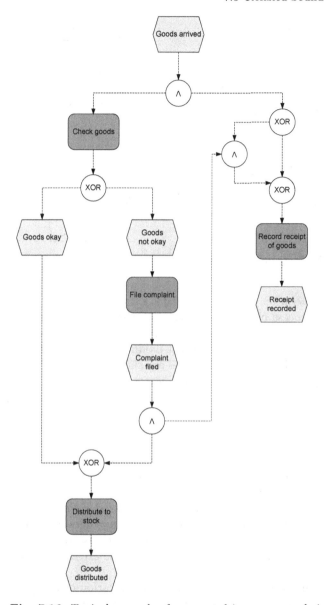

Fig. 7.16. Typical example of an event-driven process chain

event-driven process chain in a workflow net is introduced. This translation is done in three steps. In Steps 1 and 2, a translation of the event-driven process chain to Petri nets is achieved, while Step 3 translates the resulting Petri net into a workflow net.

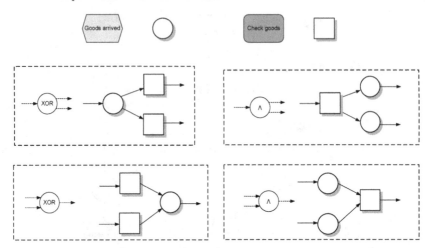

Fig. 7.17. Translation of event-driven process chain into a Petri net

Step 1, Generation of Petri Net Modules: Step 1 maps the functions of the event-driven process chain to transitions in the workflow net. Events of the event-driven process chain are mapped to places in the workflow net. Finally, the connectors are mapped to Petri net modules that realize the semantics of the connectors. These translation rules are shown in Figure 7.17.

The mapping of the *exclusive or* connector of an event-driven process chain to a Petri net module is straightforward. Two transitions share an input place, and as soon as one fires, the token is consumed, so that the other transition cannot fire, realizing an *exclusive or* split semantics.

Analogous considerations hold for the *and connector* in an event-driven process chain: an *and connector* is mapped to one transition with two output places, so that firing the transition results in a token in each of these output places, realizing *and* split semantics.

An *exclusive or* join and an *and* join are realized in Petri nets as shown in Figure 7.17. Observe that the number of outgoing edges of a split connector and the number of incoming edges of a join node is not restricted to two; the extensions to arbitrary numbers is obvious for *exclusive or* split and *and join/split* connectors.

Event-driven process chains allow the specification of (inclusive) *or* split and *or* join connectors. For these connectors, the mapping to Petri nets is not trivial, because the translation depends on the number of outgoing edges of the *or* split—or the number of incoming edges of the *or* join, respectively. The mapping for the case $n = 2$ is shown in Figure 7.18.

In this case, there are three possible behaviours of the *or* split: Either event $E1$ occurs or event $E2$ occurs or both events occur. These alternatives are represented in the Petri net by three transitions $t1, t2$, and $t3$. The case where only $E1$ occurs is represented by the firing of $t1$; the case where only

$E2$ occurs is represented by the firing of $t3$; and the case where $E1$ and $E2$ occur is represented by the firing of $t2$.

To generalize these considerations, for an *or* split with n outgoing arcs, $2^n - 1$ cases have to be considered, that is, the number of nonempty subsets of a set with n elements. Therefore, a translation of an *or* split to a Petri net is feasible only if the *or* split has few outgoing edges.

A similar observation can be made for the *or* join: all behavioural alternatives of the *or* join need to be represented by transitions. An example for $n = 2$ with three alternative cases is shown in the lower part of Figure 7.18.

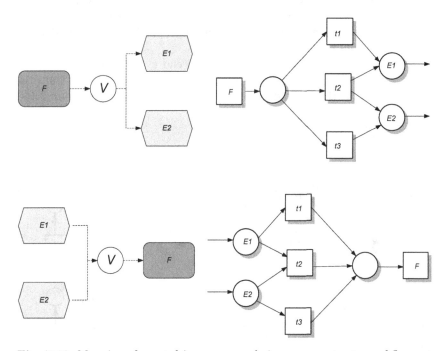

Fig. 7.18. Mapping of event-driven process chain *or connector* to workflow net

Step 2, Module Combination: In Step 2, the Petri net modules are combined. If the input and output elements of the modules are of the same kind (for example, both are places) then the elements are merged. If on the other hand the input and output elements are different (places and transitions) then the attached arcs are merged.

Step 3a, Add Source Place: In case the Petri net features multiple places without incoming edges—that is, in case the original event-driven process chain had multiple start events, a new initial place i is added. This step is required to transform a Petri net into a workflow net.

For each place p reflecting a start event in the event-driven process chain, a transition t and arcs $i \rightarrow t$ and $t \rightarrow p$ are added. It is assumed that the start events are alternative and that the occurrence of one start event suffices to start the process.

Step 3b, Add Sink Place: If the original event-driven process chain had multiple end events, a new final place o, a new transition t, and an arc $t \to o$ are added to the Petri net. For each place p representing an end event in the event-driven process chain, an arc $p \to t$ is added. It is an assumption that all end events need to occur for the process to complete.

To illustrate this algorithm, it is applied to the event-driven process chain shown in Figure 7.16. In Step 1, the elements in the event-driven process chain are translated to workflow net modules. In Step 2, the workflow modules are combined. Step 3a is not required, since there is one dedicated start event in the event-driven process chain, which can be immediately translated to the initial place of the workflow net.

Step 3b is required, because there are two end events, namely *Goods distributed* and *Receipt recorded*. By adding a new final place o and a transition $t10$ to synchronize these end events, the workflow net shown in Figure 7.19 is achieved.

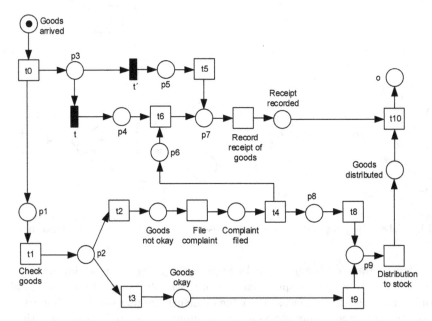

Fig. 7.19. Relaxed sound workflow net

The workflow net shown in Figure 7.19 requires some discussion. We consider a process instance in which the goods have arrived, have been checked, and are not okay. This execution sequence leads to state [p3, *Goods not ok*] of the Petri net. After a complaint is filed, the state [p3, *Complaint filed*] is reached. Since there is a token in p3, there is nothing that prevents t' from firing, leading to $[p5, Complaint\ filed]$. If $t4$ sends the filed complaint to $p6$, the Petri net reaches the state $[p5, p6, p8]$. With the tokens on $p5$ and $p8$, the process can continue, until $t10$ fires and a token is put in the final place o.

Since there still is a token at $p6$, the workflow net suffers from the improper termination problem, since from the initial state, a state $M > [o]$ can be reached, i.e. $M = [p6, o]$. This condition violates the soundness property of workflow nets. Hence, the workflow net is not sound.

At the same time, there are process instances that expose a desired behaviour: if the goods are not okay, the complaint is filed and t fires, the workflow terminates properly. If the goods are okay and t' fires, the workflow will also terminate properly. This means that there are several process instances that result in proper executions.

To capture the fact that there are desired and undesired process instances that comply with a given workflow net, a new correctness criterion is introduced: relaxed soundness. The idea of relaxed soundness is that for each transition there is a firing sequence that contains it and finally leads to a desired process instance.

Relaxed soundness includes firing sequences that do not lead to proper termination, for example, that result in a deadlock situation or in improper termination. In order to define relaxed soundness, the notion of a sound firing sequence is introduced.

Definition 7.6 Let $S = (PN, i)$ be a workflow system. A sequence of transitions σ is a *sound firing sequence* if $[i] \overset{\sigma}{\to} [o]$. The workflow system is *relaxed sound* if and only if for each transition t there exists a sound firing sequence σ which contains t. $\diamond$

The intuitive meaning of relaxed soundness is as follows: for each transition t representing an activity in a relaxed sound process model, there is at least one process instance that starts in the initial state $[i]$, contains activity t, and completes in the final state $[o]$.

If the Petri net shown in Figure 7.19 is analyzed carefully, for each transition, such a firing sequence can be found. Basically, two sound firing sequences suffice to show this for all transitions. In one such sequence, the goods are not okay and transition t is executed. In the other sequence, the goods are okay and transition t' is executed. Notice that these sequences together cover the complete set of transitions of the Petri net, which is therefore relaxed sound.

7.6 Further Soundness Criteria

In this section, further soundness criteria that cover specific aspects of business processes are introduced. In particular, weak soundness and lazy soundness are covered, before an overview of the soundness criteria introduced is provided.

7.6.1 Weak Soundness

The weak soundness property for business processes was developed in the context of process choreographies. A process choreography is realized by multiple local process orchestrations, as discussed in Chapter 6. To investigate weak soundness, we assume that each process orchestration is represented by a Web service. Each Web service exhibits conversational behaviour, and by composing these Web services, distributed business processes are developed.

Since distributed business processes are composed of existing Web services, the stipulation that every functionality provided by the process orchestrations involved is actually used is too restrictive. In contrast, we can allow process choreographies that exhibit proper behaviour, but do not use all parts of the Web services involved. This property is called weak soundness, and it is formalized as follows.

Definition 7.7 A workflow system (PN, i) is *weak sound* if and only if the following holds:

- For every state M reachable from state $[i]$ there exists a firing sequence leading from M to $[o]$, that is,

$$\forall M([i] \xrightarrow{*} M) \implies (M \xrightarrow{*} [o])$$

- State $[o]$ is the only state reachable from state $[i]$ with at least one token in place o, that is,

$$\forall M([i] \xrightarrow{*} M \wedge M \geq [o]) \implies M = [o]$$

◇

These concepts are illustrated by example originally introduced in Martens (2003a). A workflow module of a travel agency is shown on the right hand side in Figure 7.20. The process starts by getting an itinerary, providing means of travel and collecting available travel options. Concurrently rough planning and detailed planning are conducted, and the possibility to change plans is provided.

Finally, the schedule is sent. In this example, there are incoming places *Itinerary* and *Selection*, and outgoing places *Means of Travel* and *Route Planning*. Abstracting from these places and the associated arcs creates a workflow net that describes the internal process of the travel agency.

The workflow module shown can be composed with other modules. Figure 7.20 shows a default module that has one incoming place and one outgoing place; these places are in fact common with the respective places in the route planning workflow module, characterized by the identifiers of the places.

This property of workflow modules is called syntactic compatibility: workflow modules are syntactically compatible if their transitions and internal places are disjoint and each common place is an incoming place of one module and an outgoing place of the other. As a result, the default module selects

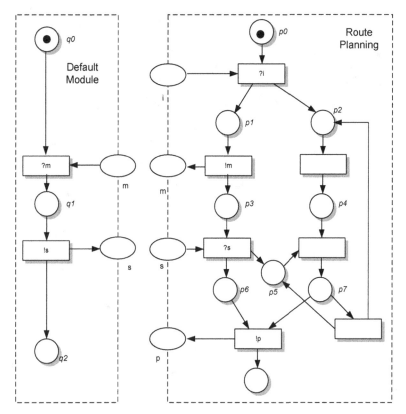

Fig. 7.20. Workflow module with syntactically compatible default module

an appropriate itinerary, so that the customer states the itinerary and gets the final travel plan.

The composition of these workflow modules is done by merging communication places, adding a new initial place to the composition as well as a transition that puts a token in each of the input places of the original workflow modules, similarly to the procedure for translating an event-driven process chain to a workflow net.

Analogously, a new final place and a transition are created and linked to the workflow modules accordingly. The transition is enabled when all output places of the original workflow modules have a token.

As a result of this composition, common places of the combined workflow modules are merged and become internal places. The incoming and outgoing places that are not common will form the new interface to the composed workflow module. The resulting composition of the route planning module and the default module is shown on the right hand side in Figure 7.21.

If workflow modules can be composed so that no interface places remain, then a distributed business process can be established. In the example, the cur-

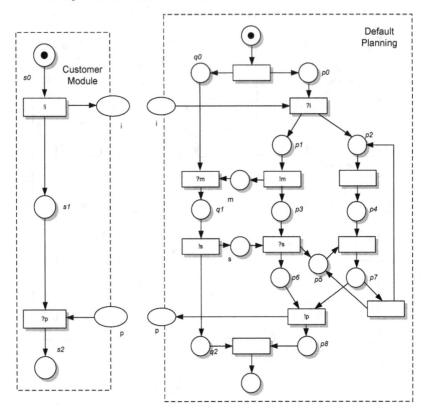

Fig. 7.21. Workflow module default planning and customer workflow module

rent workflow module *Default Planning*, developed by composing two workflow modules, requires another workflow module to attach to the interface places. Figure 7.21 shows an additional workflow module called *Customer Module* and its association with the *Default Planning* workflow module.

The customer module and the default planning module fit perfectly with each other: the incoming place i of the default planning module is matched by the outgoing place of the customer module, and the outgoing place p of the customer module matches the incoming place of the default planning module.

Workflow modules with this property are called *environments* of each other. The sample distributed business process consisting of three workflow modules—representing three Web services—is shown in Figure 7.22.

After discussing the composition of Web services, whose behaviour is represented by workflow modules, the correctness criterion weak soundness is investigated in more detail.

Figure 7.23 shows workflow modules A and B, each of which corresponds to a sound workflow net if the communication places and the associated arcs are abstracted from. A and B are syntactically compatible, since their respec-

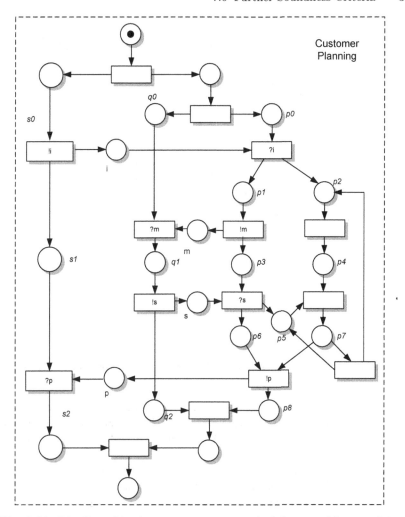

Fig. 7.22. Distributed business process composed of three workflow modules

tive incoming and outgoing places match. The composition of these workflow modules is represented in Figure 7.24, where the resulting workflow net is shown. The overall workflow net is weak sound, because the final state [*o*] can be reached from each state reachable from the initial state [*i*], and when [*o*] is reached, no other token is in the net.

While this workflow net is weak sound, it is not sound, because some transitions can never fire. In Figure 7.24, these transitions are marked by dotted rectangles. Although the original workflow modules representing the process orchestrations realized by the Web services are sound, due to the composition and the additional interface places and their attachment to the workflow modules, the resulting workflow net is not sound.

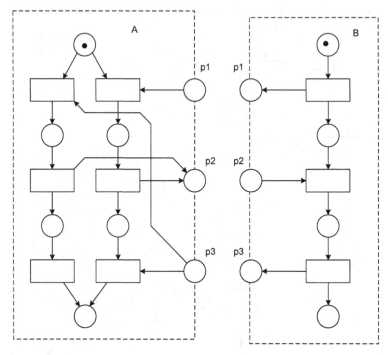

Fig. 7.23. Example of workflow modules with merged communication places

This abstract example also shows that the soundness criterion for work-flow nets is too restrictive in the context of Web services compositions. It is acceptable that certain parts of Web service A will not contribute to the overall composition.

It is also interesting to note that the two branches of Web service A are alternative, so that for each case one of these branches will be taken. However, due to the composition with a second Web service, one branch is completely ruled out.

If a composition of Web services is weak sound then the freedom from deadlock and the proper termination of the composition are guaranteed. Notice that weak soundness—just like soundness—is based on a fairness assumption: For each decision, all alternatives will be chosen eventually. This fairness assumption can to some extent be ruled out by the composition with another Web service. As shown in the example, certain decisions will simply never be made, due to the communication behaviour of the process orchestrations attached.

7.6.2 Lazy Soundness

The different kinds of soundness criteria discussed so far are tailored towards specific application environments, where the original soundness appears to be

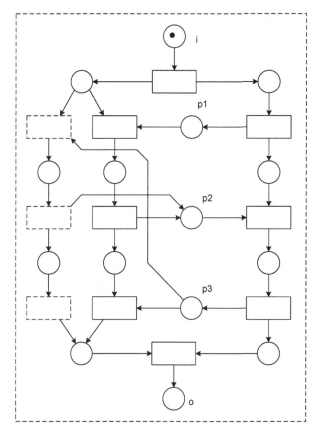

Fig. 7.24. Example of weak sound workflow net

too restrictive: relaxed soundness allows business process models that expose deadlock behaviour in some cases; but each activity can also participate in a correct process instance. Weak soundness disallows deadlocks, but it allows certain parts of the process not to participate in any process instance.

When investigating the soundness criterion for certain control flow patterns, called critical control flow patterns, it turns out that process models using these patterns cannot be sound. In addition, they cannot be weak sound. Lazy soundness has been proposed as a new soundness criterion for these critical control flow patterns.

In this section sample process models with critical control flow patterns are investigated: *Discriminator, N-out-of-M join,* and *Multiple Instances without Synchronization.*

A sample process with the discriminator pattern is shown in Figure 7.25. In this process, a manufacturer requests offers from a number of suppliers. The discriminator is used to realize a process in which the first offer is accepted, and the respective order is sent; other messages that might come in afterwards will be ignored.

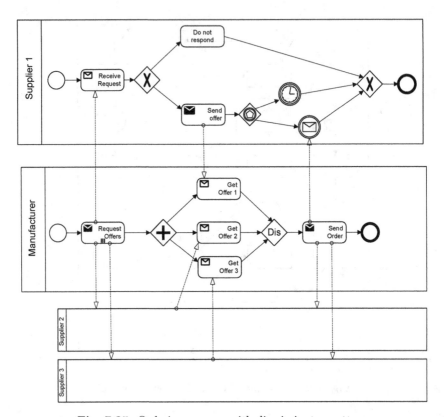

Fig. 7.25. Ordering process with discriminator pattern

The process is distributed over four parties, a manufacturer and three suppliers. The manufacturer starts the process and sends requests for offers to the suppliers. It is assumed that all suppliers share the same behaviour: they either respond by sending an offer or do not respond. The process orchestration of *Supplier 1*, as well as its interaction with the process orchestration of a *Manufacturer*, is shown in Figure 7.25.

The process orchestration of the supplier is explained as follows. After receiving a request from the manufacturer, an *exclusive or* gateway is used to decide about sending an offer. In case an offer is sent, the supplier expects to receive an order in the *Receive Order* activity. If, however, no order arrives within a defined time interval, it is assumed that the manufacturer will not respond—represented by the timer event.

The process orchestration of the manufacturer starts by its requesting offers from suppliers. Then, the manufacturer expects the arrival of messages containing the offers sent by the suppliers. It is assumed that the manufacturer is in urgent need for material, so that the first offer that arrives will be taken. This policy is realized by the discriminator pattern. Offers received after the discriminator fired will be ignored.

To see why this process is not sound, consider a concrete process instance based on the process model shown. Assume that the request messages have been sent and that *Supplier 1* was the first to respond by sending an offer. Consequently, the discriminator fires, an order is sent to *Supplier 1*, and the end event of the manufacturer's process is reached.

If an offer is received from *Supplier 2* after the manufacturing process has reached the end event, then this message is received by the *Get Offer 2* activity. This activity, however, occurs after the end of the process instance has been reached! This is an example of improper termination, because activities are executed after the process has reached its end. Therefore, the process cannot be sound.

For the same reason, the process model cannot be weak sound. But the process is relaxed sound, because relaxed sound only makes sure that there are executions that are sound. Rather than formally proving this, we argue that the process is relaxed sound.

In order to do so, we have to show that each activity can participate in a sound process instance, that is, a process instance that reaches the final state. Note that once the final state has been reached no activities can occur in the process.

Assume that *Supplier 1* sends an offer and *Supplier 2* does not send an offer. In this case, the process reaches the final state, because the manufacturer sends the order to *Supplier 1*, who can then terminate properly. Also, *Supplier 2* can terminate properly because no further activities are required after deciding not to respond to the request.

If both suppliers send an offer, and *Supplier 1* is the first to do so, then the manufacturer sends an order to *Supplier 1*. If the message by *Supplier 2* arrives and the *Get Offer 2* activity can terminate before the overall process terminates, then *Supplier 2* will detect that no message will come in.

Also, in this example, the overall process reaches the final state. Since these considerations hold for both suppliers (swapping *Suppliers 1* and *2* would have analogous results), we can conclude that all activities can participate in a process instance that reaches the final state: the process is relaxed sound.

A similar process model with an *N-out-of-M join* control flow pattern is shown in Figure 7.26. This process is a variant of the process discussed above. The business logic implements a process in which four offers are invited, and as soon as two offers have arrived, the manufacturer decides which offer to accept. Each offer, however, will get compensation, realized by the *Pay offer* activities. For ease of presentation, only one supplier is shown.

This process is not sound, because after the final state has been reached additional offers can be received by the manufacturer, and the respective payment activities are performed. These payment activities are ignored by the

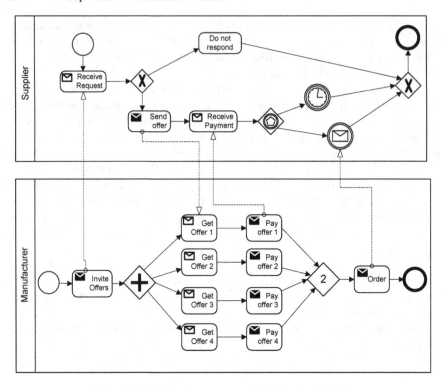

Fig. 7.26. Ordering process with N-out-of-M join

join, so that no deadlocks or livelocks will occur after the process terminates. In workflow net terminology this means that a state is reachable in which there is a token in the final place *o* while there are additional tokens in the net. Therefore, this process model is not sound.

Nevertheless this process model represents valid process instances, since the business goals are met: out of two offers an order is selected, and finally all offers which have been received have been compensated for.

Lazy soundness is designed to capture this semantics. The pay offer activities are performed after the process has completed; these activities are known as *lazy activities*.

We now investigate the *multiple instances without synchronization* pattern with respect to the lazy soundness criterion. Assume a process model in which at some point multiple instances are created that are not synchronized.

This means that the process flow continues right after the start of these multiple instances, as discussed in Section 4.1. Since there are no assumptions on the run time of the activity instances and these instances are not synchronized, it is obvious that the final activity of the process can be completed while some of the multiple instances created are still running. Therefore, process models featuring the *multiple instances without synchronization* pattern cannot be sound.

We can even argue that these instances are not even structurally sound, that is, not all nodes are on a path from i to o, in workflow net terminology. An edge $j \rightarrow k$ means that j needs to terminate before k can start. If j is an activity with the *multiple instances without synchronization* pattern, then k effectively starts before j has terminated. Therefore, the semantics of the control flow connector is violated. The multiple instances activity j spawns the instances $j_1, j_2, \ldots, j_n$, each of which is connected only to j. This means that these instances do not have any outgoing edges. Therefore they cannot be on a path from i to o, violating the workflow net property of structural soundness.

An example involving the *multiple instances without synchronization* pattern is shown in Figure 7.27, where in the upper part there is a process model shown with sequential execution of activities A, B, and C, where B is a *multiple instances without synchronization* activity.

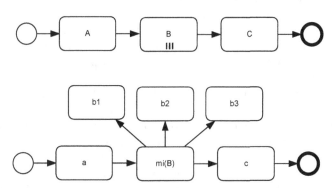

Fig. 7.27. *Multiple instances without synchronization* pattern, process model and process instance

In the lower part of Figure 7.27, a concrete process instance is shown, where three instances $b1, b2$, and $b3$ are created. The creation is done by a system activity $mi(B)$, as discussed in Section 4.1. We can assume that this system activity will spawn as many instances of b as required.

In the process instance shown, $mi(B)$ spawns the three instances and—since the instances are not synchronized—control is immediately transferred to activity instance c, whose termination completes the process. It is obvious that $b1, b2$, and $b3$ can still be running after the end event of the process has been reached. Therefore, by the structure of this process, soundness is not satisfied.

The critical control flow patterns discussed in the previous section have shown that traditional soundness criteria are not appropriate for characterizing processes using the *discriminator*, the *N-out-of-M* pattern, and the *multiple instances without synchronization* pattern.

On the other hand, these patterns are quite useful for modelling business processes, because situations like the ones shown in the examples are actually quite typical in real-world business processes. For instance, in business-to-business scenarios multiple requests for offers are sent out, and receiving responses for a proper subset of these requests is sufficient for the process to continue.

These processes are neither sound nor weak sound. They can be relaxed sound, but in environments with a high degree of automation in process enactment this is a rather weak soundness criterion, because it allows deadlocks to occur before the final state of the process has been reached.

Therefore, a new sound criterion has been proposed: lazy soundness. Lazy soundness relaxes weak soundness, because it allows activities to be executed after the final state has been reached; however, deadlocks are not permitted before the final state has been reached. Activities that are running after the final state has been reached are known as lazy activities.

Consider the example shown in Figure 7.26, and assume that the offers received from *Suppliers 1* and *2* have led to the activation of the join. Further assume that the offers from *Suppliers 3* and *4* arrive only after the final event has been reached. Then, receiving the offers for *Suppliers 3* and *4* and paying them are lazy activities.

These activities are carried out after the process has reached its final state. However, the business goals are met by this realization, since in the business scenario described all suppliers need to be paid for their offers. Lazy soundness permits the occurrence of these activities, and the resulting process model is lazy sound.

It is important to differentiate between the *completion* of a process instance and its *termination*. By completion we mean the execution of the final node. By termination we mean the point in time when all activities of the process have terminated.

Note that completion cannot occur later than termination, but a process can complete (by executing the final node) before it terminates, due to lazy activities that can still be active after the process has completed. Based on these considerations, lazy soundness is characterized as follows. A structurally sound process model is lazy sound if for each process instance the final node is executed exactly once.

Lazy soundness can be formally defined as follows.

Definition 7.8 Let (PN, i) be a workflow system, with a workflow net $PN = (P, T, F)$. (PN, i) is *lazy sound* if and only if

- $\forall M([i] \xrightarrow{*} M) \exists M' : M \xrightarrow{*} M' \land M'(o) = 1$
- $\forall M([i] \xrightarrow{*} M) : M(o) \leq 1$

◇

The first bullet makes sure that from each state reachable from the initial state $[i]$ there is a continuation of the process that leads to a state in which the final node is reached. Since the final node o has no outgoing edge, a token in o will never leave this place. The second bullet defines that no state is reachable in which there is more than one token in the final place. Therefore, this definition of lazy sound makes sure that the final node is triggered exactly once.

Lazy activities are allowed because when the state M' with $M'(o) = 1$ is reached, it is not ruled out that other places of the Petri net still have tokens. These tokens can enable transitions that represent lazy activities.

To illustrate the definition of lazy soundness, we return to Figure 7.25. This time we assume that two offers are invited and the supplier is selected, who responds first by sending an offer. This behaviour is represented by the discriminator pattern. A process instance is shown in Figure 7.28 by an event

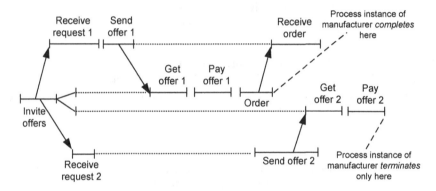

Fig. 7.28. Process instance, illustrating lazy soundness

diagram. In this diagram, a process instance is represented in which the offer by *Supplier 1* is received first. The process instance continues with the firing of the discriminator, followed by the sending of the order by the manufacturer. The order is received by *Supplier 1*, and the process completes.

The completion of the process is represented by the state M' in the definition of lazy soundness, with $M'(o) = 1$. At this point in time, *Supplier 2* decides to send an offer. This offer is received by the *Get Offer 2* activity of the manufacturer. As specified by the business policies of the manufacturer, this offer will be compensated for, represented by the *Pay Offer 2* activity instance. These activities are lazy activities. They are executed after the process instance has completed. As a result, from state M' states $M'' \neq M'$ are reachable.

The execution of the order activity by the manufacturer marks the completion of the process instance of the manufacturer. Note that this activity is executed exactly once, because the discriminator triggers its outgoing edge only after its first incoming edge is activated. Incoming edges that are activated afterwards are ignored.

This property is also required by lazy soundness, because by stating that $\forall M([i] \xrightarrow{*} M) : M(o) \leq 1$ the definition makes sure that no state transition ever puts another token in the final place, so that the completion of the process instance is signalled exactly once.

7.6.3 Soundness Criteria Overview

To summarize the considerations on soundness in business process management, the relationships between the different soundness properties are investigated. While the soundness properties are developed in the context of different formalisms, this section uses workflow nets for a concise specification.

It turns out that the soundness criteria are based on a few properties of the structure of business processes. These properties can be combined in different ways, resulting in different soundness properties.

Let $PN = (P, T, F)$ be a workflow net. The soundness criteria are based on the following criteria.

P1 *Termination*: The termination property makes sure that any process instance that starts in the initial state will eventually reach the final state. For every state M reachable from the initial state $[i]$ there exists a firing sequence leading from M to o:

$$\forall M([i] \xrightarrow{*} M) \implies (M \xrightarrow{*} [o])$$

P2 *Proper termination*: The final state is the only state reachable from the initial state in which there is a token in the final place. State $[o]$ is the only state reachable from state $[i]$ with at least one token in place o:

$$\forall M([i] \xrightarrow{*} M \wedge M \geq [o]) \implies M = [o]$$

P3 *No dead transitions*: Each transition can contribute to at least one process instance:

$$(\forall t \in T) \, \exists M, M' : [i] \xrightarrow{*} M \xrightarrow{t} M'$$

P4 *Transition participation*: Each transition participates in at least one process instance that starts in the initial state and reaches the final state: For each transition t there exists a firing sequence from $[i]$ to $[o]$ in which t participates:

$$(\forall t \in T) \, \exists M, M' : ([i] \xrightarrow{*} M \xrightarrow{t} M' \xrightarrow{*} [o])$$

There are the following relationships between these properties.

Properties P1 and P3 imply P4, because P3 states that for every transition t a state is reachable in which t is enabled. Assume that when t fires, state M' is reached. Property P1 guarantees that from any state reachable from the initial state, the final state can be reached. This property holds in particular for M'. Therefore, property P4 follows.

Note that the converse of this implication does not hold, that is, P4 does not imply P1 and P3. P4 only states that for each transition t there are states M and M', such that firing of t in state M results in state M', from which the final state can be reached.

By this definition it is not ruled out that t can be enabled in state M'', such that $M'' \xrightarrow{t} M'''$; but from the resulting state M''', the final state is not reachable.

From the definition of properties P3 and P4 it is obvious that P4 implies P3. P4 states that there are no dead transitions (P3) and, in addition, that for every state reachable by the firing of a transition t there is a continuation of the process instance that leads to the final state.

The following propositions characterize the relationships between the soundness properties.

Lemma 7.1 *Soundness* $\Leftrightarrow P1 \land P2 \land P3$ ◇

Properties P1, P2, and P3 together are used in the definition for soundness. P1 guarantees that each process instance that starts in the initial state will eventually reach the final state. When the final state is reached, there are no tokens left in the net, defined by property P2; finally, each activity can contribute to a process instance, defined by property P3.

Lemma 7.2 *Weak Soundness* $\Leftrightarrow P1 \land P2$ ◇

Weak soundness allows activities that cannot participate in any process instance. However, it states that from each state reachable, the final state can be reached and that at this point in time there are no tokens left in the net.

Lemma 7.3 *Relaxed Soundness* $\Leftrightarrow P4$ ◇

Relaxed soundness is defined by property P4. Since relaxed soundness permits deadlocks in process instances to occur, property P1 does not hold for relaxed sound processes in general. When the final node is reached, there can be tokens left in the net; these tokens can be stuck in deadlock situations. Since P3 is implied by P4, P3 also holds for relaxed sound processes.

An investigation of the relationship of the lazy soundness criterion with the traditional soundness criteria is useful. Property P1 is not satisfied, because there might be lazy activities, that is, activities that are performed concurrently to the completion of the process instance. Therefore, reaching the final state $[o]$ is not satisfied, because—in Petri net terminology—there might be additional tokens in the net, reflecting lazy activities.

On the other hand, lazy soundness guarantees that the final activity is executed exactly once, marking the completion of the process. This property—to some extent—matches the semantics of P1, because it makes sure that every process instance will complete and that there are no deadlocks that prohibit a process instance from doing so. This discussion also applies to property P2: lazy soundness violates P2, due to lazy activities. In lazy sound processes there might also be dead activities, violating properties P3 and P4.

7.7 Decision Soundness

This section investigates the impact of decision logic on behavioural properties of business processes. We show that a business process that is sound according to the soundness criterion discussed in Section 7.4 might run into a deadlock situation, if decision logic is taken into account. To incorporate decision logic into behavioural analysis of business processes, the decision soundness criterion has been established.

To illustrate the problem, a business process covering the selling of a train ticket is investigated, as shown in Figure 7.29. The process starts when a booking of a train ticket is received. The client is then offered a discount card; if she accepts, the booking will take advantage of the discount offered by the discount card. There are two discount cards available, discount card 25 and discount card 50, which provide at least 25% and 50%, respectively, discount on the train ticket price.

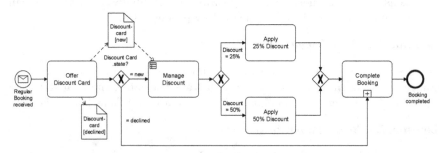

Fig. 7.29. Business process with decision task *Manage Discount*

The decision task *Manage Discount* of the business process calls a decision that returns the applicable discount. The return value of the decision task is used by the *exclusive or* gateway to implement the discount. Finally, the booking is completed by the subprocess *Complete Booking*, which also sends the ticket to the client.

To investigate the soundness of this business process, it has to be translated to a Petri net. In the classical Petri net mapping, data objects are discarded. Decisions are represented by the fairness assumption, which states that any decision possible is actually taken at some point in time. This assumption avoids starvation of Petri net transitions.

We do not need to provide this translation to a Petri net to see that the business process is sound. Along the lines of Definition 7.3 we can argue as follows:

- Each booking that is received in the start event *Regular Booking received* will inevitably lead to the end event. This holds, whether the client accepts the discount card or not.
- When the end event *Booking completed* is reached, there is no activity left in the process.
- There are no dead transitions, because all activities of the business process can participate in some process instance. Notice that the fairness assumption makes sure that both activities, *Apply 25% Discount* and *Apply 50% Discount*, will be executed in some process instance.

The logic of the *Manage Discount* decision is now included in the discussion. As shown in Figure 7.30, the decision depends on the type of discount card (25 or 50) and the number of points already collected. Depending on the distance travelled, each booking of a train ticket adds points on the card. If at least 1,000 points are on the discount card, the discount card 25 provides 30% discount, while the discount card 50 increases the discount to 60%. The decision table uses the *Unique* hit policy, discussed in Section 5.4.1.

Manage Discount			
U	*Discountcard.type*	*Discountcard.points*	*Discount*
	{25, 50}	Number	{25%, 30%, 50%, 60%}
1	25	< 1000	25%
2	50	< 1000	50%
3	25	>= 1000	30%
4	50	>= 1000	60%

Fig. 7.30. Decision table that influences the soundness of a business process

The behaviour of the train ticket purchase process including the decision logic is now investigated. By doing so, it turns out that there is a problem during process execution if the decision returns the values 30% or 60%. The problem is due to the fact that the process does not provide any option at the *exclusive or* split to deal with these values. As a result, the process will get stuck before the *xor* split, because all its alternatives are evaluated to *false*!

To cover the impact of decisions on the behaviour of business processes with decisions, decision soundness has been introduced. Let p be a business process model, where each decision task $t_d \in T$ is realized by a decision $d \in D$, where T is the set of tasks of p and D is a set of decisions. The decision task t_d is followed by an *exclusive or* split that uses the output of the decision d to decide on the branch to select. We also assume that d uses a single hit policy and that the process model p satisfies the classical soundness criterion introduced in Section 7.4.

Definition 7.9 A business process model p, where each decision task $t_d \in T$ is realized by a decision $d \in D$, is *decision sound* iff the following criteria are satisfied for each pair (t_d, d).

- *Table completeness*: Decision $d \in D$ is represented by a decision table that is complete, i.e., d provides an output value for each possible combination of input values.
- *Output coverage*: (t_d, d) satisfies the output coverage criterion if the process is able to handle all possible output values, i.e., if after t_d there is at least one branch of an *exclusive or* split for each possible output value of decision d that is associated with decision task t_d in the process model.
- *Dead Branch Absence*: (t_d, d) satisfies the dead branch absence criterion if each condition of the *exclusive or* split that follows a decision task t_d with a decision $d \in D$ appears as a possible output value of d, so that each branch can be selected.

$\diamond$

Notice that we allow situations in which a decision output satisfies multiple branches of an *exclusive or* split. In this case, the BPMN execution semantics of this control flow construct ensures that a single branch will be taken.

Decision soundness is illustrated by examples for each of its defining criteria. To discuss table completeness, a variation of the decision table introduced above is shown in Figure 7.31.

Manage Discount			
U	Discountcard.type	Discountcard.points	Discount
	{25, 50}	Number	{25%, 30%, 50%, 60%}
1	25	< 1000	25%
2	50	< 1000	50%
3	25	> 1000	30%
4	50	>= 1000	60%

Fig. 7.31. Decision table that violates the completeness criterion

The table is not complete, because there is an input combination for which there is no matching row in the decision table. Actually, there is just a single input combination with this property, the value pair $(25, 1000)$. Due to the error in the definition of row 3, there is no match for that input combination.

If the decision task *Manage Discount* calls the decision with the input pair $(25, 1000)$, the decision will not return a valid output. As a result, the business process cannot continue. Since this situation is caused by a decision, we call this situation a decision deadlock.

A second form of decision deadlock occurs if the decision returns a value that cannot be processed by the business process. In this case, the output coverage criterion introduced in Definition 7.9 is violated.

We have discussed this situation already during the motivation of decision soundness earlier in this section. The decision table shown in Figure 7.30 in combination with the train ticket purchasing process in Figure 7.29 does not satisfy the output coverage criterion, because the decision might return output value 30%, which cannot be processed by the process. Hence, the output of the decision is not covered by the process, violating decision soundness.

Finally, the third criterion of deadlock soundness is investigated, dead branch absence. This property is related to the third criterion of classical soundness definition, dead transitions. It disallows transitions in a sound business process that can never be executed. Very similarly, the dead branch criterion disallows branches in a business process that, due to the decision logic, can never be executed.

To illustrate the dead branch absence criterion, the train ticket purchasing process has to be modified. Figure 7.32 shows an excerpt of the process that can handle three different discount values, i.e., 25%, 50%, and 60%.

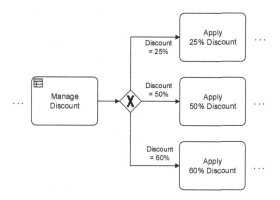

Fig. 7.32. Excerpt of train ticket purchasing process which handles three discount values

To discuss dead branch absence, a variant of the decision table is shown in Figure 7.33. The only output values of this decision are 25% and 50%. As a result, the 60%-branch of the business process can never be executed. It is a dead branch, resulting in the violation of the dead branch absence criterion and, hence, in a violation of decision soundness.

Manage Discount			
U	Discountcard.type	Discountcard.points	Discount
	{25, 50}	Number	{25%, 50%}
1	25	-	25%
2	50	-	50%

Fig. 7.33. Decision table results in violation of dead branch absence criterion

To conclude this section, a refinement of decision soundness is discussed. This is required, since in a complex organizational setting, a given decision table might be reused by different decision tasks, which can even be part of different business processes. This is a typical situation if the decision logic of a reusable business knowledge is represented by a decision table.

We assume that the decision table shown in Figure 7.30 is used for the business process in Figure 7.29 and also for the business process with four alternatives, of which an excerpt is shown in Figure 7.34.

There are no further assumptions on the activities before *Manage Discount* is executed. In particular, returning customers with several tickets already purchased might be served by that process. In any case, the decision soundness criterion is satisfied, since the table is complete, and the process and the decision satisfy the output coverage criterion and the dead branch absence criterion.

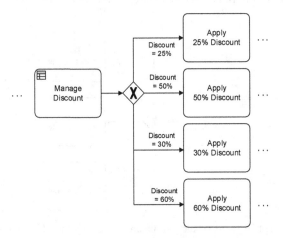

Fig. 7.34. Excerpt of train ticket purchasing process which handles four discount values

However, we have already stated a violation of the output coverage criterion due to missing alternatives in the business process to handle discount values 30% and 60% in Figure 7.29.

One might wonder if this violation can actually occur. Since the process issues the discount card immediately before the decision is invoked, the number of points has still its initial value; it cannot be equal or larger than 1,000. Hence, when taking into account the state of the business process, there is actually no problem, because all values that the decision can return *in that state*—which is 25% and 50%—are covered by the process.

To capture situations like these, a state-based decision soundness criterion is established. We can use this criterion to state that the combination of the business process in Figure 7.29 and the decision in Figure 7.30 is not decision sound, but it is state-based decision sound. Further details on different forms of decision soundness can be found in the bibliographical notes of this chapter.

Bibliographical Notes

Soundness of workflow nets has been introduced in van der Aalst (1998); further investigations on finding control flow errors in workflow specifications are reported in van der Aalst (2000). Structural correctness criteria of process models can be analyzed using the workflow analyzer Woflan, described in van der Aalst (1999) and Verbeek et al. (2001). Woflan is able to read process models specified in different process modelling languages; after internally translating the process models to a workflow net representation, the soundness properties of the process models can be analyzed.

Checking the various soundness properties is also possible with the BPM Academic Initiative software run by Signavio. It uses the soundness checking functionality provided by Lohmann and Wolf (2010) via a Web services interface. An introduction to the BPM Academic Initiative with an analysis of its process model repository can be found in Kunze et al. (2011).

Relaxed soundness was the first of the weaker soundness criteria proposed. It was published in Dehnert and Rittgen (2001). Based on this work, Siegeris and Zimmermann (2006) introduce the composition of processes, while allowing us to validate relaxed soundness. Weak soundness is introduced in Martens (2003b), where the composition of Web services is also addressed.

The general idea of lazy soundness is introduced in Puhlmann and Weske (2006b); a thorough analysis of lazy soundness and a formalization in the π-calculus is reported in Puhlmann (2007). Interaction soundness is introduced in Puhlmann and Weske (2006a); it is based on lazy soundness and takes into account the specific properties of service-oriented architectures, in which business partners can be bound dynamically, that is, at run time of the process instances. The π-calculus provides link passing mobility, a concept that represents well the dynamic structures that are found in dynamic service landscapes.

Object lifecycle conformance is introduced in Küster et al. (2007), where also techniques for generating business process models from object lifecycles are investigated. Kunze and Weske (2016) provide a comprehensive overview of behavioural models and analysis techniques, ranging from modelling state transition systems to analyzing compliance in business processes.

Decision soundness has been introduced in Batoulis and Weske (2017a). Tool support for checking decision soundness for business processes and decision tables can be found in Batoulis and Weske (2017b). An overview of several refined criteria for decision soundness was proposed in Batoulis et al. (2017).

Part III

Architectures and Methodologies

8

Business Process Management Architectures

Following our discussion of the evolution of enterprise systems architectures in Chapter 2, this chapter investigates business process management architectures and evaluates them with respect to their properties. It is organized as follows.

Section 8.1 looks at workflow management systems architectures by discussing the workflow reference architecture, an architectural blueprint for workflow management systems.

Service-oriented architectures have gained increasing popularity recently. In Section 8.2, this new architecture paradigm as well as Web services as the current implementation of service-oriented architectures are sketched. Web service composition is introduced as a realization vehicle for system workflows whose activities are realized by Web services. In Section 8.3, advanced service composition is investigated.

Data-driven approaches to the flexible enactment of business processes are discussed in Section 8.4. This approach for enactment of human interaction business processes uses data dependencies to control process enactment; it provides knowledge workers with options to design the enactment of their processes and provides additional flexibility without hampering the overall correctness of the business process.

8.1 Workflow Management Architectures

In Section 2.4, workflow management systems have been identified as an important step in the evolution of business process management systems. This section investigates the architecture of workflow management systems.

© Springer-Verlag GmbH Germany, part of Springer Nature 2019
M. Weske, *Business Process Management*,
https://doi.org/10.1007/978-3-662-59432-2_8

8.1.1 Build Time and Run Time

In traditional workflow management, the separation of build time and run time is essential. During the build time of a workflow, a workflow model is specified completely, typically using a graphical workflow modelling tool.

Workflow models are the blueprint for implemented business processes in workflow management systems. Workflow models need to be in line with business process models that capture the operational business processes; they extend the latter with technical information required to make them executable.

When a workflow model has been created that satisfies the requirements imposed by the business process, workflow modelling has completed. Depending on the workflow management system used, the workflow model is represented by a script, written in the workflow language of that system. Workflow models can also be stored in a database or workflow model repository. In any case, the workflow modelling tool is terminated after workflow modelling has completed, that is, after the build time of the workflow.

When a business process starts for which a workflow is defined that implements it, a workflow instance is created by the workflow management system; this workflow instance is based on a predefined workflow model. In the next step, the workflow instance is started, and the run time starts. The organization of the phases in build time and run time is shown in Figure 8.1, abstracting from the relationships of the workflow engine to the software layer and—in the case of human interaction workflows—to process participants.

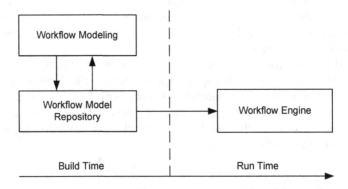

Fig. 8.1. Build time versus run time of a workflow

Workflow instances typically live in the main memory of the process engine, which controls the execution of workflow instances. The process engine decides for a given workflow instance which activities can be started, and it communicates with workflow client applications, which are accessed by process participants.

In this traditional workflow scenario, there is no link between a workflow instance and the workflow model that was used to create it. This property implies that changing the workflow model does not affect running workflow instances based on that workflow model. As a result, a strict separation between the build time of a workflow model and the run time of the respective workflow instances is realized.

The situation described is similar to traditional programming, where a program is coded in a programming language, compiled to executable code (build time), and executed (run time). Workflow modelling can be regarded as a form of programming "in the large", such that the workflow model represents a program written in a workflow language. To execute such a workflow program, the run time environment of the workflow management system is used. As a result, workflow instances correspond to program executions, realized by operating system processes.

8.1.2 Workflow Management Systems Architectures

Workflow management systems architectures organize the subsystems that are involved in the design and enactment of both system workflows and human interaction workflows. A generic workflow management systems architecture is shown in Figure 8.2.

Observe that this architecture is very similar to the conceptual systems architecture introduced in Section 3.9, used as a basis for the event-based characterization of process instances. Therefore, the workflow systems architecture presented in this section is integrated well with the definition of process models and process instances in Section 3.5.

The architecture contains the following subsystems and roles, whose responsibilities are described as follows:

The *Workflow Modelling* subsystem provides means to model the technical aspects of implemented business processes. For each activity in the operational business process model realized by software, a detailed specification of the execution environment of the software needs to be provided.

The workflow models are stored in a *Workflow Model Repository*. This repository contains the set of workflow models of the company and is therefore an important asset.

The *Workflow Engine* is responsible for enacting workflow processes. If an event occurs during the daily business of the company for which a workflow model is defined, the workflow engine creates a new workflow instance based on the defined workflow model.

Depending on whether a system workflow or a human workflow is associated with the event, different subsystems of the workflow management systems architecture are required.

If a system workflow is created, the workflow engine uses the workflow model to call the invoked applications defined for the system workflow. These calls are performed according to the process structure defined in the workflow model. The workflow engine is also responsible for transferring data between calls to different applications.

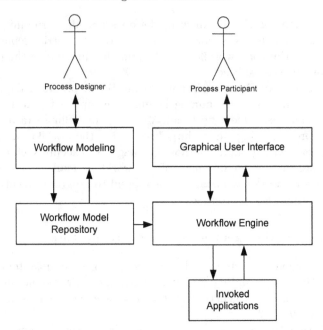

Fig. 8.2. Workflow management systems architecture

Since human interactions are not available in system workflows, the workflow engine can be regarded as an interpreter of workflow models. These workflow models need to be executable, so that complete information on the applications to invoke, including the technical execution environment, is required.

In the case of human interaction workflows, the workflow instance contains both automatically invoked applications and human interactions. These human interactions are performed using the *Graphical User Interface* subsystem. Organizational information on the *Process Participants*, their skills and competencies, can be used by the workflow engine to offer work only to knowledge workers that are available and capable of performing these activities.

8.1.3 WfMC Reference Architecture

The generic workflow management systems architecture introduced in the previous section discusses the constituents of typical workflow scenarios. To provide a common view on workflow management systems architectures, the Workflow Management Coalition—an interest group in which vendors and users of workflow management systems are organized—developed the *WfMC Workflow Reference Architecture*.

This architecture provides a high-level systems architecture blueprint for workflow management systems; it is shown in Figure 8.3.

The different subsystems of this reference architecture are discussed with their roles and responsibilities. The workflow enactment service—the WfMC

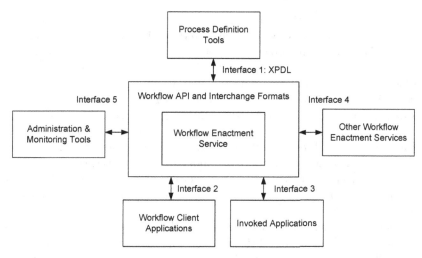

Fig. 8.3. Workflow reference architecture, proposed by the Workflow Management Coalition

term for workflow engine—is the central component of the architecture. Interfaces describe how the other subsystems connect to the workflow enactment service.

Process definition tools are used for workflow modelling; they are attached to the central component by Interface 1. The goal of this interface is to enable tools developed by different workflow system vendors to work in a standardized representation of a business process.

Interface 1 is specified in the XML language XML Process Definition Language, or XPDL. This language is based on a metamodel approach, in which the concepts of interacting business processes of multiple participants are defined. The XPDL package metamodel can be used to represent business process diagrams expressed in the BPMN.

The metamodel includes classes for pools, lanes, processes, participants, and message flow. The internal structure of processes is represented by a process metamodel. In addition to processes and activities, different types of activities and transitions are modelled to represent control flow in process models. The specification document also defines a serialization of process models to XML that includes conceptual information as well as graphics information used for rendering business process diagrams.

During the enactment of human interaction workflows, the persons involved receive work items that inform them about activities due for execution. This functionality is realized by workflow client applications, attached to the enactment service by Interface 2. The goal of standardizing Interface 2 is to allow workflow client applications of different vendors to talk to a given workflow enactment service.

Interface 3 provides the technical information to invoke applications that realize specific workflow activities. This interface should facilitate invocation of applications across heterogeneous software platforms. The reference architecture also provides an interface to other workflow enactment services. Interface 4 is used for interoperability between different workflow enactment services. The administration and the monitoring of workflows are handled by a dedicated component, accessed by Interface 5. These interfaces are not specified in detail, and their implementations remain in the prototypical stage.

The reference architecture of the Workflow Management Coalition is an important contribution to a common understanding of the components of workflow management systems and their relationships. The goal of interoperability between workflow management systems developed by different vendors, however, has yet to be achieved.

Recent achievements in service-oriented architectures fuel standardization efforts in general. The uptake of these achievements by the Workflow Management Coalition and the development of the XML Process Definition Language are important steps towards solving the workflow management system interoperability issue.

8.2 Web Services and their Composition

While service-oriented computing has been discussed from a user point of view in Chapter 2, the architectures behind this new computation paradigm are investigated in more detail.

8.2.1 Web Services Technology

Web services are the current realization of service-oriented computing. While not all features of service-oriented architectures are satisfied by current Web services technology—such as dynamic service matchmaking and binding—it provides an important milestone in the quest towards service-oriented architectures. In Mohan (2002), Web services are characterized as follows.

> Web services are self-contained, self-describing, modular applications that can be published, located, and invoked across the Web. Web services perform functions, which can be anything from simple requests to complicated business processes. Once a Web service is deployed, other applications (and other Web services) can discover and invoke the deployed service. XML messaging is used to interact with a Web service.

Commonly accepted standards are a key requirement for a successful implementation of service-oriented architectures. Web services standards are put forward as recommendations by the World Wide Web Consortium, W3C. The recommendations that provide the underpinning of Web services developments

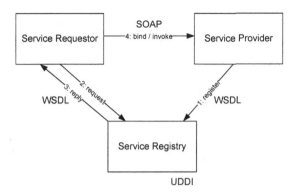

Fig. 8.4. Main World Wide Web Consortium Web services recommendations

are shown in Figure 8.4, with their role in the service-oriented architecture consisting of service provider, service requestor, and service registry.

- SOAP defines an XML messaging protocol for communicating services. SOAP takes advantage of standards to translate a SOAP message to an actual service invocation and to translate the return values of a service invocation back to a SOAP message.
- Web Services Description Language or WSDL introduces a format to specify Web services. WSDL serves the same purpose as interface definition languages in standard middleware environments. However, WSDL features a set of extensions to account for the missing centralized knowledge on transport and addressing, such as service endpoints, required to invoke Web services.
- Universal Description, Discovery, and Integration, or UDDI, provides an infrastructure to publish information about services and their providers. The UDDI application programming interface provides access information to the registry, for instance, to register a service or to search for appropriate services or service providers.

The Web Services Description Language can be used to specify how a service can be used, that is, a service contract. This contract can be separated into a logical contract and one or more physical contracts.

The logical contract defines a public interface of the service, which is independent of the service implementation. It is also independent of message formats and transport protocols used to invoke the service. These aspects are handled in the physical contract.

There can be multiple physical contracts for a service, detailing how the service can be invoked. While SOAP over the hypertext transfer protocol is the most prominent way of invoking a Web service, mail protocols and other transport protocols are also feasible.

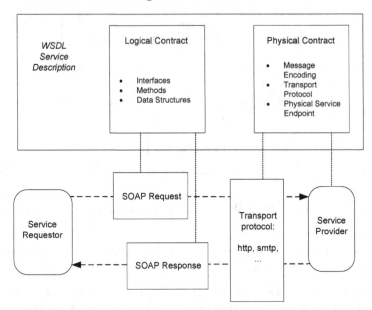

Fig. 8.5. Role of WSDL in Web service invocation

The structure of a service invocation and the role of the Web Services Description Language are shown in Figure 8.5, where the logical contract and physical contract of a service description are shown.

The provider of a Web service is responsible for preparing the WSDL file of the service. In order to invoke a Web service, service requestors need access to the WSDL specification, typically by using a service registry.

The communication of the service requestor with the service provider is also shown in Figure 8.5. The service requestor creates a SOAP message, using the information in the logical contract of the WSDL specification. The information in the physical contract is used to determine the appropriate message encoding and the transport protocol.

The message is sent to the service endpoint, which is specified in the physical contract of the WSDL file. The service provider receives the message and invokes the software that implements the service. If a response message is defined for the invoked Web service, a SOAP message holding the return values is sent to the service requestor, completing the Web service execution.

8.2.2 Web Services Composition

The Web services standards discussed so far provide the ability to define and invoke services, realizing a loose coupling of services. Service composition is an important concept to develop applications on the basis of existing services; the general idea was introduced in Section 2.5.4. Service compositions describe how a set of individual services are related to each other, that is, they describe process structures. As a result, a service composition contains a set of services, each of which realizes a process activity.

Web services composition is a concrete realization of these concepts; it can also be regarded as an implementation of system workflows (Section 2.4) in service-oriented software environments, based on Web services.

Service composition is a recursive concept: each service composition can be specified as a Web service, using the Web Services Description Language. Therefore, each service composition can participate as a building block in other, higher-level service compositions, realizing a hierarchical structuring of Web services.

The standard in Web services composition is the Business Process Language for Web Services, WS-BPEL. It is the outcome of a merger of the Web Services Flow Language by IBM and XLANG by Microsoft. To understand WS-BPEL, it is instructive to investigate these ancestor languages.

Web Services Flow Language can be considered an XML serialization of Flow Definition Language, the script language that was used in IBM's workflow product, enhanced by concepts to access Web services. It is based on a graph-based process language, where activities are ordered in an acyclic form by control flow links.

Data dependencies are specified by data flow between activities. Process behaviour is specified by transition conditions attached to control flow links. This means that there is no explicit split and join behaviour defined. However, by attaching conditions, any splitting behaviour can be realized. The graph-based language used in Flow Definition Language is similar to the one discussed in Section 4.6.

XLANG is a block structured language that was used in BizTalk, Microsoft's enterprise application integration software, focusing on the integration of heterogeneous back-end systems using processes. In block-structured languages, a strict nesting of control flow blocks is used to structure business processes. As a result, for instance, the paths following an *and* split can never be combined by a join other than an *and* join.

The main features of these ancestor languages made their way to the Business Process Execution Language for Web Services; WS-BPEL uses a block structuring to organize service compositions, and links can be defined to express graph-like structures.

The language can be used to characterize both abstract processes and concrete processes. *Abstract processes* describe the externally visible behaviour of a business process. They mainly serve communication purposes, so operational details are disregarded. On the other hand, *concrete processes* contain information required to execute the Web services of the service composition. The following types of activities are available in WS-BPEL.

- *Invoke*: Invoke an operation offered by a Web service; this invocation may or may not have a response
- *Receive*: Wait for a message to arrive

- *Reply*: Send a reply in response to a receive message
- *Wait*: Wait for a specified time period
- *Assign*: Assign data values, for instance, from received messages to process variables
- *Throw*: Indicate that an error has occurred; used for exception handling
- *Terminate*: Complete the process

Activities in WS-BPEL can be related to each other using the following control flow structures.

- *Sequence*: Define a block consisting of an ordered sequence of activities
- *Switch*: Based on an expression, select a particular activity from a set of possible alternatives
- *Pick*: Wait for a suitable message to arrive or for a time-out event. On receipt of the message (or the time-out event), start a defined activity
- *While*: Execute a set of activities as long as a condition is evaluated to true
- *Flow*: Concurrently execute a set of activities
- *Link*: Execution constraint between activities

An example of a business process expressed in WS-BPEL is graphically represented in Figure 8.6. This example originates from the WS-BPEL specification (Oasis (2007)) and is adapted to focus on the main concepts.

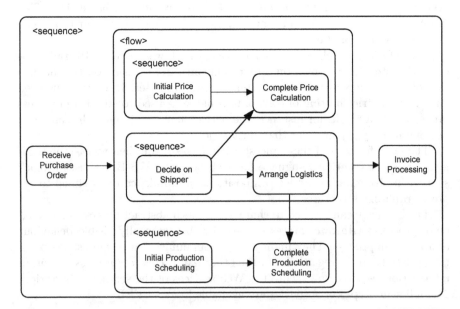

Fig. 8.6. Graphical representation of Web services composition in the WS-BPEL format

The sample service composition is activated once a purchase order is received. In this case, the initial price is calculated, production scheduling is started, and a shipper is selected that will be used to ship the ordered products to the customer.

Since the selection of the shipper has implications on the price, the complete price calculation can only be done after the shipper has been determined. Once the shipper has been determined, the logistics can be arranged. The arrangement of the logistics has implications on the production scheduling, so that the final production scheduling can only be done once the logistics has been arranged.

The block structuring of Web services compositions expressed in the WS-BPEL language is represented in Figure 8.6. The process consists of a sequence consisting of three blocks, two of which are process activities (*Receive Purchase Order* and *Invoice Processing*) and one of which is a flow block with an internal structure. The flow consists of sequences, each of which hosts two activities.

In addition to the block structure, directed arrows are drawn between activities: from the *Decide on Shipper* activity to the *Complete Price Calculation* activity and from the *Arrange Logistics* activity to the *Complete Production Scheduling* activity.

By these links, the business logic discussed above can be represented: because shippers provide shipping services at different costs, the complete price calculation can only be done when the shipper is determined, and production scheduling can only be started when the logistics have been arranged.

Figure 8.7 shows a high-level view on the purchase order Web services composition, where the communication behaviour of the service composition with the individual Web services is shown.

The purchase order process is invoked by receiving a purchase order message sent by a business partner, identified by the term purchasing. (Observe that technical aspects are not detailed, for instance, the characterization of business partners that act as providers of Web services.) The purchase order process uses three Web services: invoicing, shipping, and scheduling. The operations provided by these services as well as the WS-BPEL code to orchestrate these services are discussed next.

Figure 8.8 shows the structure of the WS-BPEL file that captures the process orchestration, abstracting from its XML representation. Observe that the block structuring as shown in Figure 8.6 is reflected by the structure of the WS-BPEL representation. While WS-BPEL uses an XML format with the respective nested elements, the simplified notion in Figure 8.8 uses indentation for structuring.

Links can be used to define execution ordering between activities that could be executed independently from each other, if no links were defined.

In the example, the links are defined in the `flow` block by, for instance, `link name = ship-to-invoice`. The source and target nodes of this link are defined for the activities. For instance, by defining `source ship-to-invoice` of the *Decide on Shipper* activity and `target ship-to-invoice` of the *Com-*

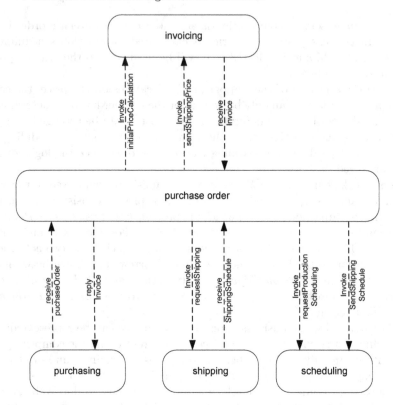

Fig. 8.7. Communication behaviour of purchase order WS-BPEL process

plete Price Calculation activity, an execution ordering of these activities can be established.

Service Composition in Enterprise Application Integration

For a better understanding of Web service composition in enterprise application integration scenarios, a sample process is investigated, dealing with the processing of a purchase order. The enterprise scenario in which multiple legacy systems contribute to the realization of a business process activity was discussed in Section 2.4. Figure 8.9 extends these considerations by assigning Web services standards to the software entities.

In this example, two legacy systems with proprietary interfaces $I1$ and $I2$ and one system with a WSDL interface $S3$ are shown. The enterprise application integration middleware provides service-enabling of legacy applications, so that the resulting services $S1$ and $S2$ can be exposed as Web services, described by WSDL files.

The *Analyze Order Service* uses these services to realize a composed service. The term composed service refers to a service that is realized by a service

```
sequence
// Receive Purchase Order, partner link purchasing
receive PO
flow
   // defining links between activities
   links
      link name = ship-to-invoice
      link name = ship-to-scheduling
   sequence
      // Decide on Shipper, partner link shipping
      invoke requestShipping(in: shippingRequest, out:shippingInfo)
         source ship-to-invoice
      // Arrange Logistics activity, partner link shipping
      receive shippingSchedule
         source ship-to-scheduling
   sequence
      // Initial Price Calculation, partner link invoicing
      invoke initialPriceCalculation (in: PO)
      // Complete Price Calculation, partner link invoicing
      invoke sendShippingPrice (in: shippingInfo)
         target ship-to-invoice
      // Receive invoice, partner link invoicing
      receive Invoice
   sequence
      // Initiate Production Scheduling, partner link scheduling
      invoke requestProductionScheduling (in: PO)
      // Complete Production Scheduling, partner link scheduling
      invoke sendShippingSchedule (in: shippingSchedule)
         target ship-to-scheduling
// Invoice Processing, partner link purchasing
reply Invoice
```

Fig. 8.8. Structure of Web services composition expressed in WS-BPEL (simplified)

composition. The *Analyze Order Service* not only uses Web services provided by the enterprise application integration middleware, but also a Web service S3 that is directly available from the Order_324 system.

The composed *Analyze Order Service* can be realized in different ways. Either a traditional programming language like Java or C# can be used to realize the application logic, or a service composition language can be employed.

As discussed above, the Business Process Execution Language for Web Services allows directly implementing the process structure in which the underlying services are orchestrated. Graphical programming tools are available to express the process structure. These tools generate a WS-BPEL file that represents the executable process.

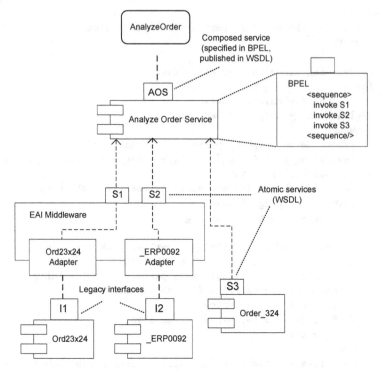

Fig. 8.9. Web services standards in service-enabling

At run time, WS-BPEL engines control the execution of the composed service. This is done by invoking the Web services according to the process orchestration, reacting to error situations, collecting replies, and so on, as specified in the executable WS-BPEL file.

The steps involved in the definition and enactment of a service composition using WS-BPEL are shown in Figure 8.10. There are Web services $S1, S2$, and $S3$ available whose WSDL specifications are stored in a registry. The designer of the composed service uses a WS-BPEL editor to assemble Web services. She might use a graphical editor that supports graphical modelling of the process and provides an export functionality to the WS-BPEL format.

WSDL specifications of Web services provide an executable process specification. In step (1), the WS-BPEL editor retrieves this information from the registry. Once the designer has finalized the service composition, the resulting WS-BPEL file is generated (2a). The composed service can now be made available by storing in the registry the respective WSDL file that describes how this new service can be used (2b).

When the composed service is executed, a WS-BPEL engine reads the respective WS-BPEL specification (3). During the enactment of the composed service, the services are invoked in sequence, as specified in the sample WS-BPEL excerpt, as indicated by messages 4a through 6b.

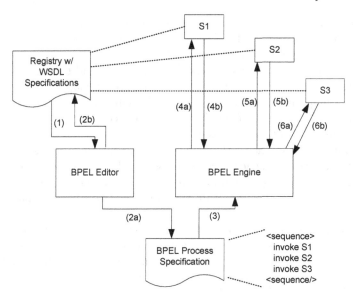

Fig. 8.10. Composed service design and enactment using Business Process Execution Language

8.3 Advanced Service Composition

So far, business process activities have been described by simple terms. What is actually meant by these terms, like *AnalyzeOrder*, is determined by the reader. The intention of the terms used by the process designer and the semantics associated with these terms by the process participants is, hopefully, similar.

To improve the understanding of business process diagrams at a non-technical level, textual explanations are associated with business process models, expressed in, for instance, event-driven process chains. In case there are ambiguities in a process model or certain process parts are not clear, the process participant can ask the process designer about the intended meaning.

The process designer will explain the rationale, and the process participant will comprehend. In some cases, these discussions might lead to a refinement of the process model, since the process participant might have identified an unclear and ambiguous part in the process model.

In this book we are very much interested in business processes that are enacted in software. Services can only be composed in a correct way, if they operate on the same domain concepts. For instance, a service that returns customer data can be combined with a service that takes customer data as input. In this case, they both operate on the same domain concept, that is, the customer.

As discussed in Section 8.2, WSDL provides a syntactic interface description language, detailing the data types of input and output parameters. Since the Web services that contribute to a service composition have most likely been developed independently of each other, the data types of these services will, in most cases, not match.

Typically, these syntactic differences are identified and the resulting problems are solved by system architects and software developers, using, for instance, data mapping techniques. If compositions involving many services need to be developed, considerable overhead can be expected due to heterogeneous data types used by the Web services.

A simple example shows that syntactic integration is not sufficient for integrating services with each other. We assume that a certain product needs to be purchased and that there are two services that return the price of the product. Assume also that the product can be identified by a unique product identifier.

A price-finding application invokes the services with the identifier of the desired product. Both services return values. Assume the textual descriptions of these services indicate that the services return the price in Euros. Note that this information about the currency is not available from the return parameter *price* of the service in WSDL file.

Even parameter names like *europrice* do not help much, since the user of the service cannot be sure that the price is really in the Euros currency.

There might be additional semantic differences in the data returned by services. Assume that one service returns 120 and the other service returns 118. Since the concept of price is not agreed upon by the providers of the services, the following issue might occur. The price 120 includes value-added tax, VAT, while the price 118 does not.

As a result, the price that appears to be lower turns out to be higher because it does not include VAT. Due to the different semantics of the return parameters, the price-finding application returns a wrong result. This problem is due to the missing semantics comparability of the two services. Since at a software layer there are few options for asking the service provider about the exact semantics of their services—as at the application process level—this is a severe problem.

Problems of this kind are the key motivation for the Semantic Web research area, where the goal is to annotate data on the Web, so that its semantics are well specified. Then the data can automatically be compared and integrated.

Based on Semantic Web concepts, recent research in Semantic Web Services looks at rich semantic specifications of services that ease their automated or semi-automated discovery and composition. Before semantic concepts are addressed, the different options of service bindings are investigated.

8.3.1 Static and Dynamic Service Binding

The dynamic discovery of services is illustrated by a set of examples in the context of a composite application in the travel domain. The travel application allows customers to select trips, make reservations, and confirm reservations by providing credit card information. In order to allow this, the travel application invokes a credit card withdrawal service provided by a bank.

This example is used to explain different types of service matchmaking and service binding, namely static binding and dynamic binding; service composition based on semantics will be discussed afterwards.

In static binding, the service is bound to the application at development time. In the travel application example shown in Figure 8.11, the service invocation in the travel application is represented by a rounded rectangle marked CCW for credit card.

There are three service providers that have implemented a credit card withdrawal service, all of which can be used by the travel application. These providers are *BankA*, *BankB*, and *BankC*, representing any institutions that provide such a service. (The services provided by the organizations are depicted by small circles, as with interfaces in UML.)

The question that developers face now is which of the three implementations of the credit card withdrawal service should they decide to use? And when should this decision be made? The former question is subject to existing legal contracts between the organizations involved as well as to costs associated with using a particular credit card withdrawal service implementation.

The latter question can be reformulated to the question about when to bind the credit card withdrawal service specification to the service implementation.

In a static binding, the external service implementation is bound to the travel application at development time. This means that the use of the credit card withdrawal service by *BankB* is hardcoded in the travel application.

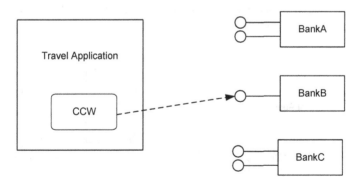

Fig. 8.11. Static binding: service provided by *BankB* coded in the travel application

Today's Web services technologies provide valuable information for coding this integration. Service specifications in the Web Services Description Language provide the information on how a particular service is invoked. Based on the textual and technical description of the service, the developer of the travel application can provide the mapping of the internal variables to the data that the external service requires.

Ambiguities in service description are effectively resolved by the programmer of the travel application by the designing of an interface to the external service. This type of static binding is appropriate in environments where the service landscape is relatively static.

Service-oriented architectures have their strengths in dynamic environments, where the service landscape is subject to change. In these settings, static binding of service implementations is not sufficient for taking advantage of a dynamically changing service landscape.

In the literature the dynamic discovery and invocation of services is generally acknowledged as being an important aspect of any service-oriented architecture, as discussed in Section 2.5.1. Dynamic discovery and invocation can also be described as dynamic binding of service specifications to service implementations.

In dynamic binding, service implementations can be discovered at run time. The application (or an advanced service middleware) asks the service registry for a list of suitable services. Once it receives this list, it selects one service provider, and binds to its service implementation. To facilitate the dynamic service matchmaking, a service request needs to be processed by the service broker. The process of selecting a set of services that fit a service request is called *service matchmaking*.

Service matchmaking crucially depends on rich specification of the services, and rich expression languages for the service request. In addition, the business partners need to have a common understanding of the concepts used. This type of a common and agreed-upon understanding can be realized by a domain ontology. While there is considerable work in ontology research and engineering, rich specification languages in general and tool support in particular have not yet reached maturity.

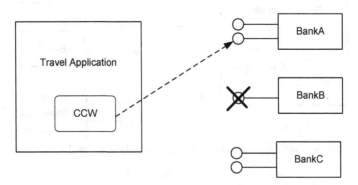

Fig. 8.12. Dynamic binding: service implementation by *BankA* is bound dynamically to travel application, due to failure of service implementation by *BankB*

Dynamic service binding allows applications to cope much better with dynamic service landscapes than static binding. Once a new service is available and registered, it can be used automatically without our changing the application (provided the legal contractual agreements between the business partners are in place).

In the example, dynamic service binding is motivated by a failing credit card withdrawal service by *BankB*. In this case, the service registry returns *BankA* and *BankC* as list of available service providers. Assuming *BankA* has a better price (or other nonfunctional property), the travel application dynamically binds the credit card withdrawal service by *BankA* to the travel application. As a result, the failure of the *BankB* service is not visible to the travel application.

There are variations of this scenario, depending on whether or not the service registry is aware of the failure of the service by *BankB*. If the registry is not aware, then the travel application would try to invoke that service. After receiving an error message or after a time-out, the travel application contacts the registry for an alternative service provider.

8.3.2 Ontologies and Data Mappings

Semantic service specifications are required that are based on domain ontologies. Domain ontologies can be considered to be data models that all process participants have agreed upon. Ontologies in computer science are characterized as data models that represent a set of concepts within a domain and the relationships between those concepts.

A domain ontology is always associated with a set of stakeholders, who need to agree on the domain ontology. An ontology has been described in Gruber (1993) as *an explicit specification of a conceptualization*.

To illustrate these considerations, Figure 8.13 shows a simple domain ontology for contacts. The concepts are represented by ellipses, and the contains relationships are shown by directed arcs.

The domain ontology shown can be used to integrate services provided by software systems. In an enterprise application integration scenario, typical systems to integrate are customer relationship management systems, or CRM systems, and enterprise resource planning systems, or ERP systems. The data structures of addresses in these systems are different, as shown in Figure 8.14.

This figure also shows a mapping of the data structures of the application systems to the data structure of the domain ontology. For instance, the full_name data field of the customer relationship management system is mapped to the Name concept in the domain ontology. Since the street address is stored in two fields of the enterprise resource planning system data structure, the field Strasse is mapped to StName, and Hausnummer is mapped to the Number concept of the ontology.

If the data fields of the application systems are mapped to the domain ontology, then a mapping of the data can be achieved automatically at run time.

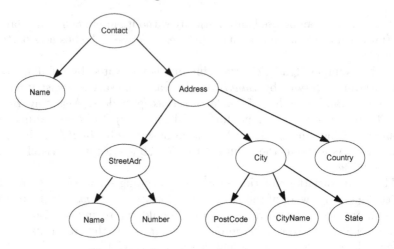

Fig. 8.13. Domain ontology for contacts

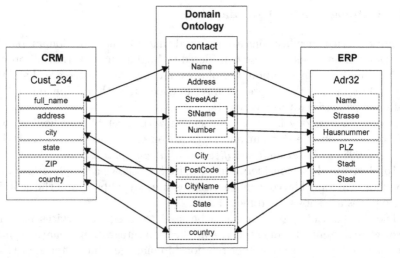

Fig. 8.14. Domain ontology facilitates data mapping, Kuropka et al. (2006)

Assume that there is a service of the customer relationship management system that returns a parameter of data type Cust_234. This data can be fed into a service that takes a parameter of data type Adr32 if the appropriate data mapping is performed.

If there is a domain ontology in place and the data structures of the systems are mapped to the domain ontology, then this data mapping can be performed automatically. This mapping process is shown in Figure 8.15 for a specific customer, Robert Miller. To indicate the application and direction of the mapping from the CRM system to the ERP system, the arrows are shown dotted and directed according to the mapping.

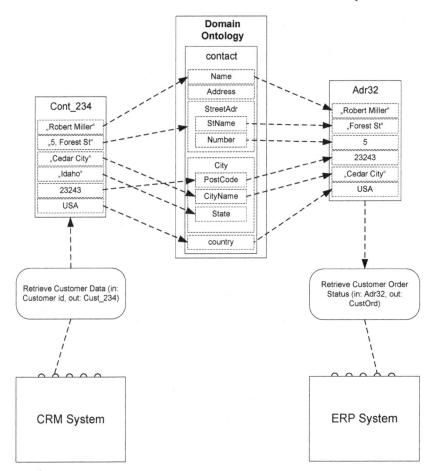

Fig. 8.15. Domain ontology used for automatic data mapping of CRM customer data to ERP customer data

8.3.3 Preconditions and Postconditions

Mapping of heterogeneous data is important in any enterprise application middleware. It provides the technical basis for integrating services with each other, so that the results returned by one service can be used by follow-up services.

The next level addresses the questions, about under what conditions a certain activity can be executed, and what the result of an activity execution is, that is, preconditions and postconditions of activities. Interestingly, in business process modelling, preconditions and postconditions are already captured. In event-driven process chains, for instance, preconditions and postconditions are represented by events, although in a relatively informal fashion.

For example, if the arrival of an order message triggers an activity to store the order, then an event *order arrived* is connected by control flow to a function *store order*. The outgoing edge of this function is connected to an event *order is stored*. The *order arrived* event characterizes the precondition of the function, while the *order is stored* event its postcondition, as shown in Figure 8.16.

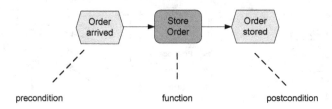

Fig. 8.16. Precondition and postcondition, expressed in event-driven process chain

This type of informally specified precondition and postcondition of a function in a business process is suitable for fostering the understanding of process models by human stakeholders. To be usable for composing services realized by software, the preconditions and postconditions need to be specified in a more precise way.

8.3.4 Advanced Service Composition by Example

This section introduces advanced service composition by an example. Our example is from the call centre domain, where phone calls by customers come in and call centre agents serve these calls using software systems, in particular, an enterprise resource planning system and a customer relationship management system. These systems realize services that make up a service composition used by the call centre agents.

The scenario is described as follows. In a call centre environment a customer calls to request certain information. Using the phone number of the incoming call, the customer relationship management system gets hold of the customer address. This address information is—after suitable data mapping is performed—fed to the enterprise resource planning system that provides information on the customer calling the call centre agent.

A domain ontology of this scenario is shown in Figure 8.17. This ontology uses the contacts ontology shown in Figure 8.13 as a building block.

This domain ontology allows us to specify a service having a phone number as input and an address as output, so that the contact information returned is not just any contact information, but the contact information for the customer with the specified phone number.

This information is required for a precise specification of the service; otherwise the relationship between input and output data is imprecise. Another

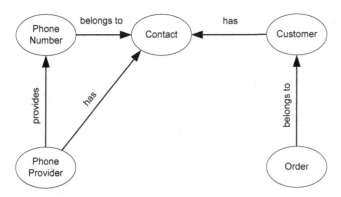

Fig. 8.17. Domain ontology of call centre example

service might exist that also has a phone number as input and an address as output, that returns the address of the phone provider for the specified phone number instead.

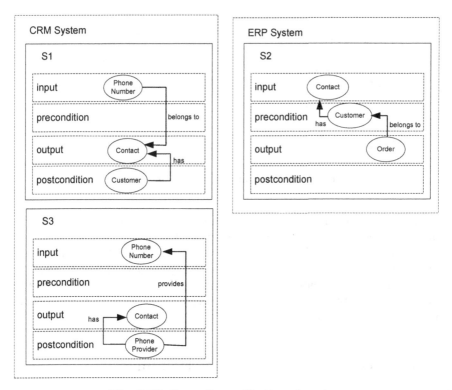

Fig. 8.18. Semantic specification of services

Figure 8.18 depicts a visualization of the semantic specifications of the services provided by the enterprise resource planning system and of the customer relationship management system.

Syntactically, service S3 is equivalent to service S1 with regard to input and output data, but instead of returning a customer's address it returns the address of the phone provider supplying the specified phone number. Such a difference of functionality is not visible in syntactic definitions, but can be represented and distinguished by semantic specifications.

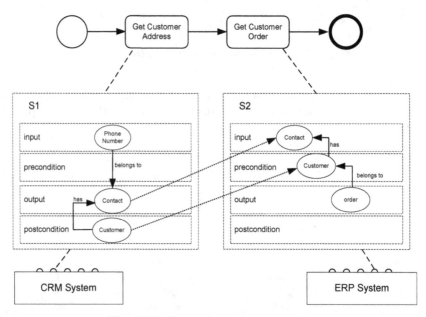

Fig. 8.19. Semantic service composition

The overall picture is shown in Figure 8.19, where the matching of the output parameter of service S1 provided by the CRM system with the service S2 provided by the ERP system is shown. In this way, these services can participate in a business process, shown in the upper part of that figure. The semantic information can be used to decide whether two services actually match semantically, so that they can be sequentially executed in the context of a given business process.

8.4 Data-Driven Processes: Case Handling

Case handling aims at balancing process orientation with data orientation to control the execution of business processes. The motivation can be derived from business process reengineering, because one of its main goals is to overcome the fragmentation of the work in organizations.

The introduction of this fragmentation of work was useful in manufacturing since the early days of industrialization, where it led to massive increases in productivity, because highly specialized workers perform isolated pieces of work with high efficiency. Once the worker has finished a piece of work, the manufactured artefact is handed over to the next worker in line.

The fragmentation of work has been transferred to the information society. Workers are expected to conduct a single piece of work in a highly efficient manner, without a complete picture on the contribution of the work to the company's goals. To control the combination of the fragmented work, complex organizational structures have been invented.

With the presence of information technology, the role of workers has changed. Now the knowledge worker is at the centre, responsible for conducting and organizing her work. The knowledge worker is highly skilled, so she can conduct a broad range of activities required to fulfill business goals of the company. An insurance claim, for example, can be processed by a single person, so that hand-over of work can be avoided. Only in specific, seldom occurring cases is expert support required.

Case handling takes into account this active role of the knowledge worker by accepting her expertise and experience to drive and control the case. Since traditional workflow technology prescribes the activities and their execution ordering, there is little room for knowledge workers to deviate from the prescribed process. As a result, traditional workflow technology appears too restrictive in these settings.

However, there is still support that flexible business process management systems can provide. Since knowledge-intensive business processes typically are centred on data processed in the context of a particular case, the handling of data requires specific attention.

A case is a product that is manufactured, and at any time knowledge workers should be aware of the overall case. Examples of cases are the evaluation of a job application, the verdict on a traffic violation, the outcome of a tax assessment, and the ruling for an insurance claim.

To illustrate the basic ideas of case handling, consider the activities A and B of a business process that are ordered by control flow $A \to B$. As a result, B can only be enabled (and therefore can only start) after A has terminated.

This type of ordering constraint is a key ingredient of business process management in general and workflow management in particular. While in many business process scenarios this traditional workflow approach is adequate, in knowledge-intensive domains, where an active role of the knowledge worker drives the process, more flexible approaches are required.

For instance, assume that A does not create its data on termination, but while it runs. Assume further that B can start working once data values created by A are available. Then, B can start working on these data, while A creates the remaining data values. In this case, the control flow constraint between A and B restricts a useful execution ordering, in which B starts working *before* A completes.

One could argue that the level of granularity of the modelled activities might not be adequate. If the generation of each data value is represented by a single activity in a business process, then the same process instances can be achieved. However, since the number of activities would become very high, complex process models that are hard to understand and maintain would result.

8.4.1 Case Handling Example

These aspects are illustrated by an example where knowledge workers use forms to interact with back-end applications. This example is shown in Figure 8.20. The business process supports the preparation of a quote after receiving a customer request.

In a traditional human interaction workflow, activities are defined to enter the customer request (*Enter Request*) and—after the customer request is entered—prepare the quote (*Prepare Quote*). These steps are ordered, so that the preparation of the quote can only be started after the request has been entered.

We now argue that this rigid definition of execution ordering might not be suitable for the business process discussed.

Assume that the received customer order is not complete. In particular, information on the zip code and the fax number are missing, while the data on the requested product is complete. In the traditional workflow with rigid control flow structures, the knowledge worker is not allowed to start working on the preparation of the quote, because the previous activity has not yet completed.

However, since only data not relevant for preparing the quote is missing, there is no reason for preventing the knowledge worker to start working on the quote. Since the preparation of the quote takes more time than registering the request, the overall execution time of the business process can be reduced if the knowledge worker starts the preparation of the quote as early as possible.

If, in an alternative setting, the fax number and the zip code is available but information on the requested item is incomplete, then the preparation of the quote should not start.

Consequently, a fine-granular definition of dependencies between data is required. This definition is based on availability of data and data constraints for activities. Thereby, the process model contains information on which data objects are mandatory for the next activity to start, and which are optional. This domain-specific knowledge needs to be provided during the design of case handling applications.

Since the case is at the centre in case handling, the abstract representations of cases are known as *case models*. A case model contains activities, data

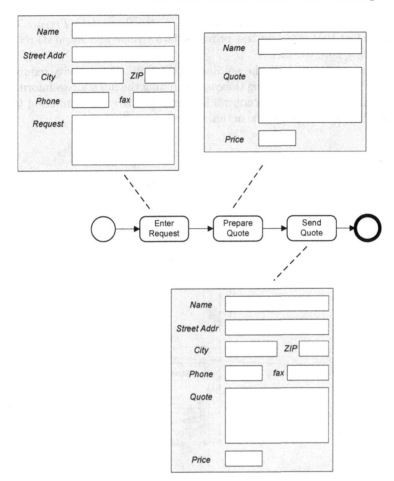

Fig. 8.20. Motivating example case handling

objects, and relationships between them, as well as different roles and other organizational and operational information.

This discussion shows that the coarse workflow level of abstraction, consisting of the two activities to enter the request and prepare the quote, is too coarse to allow efficient usage of resources. By looking at fine-grained data dependencies between activities, much more concurrency between activities is possible. In Figure 8.20, a third activity is shown that sends the quote to the customer.

Outside this simplifying example, the knowledge worker might use other software systems to prepare the quote. The important fact is that the preparation of the quote does not require address information. Therefore, this activity can be started as soon as the enter request activity has provided the name and the request information.

In the example at hand, the link from *Enter Request* to *Prepare Quote* marks the fact that enter request provides data (*Name* and *Request*) required for *Prepare Quote* to start.

The case continues with the sending of the quote. This activity requires all data that was generated during the case, including the full address information and the quotation. There is a control link from *Prepare Quote* to *Send Quote*, because the latter requires the actual quote information.

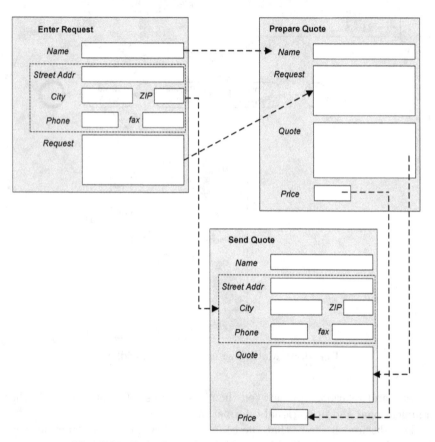

Fig. 8.21. Data dependencies in case handling example

The execution behaviour of case handling systems is sketched in Figure 8.22 by an event diagram. The case starts with an *Enter Request* activity. As soon as the name and request data fields are provided, *Prepare Quote* can start. *Send Quote* can start when the quote, including the price, is provided. In the example shown, *Prepare Quote* terminates before the *Enter Request* activity terminates. Due to the data dependencies shown, the quote can only be sent after the request is entered, that is, after the address information is available.

This example shows quite well that the set of valid execution behaviours is much larger in case handling than in traditional workflow management based solely on control flow constraints.

At the same time, there are formalized execution dependencies available in case handling systems, as depicted by the dotted arrows in Figure 8.21. By representing in case models the fine-grained data dependencies associated with activities conducted by knowledge workers, additional valid executions can be allowed without violating the overall consistency of the business process.

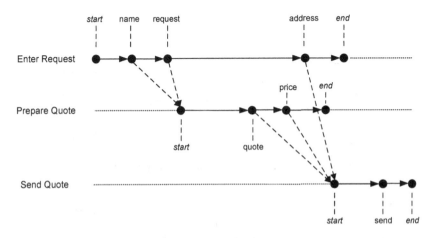

Fig. 8.22. Temporal behaviour in case handling example: overall execution time is reduced, since prepare quote can start before enter request is completed

8.4.2 Case Handling Metamodel

Following our motivating case handling and introducing the basic concepts of this paradigm by example, the main concepts in case handling are identified and organized in a case metamodel, which is shown in Figure 8.23.

Case definition is the central class of the metamodel. Case definitions are either complex (cases with internal structure) or atomic (cases without internal structure), referred to as complex case definitions and activity definitions, respectively.

Complex case definitions consist of case definitions, resulting in a hierarchical nesting of cases in subcases and activities. Each complex case definition consists of at least one case definition, and each case definition may occur in at most one complex case definition.

Since case handling is a data-driven approach, activity definitions are associated with data object definitions. Each activity definition is associated

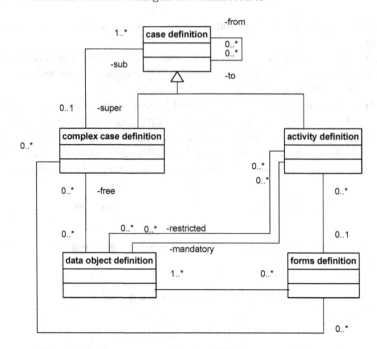

Fig. 8.23. Case metamodel, simplified version without roles

with at least one data object definition. This association is partitioned into two main types, *mandatory* and *restricted*.

If a data object is mandatory for an activity, then the respective data value has to be entered before that activity can be completed. However, it may also be entered in an earlier activity. A restricted association indicates that a data value can only be entered during a particular activity. Restricted and mandatory associations between activities and data are important vehicles for process enactment in case handling, since, for example, an activity can only be completed when its mandatory data objects are available.

As seen in the example, activities in case handling systems can be implemented using forms. Forms consist of sets of fields, each of which represents a data object. Therefore, activity definitions are associated with forms definitions. The fields displayed in a form associated with an activity correspond to mandatory as well as restricted data objects for that activity.

The definition of forms may also contain data objects that are mandatory for subsequent activities. This feature allows flexible enactment of business processes, since data values can be entered at an early stage, if the knowledge worker decides to do so.

Data objects may also be *free*, that is, associated not with particular activities but the overall case. Hence, they can be accessed at any time during the case execution. Free data objects are represented by an association of data object definition with complex case definition. The context of a case can be presented by such a form. Providing knowledge with as much information as possible is an important aspect of case handling systems. Access rights can be in place in order to limit the access to free data objects to knowledge workers.

Case handling also has an organizational facet. Rather than there being just a single type of role, as in workflow management, in case handling there are different types of roles.

- *Execute*: Roles of type execute are used for executing an activity instance.
- *Skip*: Persons who can execute an activity are not always allowed to also skip it. These knowledge workers are determined by the skip role.
- *Redo*: Activity instances can be redone. Knowledge workers able to redo a particular activity are determined by the redo role. Redoing activities allows us to somehow jump back to previous activities with the option of redoing these activities or reconfirming data values that have been entered already.

The example shown in Figure 8.24 illustrates the concepts introduced in the case handling metamodel. It shows how cases, data objects, and forms and their associations, as well as organizational aspects, play together.

There is one complex case definition $C1$, which consists of activity definitions $A1$, $A2$, and $A3$, represented by the indirect recursion of complex case definitions and case definitions in the metamodel, shown as a dotted line connecting $C1$ to its subcases. As shown in that figure, data object definition $D1$ is mandatory for $A1$, $A2$, and $A3$. $D2$ is mandatory for $A2$, and $D3$ is restricted for $A3$. Since $D1$ is mandatory for $A1$, the form definition $F1$ associated with $A1$ contains a field for $D1$. However, there is also a field for $D2$ in that form.

The knowledge worker in charge of a case based on that case definition may enter a value for $D1$ when $A1$ is ready for execution. In addition, she may also enter a value for $D2$ at that instant, which implicitly performs $A2$ as well. This is due to the fact that $D2$ is the only mandatory data object for $A2$. Note, however, that $D3$ cannot be entered, during $A1$ or during $A2$, since it is restricted to $A3$, and can therefore only be executed by $A3$, using the form associated with it.

The activities of the case are ordered: $A1$ is followed by $A2$ and $A3$, represented by the recursive association with roles to and from in the metamodel. There are five data object definitions, $D0$ through $D4$. Dotted lines marked with association type names represent the associations between activity definitions and data object definitions. $D0$ and $D4$ are free data elements, which appear in form definition $F3$, associated with the overall case definition $C1$.

Notice that form definition $F1$ contains not only a field $d1$ representing data object $D1$ (mandatory for the completion of $A1$), but also $d2$ (for data object $D2$, which is mandatory for $A2$) and $d0$ (for free data object $D0$). During the execution of $A1$, the knowledge worker may already enter a data

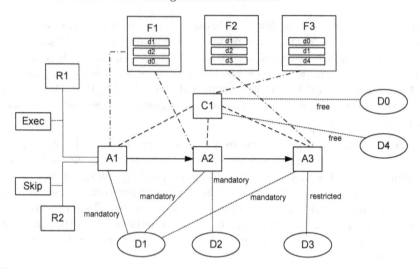

Fig. 8.24. Abstract example to illustrate case handling metamodel, van der Aalst et al. (2005b)

value for $d2$, although this is not required for the completion of $A1$. However, $A1$ cannot complete before $d1$ is entered, because $D1$ is mandatory for $A1$.

The knowledge worker may use the information presented in $d0$ to work efficiently on the case. So as not to overload the figure, the roles are not specified completely. In fact, only the roles for $A1$ are specified: $R1$ and $R2$ are associated with $A1$, where the association with $R1$ is of type *execute* (knowledge workers with role $R1$ may execute this activity), while the association with $R2$ is of type *skip*, so that persons with role $R2$ may skip this activity. To summarize, during the enactment of cases based on case definition $C1$, only knowledge workers who can play role $R1$ are permitted to perform activities based on $A1$, and only persons with role $R2$ may skip that activity.

In the context of this book, not all details of case handling systems can be discussed. For instance, case handling also allows the definition of process structures. We have concentrated on the differences between case handling and process orchestrations and did not elaborate on this particular capability of case handling. For further details, the interested reader is referred to the references in the bibliographical notes.

Bibliographical Notes

The reference architecture of workflow management systems was introduced by the Workflow Management Coalition in Hollingsworth (1995); Workflow Management Coalition (2005) introduces the XML Process Definition Language.

Flexible workflow management is addressed in Reichert and Dadam (1998) in the context of the ADEPT project; Bauer et al. (2003) discusses load balancing issues in this project. Flexible workflow management in the context of the WASA project is reported in Medeiros et al. (1995). Weske (1998) and Weske (2000) introduce the WASA approach in detail that is also reported in this chapter.

An overview of flexible workflow management is given by Rinderle et al. (2003). Dynamic changes to process types and process instances are investigated in Rinderle et al. (2004). Ly et al. (2006) discusses semantic aspects in process execution control, focusing on execution semantics rather than application semantics. Investigations regarding change patterns in business processes and features in process-aware information systems are reported in Weber et al. (2007). Reichert et al. (2009) provide an overview of flexibility in process-aware information systems.

The concepts that constitute a service-oriented architecture were introduced in Burbeck (2000). Web services standards are put forward as recommendations by the World Wide Web Consortium. The SOAP recommendation is published as Gudgin et al. (2007), while the Web Services Description Language is available as Chinnici et al. (2007). The Universal Description, Discovery, and Integration is published in Clement et al. (2004).

Web services concepts, architectures, and applications are addressed in Alonso et al. (2009), starting from conventional middleware, including enterprise application integration middleware. Newcomer and Lomow (2005) look at practical aspects of service-oriented architectures. The relationship of workflow management and service-oriented architectures is addressed in Leymann et al. (2002).

The Web Services Business Process Execution Language, developed under the guidance of the Organization for the Advancement of Structured Information Standards, is available in Oasis (2007).

Semantic service specifications and their use in service matchmaking, service composition, and flexible service enactment were addressed in the Adaptive Services Grid project, supported by the European Commission in the Sixth Framework Programme. The conceptual design of a service provisioning platform is introduced in Kuropka et al. (2006). The automated composition of services using a heuristic search algorithm is addressed in Meyer and Weske (2006). The adaptation of interfaces for composed services is addressed in Dumas et al. (2006).

In the context of semantic Web services, there are two major efforts. The Web Service Modeling Ontology has its centre of gravity in Europe, while the Web Ontology Language is mainly an American effort. In de Bruijn (2005), the Web Service Modelling Language is introduced as core part of the Web Service Modeling Ontology. An overview of the Ontology Web Language is given in McGuinness (2004). Semantics concepts are also used in Nagarajan et al. (2006) to foster the interoperability of Web services. Verma et al. (2006)

introduces an approach to adapt Web processes to external events while preserving constraints that are required for the coordination of the services.

Currently, novel software architectures for the design and implementation of business processes and of process choreographies are being discussed. Those are based on the Representational State Transfer (REST) architectural style that was introduced by Fielding (2000) and blockchains, respectively. Nikaj et al. (2015) enhance BPMN choreography diagrams with RESTful information to ease the implementation of process choreographies. Xu et al. (2019) provide an overview of different types of blockchains, before addressing architectural aspects related to the model-driven engineering of blockchain-based applications.

Case handling is introduced in van der Aalst et al. (2005b) from conceptual and technical points of view. The application of case handling is addressed in Reijers et al. (2003). Case handling is realized in the FLOWer business process management system, as reported in van der Aalst and Berens (2001). Recently, the term adaptive case management was coined, which includes concepts from case handling and flexible workflow management. Swenson (2010) presents several approaches related to adaptive case management. Hewelt and Weske (2016) introduce an approach called fragment-based case management, where cases are defined based on process fragments that are combined by knowledge workers during runtime, based on data constraints.

9

Business Process Management Methodology

So far, this book has introduced concepts, languages and architectures to develop and analyze process oriented information systems. This section broadens the scope by investigating how process management projects can be conducted, that is, we look at business process management methodologies.

Since every company is different and each process management project has to cope with different assumptions, goals, requirements, and people, the methodology shown is not meant as a blue print for all types of projects in this area. Instead, the main goal of this chapter is to generate awareness for the typical issues that people encounter in real-world process management projects. The chapter also provides hints on how these issues could be addressed.

9.1 Dependencies between Processes

As sketched in Section 2.3 in the context of process landscapes, the goal of a business process is to produce results, that is, outcomes that are of value to its customers. Results are the vehicle for the value created by a process. In order to develop these results, each process needs input from other processes. Hence, each business process has supplier processes and customer processes. Each process provides results to its customer processes. At the same time, it acts as a customer to its supplier processes.

Supplier-customer relationships can also cross organizational boundaries. This observation is in line with the structure of value systems, in which each company is represented by a value chain, and the value chains of business partners are organized as a value system, representing their relationships. A manufacturing company, for instance, orders raw material from its suppliers, adds value by manufacturing goods, and sells these goods to its customers.

This concept is visualized in Figure 9.1, which looks at cross organizational supplier-customer relationships. *Company A* has one external supplier and one

© Springer-Verlag GmbH Germany, part of Springer Nature 2019
M. Weske, *Business Process Management*,
https://doi.org/10.1007/978-3-662-59432-2_9

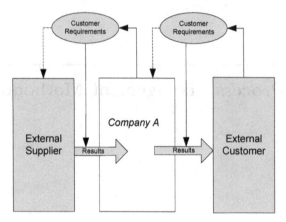

Fig. 9.1. Supplier-customer relationships between companies

external customer. It receives input (results developed by its external supplier) and produces output (results provided to its external customer).

This figure also shows requirements that define properties of the results. Starting from right to left, the external customer imposes customer requirements on the results delivered by *Company A*. By these requirements, the external customer also indirectly imposes requirements on that company, since its processes need to be designed in a way that the results satisfy the requirements. In Figure 9.1, these indirect requirements are shown as dashed lines, while the direct requirements on the results are shown as solid lines.

This approach is illustrated by an example involving a company that manufactures bikes. The company has several suppliers that provide the material required for bike production. The material is the "result" provided by the external supplier to the bike manufacturer. The customer orders well-specified bikes, imposing requirements on the results that the bike manufacturer delivers.

These relationships between companies are typically determined by contracts. An order is an example of such a contract. The external customer issues an order, that defines all details of the ordered bikes. Also, the price and further information, such as the date of delivery is determined in the contract.

After discussing supplier-customer relationships between companies, internal processes of companies are investigated, shown in Figure 9.2. Each process that a company performs has internal or external customers. The term internal refers to customers that are part of the same organization as the supplier process. An internal supplier is a process that resides in the same organization as the customer. If the delivered result crosses organizational boundaries, the terms external customer and external supplier are used.

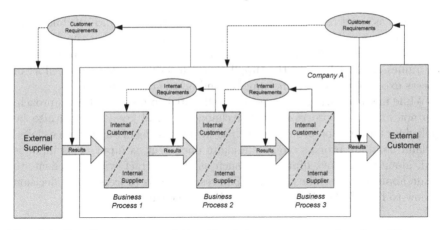

Fig. 9.2. Supplier-customer relationships between processes, based on Füermann and Dammasch (2008)

On the left-hand side of that figure, a supplier of the bike manufacturer can be found; in the centre, three internal processes are shown. On the right hand side a bike shop can play the role of external customer.

To illustrate these concepts, the bike manufacturing example is revisited. In that company, the incoming logistics process is responsible for collecting the input material, for storing it in a warehouse, and for updating an inventory database. It serves as supplier for the production process, which needs the material to build bikes. Once the bikes are manufactured, the sales process takes over. Therefore, the production process is the internal supplier for the sales process, which ships the bikes to its external customer, for instance, a bike shop.

This description goes very well with the diagram shown in Figure 9.2. However, that figure exposes a simplification, since no process has more than one supplier or customer. Real-world processes typically have multiple suppliers and multiple customers as well as multiple input and output results.

The material provided by an external supplier needs to obey the requirements as defined by the contract. This property also holds for internal processes. Well specified interfaces are also important between internal processes, since internal customer processes will only be satisfied if the results delivered match their requirements. Many companies use internal documents to state the requirements regarding the results exchanged between their internal processes. However, often these internal requirements are defined in a less precise way than contracts with external business partners.

Once the requirements are set, it is important to be able to decide whether a result actually satisfies the requirements defined. Therefore, properties of results need to be measurable with respect to their requirements.

Returning to the bike manufacturing example, a contract contains exact specifications of the bicycle frames a company orders from its suppliers. The customer has exact requirements for the products ordered. Once the bike company receives a set of frames from a supplier, it checks whether the delivered frames fulfill the specifications as specified in the order. If this is not the case, the frames are sent back to the supplier, which results in additional effort of process execution, both on the supplier and on the customer side.

While manufacturing processes are well suited to illustrate this approach, it is not limited to processes that exchange physical goods. It can also be applied for information processes, such as the processing of an insurance claim. A claim handling process requires a claim document as input. This input is used, along with other input data, such as the contract with the client, to decide about covering the damage. The result of this process is the decision on how to handle the claim, passed back to the client.

9.2 Methodology Overview

Rather than presenting a formal method for describing development processes, we use an informal notation, in which phases are represented by boxes and dependencies between phases by arcs. The methodology is shown in Figure 9.3.

The methodology starts with the *Strategy and Organization* phase, in which the organizational prerequisites for the project are established. A key activity in this phase is the setting up of a steering committee consisting of high level company officials. The most important processes are identified, and for each process, a process owner is selected, who chairs a process team that is responsible for the development of the process.

The *Process Landscape Design* phase takes a closer look at the supplier-customer relationships between the key processes. The respective process teams cooperate to identify the complete set of dependencies between the processes based on the results exchanged. The outcome of this phase is a process landscape, consisting of the main processes and their supplier-consumer relationships.

From the third phase on, the phases are conducted for each business process individually. However, the process teams still interact with each other to identify dependencies, find deficiencies, and to be able to improve their processes.

The *Process Design* phase starts by taking an in-depth look at the results produced during process execution. Results are analyzed with respect to their importance for customers and the resources required for producing them. Business processes are modeled, concentrating on activities that are required for achieving the results. The measuring of process performance is also addressed in this phase by providing a set of metrics and performance indicators that are used to measure processes in later phases.

Most business processes are performed by people and supported by information systems. Therefore, the *Process Implementation* phase looks at

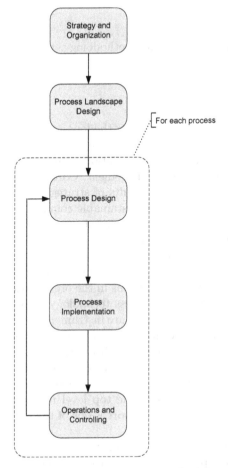

Fig. 9.3. Business process methodology

technical aspects, while also sketching organizational aspects of process implementations. An important aspect of this phase is the implementation of
measurements that were defined during the previous phase.

The daily business of the organization is conducted during the *Operations and Controlling* phase by executing business processes. Measurements
are performed and the process performance is reviewed by the process team.
Whenever there are issues with the performance—such as violation of the intended performance or negative trends that could lead to problems later—the
process team investigates the situation and proposes changes to the process.
The actual changes to the process are conducted in the design phase, which
is re-entered in this case.

9.3 Phases in Detail

After providing an overview of the methodology, this section discusses the individual phases in more detail.

9.3.1 Strategy and Organization

Strategy development aims at improving the long-term competitiveness of organizations in a way that is sustainable. The early identification of changing markets and the evaluation of the organization's strengths and weaknesses are important activities in strategic management. Core competencies are identified and strengthened. The major results of strategic management are long-term strategies and ways to achieve sustainable competitive advantage. Business process management can provide a link between the strategic goals of a company and the actual work being done.

Once the long-term strategies are set up, process management projects can be established to implement them. Any business process management effort requires the support of influential persons in the organization. Due to the outreach of new solutions based on process technology, awareness building and training involving process stakeholders are instrumental. The establishment of dedicated roles in the executive management is also important, most prominently the role of Chief Process Officer (CPO), as discussed in Section 1.2.

The CPO installs a steering committee that overlooks all process related projects and provides the resources for conducting them. The steering committee involves further members of the top level management. It has been shown that top level management support is one of the key success factors for process management projects.

Once it is set up, the steering committee identifies the most important organizational business processes. These processes have direct impact on the company's customers. They can be identified by collecting and evaluating internal and external contracts and by analyzing information systems that external partners access.

For each identified key process, a process owner is selected. It is typically the chair of the department that covers the majority of activities in the process. He or she puts together a process team, consisting of persons that are personally involved in and knowledgeable about the process. In later phases, the project team analyzes and improves the process. It makes sure that the process fulfills the requirements imposed by its customers, both internal and external.

9.3.2 Process Landscape Design

Once the key processes are identified and the process teams are established, the dependencies between the processes are investigated. Each process team looks at the most important results provided by its process and the customers for whom the results are produced. To develop a process landscape, the focus in this phase is on identifying the main dependencies between processes, while the next phase looks into the operational aspects of business processes.

In the process landscape design phase, internal and external contracts are analyzed that have been identified in the first phase. The partners of the contracts are candidate processes which have a supplier relationship or a customer relationship with the process under investigation. Dependencies between processes are identified and consolidated in a process landscape.

Fig. 9.4. Input and output results of Product Development Process

To illustrate this concept, a product development process is considered. The process team has analyzed the internal and external contracts as well as additional documentation about the process and information systems that the process uses. This analysis has shown that the process receives prototypes as well as product specifications from customer processes. Its main results are the products the company sells to its customers. These input and output results are shown in Figure 9.4.

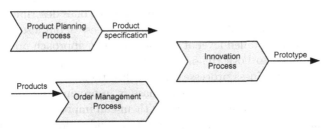

Fig. 9.5. Input and output results of other processes that are related to Product Development Process

At this stage, it is essential to communicate with other process teams. Figure 9.5 shows the input and output of other key processes. In this example, matching the inputs and outputs of the processes immediately shows the dependencies between these processes.

In general, the dependencies between processes are not as obvious as they are in this example. Different terms might be used by the process teams to define a given result. In these cases, the process teams need to discuss the core of what is exchanged between their processes. The goal of this discussion process is consolidating the results exchanged and, finally, designing a process landscape.

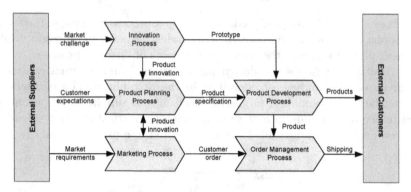

Fig. 9.6. Process landscape showing supplier-customer relationships between business processes

The resulting process landscape is shown in Figure 9.6, which is a variant of the process landscape discussed in Section 2.3.2. It contains the processes discussed above as well as their supplier-consumer relationships.

9.3.3 Process Design

Once the project landscape is set up, the process team investigates the operational processes that contribute to its organizational process. Typically, there are several operational business processes that realize one organizational business process. Supplier-customer relationships like the ones described earlier in this chapter do not only apply to organizational processes, but also operational processes on a more detailed level of abstraction. The approach presented can therefore be applied to both the organizational business processes as well as to the operational business processes that realize them.

The key goal of the process design phase is improving the interfaces between the processes, because streamlining them can improve the performance of an organization significantly. If the results provided do not match the requirements, exceptions occur, processes need to be repeated, so that time and effort is wasted. On the other hand, time and effort are also wasted, if the quality of result is higher than required. For instance, providing a ten page report is a waste of effort, if the customer desires a two page report only.

Process Modelling

To start the modelling of the business process, its results are documented and associated with customers. Then a consistency check is performed to find out whether all results actually have at least one customer and whether there is at least one result delivered to each customer.

This consistency check might lead to interesting results. If the process produces a result for which no customer can be identified, the result is obviously not required. Future versions of the process do not need to produce this result, which reduces the effort of process execution.

Once all results of the process are described and associated with customers, the process team identifies and describes the activities that produce them. If BPMN is used to represent operational business processes, results can be represented by data objects. By associating data objects with process activities, we can define which activities are responsible for creating which results. In BPMN, data objects can be marked as data output, which indicates that the results represented by the data object are used after the process has terminated.

In a next step, the process inputs are investigated in more detail. Therefore, the process suppliers are contacted and the results provided by them are analyzed. In case of an internal supplier, contacting the team does not incur problems. In case of an external supplier, the steering committee has to be involved. The goal of this contacting other process teams is to improve the interfaces between the processes. This discussion between project teams will create a shared understanding of what the results are actually used for, which leads to a more precise characterization of the input and output between processes.

The gathered information is represented in the business process model as data input, which is associated with process activities. Also in this phase, consistency checks can be performed. For instance, we can analyze whether all input data is actually used by the process. If not all input data is used, the respective supplier process needs to be informed.

The business process needs to be refined accordingly. For instance, activities responsible for the creation of data output that is not required can be dropped. This step results in a consolidated process model that only contains data objects that are actually needed, both with respect to input data and output data.

Process Improvement and Measurement Definition

In this phase, the process model is enhanced by activities that are also required by the process. Often, a result is not delivered in one step, but several activities are required that, for instance, produce intermediate results or perform additional checks. The business process model is enriched by these activities.

Since process improvement is about effort, the resources required to produce its results also have to be taken into account. Therefore, the next step involves the estimation of resources required to perform process activities. This effort can then be associated with results, so that for each result delivered the effort to obtain it is determined.

Options for process improvement are investigated next. For each such option, the effect on the overall cost of the process can be estimated. For instance, dropping activities that are no longer required reduces the effort of the process, while adding activities or enhancing the work done in an activity—for instance, to provide results of higher quality—adds to the effort.

At this point, the value of process activities is analyzed. Activities that do not contribute to the value creation, that is, to the development of the process results, are candidates for being dropped.

There are further approaches to improve the performance of business processes. The most important one has already been discussed, that is, producing results in exactly the quality that is required by the process customers. This goes along with identification and elimination of over production. For instance, results might be produced for which persons think that they might eventually be useful. However, if results are not required then the process should not produce them in the first place.

Many business processes contain approvement steps that were introduced a long time ago and never reviewed. Not all of them might be required and some of them could be performed by information systems. These steps add to the execution time of the process, because they typically require hand-overs between persons. For instance, a document is prepared by a clerk and given to a manager for approval. If the manager is currently busy, he or she might sign the document only later, delaying the process.

In general, the hand-over of work needs to be investigated carefully and dropped whenever possible. This was already discussed in the context of resource allocation patterns, where the case handling pattern was introduced to assign related process activities to one person only.

After applying these process improvement steps, the process model is updated accordingly and reviewed, resolving any ambiguities that might have emerged.

The process design phase also involves the definition of measures. Each process should be measured with one or two metrics that characterize the essentials of its performance. Such a metric is called *Key Performance Indicator* or *KPI*. For each KPI, the following aspects need to be defined.

- Business goal that the key performance indicator contributes to
- Name and data type
- Algorithm that exactly defines how to measure the KPI
- Target value of the key performance indicator
- Upper and lower target margins that define a corridor of the intended performance

Consider a sample key performance indicator named *QuoteIssueTime*, which contributes to a goal *ExcellentCustomerService* by defining a service level regarding the preparation of quotes.

This performance indicator states that 90% of all quote requests should be processed within two working days, which is the target value. The KPI allows an upper target margin of 4% and a lower target margin of 6%. This means that the KPI is still satisfied, if 93.6% (90% plus 4% of 90%) of the quote processes are completed within two working days. Since the KPI has the lower target margin of 6%, it is still satisfied if only 84.6% (90% minus 6%) of the service processes are completed within two working days.

The interval from 93.6% to 84.6% defines the corridor of intended performance of the service process. If the performance of the process leaves this corridor or if a trend emerges that indicates leaving the corridor soon, the process team investigates the reasons for this change in performance and either updates the process or reviews the resources allocated to the process.

9.3.4 Process Implementation

After the operational business process models have been developed, the implementation phase investigates how these processes can be realized.

Each process implementation has organizational aspects as well as technical aspects. Organizational aspects concern persons, their roles and responsibilities. Technical aspects include the use of systems in the process. In our area, information systems play the most prominent role, but it might also be systems that deal with physical objects, such as production systems.

Implementing a process in an organization is a broad topic, which cannot be covered completely in a text book. It involves setting up the organizational structures that are in line with the process. The persons involved need to be trained to be able to play their role in the process effectively. Working guidelines are used as an instrument to communicate processes. Depending on the scenario, these guidelines might also contain just the goal of an activity rather than a detailed recipe on how to reach it. Knowledge workers know very well how to solve problems during process execution, as they emerge.

Platform Selection

Since this book concentrates on concepts and architectures of process oriented information systems, technical aspects are discussed in more detail. In this context, a platform suitable to run the business process has to be selected.

If the organization plans to base its information systems on a service-oriented architecture, the business process can be realized using service composition techniques. If human interaction is required and the process is well structured, then an appropriate platform is a workflow management system. In case the process structure is rather flexible and data plays a key role during process enactment, a case handling system should be selected. The process might also be implemented without a dedicated process oriented information system, in which case the process is used as requirements document in the respective software development process.

In real-world projects, the selection of an enactment platform is often done at an early project stage, either by an extensive selection process or by using existing relationships with specific vendors. The early selection of a system, however, is one of the main problems in process implementation, since at this point in time there is little information available on the business processes and their execution environment. Consequently, it is not possible to choose a workflow management system according to the specific needs of the business processes under consideration.

Therefore, the methodology proposes not to select the enactment platform up front, but after the business process and the technical environment of its execution have been established. The selection process starts with the defining of selection criteria based on the identified business processes. Obviously, there are many criteria for selecting a suitable workflow management system, ranging from integration criteria to the interface design of the systems.

Based on the identified selection criteria and on market analysis data, an initial set of workflow management systems can be selected. However, if the systems available do not meet the criteria—or the systems cannot be used in the particular technological infrastructure—then the selection criteria have to be redesigned. If a system is found that satisfies the criteria, it is installed and tested against the criteria. If the tests are successful, a review meeting is organized in which the final decision on the system to be used is made.

Implementation Aspects

The activities in the operational business process are mapped to activities at the workflow level. There are complex relationships possible between the operational level of a business process and its implementation. In some cases, an activity in the operational level can be mapped to a subprocess in the implementation level, resulting in a hierarchical decomposition. However, in the general case, relationships between processes might be more complex, as recently formalized as complex correspondencies between activities of related business processes.

In addition to the process aspect, the organizational environment needs to be represented if human interaction workflows are used to realize the operational business process. Depending on the functionality provided by the enactment platform, either the organizational information is entered in the system or an interface to an existing system that manages organizational information is established.

An important activity in this phase is concerned with the integration of external applications. Depending on the support provided by the selected workflow system and enterprise application integration platform, application integration may require considerable coding and extensive testing.

Measurement Implementation

The implementation phase does not only concern the realization of the actual business process, but also of the key performance indicators defined for it. This can be achieved by implementing measurement points that provide execution information while the process runs and by aggregating this information as defined in the performance indicator.

To illustrate this approach, the key performance indicator *IssueQuoteTime* is revisited. The *Issue Quote* process, responsible for issuing quotes is shown in Figure 9.7. It starts by receiving a request message from a customer, followed by an activity to prepare the quote. Once the quote is prepared, it can be approved. The process ends by sending the quote to the customer.

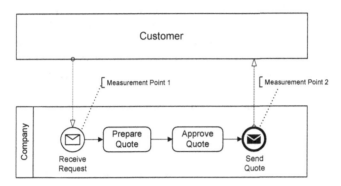

Fig. 9.7. Process diagram containing measurement points for key performance indicator *IssueQuoteTime*

For this process, measurement points can be implemented by creating a log entry each time a request-for-quote message is received (*Measurement Point 1* in Figure 9.7). This log entry contains information about the request, most prominently an identifier, and a time stamp taken when the message arrived.

Another log entry is written when the quote is sent (*Measurement Point 2*). This entry contains the identifier and a time stamp, taken when the quote was sent. The identifier allows to correlate log entries that belong to the same process instance. The measurement points are represented in Figure 9.7 by annotations of the respective events.

Test and Deployment

Testing comprises the two subphases lab simulation and field testing. The overall goal of the testing subphase is to obtain information about the technical stability, performance, and the usability of the solution in the target environment. A field test is performed to show that the workflow application is able to handle real-world situations, characterized by problems which (at least partially) cannot be planned or predicted beforehand in laboratory environments. Therefore, the application is tested against real-world conditions. After defining the goals of the field test, the business processes to be tested are selected.

For each such process, a backup solution must be provided to cope with potential error situations in the application. In case of human interaction workflows, the employees involved in the tested processes are trained on the new business process application. If the training is completed and the backup solution is tested extensively and is considered stable, the field test can be performed. After its completion, the test data generated is analyzed. Depending on the analysis, the project team may decide to create new test goals. This process can iterate, so that the field tests become increasingly accurate.

Once the process and the measuring points required for computing its KPI are implemented and tested, the process needs to be deployed and the related technical and organizational changes have to be performed. These activities include communication of the improved process in the organization. It also involves user training on new or modified information systems that support the process. In addition to these organizational aspects, application data might need to be migrated to new systems. If the training and the data migration are finished successfully, the new process can go live.

9.3.5 Operations and Controlling

In the operations and controlling phase, the daily business of the organization is conducted.

In this phase, it is essential that the process is performed as designed. Any bypassing of the process by employees needs to be identified. Once a bypass has been identified, the reasons for bypassing the process need to be carefully investigated. In many cases, there is a valid reason for not executing the process as planned. A typical reason is a new software system that has no intuitive user interface or the employees that are expected to work with the system have not been trained properly.

Identifying such a bypass puts a work item on the agenda of the process team. Typically, either there is a problem with the usability of the software, as discussed above. Or the process structure is not adequate to conduct the business process. Whenever a structural issue is discovered, the process team re-enters the design phase and looks for ways of improving the process so that its structural problems vanish. Any further problems that emerge are also reported to the process team that takes care of them. Since the members of the process team are themselves heavily involved in the process, they will be able to spot any issue that might arise in the process.

Controlling is an important aspect of this phase, that is, measuring of the performance indicators. Following up on the example, the measurement points are used to compute the key performance indicator *IssueQuoteTime* as follows. Pairs of events that belong to the same process instance are identified, and the time stamp of the receive event is subtracted from the time stamp of the send event, resulting in the time span between receiving the request and sending the quote.

If the reporting period is, for instance, twice a month, this information is gathered, before computing the performance indicator two times a month. As long as the measured KPI is within the range 84.6% through 93.6%, things are fine and we can report this information to the management. However, once the lower threshold value or the upper threshold value is reached, a signal will be shown to the process owner to indicate the need for action on this process.

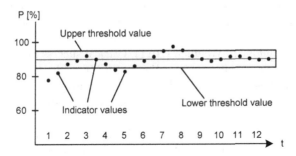

Fig. 9.8. Process performance diagram showing the percentage P of process instances that have completed within the desired time

Using diagrams like the one shown in Figure 9.8, the process owner gets a visual impression of the process performance over time; he or she can detect trends in the performance of the process as they develop.

In this diagram, the performance values are shown as black dots for one year. The calculation was done two times a month. For instance, a black dot at the coordinates (9, 90%) means that during the reporting period in September, 90% of all quotes have been sent within two working days.

In January, the KPI was not met. By the appropriate measures taken by the process team, the performance improved to reach about 90% in March. Then the performance deteriorated, so that the lower threshold value was missed in May. This fact was detected by the performance team, and appropriate measures were taken to improve the process. Performance rose again, and even left the KPI corridor in August, so that measures were taken to save effort, which is not required to reach the KPI. Finally the system is in a stable state, indicated by the sequence of measures in the target zone of the KPI.

This discussion shows how the measured values can be used to constantly monitor the performance of the process. Whenever the KPI corridor is left or a trend is detected that could lead to this situation in the near future, the process team investigates the reasons for this situation. Once the reasons are found, the process team re-enters the process design phase. If the problem can be solved by changing the resources allocated to the process, the respective measures are taken. The modifications are implemented and deployed, so that the business process again meets its key performance indicator.

Bibliographical Notes

Workflow application development processes have been discussed in Weske et al. (2001). The material presented in Chapter 9 extends the work presented therein and combines it with a methodology focusing on supplier-customer relationships of processes, developed in Füermann and Dammasch (2008). Pulier and Taylor (2006) investigate development methodologies for enterprise application integration scenarios in service-oriented architectures from a practical point of view, using a fictious enterprise. Complex correspondencies between business processes on different levels of abstraction are investigated with respect to their behaviour in Weidlich (2011). Critical success factors of process oriented information systems are investigated in Mutschler et al. (2008). Process improvement has been addressed in Mansar and Reijers (2005) and Reijers (2005), where best practices of process improvement based on heuristic rules were identified.

In the context of the Integrated Definition Methods (IDEF) approach, an IDEF3 process description capture method is proposed in Meyer et al. (1995). This method comes with dedicated organizational regulations, forms to describe processes and activities, and a process description language.

References

van der Aalst W (1998) The Application of Petri Nets to Workflow Management. The Journal of Circuits, Systems and Computers 8(1):21–66

van der Aalst W (1999) Woflan: A Petri-net-based Workflow Analyzer. Systems Analysis - Modelling - Simulation 35(3):345–357

van der Aalst W, Basten T (2002) Inheritance of Workflows: An Approach to Tackling Problems Related to Change. Theor Comput Sci 270(1-2):125–203

van der Aalst W, Berens P (2001) Beyond Workflow Management: Product-driven Case Handling. In: Ellis S, Rodden T, Zigurs I (eds) International ACM SIG-GROUP Conference on Supporting Group Work (GROUP 2001), pp 42–51

van der Aalst W, van Hee K (2004) Workflow Management: Models, Methods, and Systems. Cooperative Information Systems Series, MIT Press

van der Aalst W, ter Hofstede A (2005) YAWL: Yet Another Workflow Language. Information Systems 30(4):245–275

van der Aalst W, Weske M (2001) The P2P Approach to Interorganizational Workflows. In: Dittrich KR, Geppert A, Norrie MC (eds) Proceedings of the 13th Conference on Advanced Information Systems Engineering (CAiSE'01), Springer Lecture Notes in Computer Science 2068, pp 140–156

van der Aalst W, Hofstede A, Weske M (2003a) Business Process Management: A Survey. In: Aalst W, Hofstede A, Weske M (eds) International Conference on Business Process Management (BPM 2003), Springer-Verlag, Berlin, Lecture Notes in Computer Science, vol 2678, pp 1–12

van der Aalst W, ter Hofstede A, Weske M (eds) (2003b) Proceedings of the International Conference on Business Process Management., no. 2678 in Lecture Notes in Computer Science, Springer, Heidelberg

van der Aalst W, ter Hofstede AHM, Kiepuszewski B, Barros AP (2003c) Workflow Patterns. Distributed and Parallel Databases 14(1):5–51

van der Aalst W, Aldred L, Dumas M, ter Hofstede A (2004) Design and Implementation of the YAWL System. In: Proceedings of The 16th International Conference on Advanced Information Systems Engineering (CAiSE 04), Springer-Verlag, Lecture Notes in Computer Science, vol 3084, pp 142–159

van der Aalst W, Benatallah B, Casati F, Curbera F (eds) (2005a) Proceedings of the Third International Conference on Business Process Management., no. 3649 in Lecture Notes in Computer Science, Springer, Heidelberg

© Springer-Verlag GmbH Germany, part of Springer Nature 2019
M. Weske, *Business Process Management*,
https://doi.org/10.1007/978-3-662-59432-2

van der Aalst W, Weske M, Grünbauer D (2005b) Case Handling: A New Paradigm for Business Process Support. Data and Knowledge Engineering 53:129–162

van der Aalst W, de Medeiros AKA, Weijters AJMM (2006) Process Equivalence: Comparing Two Process Models Based on Observed Behavior. In: Business Process Management, Springer, Lecture Notes in Computer Science, vol 4102, pp 129–144

van der Aalst W, Reijers H, Weijters A, van Dongen B, de Medeiros AA, Song M, Verbeek H (2007) Business Process Mining: An Industrial Application. Information Systems

van der Aalst WMP (2000) Workflow Verification: Finding Control-Flow Errors Using Petri-Net-Based Techniques. In: van der Aalst et al. (2000), pp 161–183

van der Aalst WMP (2011) Process Mining: Discovery, Conformance and Enhancement of Business Processes. Springer

van der Aalst WMP (2016) Process Mining - Data Science in Action, Second Edition. Springer

van der Aalst WMP, Stahl C (eds) (2011) Modeling Business Processes – A Petri Net-Oriented Approach. MIT Press

van der Aalst WMP, Desel J, Oberweis A (eds) (2000) Business Process Management, Models, Techniques, and Empirical Studies, Lecture Notes in Computer Science, vol 1806, Springer

van der Aalst WMP, Casati F, Conforti R, de Leoni M, Dumas M, Kumar A, Mendling J, Nepal S, Pentland BT, Weber B (eds) (2018) Proceedings of the Dissertation Award, Demonstration, and Industrial Track at BPM 2018 co-located with 16th International Conference on Business Process Management (BPM 2018), Sydney, Australia, September 9-14, 2018, CEUR Workshop Proceedings, vol 2196, CEUR-WS.org

Abramowicz W, Paschke A (eds) (2018) Business Information Systems - 21st International Conference, BIS 2018, Berlin, Germany, July 18-20, 2018, Proceedings, Lecture Notes in Business Information Processing, vol 320, Springer

Alonso G, Dadam P, Rosemann M (eds) (2007) Business Process Management, 5th International Conference, BPM 2007, Brisbane, Australia, September 24-28, 2007, Proceedings, Lecture Notes in Computer Science, vol 4714, Springer

Alonso G, Casati F, Kuno H, Machiraju V (2009) Web Services: Concepts, Architectures and Applications. Data-Centric Systems and Applications Series, Springer

Baesens B, Setiono R, Mues C, Vanthienen J (2003) Using neural network rule extraction and decision tables for credit - risk evaluation. Management Science 49(3):312–329

Barros AP, Dumas M, ter Hofstede AHM (2005) Service Interaction Patterns. In: van der Aalst W, Benatallah B, Casati F, Curbera F (eds) Business Process Management, Springer, Heidelberg, Lecture Notes in Computer Science, vol 3649, pp 302–318

Basten T, van der Aalst W (2001) Inheritance of Behavior. JLAP 47(2):47–145

Batoulis K, Weske M (2017a) Soundness of decision-aware business processes. In: Carmona et al. (2017b), pp 106–124

Batoulis K, Weske M (2017b) A tool for checking soundness of decision-aware business processes. In: Clarisó et al. (2017)

Batoulis K, Weske M (2018a) Disambiguation of DMN decision tables. In: Abramowicz and Paschke (2018), pp 236–249

Batoulis K, Weske M (2018b) A tool for the uniqueification of DMN decision tables. In: van der Aalst et al. (2018), pp 116–119

Batoulis K, Meyer A, Bazhenova E, Decker G, Weske M (2015) Extracting decision logic from process models. In: Zdravkovic et al. (2015), pp 349–366

Batoulis K, Haarmann S, Weske M (2017) Various notions of soundness for decision-aware business processes. In: Mayr et al. (2017), pp 403–418

Bauer T, Reichert M, Dadam P (2003) Intra-Subnet Load Balancing in Distributed Workflow Management Systems. International Journal of Cooperative Information Systems 12(3):295–324

Becker J, Kugeler M, Rosemann M (2011) Process Management. A Guide for the Design of Business Processes, 2nd edn. Springer

Boehm BW (1981) Software Engineering Economics. Pearson Education

Booch G, Jacobson I, Rumbaugh J (2005) The Unified Modeling Language User Guide, 2nd edn. Addison-Wesley

BPM Offensive Berlin (2011) BPMN 2.0 Business Process Model and Notation, Poster. http://www.bpmb.de/index.php/BPMNPoster

Bravetti M, Núñez M, Zavattaro G (eds) (2006) Web Services and Formal Methods, Third International Workshop, WS-FM 2006 Vienna, Austria, September 8-9, 2006, Proceedings, Lecture Notes in Computer Science, vol 4184, Springer

de Bruijn J (2005) The Web Service Modeling Language WSML. Available at http://www.wsmo.org/TR/d16/d16.1/v0.21/. Tech. rep., University of Innsbruck

Burbeck S (2000) The Tao of E-Business Services – The Evolution of Web Applications into Service-Oriented Components with Web Services. Tech. rep., IBM Software Group

Calvanese D, Dumas M, Laurson Ü, Maggi FM, Montali M, Teinemaa I (2018) Semantics, analysis and simplification of DMN decision tables. Inf Syst 78:112–125

Carmona J, Engels G, Kumar A (eds) (2017a) Business Process Management - 15th International Conference, BPM 2017, Barcelona, Spain, September 10-15, 2017, Proceedings, Lecture Notes in Computer Science, vol 10445, Springer

Carmona J, Engels G, Kumar A (eds) (2017b) Business Process Management Forum - BPM Forum 2017, Barcelona, Spain, September 10-15, 2017, Proceedings, Lecture Notes in Business Information Processing, vol 297, Springer

Chappell DA (2004) Enterprise Service Bus. Theory in Practice, O'Reilly

Chen PP (1976) The Entity-Relationship Model - Toward a Unified View of Data. ACM Trans Database Syst 1(1):9–36

Chinnici R, Moreau JJ, Ryman A, Weerawarana S (2007) Web Services Description Language (WSDL) Version 2.0. W3C

Clarisó R, Leopold H, Mendling J, van der Aalst WMP, Kumar A, Pentland BT, Weske M (eds) (2017) Proceedings of the BPM Demo Track and BPM Dissertation Award co-located with 15th International Conference on Business Process Modeling (BPM 2017), Barcelona, Spain, September 13, 2017, CEUR Workshop Proceedings, vol 1920, CEUR-WS.org

Clement L, Hately A, von Riegen C, Rogers T (2004) UDDI Version 3.0.2. OASIS

Cuntz N, Kindler E (2005) On the Semantics of EPCs: Efficient Calculation and Simulation. In: van der Aalst W, Benatallah B, Casati F, Curbera F (eds) Business Process Management, Springer, Heidelberg, Lecture Notes in Computer Science, vol 3649, pp 398–403

Davenport TH (1992) Process Innovation – Reengineering Work through Information Technology. Havard Business School Press

Dayal U, Eder J, Koehler J, Reijers HA (eds) (2009) Business Process Management, 7th International Conference, BPM 2009, Ulm, Germany, September 8-10, 2009. Proceedings, Lecture Notes in Computer Science, vol 5701, Springer

Decker G (2009) Design and Analysis of Process Choreographies. PhD thesis, Hasso Plattner Institut, University of Potsdam

Decker G, Barros AP (2007) Interaction Modeling Using BPMN. In: ter Hofstede et al. (2008), pp 208–219

Decker G, Mendling J (2009) Process Instantiation. Data Knowl Eng 68(9):777–792

Decker G, Weske M (2007) Behavioral Consistency for B2B Process Integration. In: Krogstie et al. (2007), pp 81–95

Decker G, Weske M (2011) Interaction-centric Modeling of Process Choreographies. Inf Syst 36(2):292–312

Decker G, Zaha JM, Dumas M (2006) Execution semantics for service choreographies. In: Bravetti et al. (2006), pp 163–177

Dehnert J, Rittgen P (2001) Relaxed Soundness of Business Processes. In: Dittrich K, Geppert A, Norrie (eds) Proceedings of the 13th International Conference on Advanced Information Systems Engineering (CAiSE), Springer, Lecture Notes in Computer Science, vol 2068, pp 157–170

Desel J, Pernici B, Weske M (eds) (2004) Business Process Management: Second International Conference, BPM 2004, Potsdam, Germany, June 17-18, 2004. Proceedings, Lecture Notes in Computer Science, vol 3080, Springer

Dijkman RM, Hofstetter J, Koehler J (eds) (2011) Business Process Model and Notation - Third International Workshop, BPMN 2011, Lecture Notes in Business Information Processing, vol 95, Springer

Dijkstra EW (1982) EWD 447: On the Role of Scientific Thought. In: Selected Writings on Computing: A Personal Perspective, Springer-Verlag

Dubray JJ, Amand SS, Martin MJ (2006) ebXML Business Process Specification Schema Technical Specification v2.0.4. OASIS

Dumas M, van der Aalst W, ter Hofstede AH (eds) (2005) Process Aware Information Systems: Bridging People and Software through Process Technology. John Wiley & Sons

Dumas M, Spork M, Wang K (2006) Adapt or Perish: Algebra and Visual Notation for Service Interface Adaptation. In: Business Process Management, Springer, Lecture Notes in Computer Science, vol 4102, pp 65–80

Dumas M, Reichert M, Shan MC (eds) (2008) Business Process Management, 6th International Conference, BPM 2008, Lecture Notes in Computer Science, vol 5240, Springer

Dumas M, Rosa ML, Mendling J, Reijers HA (2018) Fundamentals of Business Process Management, Second Edition. Springer

Dustdar S, Fiadeiro JL, Sheth A (eds) (2006) Proceedings of the Fourth International Conference on Business Process Management., no. 4102 in Lecture Notes in Computer Science, Springer, Heidelberg

Ellis CA, Bernal M (1982) OfficeTalk-D: An Experimental Office Information System. In: Proceedings of the SIGOA conference on Office Information Systems, ACM Press, New York, NY, USA, pp 131–140

Fielding RT (2000) REST: architectural styles and the design of network-based software architectures. Doctoral dissertation, University of California, Irvine

Forst A, Kühn e, Bukhres O (1995) General Purpose Work Flow Languages. Distributed and Parallel Databases 3(2):187–218

Füermann T, Dammasch C (2008) Process Management: Roadmap to Continuous Process Improvement *(in German)*. Hanser

García-Bañuelos L, Ponomarev A, Dumas M, Weber I (2017) Optimized execution of business processes on blockchain. In: Carmona et al. (2017a), pp 130–146

Georgakopoulos D, Hornick MF, Sheth AP (1995) An Overview of Workflow Management: From Process Modeling to Workflow Automation Infrastructure. Distributed and Parallel Databases 3(2):119–153

Georgakopoulos D, Prinz W, Wolf A (eds) (1999) Proceedings of the International joint Conference on Work Activities Coordination and Collaboration 1999, San Francisco, California, USA, February 22-25, 1999, ACM

Gfeller B, Völzer H, Wilmsmann G (2011) Faster or-join enactment for bpmn 2.0. In: Dijkman et al. (2011), pp 31–43

Girault C, Valk R (2010) Petri Nets for System Engineering: A Guide to Modeling, Verification, and Applications. Springer

van Glabbeek R, Weijland W (1996) Branching Time and Abstraction in Bisimulation Semantics. Journal of the ACM 43(3):555–600

Grefen P, Aberer K, Hoffner Y, Ludwig H (2000) CrossFlow: Cross-Organizational Workflow Management in Dynamic Virtual Enterprises. International Journal of Computer Systems Science & Engineering 15:277–290

Gruber T (1993) A Translation Approach to Portable Ontologies. Knowledge Acquisition 5(2):199–220

Gudgin M, Hadley M, Mendelsohn N, Moreau JJ, Nielsen HF, Karmarkar A, Lafon Y (2007) SOAP Version 1.2. http://www.w3.org/TR/soap

Haarmann S, Batoulis K, Nikaj A, Weske M (2018) DMN decision execution on the ethereum blockchain. In: Krogstie and Reijers (2018), pp 327–341

Hammer M, Champy J (1993) Reengineering the Corporation: A Manifesto for Business Revolution. Harper Business

Havey M (2005) Essential Business Process Modeling. O'Reilly Media

Henning M, Vinoski S (1999) Advanced CORBA Programming with C++. Professional Computing Series, Addison-Wesley

Hewelt M, Weske M (2016) A hybrid approach for flexible case modeling and execution. In: Rosa et al. (2016), pp 38–54

Hidders J, Dumas M, van der Aalst W, ter Hofstede AH, Verelst J (2005) When Are Two Workflows the Same? In: Proceedings 11th Australasian Theory Symposium (CATS 2005), Newcastle, Australia

ter Hofstede AHM, Benatallah B, Paik HY (eds) (2008) Business Process Management Workshops, Lecture Notes in Computer Science, vol 4928, Springer

ter Hofstede AHM, van der Aalst WMP, Adams M, Russell N (eds) (2010) Modern Business Process Automation – YAWL and its Support Environment. Springer

Hollingsworth D (1995) The Workflow Reference Model. Tech. Rep. Document Number TC00-1003, Workflow Management Coalition

Hull R, Mendling J, Tai S (eds) (2010) Business Process Management - 8th International Conference, BPM 2010, Lecture Notes in Computer Science, vol 6336, Springer

Jablonski S (1997) Architecture of Workflow Management Systems (in German). Informatik Forschung und Entwicklung 12(2):72–81

Jensen K, van der Aalst WMP (eds) (2009) Transactions on Petri Nets and Other Models of Concurrency II, Special Issue on Concurrency in Process-Aware Information Systems, Lecture Notes in Computer Science, vol 5460, Springer

Jensen K, Kristensen LM (2009) Coloured Petri Nets - Modelling and Validation of Concurrent Systems. Springer

Kindler E (2004) On the Semantics of EPCs: A Framework for Resolving the Vicious Circle. In: Desel et al. (2004), pp 82–97

Kosiol E (1962) Organization of the Corporation (in German). Gabler, Wiesbaden

Krogstie J, Reijers HA (eds) (2018) Advanced Information Systems Engineering - 30th International Conference, CAiSE 2018, Tallinn, Estonia, June 11-15, 2018, Proceedings, Lecture Notes in Computer Science, vol 10816, Springer

Krogstie J, Opdahl AL, Sindre G (eds) (2007) Advanced Information Systems Engineering, 19th International Conference, CAiSE 2007, Trondheim, Norway, June 11-15, 2007, Proceedings, Lecture Notes in Computer Science, vol 4495, Springer

Kunze M, Weske M (2016) Behavioural Models - From Modelling Finite Automata to Analysing Business Processes. Springer

Kunze M, Luebbe A, Weidlich M, Weske M (2011) Towards Understanding Process Modeling - The Case of the BPM Academic Initiative. In: Dijkman et al. (2011), pp 44–58

Kuropka D, Bog A, Weske M (2006) Semantic Enterprise Services Platform: Motivation, Potential, Functionality and Application Scenario. In: Proceedings of the thenth IEEE international EDOC Enterprise Computing Conference. Hong Kong, October 2006, pp 253–261

Kuropka D, Tröger P, Staab S, Weske M (eds) (2008) Semantic Service Provisioning. Springer

Küster JM, Ryndina K, Gall H (2007) Generation of business process models for object life cycle compliance. In: Alonso et al. (2007), pp 165–181

Lamport L (1978) Time, Clocks, and the Ordering of Events in a Distributed System. Communications of the ACM 21(7):558–565

Leymann F, Altenhuber W (1994) Managing Business Processes as Information Resources. IBM Systems Journal 33(2):326–348

Leymann F, Roller D (1997) Workflow-based Applications. IBM Systems Journal 36(1):102–123

Leymann F, Roller D (1999) Production Workflow: Concepts and Techniques. Pearson Education

Leymann F, Roller D, Schmidt MT (2002) Web Services and Business Process Management. IBM Systems Journal 41(2):198–211

Lohmann N, Wolf K (2010) How to Implement a Theory of Correctness in the Area of Business Processes and Services. In: Hull et al. (2010), pp 61–77

Lohmann N, Massuthe P, Stahl C, Weinberg D (2006) Analyzing Interacting BPEL Processes. In: Business Process Management, Springer, Lecture Notes in Computer Science, vol 4102, pp 17–32

Ly LT, Rinderle S, Dadam P (2006) Semantic Correctness in Adaptive Process Management Systems. In: Business Process Management, Springer, Lecture Notes in Computer Science, vol 4102, pp 193–208

Mansar SL, Reijers HA (2005) Best practices in business process redesign: validation of a redesign framework. Computers in Industry 56(5):457–471

Martens A (2003a) On Compatibility of Web Services. In: 10th Workshop on Algorithms and Tools for Petri Nets (AWPN 2003), Eichstätt, Germany

Martens A (2003b) On Usability of Web Services. In: Calero C, Daz O, Piattini M (eds) Proceedings of 1st Web Services Quality Workshop

Martens A (2005a) Analyzing Web Service based Business Processes. In: Cerioli M (ed) Proceedings of Intl. Conference on Fundamental Approaches to Software Engineering (FASE'05), Part of the 2005 European Joint Conferences on Theory and Practice of Software (ETAPS'05), Springer-Verlag, Edinburgh, Scotland, Lecture Notes in Computer Science, vol 3442

Martens A (2005b) Consistency between Executable and Abstract Processes. In: Proceedings IEEE International Conference on e-Technology, e-Commerce, and e-Services (EEE 2005), IEEE Computer Society, Hong Kong, China, pp 60–67

Massuthe P, Schmidt K (2005) Operating Guidelines - an Automata-Theoretic Foundation for the Service-Oriented Architecture. In: Proceedings Fifth International Conference on Quality Software (QSIC 2005), IEEE Computer Society, Washington, DC, USA, pp 452–457

Massuthe P, Reisig W, Schmidt K (2005) An Operating Guideline Approach to the SOA. Annals of Mathematics, Computing & Teleinformatics 1(3):35–43

Mayr HC, Guizzardi G, Ma H, Pastor O (eds) (2017) Conceptual Modeling - 36th International Conference, ER 2017, Valencia, Spain, November 6-9, 2017, Proceedings, Lecture Notes in Computer Science, vol 10650, Springer

McGuinness FE D; van Harmelen (2004) OWL Web Ontology Language Overview. Tech. rep., Web Ontology Working Group at the World Wide Web Consortium (W3C)

Medeiros CB, Vossen G, Weske M (1995) WASA: A Workflow-Based Architecture to Support Scientific Database Applications (Extended Abstract). In: Revell and Tjoa (1995), pp 574–583

Mendling J, van der Aalst W (2007) Formalization and Verification of EPCs with OR-Joins Based on State and Context. In: Krogstie et al. (2007), pp 439–453

Mendling J, Weidlich M, Weske M (eds) (2011) Business Process Modeling Notation - Second International Workshop, BPMN 2010, Lecture Notes in Business Information Processing, vol 67, Springer

Mendling J, Weber I, van der Aalst WMP, vom Brocke J, Cabanillas C, Daniel F, Debois S, Ciccio CD, Dumas M, Dustdar S, Gal A, García-Bañuelos L, Governatori G, Hull R, Rosa ML, Leopold H, Leymann F, Recker J, Reichert M, Reijers HA, Rinderle-Ma S, Solti A, Rosemann M, Schulte S, Singh MP, Slaats T, Staples M, Weber B, Weidlich M, Weske M, Xu X, Zhu L (2018) Blockchains for business process management - challenges and opportunities. ACM Trans Management Inf Syst 9(1):4:1–4:16

Meyer H, Weske M (2006) Automated Service Composition Using Heuristic Search. In: Business Process Management, Springer, Lecture Notes in Computer Science, vol 4102, pp 81–96

Meyer R, Menzel C, Painter M, deWitte P, Blinn T, Perakath B (1995) Information Integration for Concurrent Engineering IDEF3 Process Description Capture Method Report. Tech. rep., Knowlege Based Systems, Inc.

Mohan (2002) Dynamic E-business: Trends in Web Services. In: Buchmann A, Casati F, Fiege L, Hsu MC, Shan MC (eds) Proceedings of the third VLDB workshop on Technologies for E-Services, vol Springer Lecture Notes in Computer Science 2444, pp 1–5

Mutschler B, Reichert M, Bumiller J (2008) Unleashing the effectiveness of process-oriented information systems: Problem analysis, critical success factors, and implications. IEEE Transactions on Systems, Man, and Cybernetics, Part C 38(3):280–291

Nagarajan M, Verma K, Sheth AP, Miller J, Lathem J (2006) Semantic interoperability of web services - challenges and experiences. In: ICWS '06: Proceedings of the IEEE International Conference on Web Services (ICWS'06), IEEE Computer Society, Washington, DC, USA, pp 373–382

Newcomer E, Lomow G (2005) Understanding SOA with Web Services. Addison Wesley

Nikaj A, Mandal S, Pautasso C, Weske M (2015) From choreography diagrams to restful interactions. In: Norta et al. (2016), pp 3–14

Nikaj A, Hewelt M, Weske M (2018) Towards implementing rest-enabled business process choreographies. In: Abramowicz and Paschke (2018), pp 223–235

Nordsieck F (1932) The Figurative Collection and Investigation of the Operational Organization. (in German). C. E. Poeschel, Stuttgart

Norta A, Gaaloul W, Gangadharan GR, Dam HK (eds) (2016) Service-Oriented Computing - ICSOC 2015 Workshops - WESOA, RMSOC, ISC, DISCO, WESE, BSCI, FOR-MOVES, Goa, India, November 16-19, 2015, Revised Selected Papers, Lecture Notes in Computer Science, vol 9586, Springer

Oasis (2007) Web Services Business Process Execution Language Version 2.0. OASIS Standard

Object Management Group (2011) Business Process Model and Notation (BPMN) Version 2.0. formal/2011-01-03 edn

Object Management Group (2018) Decision Model and Notation (DMN) Version 1.2. dtc/2018-06-01 edn

O'Neil P, O'Neil E (2000) Database: Principles, Programming, and Performance, 2nd edn. Elsevier Science & Technology Books

Parnas DL (1972) On the Criteria to be Used in Decomposing Systems into Modules. Communications of the ACM 15(12):1053–1058

Petri CA (1962) Communication with Automata (in German). PhD thesis, Universität Bonn, Institut für Instrumentelle Mathematik, Schriften IIM Nr.2

Porter ME (1998) Competitive Advantage. Free Press

Puhlmann F (2007) On the Application of a Theory for Mobile Systems to Business Process Management. PhD thesis, Hasso Plattner Institute for IT Systems Engineering at the University of Potsdam

Puhlmann F, Weske M (2006a) Interaction Soundness for Service Orchestrations. In: Dan A, Lamersdorf W (eds) Proceedings of the 4th International Conference on Service Oriented Computing (ICSOC 2006), Springer Verlag, LNCS, vol 4294, pp 302–313

Puhlmann F, Weske M (2006b) Investigations on Soundness Regarding Lazy Activities. In: Business Process Management, Springer, Lecture Notes in Computer Science, vol 4102, pp 145–160

Pulier E, Taylor H (2006) Understanding Enterprise SOA. Manning

Ramakrishnan R, Gehrke J (2002) Database Management Systems, 3rd edn. McGraw-Hill

Reichert M, Dadam P (1998) ADEPT$_{flex}$-Supporting Dynamic Changes of Workflows Without Losing Control. J Intell Inf Syst 10(2):93–129

Reichert M, Weber B (2012) Enabling Flexibility in Process-Aware Information Systems - Challenges, Methods, Technologies. Springer

Reichert M, Rinderle-Ma S, Dadam P (2009) Flexibility in Process-Aware Information Systems. In: Jensen and van der Aalst (2009), pp 115–135

Reijers HA (2005) Process Design and Redesign, chap 9. In: Dumas et al. (2005)

Reijers HA, Rigter JHM, van der Aalst W (2003) The Case Handling Case. Int J Cooperative Inf Syst 12(3):365–391

Revell N, Tjoa AM (eds) (1995) Database and Expert Systems Applications, 6th International Conference, DEXA'95, London, United Kingdom, September 4-8, 1995, Proceedings, Lecture Notes in Computer Science, vol 978, Springer

Rinderle S, Reichert M, Dadam P (2003) Evaluation of Correctness Criteria for Dynamic Workflow Changes. In: van der Aalst W, ter Hofstede AHM, Weske M (eds) Business Process Management, Springer, Lecture Notes in Computer Science, vol 2678, pp 41–57

Rinderle S, Reichert M, Dadam P (2004) On Dealing with Structural Conflicts between Process Type and Instance Changes. In: Desel et al. (2004), pp 274–289

Rinderle-Ma S, Toumani F, Wolf K (eds) (2011) Business Process Management - 9th International Conference, BPM 2011, Clermont-Ferrand, France, August 30 - September 2, 2011. Proceedings, Lecture Notes in Computer Science, vol 6896, Springer

Rosa ML, Loos P, Pastor O (eds) (2016) Business Process Management Forum - BPM Forum 2016, Rio de Janeiro, Brazil, September 18-22, 2016, Proceedings, Lecture Notes in Business Information Processing, vol 260, Springer

Russell N, van der Aalst W, ter Hofstede AHM, Edmond D (2005) Workflow Resource Patterns: Identification, Representation and Tool Support. In: CAiSE, pp 216–232

Russell N, ter Hofstede A, van der Aalst W, Mulyar N (2006) Workflow Control-Flow Patterns: A Revised View. Tech. Rep. BPM Center Report BPM-06-22, BPMcenter.org

Russell N, van der Aalst WMP, ter Hofstede AHM (2016) Workflow Patterns: The Definitive Guide. MIT Press

Scheer AW (2000) ARIS – Business Process Frameworks, 3rd edn. Springer

Scheer AW, Kirchmer M, Abolhassan F, Jost W (eds) (2004) Business Process Automation. Springer

Scheer AW, Thomas O, Adam O (2005) Process Aware Information Systems: Bridging People and Software through Process Technology, chap Process Modeling Using Event-Driven Process Chains, pp 119–145. In: Dumas et al. (2005)

Schmelzer H, Sesselmann W (2010) Practical Use of Business Process Management (in German), 7th edn. Hanser

Schumacher H, Sevcik KC (1976) The synthetic approach to decision table conversion. Commun ACM 19(6):343–351

Siegeris J, Zimmermann A (2006) Workflow Model Compositions Preserving Relaxed Soundness. In: Business Process Management, Springer, Lecture Notes in Computer Science, vol 4102, pp 177–192

Silberschatz A, Galvin PB (2008) Operating System Concepts, 8th edn. Addison-Wesley

Silver B (2011) BPMN Method and Style, 2nd edn. Cody-Cassidy Press

Silver B, Tirelli E (2018) DMN Cookbook. Cody-Cassidy

Smith H, Fingar P (2006) Business Process Management: The Third Wave. Meghan-Kiffer Press

Stallings W (2004) Operating Systems. Prentice Hall

Swenson KD (ed) (2010) Mastering the Unpredictable: How Adaptive Case Management will revolutionize the way that knowledge workers get things done. Meghan-Kiffer

Tanenbaum AS (2007) Modern Operating Systems, 3rd edn. Prentice-Hall, International

Taylor FW (1967) The Principle of Scientific Management. Norton & Company

Taylor J, Purchase J (2016) Real-world Decision Modeling with DMN. Meghan-Kiffer

Verbeek H, Basten T, van der Aalst W (2001) Diagnosing Workflow Processes using Woflan. The Computer Journal 44(4):246–279

Verma K, Doshi P, Gomadam K, Miller J, Sheth A (2006) Optimal Adaptation in Web Processes with Coordination Constraints. In: ICWS '06: Proceedings of the IEEE International Conference on Web Services (ICWS'06), IEEE Computer Society, Washington, DC, USA, pp 257–264

Weber B, Rinderle S, Reichert M (2007) Change Patterns and Change Support Features in Process-Aware Information Systems. In: Krogstie et al. (2007), pp 574–588

Weidlich M (2011) Behavioural Profiles: A Relational Approach to Behavioral Consistency. PhD thesis, Hasso Plattner Institut at the University of Potsdam

Weidlich M, Mendling J, Weske M (2011) Efficient Consistency Measurement Based on Behavioral Profiles of Process Models. IEEE Trans Software Eng 37(3):410–429

Weikum G, Vossen G (2001) Transactional Information Systems: Theory, Algorithms, and the Practice of Concurrency Control and Recovery. Elsevier Science & Technology Books

Weske M (1998) Formal Foundation and Conceptual Design of Dynamic Adaptations in a Workflow Management System. In: Sprague (ed) Proceedings of the Thirty-Fourth Annual Hawaii International Conference on System Science (HICSS-34) Minitrack Internet and Workflow Automation: Technical and Managerial Issues., IEEE Computer Society Press

Weske M (2000) Workflow Management Systems: Formal Foundation, Conceptual Design, Implementation Aspects. Habilitation Thesis, University of Münster

Weske M, Goesmann T, Holten R, Striemer R (2001) Analysing, modelling and improving workflow application development processes. Software Process: Improvement and Practice 6(1):35–46

Weske M, Vossen G, Puhlmann F (2005) Workflow and Service Composition Languages. In: Bernus P, Mertins K, Schmidt G (eds) Handbook on Architectures of Information Systems, Springer, Berlin, pp 369–390

Woods D, Mattern T (2006) Enterprise SOA – Designing IT for Business Innovation. O'Reilly

Workflow Management Coalition (2005) Process Definition Interface - XML Process Definition Language. Document Number WFMC-TC-1025

Xu X, Weber I, Staples M (2019) Architecture for Blockchain Applications. Springer

Zaha JM, Barros A, Dumas M, ter Hofstede A (2006a) Let's Dance: A Language for Service Behavior Modeling. In: Proceedings 14th International Conference on Cooperative Information Systems (CoopIS 2006), Springer Verlag, Montpellier, France

Zaha JM, Dumas M, ter Hofstede A, Barros A, Decker G (2006b) Service Inter-
    action Modeling: Bridging Global and Local Views. In: Proceedings 10th IEEE
    International EDOC Conference (EDOC 2006), Hong Kong
Zdravkovic J, Kirikova M, Johannesson P (eds) (2015) Advanced Information Sys-
    tems Engineering - 27th International Conference, CAiSE 2015, Stockholm, Swe-
    den, June 8-12, 2015, Proceedings, Lecture Notes in Computer Science, vol 9097,
    Springer

Index

© Springer-Verlag GmbH Germany, part of Springer Nature 2019
M. Weske, *Business Process Management*,
https://doi.org/10.1007/978-3-662-59432-2

Printed in the United States
By Bookmasters